AMERICAN S

C000153349

US intelligence agencies — the eponymous American spies — are exceedingly aggressive, pushing and sometimes bursting through the technological, legal and political boundaries of lawful surveillance. Written for a general audience by a surveillance law expert, this book educates readers about how the reality of modern surveillance differs from popular understanding. Weaving the history of American surveillance — from J. Edgar Hoover through the tragedy of September 11th to the fusion centers and mosque infiltrators of today — the book shows that mass surveillance and democracy are fundamentally incompatible. Granick shows how surveillance law has fallen behind while surveillance technology has given American spies vast new powers. She skillfully guides the reader through proposals for reining in massive surveillance with the ultimate goal of surveillance reform.

JENNIFER STISA GRANICK is Director of Civil Liberties at Stanford Law School. Jennifer practices, speaks and writes about computer crime and security, electronic surveillance, consumer privacy, and data protection. Before teaching at Stanford, Jennifer spent almost a decade practicing criminal defense law in California. She received a 2016 Women in Security award from Duo Security. She earned her law degree from the University of California, Hastings College of the Law and her undergraduate degree from the New College of Florida.

AMERICAN SPIES

Modern Surveillance, Why You Should Care,
and What to Do about It

JENNIFER STISA GRANICK

CAMBRIDGE
UNIVERSITY PRESS

CAMBRIDGE
UNIVERSITY PRESS

University Printing House, Cambridge CB2 8BS, United Kingdom

One Liberty Plaza, 20th Floor, New York, NY 10006, USA

477 Williamstown Road, Port Melbourne, VIC 3207, Australia

4843/24, 2nd Floor, Ansari Road, Daryaganj, Delhi – 110002, India

79 Anson Road, #06-04/06, Singapore 079906

Cambridge University Press is part of the University of Cambridge.

It furthers the University's mission by disseminating knowledge in the pursuit of
education, learning, and research at the highest international levels of excellence.

www.cambridge.org
Information on this title: www.cambridge.org/9781107103238
DOI: 10.1017/9781316216088

First published 2017

Printed in the United Kingdom by Clays, St Ives plc

A catalogue record for this publication is available from the British Library.

Library of Congress Cataloging-in-Publication Data
Names: Granick, Jennifer Stisa.
Title: American spies : modern surveillance, why you should care, and
what to do about it / Jennifer Stisa Granick.
Description: Cambridge [UK] ; New York : Cambridge University Press, 2017.
Identifiers: LCCN 2016036440 | ISBN 9781107103238 (hardback)
Subjects: LCSH: Intelligence service – Law and legislation – United States. |
Domestic intelligence – United States. | Espionage, American – United States. |
Wiretapping – Law and legislation – United States. | Electronic surveillance –
Law and legislation – United States. | Privacy, Right of – United States. |
United States. Constitution. 4th Amendment. | Snowden, Edward J., 1983– |
Leaks (Disclosure of information) – United States. | BISAC: LAW / General.
Classification: LCC KF4850 .G725 2016 | DDC 363.2/32–dc23
LC record available at https://lccn.loc.gov/2016036440

ISBN 978-1-107-10323-8 Hardback
ISBN 978-1-107-50185-0 Paperback

CONTENTS

    Amendment   240

15 The Failures of External Oversight   244

16 The National *In*Security Agency   263

17 The Future of Surveillance   290
    Ending Secret Law and Increasing Public Accountability   292
    Oversight   294
        Internal Oversight   294
        Oversight by Congress   296
        Oversight by Courts   297
    The Risks and Rewards of Surveillance   300
        Updating Our Laws to Take into Account the Power of
            Metadata   302
        The Interests of Foreigners   303
    FISA Amendments Act Reform   304
        Purpose of Collection   305
        Upstream and Abouts   305
        Minimization and Back Door Searches   307
        EO 12333 Reform   309
        Transparency   310

    Glossary of Selected Terms   314
    Further Reading   317
    Index   318

ACKNOWLEDGMENTS

While writing this book, I thought a lot about Caspar Bowden, who passed away in 2015 well before his business was completed. We will carry on, Caspar, and I hope we will make you proud.

I'm grateful to Fred von Lohmann for the idea that I should write this book, for his tolerance of the time and effort it took, for his rigorous proof-reading, and for his steadfast love in the face of my preoccupation. Barbara van Schewick, the Director of our Center for Internet and Society, gave me great leeway to have time to write and was incredibly supportive and enthusiastic. I couldn't ask for a more empowering boss. I'm grateful to Ryan Harbage, my agent, for encouraging me and guiding me through the process.

Editors Nan Weiner and Ruth Starkman guided me at various points of the project, helping me make the book more accessible and better organized.

I was ably assisted by Gabe Schlaback and Marta Belcher who helped with early research. Thank you to my footnoting assistants, Alec Pallin, Wesley Tiu, Taylor Goodman, and Alex Zaheer. Elliot Serbin was especially helpful with footnoting and with ensuring stylistic consistency throughout.

A number of friends and colleagues read the book and provided invaluable commentary and demands for clarifications. Thank you to readers Mark Seiden, Ethan Watters, Kim Magowan, Van Harvey, Hal Murray, Neil Richards, and Margaret Hu.

To my colleagues in the surveillance, civil liberties, and human rights communities – whistleblowers, reporters, lawyers, activists, government officials past and present: I wrote this book to bring your ideas to the general public in an effort to get more people to understand and care about surveillance. I hope you see your hard work and ideas fairly and eloquently reflected here.

LEGAL DECISIONS RELATED
TO SURVEILLANCE

ACLU v. Clapper, 959 F.Supp.2d 724 (SDNY 2013)

A lawsuit in the Southern District of New York by the American Civil Liberties Union and its affiliate, the New York Civil Liberties Union, against the US government challenging the legality of the National Security Agency's bulk phone metadata collection program.

Berger v. New York, 388 U.S. 41 (1967)

A United States Supreme Court decision holding that New York's wiretapping statute was insufficiently protective of privacy rights in telephone calls. *Berger* was the precursor for federal and state adoption of so-called super warrants required to authorize wiretapping.

Clapper v. Amnesty Int'l USA, 133 S.Ct. 1138 (2013)

A United States Supreme Court decision holding that Amnesty International USA and others lacked standing to challenge section 702 of the Foreign Intelligence Surveillance Act because the plaintiffs could neither prove that they were spied on, nor, if they were, that it was because of section 702. The decision interferes with the ability to challenge the constitutionality of secretive surveillance programs.

Hepting v. AT&T aka In re Nat. Sec. Agency Telecommunications Records Litigation, 633 F.Supp.2d 949 (NDCal 2009)

A class action lawsuit filed in January 2006 by the Electronic Frontier Foundation (EFF) against the telecommunications company AT&T alleging that AT&T permitted and assisted the NSA in unlawfully monitoring communications of AT&T customers and others routed through AT&T's network. The lawsuit was dismissed on June 3, 2009 due to immunity provisions passed in the Foreign Intelligence Surveillance Act Amendments Act of 2008.

Jewel v. NSA [See the Electronic Frontier Foundation case page available at www.eff.org/cases/jewel]

A class action lawsuit filed by the EFF against the NSA and several high-ranking officials in Bush Administration alleging an illegal and unconstitutional program of dragnet communications surveillance based in part on testimony from former AT&T technician Mark Klein. The case is ongoing.

Katz v. United States, 389 U.S. 347 (1967)

A United States Supreme Court decision legally defining a Fourth Amendment search as interference with a reasonable expectation of privacy. The case is the foundation of modern Fourth Amendment jurisprudence. It overruled *Olmstead v. United States.*

Korematsu v. United States, 321 U.S. 760 (1944)

A United States Supreme Court decision upholding the constitutionality of the internment of Japanese Americans during World War II.

Kyllo v. United States, 533 U.S. 27 (2001)

A United States Supreme Court decision holding that the use of a thermal imaging device from a public vantage point to monitor the radiation of heat from a person's home was a "search" within the meaning of the Fourth Amendment, and thus required a warrant.

Obama v. Klayman, 800 F.3d 559 (DCCir. 2015)

A case pending in the United States District Court for the District of Columbia challenging the legality of the bulk collection of both phone and Internet metadata by the United States.

Olmstead v. United States, 277 U.S. 438 (1928)

A United States Supreme Court decision in which the Court reviewed whether the use of wiretapped private telephone conversations, obtained by federal agents without judicial approval and subsequently used as evidence, constituted a violation of the defendant's rights. The Court held that the Fourth Amendment rights of the defendant were not violated. This decision was overturned by *Katz v. United States* in 1967.

Riley v. California, 134 S.Ct. 2473 (2014)

A United States Supreme Court decision unanimously holding that – despite the doctrine saying that warrantless searches incident to arrest do not violate the Fourth Amendment – officers may not conduct a warrantless search of the digital contents of a cell phone incident to arrest. Digital is different.

Schrems v. Facebook, Case No. C-362/14 (2015)

A Court of Justice of the European Union decision invalidating the Safe Harbor framework underlying data transfers between Europe and the United States on the grounds that section 702 of the FISA Amendments Act inadequately protects European citizens' privacy rights.

Smith v. Maryland, 442 U.S. 735 (1979)

A United States Supreme Court decision holding that the installation and use of the pen register was not a "search" within the meaning of the Fourth Amendment, and hence no warrant was required. The pen register did not violate the defendant's reasonable expectation of privacy because the numbers were already available to and recorded by the phone company.

United States v. Ganias, 755 F.3d 125 (2d Cir. 2014)

A United States Court of Appeals for the Second Circuit case in which the IRS obtained a search warrant allowing its agents to review files seized earlier and retained by the government. A three-judge panel of the Second Circuit Court of Appeals suppressed the evidence, holding that the government could not seize and keep evidence only to search it later in unrelated matters. As of this writing, the ruling is on appeal to the Second Circuit *en banc*, 791 F.3d 290 (2d Cir. 2015).

United States v. Jacobsen, 466 U.S. 109 (1984)

A United States Supreme Court decision holding that people have a reasonable expectation of privacy in their letters and therefore that warrantless searches are presumptively unreasonable under the Fourth Amendment.

United States v. Jones, 32 S.Ct. 945 (2012)

A United States Supreme Court decision holding that the installation of a Global Positioning System (GPS) tracking device on a vehicle and using the device to monitor the vehicle's movements constitutes a search under the Fourth Amendment. The majority opinion was based on the view that installing and using the device interfered with the defendant's property interest in the vehicle. The concurrence, joined by five Justices, suggested that investigations have a tipping point where otherwise lawful surveillance becomes so extensive that the Fourth Amendment applies.

United States v. Miller, 425 U.S. 435 (1976)

A United States Supreme Court decision holding that there is no reasonable expectation of privacy in one's bank records, so the government could obtain the records without first getting a search warrant. In conjunction with *Smith v. Maryland*, this case is the foundation of the so-called third party doctrine, the assertion that people have no constitutionally protected privacy interest in materials held by third parties.

United States v. Muhtorov, 2-cr-00033-JLK (D. Colo.)

A United States criminal case charging the defendant with providing and attempting to provide material support and resources to a foreign terrorist organization. The defendant was one of the few given notice that he was subject to surveillance under section 702 of the FISA Amendments Act. As a result, Mr. Muhtorov is one of the few people with standing to challenge the surveillance on statutory and constitutional grounds.

United States v. Truong, 629 F.2d 908 (4th Cir. 1980)

A United States Court of Appeals for the Fourth Circuit decision holding there was at the time a foreign intelligence exception to Fourth Amendment, which applied only in those situations in which interests of the executive are paramount, when object of search or surveillance is a foreign power, its agent, or collaborators, and when surveillance is conducted primarily for foreign intelligence reasons.

United States v. United States District Court (Keith case), 407 U.S. 297 (1972)

A United States Supreme Court decision that unanimously held that the Fourth Amendment applied in investigations of domestic surveillance targeting a domestic threat. The *Keith* case nevertheless left open important constitutional questions that are still not answered today.

United States v. Warshak, 631 F.3d 266 (6th Cir. 2010)

A United States Court of Appeals for the Sixth Circuit decision holding that government agents violated the defendant's Fourth Amendment rights by compelling his Internet Service Provider (ISP) to turn over his emails without first obtaining a search warrant. However, constitutional violation notwithstanding, the evidence obtained with these emails was admissible at trial because the government agents relied in good faith on part of the Electronic Communications Privacy Act (ECPA), the Stored Communications Act (SCA), which allowed warrantless seizure of email content. At the time of writing, this is the only Article III court case reaching a decision on whether email is protected by the reasonable expectation of privacy.

Introduction

Technology can be a force for good – connecting people, enabling creativity, making knowledge widely available, and empowering communities to work together. But the Internet and other digital technologies have also profoundly transformed government capabilities to spy on people, in ways that raise important questions about how to protect civil rights and political freedoms. This book explains the law and policy of American digital surveillance in the modern era. It invites the general public to participate intellectually and politically in securing a future where technology promotes free and open exchanges, while also protecting citizens in their daily lives, and providing for law enforcement and national security.

When I first began researching the relationship between surveillance, technology, and civil liberties, the digital era was in its infancy. I became a lawyer in the 1990s in the early years of the public Internet. I represented people charged with crimes related to the Internet in state and federal courts. I also litigated Fourth Amendment privacy claims, seeking constitutional protection for the wealth of personal data that new technologies were just beginning to generate. My clients included computer security experts, who were being investigated for technology research that scared judges unfamiliar with the Internet, as well as run-of-the-mill criminal defendants facing digital evidence like door access logs, hard drive searches, and more. I learned how hard it was to educate judges about technology. Once, when questioning the forensic reliability of a document purporting to log user access to an important computer server, I argued that the entries were not authenticated, but cut and pasted into a Microsoft Word document and thus could be incomplete or manipulated by a police officer or prosecutor. "Cut and paste?" the judge asked. "Like, with a scissor?"

I came to Stanford in 2001 to teach, research, and advocate for better technology-related policies. One of the major mysteries scholars and civil libertarians were confronting was surveillance policy. A major obstacle to understanding government surveillance is the veil of secrecy that surrounds our national security policies. I am concerned with the toll surveillance can take on personal freedom. How can we know whether surveillance conducted in secret is constructive or destructive? For years, surveillance and civil liberties lawyers like me have been wondering what the US government is really doing when it spies on regular people. We've submitted Freedom of Information Act (FOIA) requests for records about surveillance technologies. We've filed lawsuits challenging certain surveillance statutes as indiscriminate. We've interviewed whistleblowers, who have revealed how US spying impacts the privacy and freedom of people around the world. Still, the big picture was hazy. Each time surveillance news broke, lawmakers and the public cared more about other things and the story faded off the front pages. As with our government's top-secret classification of other "war on terror" policies – drone strikes, waterboarding and other torture techniques, kidnapping people and bringing them to off-the-books black sites for imprisonment, interrogation, or worse – we suspected that the secrecy was hiding ill-advised, illegal, and even dangerous activity.

Then came June 2013 and Edward Snowden. Snowden, a former contractor for the secretive National Security Agency (NSA), gave reporters documents, evidence that can't be ignored, and demonstrated clearly that American spying is out of control. The United States is collecting vast amounts of private data, including about American citizens and even more about people around the world. Behind closed doors, judges are making secret law, adopting laughably bad interpretations of statutes, and invalidating constitutional privacy protections in the name of spying on innocent people. Spies are hacking the Internet, installing malicious software, and stealing encryption keys so that they can carry on mass surveillance. Computers are collecting sensitive, detailed data, reading emails and recording the phone calls of millions of people. Social welfare organizations, groups we think of as doing good – UNICEF, Doctors Without Borders, the Council on American Islamic Relations (CAIR) – are surveillance targets. Snowden's disclosures also revealed that the NSA had proposed using the information it serendipitously collects on pornography viewing and personal foibles to discredit people the agency says hold radical, albeit peaceful, political beliefs. We're reminded of the Federal Bureau of Investigation's (FBI) dirty tricks campaigns against the civil rights and antiwar movements of the 1960s and 1970s. Now, as then, agents use data gleaned from potentially illegal spying in criminal courts and mislead defendants and even judges about where it comes from.

As University of Pennsylvania computer science professor and cryptographer, Matt Blaze, said to me soon after the Snowden stories started to break: "Isn't finally knowing all this great? ... Except for how terrible it all is."

Yes, it is great. It's great to finally have some answers. After years of being told that civil libertarians were needlessly alarmist about surveillance, policy makers are finally acknowledging the validity of our concerns. We are learning what kind of spying the US government has been doing in our name. It's great, as a surveillance lawyer, to finally get behind the veil of secrecy to learn what courts think our privacy laws actually mean. It's great to have an opportunity to debate openly as a democracy how to protect our privacy and security, how to promote civil liberties and human rights around the world.

But as Matt's quip pointed out, the Snowden revelations also confirmed civil libertarians' worst fears. Modern surveillance is truly different and far more dangerous than we had previously understood. Modern surveillance uses more powerful spying technology, operates under weaker privacy laws, is motivated by a far greater hunger for data following the terrorist attacks of September 11th, and is shrouded in secrecy. For these reasons, the truth about modern surveillance is different from what the public might understand in important ways.

First, modern surveillance is mass surveillance. It used to be that governments did not collect much information on regular people. Governments were technologically limited in their capacity to spy. Now, the NSA can collect vast amounts of information, and then parse through it for matters of interest. Increasingly, protections against abuse, if there are any, operate after-the-fact. That means the US government used to lack the *capacity* for widespread abuse of information because it had limited ability to collect the data. Now, the government has limited *permission* to misuse the massive amount of information it obtains through surveillance.

Next, modern surveillance targeting foreigners has a huge impact on American privacy, as our data gets caught in any dragnet installed on the global Internet. Many people do not realize that our failure to respect the privacy of foreigners impacts Americans too. This is because the image of Spy vs. Spy is now outdated. Modern surveillance means spying on regular people around the world, not just government agents, terrorists, and other spies.

Third, spying is thriving, in part because of technology. Modern surveillance is rapidly defeating constraints posed by either technology or economics. It used to be impossible to follow thousands of people 24 hours a day while ensuring that none of them would ever find out. Today it's not only possible, it's cheap and it's easy. It's not that much more trouble to track hundreds of thousands or millions of people than it is to follow a few.

Spying is thriving not only because of technology, but also because of modern business models. Much of the modern privacy problem is the result of people giving up their data – knowingly or otherwise – to obtain cool new products and services. American spies are successfully deploying surveillance-friendly communications tools even where we could have more privacy-protecting ones. That means building secret spying rooms inside phone company offices, compromising encryption standards, forcing back doors in communications products like Skype, weakening encryption protection for iPhones and Android devices, and more. Modern surveillance is increasingly hard coded into technology and wedded with business models, making it more resistant to legal and political change and capable of abuse on an ongoing basis.

Fourth, in the face of these imperatives – technology, economics, and consumer demand – law has fallen way behind. Modern surveillance is regulated by a confusing patchwork of laws that nevertheless fails to provide meaningful limits on government power, and which therefore invites abuse. After September 11th, laws that should have protected people's privacy and stopped surveillance abuses were weakened via the USA PATRIOT Act. When technology and economics gave spies vastly more power, rather than have law step up to the challenge of constraining that power, Congress and the courts did nothing, or the laws were softened even further. American spies have flooded into the power vacuum left by powerful technology and weak legal protections. While the public knew Congress was rolling back privacy laws to some extent with the USA PATRIOT Act, those decisions actually have led to far greater privacy invasions than anyone understood before now.

Finally, modern surveillance depends on an untenable level of secrecy. Spying has always protected legitimate secrets from the targets. But now since everyone is subject to spying, modern surveillance has to be hidden from everyone. The activities of American spies remain hidden from public oversight. That means secret court opinions, classified policies, misleading use of language, aggressive prosecution of whistleblowers, spying on journalists, and suppressing court challenges. These practices are fundamentally incompatible with a free society.

The call is clear. We need a comprehensive public investigation into what American spies are doing in our name, and we need far stronger regulation of surveillance activities to protect innocent people's privacy and to guard against abuses of sensitive, personal data.

But stunned and alarmed as many people were by Snowden's revelations, it seems that some of my friends and colleagues are in denial. They are comforted by deceptive reassurances, like when President Obama intones that "no one is listening to your phone calls." Or they insist: "I'm just a regular person, why would the government be spying on me?" They say, "massive surveillance is just the price we have to pay to keep our country safe from terrorists." Or they believe that legal reforms adopted after the surveillance abuses of the 1960s and 1970s – when the US government spied on and attempted to blackmail Dr. Martin Luther King, Jr. – remain effective today, and that the courts and Congress exercise sufficient oversight of American spies.

The truth is sobering. American spies collect billions of calls, emails, and other communications data on hundreds of thousands or millions of people without any reason for suspicion. American spies compile details that reveal the identities of people you talk with, what you read, what you buy, what you believe, and where you go. In conducting all this surveillance, American spies end up spying on Americans and are increasingly omniscient.

No doubt, terrorism is terrible. It violently destroys lives, inflicts economic loss, and robs the public of peace of mind and quality of life. It exacerbates social and class divisions and tears at the fabric of national unity. The attacks of September 11 were horrific. To this day, I cannot think about them without tearing up. But the risk terrorism poses to American lives is actually tiny. In the past decade, the number of people in the United States killed by terrorists is less than 100.[1] So why have the American people sacrificed so much of our liberty, and endangered the liberties of others, in the fight against terrorism?

America can survive terrorism. But American democracy cannot survive modern surveillance. Privacy is key to the exercise of individual

---

[1] Counting terrorist deaths depends on definitions. In October of 2015, an expansive definition that included non-jihadist attacks tallied seventy-one. See L. Qiu. "Fact-checking a comparison of gun deaths and terrorism deaths." *PolitiFact*. October 5, 2015. www.politifact.com/truth-o-meter/statements/2015/oct/05/viral-image/fact-checking-comparison-gun-deaths-and-terrorism-/. If you add the fourteen people slain in the December San Bernardino shooting and the three killed in the Planned Parenthood attack in November of that year, the number is still less than 100.

freedoms – to read, to think, to express oneself, to conduct intimate relationships, to be let alone. But privacy is also key to political evolution. Without a zone of protection, those who seek to evolve the country's laws and policies, to challenge the status quo, are at risk of imprisonment or blackmail by those in power. Those in power are at risk of blackmail or embezzlement by other powerful people. Americans natively understand this is true in despotic countries. We worry that China is punishing religious minorities, political upstarts, and artists. We know that in Russia journalists and business leaders with political ambitions are imprisoned or worse. These kinds of civil liberties attacks have happened here in the United States, too, still happen more than they should, and could become a serious challenge to our democracy in the future. This claim may seem hyperbolic, but while the US government is not going to dissolve into despotism overnight, the encroaching loss of liberty is profound.

This book offers a historical account of an extraordinarily complex policy and legal debate on modern surveillance. There are multiple federal agencies charged with protecting the United States' national security and foreign affairs interests as part of the so-called "intelligence community." Data collection of all kinds, including electronic surveillance, signals intelligence (SIGINT), and human intelligence (HUMINT), are part of this work. The agencies' roles can be overlapping, coordinating, or exclusive, and each of the agencies has its own mission, its own jurisdiction, and its own rules. The NSA is responsible for SIGINT. The Central Intelligence Agency (CIA) is responsible for "national foreign intelligence." The Department of Defense collects both national and military foreign intelligence. The FBI conducts counterintelligence inside the United States and when requested by other intelligence community agencies, assists with the collection of foreign intelligence inside the United States. Other members of the seventeen agencies comprising the intelligence community include the Department of Treasury, the Department of State, and the Department of Energy.[2] Collectively, I call the federal agencies involved in SIGINT collection "American spies."

Against this complicated backdrop, my job is to assess and, where appropriate, debunk American spies' best arguments for the legality and

---

[2] See www.dni.gov/index.php: Air Force Intelligence, Army Intelligence, Central Intelligence Agency, Coast Guard Intelligence, Defense Intelligence Agency, Department of Energy, Department of Homeland Security, Department of State, Department of the Treasury, Drug Enforcement Administration, Federal Bureau of Investigation, Marine Corps Intelligence, National Geospatial-Intelligence Agency, National Reconnaissance Office, National Security Agency, and Navy Intelligence.

acceptability of their actions. I hope to answer the questions I've been hearing from colleagues, students, friends, and the general public ever since the first news story based on Snowden documents, and enable readers to participate meaningfully in the sometimes seemingly arcane policy debates around modern surveillance.

My first goal in writing this book is to give the American voter the information she needs to understand and participate in this debate, and to make a difference. Second, I believe that by explaining the policy debates taking place in the United States, people in other nations will be able to learn from our experience, and avoid making the same mistakes that we have made.

The rules by which the government decides whether and when to respect our privacy and leave us alone, or collect information on us and eavesdrop in our private affairs, are byzantine. Today, a smattering of sparse, mostly secret internal rules is the only thing standing between people and abusive exercise of that power. As Edward Snowden said, in explaining his decision to come forward, "I believe that at this point in history, the greatest danger to our freedom and way of life comes from the reasonable fear of omniscient State powers kept in check by nothing more than policy documents." In other words, massive surveillance used to be impossible. Today, it's happening, and the risks of this extensive spying are managed with internal policies. It is not enough to try to contain overbroad surveillance with government agency protocols. These protocols are complicated and secret. When people break them, it has taken the public years to find out, and no one gets punished.

But an informed electorate is a powerful electorate. Public pressure stymied the rampant political spying of the 1960s and 1970s. In 2012, public pressure stopped SOPA and PIPA, seemingly unstoppable draconian copyright laws that would have improperly censored the Internet. And in 2015, public pressure turned network neutrality, an arcane but important issue of government regulation of Internet service providers, into a concrete rule intended to preserve and promote a free and open Internet. Similarly, Congress put an end to the NSA's bulk collection of Americans' phone records with 2015's USA Freedom Act. It can be done.

And it must. John Gilmore, one of the founders of the Electronic Frontier Foundation, is quoted as having said, "*never give a government a power you would not want a despot to have.*" The American government has such powers. It has huge and growing technological capability to collect and analyze vast amounts of data. The stakes are incredibly high and time for change is short. Otherwise, mass surveillance will become – technologically and politically – the new normal.

Mass surveillance and democracy are fundamentally incompatible. It is impossible to know whether judges, lawmakers, and presidents are acting out of principle and allegiance to their understanding of what the public wants or out of fear that spies will disclose embarrassing or illegal behavior. Massive surveillance thwarts citizens pressuring for political change through the risk of criminal prosecution, blackmail, or other threats. The secrecy and the lies required to spy on everyone are inconsistent with a democratic government of, by, and for the people.

I hope this book will enable people to fight for democracy.

1

Modern Surveillance: Massive, Classified, and Indiscriminate

Information is power. Foreign intelligence collection aims to help government officials understand what goes on outside the country. Officials can use this information to inform foreign policy, to prevent terrorist attacks, to influence, or even to control events in other nations. In our conduct of information collection for foreign intelligence purposes, the United States casts a wide net, relying not only on human intelligence – spies, informants, and analysts – but increasingly on signals intelligence. Signals intelligence (SIGINT) includes collection and analysis of phone calls, emails, iMessages, texts, cell phone tower data, web browsing histories, and more. Once, SIGINT was difficult and expensive. Now, collection is easy and cheap. Surveillance in the name of foreign intelligence has metastasized, and now includes vast SIGINT collection on Americans and on everyday people in other nations. The public is rightly concerned about broad, suspicionless surveillance, so the intelligence community has built technological, legal, and political support for massive surveillance in secret.

Before June 2013, even surveillance law experts didn't know the full scope of US government spying on American citizens. But on June 5, 2013, an amazing news story opened a new window on secret spy programs. That morning, reporter Glenn Greenwald dropped a bombshell in the digital pages of *The Guardian*, an opinionated UK-based newspaper known for its liberal politics and investigative scoops. Greenwald had proof that the US telecommunications company Verizon was handing "call detail records" from every one of its US customers over to the Federal Bureau of Investigation (FBI) pursuant to a classified court order from a top-secret federal intelligence tribunal. The FBI was then giving this information to the National Security Agency (NSA). The NSA is a *foreign* intelligence agency prohibited from spying on Americans without a court order. The "call detail records" included the phone numbers that Americans call and are called by, as well as the date, time, and length of the calls.

It wasn't the first time that a news outlet had reported that surprisingly large numbers of people's phone calling data were being collected by the US government. In 2006, *USA Today* reported that American spies were collecting tens or hundreds of thousands of people's calling records. But the paper didn't offer any documentary proof. The issue eventually faded off the front pages. This time, however, Greenwald provided evidence. *The Guardian* published the actual court order on *The Guardian's* website. It was marked "TOP-SECRET//SI//NOFORN" across the top. Top-secret. Special Intelligence. Not Releasable to Foreign Nationals. These designations made the order one of the most closely held secrets of the US government.

The scope of the government's call records collection was shocking. It was everything. Americans' domestic and international calls were being collected in bulk. The order did not limit the government to obtaining information on particular phone numbers or specified suspects. Rather, the collection was indiscriminate, giving the FBI information on all of Verizon Business's 100 million phone service customers, the vast majority of whom are surely not under any kind of suspicion. [A few months later, the public learned that AT&T and Sprint were also receiving similar orders.] Then, apparently, the FBI was just handing those records over to the NSA. This surveillance program was a dragnet, capturing any and every phone record. But why? The US government isn't supposed to spy on its own citizens – never mind on *every* citizen – for no reason. And the NSA in particular is a *foreign* intelligence agency. Why was it collecting purely *domestic* telephone records?

The next morning, California's senior Senator, Democrat Dianne Feinstein, and Georgia Republican Senator Saxby Chambliss appeared at a hastily arranged press conference.[1] Feinstein and Chambliss were co-heads of the Senate Intelligence Committee, charged with overseeing federal intelligence activities. It was true, the two Senators said, the NSA was collecting Americans' phone records via the FBI. But this was nothing new. Collection of Americans phone call records had been going on secretly for the past seven years under the auspices of the secretive Foreign Intelligence Surveillance Court, or FISC.

The NSA was only collecting "metadata" under this program – phone numbers called, but not listening to what people said during the call

---

[1] E. O'Keefe. "Transcript: Dianne Feinstein, Saxby Chambliss explain, defend NSA phone records program." *The Washington Post*. June 6, 2013. www.washingtonpost.com/news/post-politics/wp/2013/06/06/transcript-dianne-feinstein-saxby-chambliss-explain-defend-nsa-phone-records-program/

– so according to the Senators there is no privacy concern whatsoever. Metadata doesn't violate your privacy, they said. Further, the Senators said, the NSA couldn't just search these records willy-nilly. Instead, it has to have "reasonable articulable suspicion" (RAS) that a phone number was connected with certain terrorist activity before it could check what numbers that number called. The FISC had imposed the RAS requirement on all intelligence searches of the dragnet data as a safeguard to ensure analysts only used the data for the court-approved counterterrorism purpose, presumably investigating certain al-Qaeda related groups.

They also assured the public that every member of the Senate had been briefed about this program. So this wasn't a secret NSA program hidden from democratic oversight. Rather, the NSA was keeping its sources and methods secret from the general public, as was common and necessary when spying on terrorists.

No one, they added, had ever complained.

Still, the Senators were unable to put public concerns completely to rest. Eventually, through a series of further disclosures and public hearings before Congress, Americans would learn that almost everything the Senators said was misleading or incomplete.

First, phone records *are* private. Federal privacy laws explicitly command phone companies not to use, disclose, or permit access to customer proprietary network information, or CPNI, except as part of providing the telecommunications services.[2] Further, the information phone records reveal about us can be incredibly revealing. Did you call a suicide hotline or Narcotics Anonymous? Did you call your boyfriend ten times in the middle of the night, and then call Planned Parenthood? Of course phone numbers are sensitive and revealing. That's exactly why the NSA wants them.

Furthermore, the NSA had been collecting this information about Americans for far longer than seven years. The Bush Administration started the NSA's domestic phone record collection fourteen years earlier, in 2001, after the attacks of September 11th. Initially, Bush did so without any statutory authority, court approval, or external oversight as part of a broader illegal surveillance program codenamed STELLARWIND. Instead, phone companies were voluntarily turning over the data without a court order. This kind of private cooperation with government surveillance historically has been characteristic of the highly regulated telecommunications industry, but especially so after September 11th.

---

[2] 47 U.S.C. § 222.

Only in May of 2006 did the Administration seek a court order, based on a novel argument that intelligence agencies were authorized by Congress to compel companies to disclose customer phone records in bulk.[3] Officials had to concoct this argument after the *USA Today* reported earlier that month that that the government was engaging in large-scale collection of Americans' phone records.[4] This news report scared previously compliant phone companies away from continuing to turn the information over to the government voluntarily. So now the Bush Administration needed something that would compel compliance and insulate the telecoms from legal liability were they to be sued by their customers.

So the Bush Administration argued that section 215 of the USA PATRIOT Act allowed the government to compel the collection. Congress had passed the USA PATRIOT Act (colloquially called the Patriot Act) in the days immediately following the September 11th attacks. The law, hundreds of pages long, changed many aspects of intelligence operations. The most controversial changes were to existing rules meant to protect American citizens' privacy. One change was codified in section 215 of the Patriot Act. Section 215 amended an existing statute to expand the scope of business records and other "tangible things" that the FBI could compel a business to disclose pursuant to an order from the FISC.[5]

Section 215 was quite controversial, so much so that Congress gave it an automatic expiration date for five years after the Patriot Act passed. It was subsequently renewed several times. But in the vigorous public debate about section 215, no one ever raised the idea that the FBI could obtain business records or other tangible things about millions or hundreds of millions of Americans. Rather, the public debate was over whether sensitive records like library lending logs should be covered by section 215. For that reason, the law was called the "library provision," but never the "bulk collection" law.

Nor was there any reason to believe that the FBI would give a huge database of *domestic* phone call information to the NSA, an intelligence agency charged with conducting *foreign* intelligence and generally prohibited from spying on Americans.

---

[3] C. Savage. *Power Wars: Inside Obama's Post-9/11 Presidency*. (New York: Little, Brown and Company, 2015) p. 771, citing *In re Application of the Federal Bureau of Investigation for an Order Requiring the Production of Tangible Things from [redacted]*, No. BR 06-05. (FISC, May 24, 2006) www.aclu.org/files/assets/2013.10.11_fisa_court_memorandum.pdf

[4] L. Cauley. "NSA has massive database of Americans' phone calls." *USA Today*. May 11, 2006. usatoday30.usatoday.com/news/washington/2006-05-10-nsa_x.htm

[5] Section 215 amended 50 U.S.C. § 1861.

The "reasonable articulable suspicion", or "RAS", requirement for search-ing the phone data was also a lot less comforting than it may have initially sounded. First, no such rule existed from 2001 to 2006 when the Bush Administration was collecting the data without a court order or judicial oversight. "Reasonable articulable suspicion" was something that the FISC judge approving the collection program in May of 2006 imposed.[6] Further, Senator Chambliss didn't make clear how the rule actually worked. People listening to him may have thought that a judge assesses whether there is adequate cause for investigating a particular phone number. This kind of factual check by an officer from an independent branch of government – either a magistrate or a judge – is typical in criminal investigations. It's one of the few tools we have to ensure that surveillance isn't undertaken for arbitrary and capricious reasons. But that wasn't a role the FISC was playing here. The FISC never reviewed the NSA's RAS determination, or any of its reasons for looking up a number.[7] Instead, it was up to the spies themselves to decide whom to target and to police their own compliance with the FISC-imposed rules.

From a civil liberties perspective, this isn't a small omission for Senator Chambliss to have made. Having an independent branch of government – a judge – oversee and approve executive branch surveillance decisions is one of the only effective checks our legal system has to guard against arbitrary spying. This is the approach required by the Fourth Amendment and almost every surveillance statute on the books. Section 215 requires a FISC judge to ensure that the business records the government wants are "relevant to an ongoing investigation." But instead of following an approach that ensures checks and balances, American spies – the FBI and the NSA working together with lawyers at the Department of Justice – got a most improbable order compelling phone company disclosure of *every* phone record.

Without court oversight, how well had American spies done at over-seeing themselves? The Senators didn't mention it in their press confer-ence, but even after the FISC required RAS, the NSA broke the RAS rule for over three years from 2006 to 2009. Only in response to a motion to

---

6 *In re Application of the Federal Bureau of Investigation for an Order Requiring the Production of Tangible Things from [redacted]*, No. BR 06-05. (FISC, May 24, 2006) www.dni.gov/files/documents/section/pub_May%2024%202006%20Order%20from%20FISC.pdf
7 "Report on the Telephone Records Program Conducted under Section 215 of the USA PATRIOT Act and on the Operations of the Foreign Intelligence Surveillance Court." Privacy and Civil Liberties Oversight Board. January 23, 2014. www.pclob.gov/library/215-Report_on_the_Telephone_Records_Program.pdf

unseal filed by the American Civil Liberties Union (ACLU) in the FISC in late 2013, did the Office of the Director of National Intelligence (ODNI) release FISC opinions detailing the NSA's failure to comply with the court's section 215 rules. The ODNI oversees the executive branch agencies and organizations that conduct intelligence activities. A 2009 FISC opinion written by FISC Judge Reggie Walton chastised the agency for violating the RAS rule. Instead of only searching for phone numbers that met the RAS standard, analysts compared the information on a daily basis with non RAS-approved numbers on an "alert list" as the numbers rolled into the NSA database. If there was a hit, then the NSA analysts would look to see if they had RAS-approval for the alerting number. If they did, they would conduct further contact chaining – three hops analysis – on the Americans' flagged number.

The alert list contained 17,835 numbers, of which only 1,935 met the FISC's RAS-approved requirement. The "station table," a list of all RAS evaluations, had about 27,000 RAS-approved selectors and 63,000 nonapproved.[8] Thus, the NSA did not have an approved factual basis for approximately 89 percent of the numbers they were using to search the phone records data. And, the NSA's illegal practice continued from 2006 until 2009. Only then did the NSA inform the FISC about it.

This may seem – and is – very technical. But it is important. The compliance failure doesn't just indicate that the first time a court gave the intelligence community bulk collection powers, the NSA and the FBI broke the rules from the very beginning and then hid their mistakes from the public. The compliance failure is also a civil liberties failure. The reason the FISC would insist on RAS approval in the first place is to ensure that NSA analysts had a good reason for closer scrutiny of Americans' calls. Why were numbers for which there was no RAS approval on the alert list or station table? They could be unconnected to terrorism, and merely related to trade issues, the price of oil, or even foreign political, religious, or environmental movements. Running those numbers could bring Americans under scrutiny for lawful, even constitutionally protected, associational and political activity.

Another surprise for those who listened to Senators Feinstein's and Chambliss's press conference was the extent of the NSA's "contact chaining." Once the NSA decided that there was RAS for a phone number,

---

[8] "Business Records FISA, NSA Review." National Security Agency. June 25, 2009, p. 3. www.aclu.org/files/assets/pub_NSA%20Business%20Records%20FISA%20Review%20 20130909.pdf

the agency could search for numbers "three hops" out. This means that the NSA looks at the first number, every number that number calls (one hop), every number those numbers call (second hop), and then every number those numbers call (third hop). The goal of contact chaining is to create a social network map of who might know whom. Contact chaining brought exponentially more people into the NSA's databases for intelligence analyst review and further "tradecraft."[9] But how many, if any, people three hops out from the original number might also be involved in terrorism?[10] The Senators' press conference created a misperception that only people who call known terrorists draw government attention under the section 215 program. In truth, contact chaining brought exponentially more innocent Americans under the government's microscope.

The assertion that no one ever complained about the classified bulk spying program also turned out to be misleading. While there was much squabbling over whether legislators had been given a chance to learn about the program, the fact was that the public, including most of our representatives in Congress, knew nothing of it.

Inevitably, such a program opened the door to abuse. Some NSA employees had used databases of phone calls to stalk their ex-lovers and spouses. The practice was common enough that the agency developed a tongue-in-cheek name for it, LOVEINT, a play on spy lingo for signals intelligence (SIGINT) and human intelligence (HUMINT).[11]

Even more disturbing, however, was that members of Congress, surveillance law professors, and the general public had no idea there was any law on the books that could allow the US government to conduct dragnet spying on Americans. You would think that a statute authorizing domestic dragnets for the very first time would be something that Congress debated. Yet, bulk collection was not debated on the House or Senate floor, even when the USA PATRIOT Act was passed.

---

[9] "Report on the Telephone Records Program Conducted under Section 215 of the USA PATRIOT Act and on the Operations of the Foreign Intelligence Surveillance Court." Privacy and Civil Liberties Oversight Board. January 23, 2014. www.pclob.gov/library/215-Report_on_the_Telephone_Records_Program.pdf

[10] After public outcry, President Obama ordered this practice changed from three hops to two hops.

[11] Officials have taken pains to stress that LOVEINT mostly involved databases of international and not domestic phone calls collected under section 215. But the point that these databases are susceptible to unofficial as well as official abuse remains. S. Gorman. "NSA officers spy on love interests." *The Wall Street Journal*. August 23, 2013. blogs.wsj.com/washwire/2013/08/23/nsa-officers-sometimes-spy-on-love-interests/

The Bush Administration was concerned about the aftermath of the 2006 *USA Today* phone records story, as well as a December 2005 *New York Times* article revealing warrantless wiretapping under another aspect of the illegal STELLARWIND spying program. So, Bush's Attorney General Alberto Gonzales and his Office of Legal Counsel (OLC) at the Department of Justice (DOJ) created a legal argument that section 215 of the Patriot Act authorized a bulk domestic spying dragnet. Judges appointed to the FISC went along with that story. Telephone companies felt comfortable continuing to disclose private records after a judge had signed off on the dragnet. The incoming Obama Administration, when informed of the program, decided to continue believing that same unbelievable story. Senators Feinstein and Chambliss also agreed, as heads of the Senate Select Committee on Intelligence. The public, however, knew nothing of these legal machinations. No one would have imagined that the law could be used for bulk information collection on *everyone* since there is nothing in the statutory language or the legislative history suggesting that with its passage, Congress authorized for the first time mass spying on Americans.

Even Representative James Sensenbrenner, a Wisconsin Republican and one of the main architects of the USA PATRIOT Act with a well-deserved reputation for being hawkish about surveillance and national security, thought the law was being abused. Sensenbrenner, former Chairman of the House Judiciary Committee, once abruptly ended and walked out of a debate on renewal of the USA PATRIOT Act because Democratic members raised the problem of human rights violations at the Guantanamo Bay detainment camp. But the first time he found out from Greenwald's reporting that his law was being used for bulk phone collection against Americans, the legislator angrily denounced the program: "Congress intended to allow the intelligence communities to access targeted information for specific investigations. How can every call that every American makes or receives be relevant to a specific investigation?" Rep. Sensenbrenner railed: "I authored the Patriot Act, and this is an abuse of that law."[12]

In response, the Obama Administration indirectly blamed Sensenbrenner and other members of Congress for their ignorance. Since 2009, the White House had provided the House and Senate Judiciary and Intelligence Committees with FISC opinions revealing how the court was

---

[12] J. Sensenbrenner. "This abuse of the Patriot Act must end." *The Guardian.* June 9, 2013. www.theguardian.com/commentisfree/2013/jun/09/abuse-patriot-act-must-end

interpreting section 215. The Obama DOJ also prepared classified briefings for the broader members of Congress as a whole and made them
available for lawmakers who wanted to take the time to come to a secure
location and read the documents. Apparently very few, if any, did. That's
their fault, not ours, implied the White House.[13]

There are many reasons why Rep. Sensenbrenner and others may have
failed to review and understand the classified briefings on how section 215
had mutated. Legislators' working hours are busy handling the issues most
salient to their constituents – who also know nothing of dragnet surveillance. Staffers who lack a security clearance cannot help their bosses in the
document review. Legislators are not allowed to discuss documents outside of the secure facility, meaning they cannot explore the issue with their
colleagues. Members of Congress may have had no idea that the memos
they were invited to see contained shocking information that the law was
being twisted out of recognition. For whatever reasons, Congress nevertheless reauthorized section 215 twice after the DOJ made the briefings
available.

There is now secret law in the United States. The Department of Justice's
Office of Legal Counsel writes secret memos that not only guide the
national security actions of the executive branch, but also provide legal
immunity for those actions. If even one FISC judge signs off on a spying
program crafted by DOJ lawyers, other FISC judges are loath to disagree
or to put a stop to the program. FISC judges sometimes write opinions but
also commonly sign orders that authorize surprising invasions of privacy
in the name of national security – and practically no one knows about it,
not even the people who wrote the law that purports to justify the spying.
You have to ask yourself: what's the difference between secret law and no
law at all?

On the morning of June 6, 2013 when Senators Feinstein and Chambliss
sought to put the phone dragnet story to rest with their reassurances,
they managed the leak as the intelligence community usually did: Put a
respected figure on television to issue reassuring statements that leave
the American public with an inaccurate understanding of what is actually going on. This is what President Bush did in 2005 and 2006, when
the *New York Times* and *USA Today* reported on STELLARWIND. He
renamed it the media-friendly Terrorist Surveillance Program, admitted

---

[13] "Bulk Collection of Telephony Metadata Under Section 215 of the USA PATRIOT
Act." Obama Administration White Paper. August 9, 2013. assets.documentcloud.org/
documents/750210/administration-white-paper-section-215.pdf

to listening when al-Qaeda calls, and refused to confirm or deny that other surveillance was ongoing. President Obama took the same tack in 2013. He appeared on television to echo Feinstein's and Chambliss' reassurances, telling the public on June 7th that "[n]obody is listening to your telephone calls."[14]

But this time, the soothing misinformation campaign was ill-advised. The next round of revelations seemed to contradict what Feinstein, Chambliss, and Obama had just told the American people. The government officials had just finished assuring the American public that the NSA was only gathering phone records and not the content of our communications. Yet, the very next day, reporter Barton Gellman and documentary filmmaker and journalist Laura Poitras published a new revelation in the *Washington Post*. Gellman and Poitras had top-secret NSA slides describing a classified program called "PRISM." PRISM routes emails, instant messages, and other digital communications from nine online platforms – Google, Yahoo!, Microsoft, Facebook, PalTalk, YouTube, Skype, AOL, and Apple – to the spies at the NSA. The NSA was getting the content of communications via PRISM, not just metadata. PRISM wasn't about "listening to Americans' phone calls," but it was about NSA analysts having access to Americans' emails. The news made President Obama's press conference attempts to reassure the public feel contrived. Greenwald posted his own version of the PRISM story at *The Guardian* just a few minutes later.[15]

The PRISM story was alarming. The slides showed the world that the NSA operates with the collaboration of some of the best-known Internet companies, putting front and center the role of these platforms in protecting – or failing to protect – their global users' privacy.

The PRISM slides mentioned a related collection program, Upstream surveillance, in which the NSA has obtained access to critical chokepoints on the global communications networks through which hundreds

---

[14] J. Favole and P. A. Nicholas. "Obama: 'Nobody is listening to your telephone calls'." *The Wall Street Journal*. June 7, 2013. www.wsj.com/articles/SB10001424127887323848045785313 43379996824

[15] B. Gellman and L. Poitras. "U.S., British intelligence mining data from nine U.S. Internet companies in broad secret program." *The Washington Post*. June 7, 2013. www.washington-post.com/investigations/us-intelligence-mining-data-from-nine-us-internet-companies-in-broad-secret-program/2013/06/06/3a0c0da8-cebf-11e2-8845-d970ccb04497_story. html; G. Greenwald and E. MacAskill. "NSA Prism program taps into user data of Apple, Google, and others." *The Guardian*. June 7, 2013. www.theguardian.com/world/2013/jun/06/us-tech-giants-nsa-data

of millions or billions of messages and calls flow. In some countries, the NSA can collect from these points in bulk, grabbing anything and everything. But in the United States, the NSA must use "selectors" or search terms to identify interesting data in the streams of information it can access. The agency pulls this raw data into government-controlled databases where it can be further mined, analyzed, shared, and disseminated. Analysts' collection and searches are not limited to national security purposes. As a result, the NSA collects staggering numbers of wholly innocent conversations.

Finally, the PRISM story showed that Greenwald's phone dragnet story was not a one-off. Someone with access to classified NSA information had given multiple journalists documents, maybe a lot of documents, and there was no telling what the public was about to learn next.

On June 11th, Edward Snowden, a 29-year-old former contractor to the NSA, revealed that he was the source of these documents. Snowden had traveled to Hong Kong, and in an unremarkable hotel room there, gave Glenn Greenwald and Laura Poitras a trove of classified documents on top-secret American spying programs, spending the subsequent days helping explain to the reporters what they were seeing. Poitras' film about those tense days, *CitizenFour*, would go on to win the Academy Award for Best Documentary in 2014.

Snowden's disclosures have changed the way the public understands what surveillance means today. There has been a flood of troubling revelations detailing illegality, mass surveillance, espionage, and government hacking. Snowden has also revealed a number of clandestine activities that call into question whether the NSA is actually undermining US interests and public safety in the name of counterterrorism.

The NSA documents detail the massive scope of US surveillance around the globe. The US government promiscuously spies on regular people in other countries. In a single month in 2011, the NSA collected 71 million calls and emails from Poland alone.[16] The NSA collects hundreds of millions of text messages per day and then data mines them for location information, contacts, travel activity, and financial transactions, including credit card numbers.[17] For the Bahamas and one undisclosed country,

---

[16] G. Greenwald. *No Place to Hide: Edward Snowden, the NSA, and the U.S. Surveillance State.* (New York: Metropolitan Books, 2014) p. 91.

[17] "Secret Surveillance: Five Large-Scale Global Programs." Joint Submission to the United Nations, Twenty-Second Session of the Universal Periodic Review Working Group. May 2015. d1ovv0c9tw0h0c.cloudfront.net/files/2014/09/cdt-aclu-upr-9152014.pdf

the United States is recording (or has recorded) the full audio content of every single mobile telephone call placed to, from, or within these countries. Computers analyze the voice recordings and pick out those calls that the software identifies as containing trigger words and phrases for closer inspection by human analysts.[18] Each of these foreign collection capabilities is referred to by a classified code name such as DISHFIRE and MYSTIC.

XKEYSCORE is a global tool that takes in billions of records every day. The tool is able to temporarily store whole Internet flows – everything – to allow NSA computers to search through the trove using keywords and other query terms to find a subset of this huge amount of data to save and analyze further. If XKEYSCORE is effective, it means that nothing that happens online can go unnoticed. Other massive international programs that worry human rights activists include QUANTUM, the capability to monitor traffic on the Internet and respond automatically with network attacks, including sending malicious software to individual mobile devices and computers, and CO-TRAVELER, where the United States captures billions of location updates daily from mobile phones around the world.[19]

How much data does the NSA eventually save? According to the NSA's BOUNDLESS INFORMANT tool, over 97 billion pieces of intelligence were collected over a 30-day period ending in March 2013. The NSA is building a massive data center in Utah to store this information, information it will measure in yottabytes. A yottabyte is a septillion bytes, approximately equal to about 500 quintillion (500,000,000,000,000,000,000,000) pages of text.[20]

Today, content collection – what people say or write – is not the most important kind of data the NSA collects. Metadata is the word for information about communications: sender, recipient, time of day, language, and more. Metadata is revealing, sensitive, and highly coveted by intelligence analysts. Metadata collection is a huge part of what the intelligence community gathers. In a one-month period alone in 2013, a single unit of

---

[18] D. Froomkin. "The computers are listening." *The Intercept*. May 11, 2015. theintercept.com/2015/05/11/speech-recognition-nsa-best-kept-secret/

[19] "Secret Surveillance: Five Large-Scale Global Programs." Joint Submission to the United Nations, Twenty-Second Session of the Universal Periodic Review Working Group. May 2015. d1ovv0c9tw0h0c.cloudfront.net/files/2014/09/cdt-aclu-upr-9152014.pdf

[20] J. Bamford. "The NSA is building the country's biggest spy center (watch what you say)." *Wired*. March 15, 2012. www.wired.com/2012/03/ff_nsadatacenter/

the NSA, the Global Access Operations unit, collected metadata on more than 97 billion emails and 124 billion phone calls from around the world. More than 3 billion of those calls and emails were collected as they passed through the United States, suggesting that some significant percentage of that information was either to or from Americans.[21]

According to the Snowden documents and confirmed by intelligence officials,[22] the NSA gathers nearly 5 billion records a day on the whereabouts of cell phones around the world. The NSA gets this data from tapping the cables that connect cell phone networks and from intercepting communications between the cell phones and the towers. The NSA improves the accuracy and completeness of this data by using drones equipped with cell network interception equipment, especially in areas of active military interest.[23] Documents revealed by Snowden show the NSA considered collecting phone and Internet data, including geolocation, from cell phones domestically and in bulk. The public does not know whether the agency does this today. The NSA is also able to get location information from people's Internet usage. Many applications leak location data – including GPS coordinates and wifi networks – and spies can collect this information and intuit physical location from it. The NSA and its British counterpart, the Global Communications Headquarters or GCHQ, have been collaborating since 2007 to build this capability. One NSA slide enthuses about the data available from iPhone and Android devices as a "Golden Nugget!"[24] British classified documents say that spies can not only glean location data from applications' data leakage, but also learn sexual orientation and political affiliation.[25] The accuracy of geolocation information varies, however.

[21] C. Stöcker. "Declassified documents: NSA wanted to collect geolocation data." *Spiegel Online.* November 19, 2013. www.spiegel.de/international/world/declassifed-documents-nsa-sought-to-collect-mobile-location-data-a-934514.html; Greenwald, *No Place to Hide,* p. 92.

[22] B. Gellman and A. Soltani. "NSA tracking cellphone locations worldwide, Snowden documents show." *The Washington Post.* December 4, 2013. www.washingtonpost.com/world/national-security/nsa-tracking-cellphone-locations-worldwide-snowden-documents-show/2013/12/04/5492873a-5cf2-11e3-bc56-c6ca94801fac_story.html

[23] G. Greenwald and J. Scahill. "The NSA's secret role in the US assassination program." *The Intercept.* February 2, 2014. theintercept.com/2014/02/10/the-nsas-secret-role/

[24] J. Ball. "Angry Birds and 'leaky' phone apps targeted by NSA and GCHQ for user data." *The Guardian.* January 28, 2014. www.theguardian.com/world/2014/jan/27/nsa-gchq-smartphone-app-angry-birds-personal-data

[25] J. Glanz, J. Larson, and A.W. Lehren. "Spy agencies tap data streaming from phone apps." *The New York Times.* January 1, 2014. www.nytimes.com/2014/01/28/world/spy-agencies-scour-phone-apps-for-personal-data.html

Geolocation data is sometimes used to target missiles from assassination drones.[26] Americans' data when we travel overseas is part of the geolocation trove.

The GCHQ contributes to the phone surveillance. In one operation, it hacked employees of telephone companies. After a lengthy investigation, the British spies hijacked these employees' Internet connections to display a fake LinkedIn page. What the employee saw looked normal, but it contained malware the GCHQ used to take over their machines and get access to the database of calling data held by their employers. Using this QUANTUM technique, the GCHQ was able to break into databases containing call detail records, which do not have the content of the call, but include caller number, called number, duration, and sometimes caller location. This information is useful to determine who might be part of a criminal plot and who foreign leaders are in contact with, as well as to track political activism, personal friendships, and other social network connections.[27]

MAINWAY is allegedly one of the most utilized tools the NSA has.[28] It is a database where the NSA stores the phone record data it collects globally. In 2011, MAINWAY was taking in 700 million phone records per day; by August 2011, it began receiving an additional 1.1 billion cell phone records daily, likely thanks to the cooperation of an unnamed corporate partner. We know that US intelligence authorities collect billions of location updates from hundreds of millions of devices each day.[29] As of 2012, the NSA was processing more than 20 billion telecommunications per day.

On the global Internet, unlike the telephone network, individuals' data routinely travels outside the country in which the person lives. For Americans, that means that the NSA's SIGINT technologies can indiscriminately grab US persons' data when it travels overseas. One State Department whistleblower, John Tye, came forward in 2014 to report that the NSA was able to collect all Gmail, video chats, and buddy lists from

[26] J. Scahill and G. Greenwald. "The NSA's secret role in the U.S. assassination program." *The Intercept*. February 9, 2014. theintercept.com/2014/02/10/the-nsas-secret-role/

[27] P. Langlois. Interview with C. Stöcker. "Passively sniffing data: How mobile network spying works." *Der Spiegel*. November 15, 2015. www.spiegel.de/international/europe/interview-telecom-security-expert-philippe-langlois-on-gchq-spying-a-933870.html

[28] L. Poitras and J. Risen. "NSA gathers data on social connections of US citizens." *The New York Times*. September 28, 2013. www.nytimes.com/2013/09/29/us/nsa-examines-social-networks-of-us-citizens.html

[29] "Secret Surveillance: Five Large-Scale Global Programs." Joint Submission to the United Nations, Twenty-Second Session of the Universal Periodic Review Working Group. May 2015. d1ovv0c9tw0h0c.cloudfront.net/files/2014/09/cdt-aclu-upr-9152014.pdf

overseas. When Google, Yahoo!, and other companies store their data overseas, American data was part of the haul. Before Snowden, it was not immediately obvious to people that *foreign* collection could have such a big *domestic* impact.

MAINWAY, DISHFIRE, CO-TRAVELER, and other massive foreign collection programs take place within the US legal framework for permitting and regulating signals intelligence or SIGINT. Until recently, the American public didn't pay a lot of attention to SIGINT collection. Regulation of intelligence collection historically was looser than that for law enforcement investigations. Americans have been comfortable with these looser rules for a variety of reasons. We've assumed that foreign surveillance outside the United States mostly only impacts foreigners. Why should Americans – or Congress – care about foreigners subject to foreign intelligence spying? These are people who do not vote and who do not have any Fourth Amendment rights under the US Constitution.[30] Theoretically, these are also people who are less susceptible to abuse at the hands of US police.

Another reason for a looser approach is the view that intelligence is essentially a predictive sport. Spies are looking to understand a situation, not investigate a crime. The topics you want your government to understand can be both broad and innocent. Intelligence topics include things like oil prices, trade, and economic trends.[31]

As a result, intelligence-oriented spying that takes place outside the United States and which doesn't target particular Americans has been only lightly regulated. Foreign US spying takes place under a presidential order called Executive Order 12333 (EO 12333, pronounced "twelve triple three"). EO 12333 was issued during the Reagan era and has not been substantially amended since. It generally authorizes the federal agencies that make up the intelligence community to collect information on which the federal government can base decisions concerning the conduct and development of foreign, defense, and economic policy, and the protection of national security from foreign threats. EO 12333 operates in conjunction with other executive branch rules, some public, some still classified, that regulate what each intelligence community agency is allowed to do,

---

[30] *United States v. Verdugo-Urquidez*, 494 U.S. 259 (1990); see also M. L. Cohen. "*United States v. Verdugo-Urquidez*, the Fourth Amendment Has Limited Applicability to Aliens Abroad." *Md. J. Int'l L.* 14 (1990).

[31] Untitled NSA PowerPoint, The Office of the General Counsel. www.dni.gov/files/documents/1118/CLEANED021.extracts.%20Minimization%20Pr...cted%20from%20file%20021-Sealed.pdf

including how it may use and share data collected from surveillance. These post-collection rules are generally called "minimization procedures." Minimization procedures are full of loopholes that allow the intelligence community not only to collect, but also to use, analyze, and share Americans' communications data opportunistically collected as part of foreign spying. They are generally classified, can be changed in secret, and are inordinately complex. There are effectively no remedies for violations of minimization procedures.

Edward Snowden explains the scope of the collection this way:

> [T]he NSA specifically targets the communications of everyone. It ingests them by default. It collects them in its system and it filters them and it analyzes them and it measures them and it stores them for periods of time simply because that's the easiest, most efficient and most valuable way to achieve these ends. So while they may be intending to target someone associated with a foreign government, or someone that they suspect of terrorism, they are collecting YOUR communications to do so.[32]

The takeaway is that modern surveillance is both *massive* and *indiscriminate*. Where once we might have thought of international spying as government versus government, today it's governments versus individuals around the globe. Once we might have thought of spying as eavesdropping on known targets. Today, spying means opportunistically collecting information on everyone, in the hopes of finding the known and unknown threats among them. Instead, in the name of spying on drug dealers and terrorists, the government opportunistically captures voluminous amounts of data about hundreds of millions of innocent people, along with a smattering of the guilty. Then, computers comb through the mass, trying to find needles in the haystack, looking for patterns, seeking to turn billions and billions of pieces of "information" into usable "intelligence." In the words of law professor David Cole, the US government's surveillance capabilities are, "already well beyond our greatest fears."[33]

---

[32] E. Snowden. Interview with G. Greenwald and L. Poitras. "NSA whistleblower Edward Snowden: 'I don't want to live in a society that does these sort of things' – video." *The Guardian.* Online video clip. June 9, 2013. www.theguardian.com/world/video/2013/jun/09/nsa-whistleblower-edward-snowden-interview-video

[33] D. Cole. "Collect it all!: Newly released NSA documents reveal omnivorous appetite for our private data." *Just Security.* May 13, 2014. www.justsecurity.org/10396/newly-released-nsa-documents-reveal-omnivorous-appetite-private-data/

There are two main reasons for this change: technology and motivation. Today, technology has advanced to the point where governments can do massive surveillance, whether through Internet monitoring, capitalizing on the data collection by private companies, or using cameras and sophisticated software for license plate detection or facial recognition. The US government's stated motive for this collection is the problem of "asymmetrical warfare."

When EO 12333 was issued in 1981, the world was a different place. The threats were from nation states, like the Soviet Union, and diplomatic and military officials did not necessarily use the same communications networks as the general public. Today stateless terrorists can cause great harm. These non-state threats communicate over the global Internet. Terrorists can hide among a civilian population, so the theory is that ferreting out would-be evildoers requires listening thoroughly to that same population.

Even democratic governments will sometimes spy on regular people – when innocents talk to targets, when our behavior is sufficiently similar to that which characterizes dangerous people, in emergencies, and when government agents make mistakes. The question that the Snowden revelations brought into sharp relief is whether spying on routine people should be a routine practice. Does the kind of massive spying the United States is doing actually help protect the public from terrorism, and if so, at what countervailing social and political cost?

Using citizens' data to find terrorists presents a myriad of legal, ethical, and practical questions – who authorizes and polices the collection? If it has to be secret, how can we ensure it is also democratic, and how can people trust in what the government is doing with the data in our name? In a mass surveillance world, are post-collection rules adequate to protect civil liberties? The few internal policies we've seen, vague and permissive as they are, do not recognize the rights of foreigners at all, disregard attorney-client and other legal privileges, and allow data collected for national security reasons to be repurposed for dirty tricks, defamation, and run-of-the-mill criminal investigations. Could these regulations be strengthened, or are such usage rules inadequate to stop abuses? Does massive collection even work to keep the nation safer? Can a democracy survive a government with a rapacious appetite for personal data? Modern surveillance – its blanket approach to collection and its secretive nature – evades these questions.

In one slide presented at a 2011 meeting of the United States' closest spying partners, the NSA itself described its break from the old-fashioned investigate-the-bad-guy approach. The slide, entitled "New Collection Posture," entreats: "Collect it All," "Process it All," "Exploit it All," "Partner it All," "Sniff it All" and, ultimately, "Know it All."[34] We shouldn't shrink from considering the full implications of this terrifying mindset. To have any hope of properly managing modern surveillance, we need to admit and understand that American spies have an insatiable hunger for data.

[34] Greenwald, *No Place to Hide*, p. 97.

2

Word Games

Unfortunately, the public can't take the US government at its word when it comes to its surveillance practices. Of course, some of what the government does has to be secret. The public generally doesn't need to know, and generally can not know, whom the government targets without compromising investigations. We need to rely on other oversight mechanisms to ensure that the government doesn't go after the wrong people.

But American spies obscure far too much information about their collection practices and their legality. When the intelligence community talks about surveillance, it uses misleading vocabulary and relies on partial disclosures to hide the scope of the spying and its impact on individual privacy.

American spies have evolved a whole coded vocabulary that deflects any nonexpert, and sometimes experts as well, from learning the truth. Words like "collect," "target," "in bulk," and "surveillance" all have concocted meanings in the intelligence gathering context. If you rely on your common understanding of the words as they are generally used, you will not understand what in fact happens in the surveillance world. The public often does not know, though we are learning, what secret definitions the intelligence community has given to these words. Different agencies use the same words to mean different things. And, given how complex surveillance can be, there may not be clear words or phrases that concisely and accurately describe actual government practices. That means, when describing and debating intelligence spying, it's easy to misunderstand.

American spies know that they use counterintuitive and coded language. The Defense Intelligence Agency's "intelligence law handbook" explains and embraces this fact. In setting out rules for defense related spying, the handbook begins:

> To begin the journey, it is necessary to stop first and adjust your vocabulary. The terms and words used in DoD 5240.1-R[1] have very specific meanings,

[1] DOD 5240.1-R is entitled "Procedures Governing the Activities of DOD Intelligence Components that Affect United States Persons" and is the Department of Defense document that implements Executive Order 12333.

and it is often the case that one can be led astray by relying on the generic or commonly understood definitions of a particular word.

Along with the problem of "vocabulary adjustment" rides the problem of secrecy. Most of the definitions and the rules that one needs to know to understand modern surveillance were top secret just a few months or years ago, and could be again. In secret, the rules are still evolving. So something that was true in 2014 may no longer be the case and the public has no way of knowing that things have changed.

Rather than throw up our hands in exasperation, however, we have to make an effort to understand modern surveillance. The risks to our freedoms and democracy are too great not to pay attention. In the service of understanding, the public needs some clear, shared definitions of important terms. But the public also needs to understand the varying or nonintuitive definitions used by the intelligence or law enforcement communities. Otherwise, when listening to debates and doing research outside this book, readers will not be able to understand and assess what they are being told.

Let's start with the word *surveillance*. In this book, I use surveillance to mean government collection of private and personal information: address books, buddy lists, photos, phone numbers, web history, geolocation data, and more. I also call this spying. But in policy and legal discussions, most of this information gathering is not called "surveillance." Experts use "surveillance" as a term of art with a specialized legal meaning. "Surveillance" is a shorthand for "electronic surveillance." "Electronic surveillance" or ELSUR is a statutorily defined in the Foreign Intelligence Surveillance Act (FISA). There are four collection activities that FISA defines as "electronic surveillance." The definitions are complicated and narrow and do not include many kinds of data collection. So by using "surveillance" to mean only ELSUR governed by FISA, officials can say that they do not conduct "surveillance" even when they are collecting personal data like phone numbers, Internet transactional records, face prints, or geolocation data. The intelligence community might call its acquisition of this kind of information "collection," which sounds milder than "surveillance."

Let me explain the intelligence officials' reasoning in more detail. FISA defines four collection activities as ELSUR. Each activity has a multipart, complicated definition. Each definition identifies a type of information that might be subject to collection: a wire communication, a radio communication, or other information. Each subsection then further identifies the conditions under which collecting that type of information constitutes ELSUR. The conditions revolve around (1) whether the collection takes place inside the United States, (2) whether the collection targets Americans, or the government knows that an American is a party to the communication, and (3) whether an individual has "a reasonable expectation of privacy such that a warrant would be required for law enforcement purposes" before the government might collect this information.

As an example, consider the NSA's eavesdropping on phone calls. Landline phone calls are "wire communications." There are two parts of the ELSUR definition that set forth when the government's collection of wire communications (e.g. phone calls) constitutes ELSUR and thus must comply with FISA regulations. It's ELSUR if the government is targeting a known US person who is in the United States and that person has a reasonable expectation of privacy in the communication. It's also ELSUR if the government collects the phone call from inside the United States without consent. But collecting wire communications from outside the United States when the NSA doesn't have an American target is not ELSUR. So, eavesdropping on a Canadian law professor's phone calls from a vantage point in Canada is not "electronic surveillance." Intelligence officials would not call the collection "surveillance."

That example uses a relatively familiar technological and legal scenario, telephone wiretapping. But things get complicated – very complicated – when the NSA wants to collect electronic data. Under FISA, emails and other digital data being carried on a wire or fiber optic cable are treated as wire communications.[2] But it's only ELSUR to collect wire communications to or from a US person if (a) collection takes place inside the United States or (b) a particular, known US person in the United States is intentionally targeted AND has a reasonable expectation of privacy in the United States.

Now, let's explore how this narrow definition of surveillance means that even highly invasive government spying may be neither regulated by law nor acknowledged by intelligence community officials. The CO-TRAVELER program collects vast amounts of location data overseas. Is it

---

[2] 50 U.S.C. § 1801(l). In contrast to intelligence gathering, for criminal investigations, wire communications are limited to phone calls and other aural messages. "Wire communication" means "any aural transfer made in whole or in part through the use of facilities for the transmission of communications by the aid of wire, cable, or other like connection between the point of origin and the point of reception (including the use of such connection in a switching station) furnished or operated by any person engaged in providing or operating such facilities for the transmission of interstate or foreign communications or communications affecting interstate or foreign commerce." See 18 U.S.C. § 2510.

surveillance under the intelligence agencies' definition of that term? No, it is not. The collection takes place outside the United States. No US person is targeted because it's a bulk collection program. And most perniciously, the US government's official position is that individuals generally do not have a reasonable expectation of privacy in location data generated by their cell phones.

First, the legal consequence of CO-TRAVELER falling outside of the FISA definition of ELSUR is that the collection activity is unregulated by FISA. Unless it is covered by the Fourth Amendment or some other privacy-protecting statute, the collection of location information overseas is only limited by executive order. The political consequence of a collection practice falling outside of the "surveillance" definition is that intelligence community officials and lawmakers just won't use the word "surveillance" to describe the activity. So government agents can say with a straight face that they don't surveil Americans even if they are operating dragnets that routinely collect location data about Americans.

More broadly, the "reasonable expectation of privacy" loophole is a real problem. It could allow a lot of invasive government collection to evade FISA regulation. Here's an example. There's only one subpart of the ELSUR definition that covers the government's access to information on computer servers. That subpart says it's only ELSUR if people have a reasonable expectation of privacy in the information and a warrant would be required to obtain it in a criminal law context. However, the Department of Justice does not believe that people have a reasonable expectation of privacy in phone calling records, Internet transactions, financial records, hard drive backups, or other sensitive data stored with "cloud" Internet services. So, if that argument won the day, then government officials would not call their collection of Dropbox files, bank records, and other personal, revealing data "surveillance."

The word *bulk* is another opportunity for mischief. People use the word "bulk" as a synonym for massive, vast, or large-scale collection. But the intelligence agencies have a special definition of the word "bulk." They only use bulk to mean acquisition that takes place without using a selection term or "discriminator." In other words, grabbing *everything* is bulk. But if the government uses search terms, key words, or selection terms, it's not bulk. So, if, when wiretapping a particular fiber optic cable, the NSA selects or "tasks" all communications with the word "Syria" or "China" in them, the NSA lawyers might not call that "bulk," even though hundreds of millions of innocent people's irrelevant messages are going to be collected and analyzed. Similarly, the government won't say that its collection is *indiscriminate* if it uses any kind of selection term.

The opposite of "bulk" is *targeted*. If a collection technique is based on discriminators or selectors, it is "targeted." So surveillance experts call programs like PRISM, Upstream, and even some EO 12333 programs "targeted." The public might misunderstand, thinking that targeted collection means spying on a particular person – a computer query for "everything to or from Jennifer at granick dot com." But the targets could be Doctors Without Borders, or the Syrian government, or "people in Yemen who speak Arabic," or "anyone who has viewed this ISIS beheading video." Even if only one in ten thousand individuals spied on is a target, intelligence officials will still refer to the collection as "targeted."

These definitional subtleties render it difficult for people seeking surveillance reform to understand exactly how to accomplish those goals. In June 2015, Congress managed to pass a law called the USA Freedom Act in response to the section 215 phone dragnet. The idea behind the law was to stop massive collection of phone records, Internet data, and other personal data. To do this, the statute couldn't just end "bulk collection." That leaves open the possibility that the NSA will issue orders for all information from "Western Union" or "Visa." This kind of surveillance request would not be "bulk" in the NSA's dictionary, but it would still be massive collection affecting millions of innocent people. Instead, the statute took the approach of requiring a "specific selection term" and trying very carefully to define that phrase so that the search term couldn't be a communications provider, a language, or a country. Congress cannot be sure that the USA Freedom Act was successful until it reviews the actual operation of the new program.

Also ambiguous is the way American spies use the word *target*. Target is a key concept in surveillance law. But it is not defined in FISA or any other surveillance statute and it is used both as a noun and a verb. To be clear, the target is the individual or entity about which the United States seeks information. It is not the individuals wiretapped. Rather, spies can wiretap people who are talking about the target. The people whose communications the NSA collects are "monitored," but they are not called targets. That means that government officials can say that PRISM does not target Americans. The public may believe that that means that PRISM has little to do with American privacy. But in fact, the very purpose of the statute that authorized PRISM, section 702 of the Foreign Intelligence Surveillance

Act Amendments Act, is to allow warrantless wiretapping of Americans when we talk to people overseas.

The fact that the target is the person or entity *about* which the government seeks information makes the question of what constitutes a *selector* very important. It's one thing to collect on a person, like Osama bin Laden. But targets don't need to be individuals. They can be groups, like al-Qaeda. Targets can also be countries, like France or Germany. Selectors could also be the digital indications that a cybersecurity attack is underway. When talking about selectors, the NSA uses the phrase, "such as an email address or phone number" as an example. A designated selector could be something like BadGuy@ISP.com in the body of the email. The NSA could look for details about a user's computer software in order to uniquely identify people online – a so-called web browser fingerprint. But that doesn't mean that selectors can't be much broader than that. A selector can also include some other element believed to reflect a foreign intelligence or terrorism connection.[3]

The public has very little information about what kind of selectors intelligence analysts use. But we know that in one case, classified as a mistake by NSA internal auditors but not reported to Congress or to the FISC, NSA personnel queried a database for any communications that mentioned both the Swedish manufacturer Ericsson and "radio" or "radar." Because one of the PRISM/section 702 certifications issued by the FISC allows surveillance for cybersecurity purposes, experts intuit that hacking attack signatures may be selection terms. Even if the threat signature is pretty specific, using this type of information as a selector means that data hackers are stealing from victim's computers could constitute part of section 702 collection. We just don't know. Clearly, though, the risk of over-collection is huge: personal information or intellectual property could be part of that data collection.

Intelligence officials have told us that under PRISM and other section 702 surveillance, selectors are not keywords like "Yemen" or generic names like "Osama bin Laden."[4] Nothing in the statute would limit broad selectors or generic foreign intelligence topics. Nevertheless, it appears that through 2015, the FISC, which must approve the categories of foreign intelligence surveillance under section 702 and which exercises some

[3] D. Kris and J.D. Wilson. *National Security Investigations and Prosecutions*. 2d ed. (Eagan, MN: Thomson West 2012) §17.5.

[4] R. De. Testimony at "Public Hearing Regarding the Surveillance Program Operated Pursuant to Section 702 of the Foreign Intelligence Surveillance Act." PCLOB Board. March 19, 2014. p. 57.

oversight over the targeting procedures the NSA uses, would not approve broad or generic selectors as part of the targeting procedures.

For foreign collection, the public knows very little about what kinds of selectors are used, other than email addresses and phone numbers. A selector could be designed to capture all messages to people living in Yemen, for example. Former NSA cryptographer-turned-whistleblower William Binney has said that analysts search collected data for terms they believe their targets use. But the search terms can be quite broad. In 2012, the Department of Homeland Security (DHS) released search terms it uses to identify potential terrorists on social networking sites. Most of the terms were generic, like "cops" or "dirty bomb" and some were entirely innocuous, like "pork" or "subway."[5] Binney was highly critical of using these kinds of words to pull data out of NSA databases. "This buries you in data, you can never get through this. It's a waste of time."[6]

Selectors matter not just because their selection poses a risk of over-collection, but because there are different rules for selector-based and selectorless collection. The NSA has some limits on how it can analyze and share Americans' data it obtains via bulk collection overseas.[7] But those limits don't apply to "targeted" collection, even if the collection is huge. In other words, no matter how massive the collection is, the bulk collection rules don't apply if the analyst uses selectors.

I use the term *collect* to mean gather or acquire information. It's hard to come up with a simpler definition of the term. But the intelligence community sometimes defines collection in a way that occludes its actual dragnet approach. No matter how much data the NSA gathers, stores, data mines, and more, the intelligence agencies sometimes assert that "collection" doesn't happen until a human looks at it.

In March of 2013, Senator Ron Wyden (D-OR) asked Director of National Intelligence James Clapper in a congressional hearing whether the NSA collects any information at all on millions or hundreds of millions of Americans. Clapper knew the question was coming. Wyden had warned him he would ask it. In response, Clapper said, "[N]o, not wittingly."[8]

---

[5] "Analysts Desktop Binder." Department of Homeland Security. 2011. pp. 20–23 epic.org/foia/epic-v-dhs-media-monitoring/Analyst-Desktop-Binder-REDACTED.pdf

[6] A. O'Brien. "Retired NSA technical director explains Snowden docs." *alexaobrien.com.* September 30, 2014. alexaobrien.com/archives/900

[7] "Presidential Policy Directive 28 – Signals Intelligence Activities." White House Office of the Press Secretary. January 17, 2014.

[8] G. Kessler. "Clapper's 'least untruthful' statement to the Senate." *The Washington Post.* June 12, 2013. www.washingtonpost.com/blogs/fact-checker/post/james-clappers-least-untruthful-statement-to-the-senate/2013/06/11/e50677a8-d2d8-11e2-a73e-826d299ff459_blog.html

That answer sat in the public record until June 2013. After the Snowden revelations, we know that the NSA does in fact collect such information – specifically phone records, if not other categories of data, too – as Wyden, the Senate Intelligence Committee members, the DNI, and Clapper all knew at the time. Yet, Clapper refuses to admit that he had lied to Congress. Rather, in an interview with NBC's Andrea Mitchell,[9] he justified his answer with a legalism. He said that, "I responded in what I thought was the most truthful, or least untruthful manner, by saying no." Clapper indicated that his response to Wyden turned on a definition of "collect": "There are honest differences on the semantics of what – when someone says 'collection' to me, that has a specific meaning, which may have a different meaning to him." Clapper said that "collect" doesn't mean acquire or gather. It means "taking the book off the shelf and opening it up and reading it." And, information isn't collected if a machine is analyzing it, only if a human is.

Clapper didn't make this up, exactly. The Department of Defense intelligence handbook says information isn't "collected" until it is received for use by an employee of a DoD intelligence component in the course of his official duties. Electronic data is "collected" only when it has been processed into intelligible form.[10] Since so many of US intelligence law's safeguards and privacy protections hinge on the word "collect," Clapper's soft shoe routine would allow the NSA to gather, store, and use computers to data mine and analyze *everything*, and the law wouldn't kick in until a human read it.

In a similar incident, former NSA Director General Keith Alexander had told Congress that "we don't hold data on U.S. citizens." His statement didn't use the word "collect," and the world found out in June 2013 that his claim is entirely false. But some Obama Administration officials said that the NSA's internal definition of the word "*data*" doesn't include metadata. Later documents would show that their definition of SIGINT does include metadata.

[9] J. R. Clapper. Interview with A. Mitchell. "Director James R. Clapper Interview with Andrea Mitchell, NBC News Chief Foreign Affairs Correspondent." Office of the Director of National Intelligence. June 10, 2013. www.dni.gov/index. php/newsroom/speeches-and-interviews/195-speeches-interviews-2013/874-director-james-r-clapper-interview-with-andrea-mitchell

[10] "Procedures Governing the Activities of the DOD Intelligence Components that Affect United States Persons." Department of Defense: Under Secretary of Defense for Policy. December 1982. fas.org/irp/doddir/dod/d5240_1_r.pdf

There was an outcry in Clapper's and Alexander's defense. The officials were trying to adhere to the requirement to protect classified information while also answering the questions asked. The legalisms were just a way to get out of a difficult situation. But in doing so, the officials revealed that the public cannot believe what intelligence officials say.

About nine months later, the Privacy and Civil Liberties Oversight Board (PCLOB) held a hearing about PRISM and section 702. The PCLOB is an independent, bipartisan agency within the executive branch and established in August 2007. It is comprised of four part-time members and a full-time chairman. The PCLOB has two missions: (1) To review and analyze actions the executive branch takes to protect the Nation from terrorism, ensuring the need for such actions is balanced with the need to protect privacy and civil liberties, and (2) To ensure that liberty concerns are appropriately considered in the development and implementation of laws, regulations, and policies related to efforts to protect the Nation against terrorism.

At the March 2014 hearing, a PCLOB board member asked the NSA General Counsel Rajesh De to clarify what the agency meant by "collect." In his answer, De narrowly disavowed Clapper's definition of "collect." De said that, "for these purposes" acquisition and collection mean the same thing.[11] That won De some credibility in the PCLOB hearing. It also made the testimony and subsequent PCLOB report on section 702 easier to understand. But what did De mean by "for these purposes"? When does "collect" mean collect?

The Department of Defense procedures for handling Americans' information considers data "collected" only when "it has been processed into intelligible form." But the NSA's signals intelligence directive has a different definition. "Collection" is the "intentional tasking or selection of identified nonpublic communications for subsequent processing aimed at reporting or retention as a file record."[12] NSA General Counsel De confirmed in his March 2014 testimony before the PCLOB that the NSA uses the common definition of "collect" for section 702 spying.

> There are some theories out there that when the government receives the data it doesn't count as collection or acquisition. That is incorrect. Acquisition and collection for these purposes are the same thing.

[11] R. De. Testimony at "Public Hearing Regarding the Surveillance Program Operated Pursuant to Section 702 of the Foreign Intelligence Surveillance Act." PCLOB Board. March 19, 2014, p. 38.

[12] "USSID-18: Legal Compliance and U.S. persons Minimization Procedures." National Security Agency. July 25, 2011. § 9.2.

De sounded clear. But given how the intelligence community talks about surveillance, we should not overlook De's use of the qualifier "for these purposes." Given the definition of "collect" in the Department of Defense handbook, there almost certainly are surveillance programs other than section 702 for which the NSA and the Department of Defense do not call information *collected* until a human analyst takes a look at it. In other words, the public cannot assume that the definition the NSA uses for "collect" in the section 702 context is the same definition it uses for other programs, nor that the NSA's definitions bind the Department of Defense or other agencies in the intelligence community.

If an American is talking to, or sometimes even just about, a surveillance target, the American will be monitored. The intelligence community calls the monitoring of Americans that happens as a result of surveillance targeting foreigners *incidental collection*. The phrase makes it sound like there are only a few *incidents* when this kind of collection happens. In other words, incidental sounds unintentional and insignificant. In fact, incidental collection is the whole point of section 702 surveillance: the law was passed to enable the NSA to collect communications between Americans and foreigners. Collecting on Americans is a natural and intended consequence of targeting the international communications of foreigners. Further, there are far more than a few incidents. Incidental collection can overwhelm collection about the target. The *Washington Post* did an analysis of data Snowden provided that the NSA had collected pursuant to PRISM.[13] Only one out of ten people in the sample set was the target of the surveillance. Everyone else was "incidental" by-catch. From Snowden the public learned that spying on foreigners has a huge impact on American privacy. Use of the word "incidental" obscures that.

Another NSA obfuscation is the word *inadvertent*. In 2009, the *New York Times* reported that the NSA had been collecting Americans' messages to each other under section 702 and that this collection had been "significant and systemic."[14] The public later learned that the NSA told the FISC that the technological design of its Upstream collection devices mean that purely domestic communications are routinely captured. That doesn't sound "inadvertent," but that's what surveillance experts call it.

---

[13] B. Gellman, J. Tate, and A. Soltani. "In NSA-intercepted data, those not targeted far outnumber the foreigners who are." *The Washington Post*. July 5, 2014. www.washingtonpost.com/world/national-security/in-nsa-intercepted-data-those-not-targeted-far-outnumber-the-foreigners-who-are/2014/07/05/8139adf8-045a-11e4-8572-4b1b969b6322_story.html

[14] E. Lichtblau and J. Risen. "Officials say US wiretaps exceeded law." *The New York Times*. April 15, 2009. www.nytimes.com/2009/04/16/us/16nsa.html

Once information is collected – intentionally, incidentally, or inadvertently – so-called *minimization procedures* govern what different government agencies are allowed to do with the information, specifically information "concerning any United States person." In the criminal wiretap context, minimization means that the investigators have to take steps to limit – minimize – collection of information irrelevant to the approved investigation. But in the foreign intelligence context, the NSA maximizes the data it collects. Here, the word *minimization* doesn't mean a prohibition on collecting irrelevant information. Instead it means the procedures and regulations for analyzing, sharing, and keeping data after it has been collected. In other words, "minimizing" doesn't mean narrowing collection, and it doesn't necessarily mean throwing away irrelevant data. It means applying the so-called minimization rules for using, analyzing, sharing, or sometimes discarding data. In other words, minimizing can mean analyzing or sharing even though it sounds like it means discarding or deleting.

Another way the intelligence community confuses the public about the impact of minimization is when it lauds the minimization procedures that limit the NSA from certain uses of collected data concerning Americans. Of course, the NSA may only act in accordance with its foreign intelligence mission. But there are other agencies in the government that also have access to Americans' data that the NSA collects. The FBI has far more liberal rules for accessing and using Americans' data than the NSA does. Under rules declassified in 2015, the FBI can not only search PRISM databases for US-person information as part of routine criminal investigations, it may also do so to initiate an investigation without any suspicion of wrongdoing. The FBI may then share that information with the Drug Enforcement Administration (DEA), Internal Revenue Service (IRS), and other law enforcement agencies. In short, minimization rules may limit what the NSA can do given its foreign intelligence mission. But they don't stop the NSA from making its broad collection of data including information about Americans available to the FBI and the DEA for use in criminal cases.

Minimization rules allow the NSA to keep American data indefinitely if they include "foreign intelligence information," a term that encompasses any conversation relating to the conduct of foreign affairs. And even communications that don't include foreign intelligence information can be retained for as long as five years unless the analysts are confident that it could not be foreign intelligence. At that point the information is *purged* from NSA systems. But purged doesn't necessarily mean deleted. Purged means "deindexed" or otherwise made unavailable. So purged can mean kept, but not findable. Supposedly.

Spy program code names have a similarly confusing effect. The MAINWAY database holds one kind of information, while the CO-TRAVELER database holds another. Talking about specific programs generally means talking about surveillance in pieces. It doesn't help the public understand surveillance if we view government collection as this or that program taking place under one or another legal authorities. It can also be misleading to talk about the legal limitations for a particular surveillance program when there are other surveillance programs that collect similar data and do not have those same limitations. That's seeing the trees instead of the forest. The truth is that surveillance programs interact and feed data to each other. What's important is the big picture. Surveillance takes place under multiple legal authorities and is robust and comprehensive. For that reason, I tend not to use program names in this book because, while they sound cool, they aren't very enlightening.

That brings us to another important term, *search*. American spies hate to use the term "search." That's because searches are governed by the Fourth Amendment. If something is a search then government agents probably need a warrant to do it. And spies don't want to get warrants. So they have a different word they use for this kind of data analysis, a *query*. A query is what an analyst does when she is looking through or analyzing information already in the government's custody.

Consider President Obama telling Americans they have nothing to fear from the NSA's foreign intelligence spying. His claim is based on the fact that SIGINT law generally establishes special protections for "United States persons" (US persons) defined as citizens, permanent resident aliens, US corporations, and associations substantially comprised of US persons. These protections are less robust than they should be. But more fundamentally, who gets to be one of these *US persons*? Incredibly, the answer to this question is another spy word game. Despite a clear statutory definition of "US persons," we do not know to whom the FBI extends the statutory protections. That is because the FBI has a classified definition of who is and who is not a US person.[15]

---

[15] "A Review of the FBI's use of Section 215 Orders: Assessment of Progress in Implementing Recommendations and Examination of Use in 2007 through 2009." US Department of Justice: Office of the Attorney General. May 2015, p. vi.

We know this from the NSA inspector general. Inspectors general perform oversight of the NSA and the FBI under the auspices of the Department of Justice. In May of 2015, an inspector general report looking at the government's use of the section 215 phone dragnet was partially declassified. The report makes clear that the FBI has secret criteria for who it treats as a US person. At one point, the report makes reference to a "classified directive to the definition of U.S. persons," and then blacks out the remainder of the sentence detailing what that directive says.[16] If there is a secret definition of "U.S. persons," then how can we feel reassured when the President says Americans need not worry? Who is in that group that enjoys special protections, and who is left out?

***

Surveillance law and technology are complicated to begin with, but the agency language exacerbates the lack of trust between the public and the intelligence community. Nonexperts are confused and excluded from the discussion. And even potential experts like Congress or the PCLOB have to struggle mightily to understand what it is that they are being told.

Is the doublespeak intentional? Take, for example, Senators Feinstein and Chambliss telling Americans that the NSA was not getting the content of their messages "under the 215 program," when they knew full well that content is collected, just under a different law. Or President Obama saying that no one is listening to our phone calls when he is fully aware that the NSA is gathering our international emails and instant messages. The concern was not that a human was listening to everything Americans say. It was that our emails and instant messages were being collected and potentially screened for communications with foreigners that have no connection with counterterrorism, or for key words and phrases like "bomb," "marijuana," "protest," or "fuck the police." We're worried about new technologies which allow all our calls to be recorded, run through a speech-to-text translation,[17] and computer-analyzed for foreign intelligence selectors, criminal activity, political activism, and more.

Former Representative Mike Rogers, who once chaired the House Intelligence Committee, told CBS's *Face the Nation* that there was no government surveillance of phone calls or emails. "They do not record your

---

[16] Ibid.
[17] D. Froomkin. "The computers are listening: How the NSA converts words into searchable text." *The Intercept.* May 5, 2015. theintercept.com/2015/05/05/nsa-speech-recognition-snowden-searchable-text/

e-mails ... None of that was happening, none of it – I mean, zero."[18] Rogers, during the debate over whether to reauthorize section 702, also downplayed its effect on American privacy, saying that spying on Americans "has not happened frequently at all."[19] Today, we know that was grossly misleading.

The evidence suggests that the misdirection is intentional, at least on the part of some officials. The misstatements go well beyond the kind of obfuscation needed to keep terrorists complacent about using surveilled networks. American spies know they have to maintain public acquiescence, and they believe that if people knew the truth, the programs would lose support. But in order to make informed decisions about surveillance, the public needs to be able to penetrate the lingo and legal concepts and to decipher the evasive answers it receives. As cryptographer Matt Blaze once said, crafting a question to get meaningful answers from the NSA is a lot like crafting a wish to get a genie to give you what you actually want. Trying to avoid the realm of the magical and esoteric, the public must tread very carefully, and ask for documentation, declassification, and multiple sources of information before we can truly be confident that we know what kind of spying is going on in our names.

[18] "Face the Nation Transcripts July 28, 2013: Rogers, Udall, and the latest from Egypt." *CBS News*. July 28, 2013. www.cbsnews.com/news/face-the-nation-transcripts-july-28-2013-rogers-udall-and-the-latest-from-egypt/

[19] J. Sanchez. "Our dishonest debate over NSA spying." *The Hill*. September 24, 2012. thehill.com/blogs/congress-blog/technology/251301-our-dishonest-debate-over-nsa-spying

3

Snowden, Surveillance Whistleblowers, and Democracy

Edward Snowden, a twenty-nine-year-old NSA contractor and computer security expert, used his position as a contractor and system administrator to take voluminous classified documents detailing secret US government spying programs. Snowden broke the law by disclosing classified information. He did so because he believed it was the lesser of two evils. Edward Snowden came into the NSA with fresh eyes and a libertarian political philosophy steeped in our Founding Fathers' fear of a government grown too powerful. Snowden has been able to explain very succinctly exactly what the NSA is capable of, and why it scared him.

> "The NSA has built an infrastructure that allows it to intercept almost everything."
> "... I believe that at this point in history, the greatest danger to our freedom and way of life comes from the reasonable fear of omniscient State powers kept in check by nothing more than policy documents."

Snowden has said he hoped for a systematic debate about the danger that massive and robust surveillance poses to American liberty. Snowden saw something, and he said something.[1]

Snowden gave those documents to reporters including Glenn Greenwald, Laura Poitras, and Barton Gellman, who used them to discover and report on massive domestic and international spying. Snowden fled the United States, eventually ending up in Russia. Almost immediately after the public learned that Snowden was the source of the leaked documents, the surveillance debate started to veer from the question of whether what the United States was doing was legal and right to the question of whether what Edward Snowden did was legal and right.

This debate is misguided and facile. Is Snowden a traitor or a hero? Does he deserve to be called a whistleblower, or did he take too many documents? Is he denied that status because most of the programs he revealed were legal,

---

[1] "If You See Something, Say Something." *dhs.gov.* Department of Homeland Security. www.dhs.gov/see-something-say-something

albeit highly disturbing? Why didn't Snowden pursue alternative means of raising his concerns internally, rather than go to the press? If Snowden was so sure that what he did was right, why didn't he come home and face the music? Amazingly, there has been a vigorous public debate about whether Snowden is a conceited jerk, mostly fueled by people who have fewer Twitter followers than Snowden has. After Snowden ended up in Russia, the demonizers turned up the volume. Putin is way worse than Obama. Surely Snowden was a Russian spy. He should come home and take his punishment.

These criticisms are mostly unfounded. Snowden didn't bring documents with him to Russia. He had nothing with him when he left Hong Kong.[2] Snowden didn't want to go to Russia. That was one of the only options left to him after the US government cancelled his passport and brought down the Bolivian President's plane over France, having received a false tip that Snowden was aboard. Snowden would not get fair treatment in a trial in the United States. He would likely be held in solitary confinement and would be prohibited from talking – even in court in his own defense – about the surveillance abuses that motivated his disclosures.

Whistleblowers like Snowden aren't well protected under US law. Instead, they face great personal danger in coming forward. The information they are revealing is usually classified or covered by a nondisclosure agreement, as employers don't want their wrongdoing widely known. The law generally will not protect whistleblowers from retaliation or prosecution if they make public allegations. Whistleblower protection laws, including the 1998 Intelligence Community Whistleblower Protection Act that former Secretary of State Hillary Clinton has pointed to,[3] would only have allowed Snowden to talk to an inspector general or to the congressional intelligence committees. These entities were presumably aware of at least some domestic spying, and had done nothing about it. Further, whistleblower protection generally does not extend to contractors like Snowden. Even so, the law would only protect Snowden if his report was of "urgent concern." Policy disagreements are not matters of "urgent concern." It's unlikely the law would cover Snowden's reports about programs that had been ongoing in one form or another for fifteen years.

But the negative, misguided statements have an impact. When comedian John Oliver asked tourists in New York's Times Square who Snowden

---

[2] J. Risen. "Snowden says he took no secret files to Russia." *The New York Times*. October 17, 2013. www.nytimes.com/2013/10/18/world/snowden-says-he-took-no-secret-files-to-russia.html

[3] "CNN Democratic Debate – full transcript." *CNN*. October 13, 2015. cnnpressroom.blogs.cnn.com/2015/10/13/cnn-democratic-debate-full-transcript/

was, many people didn't know, but those who thought they did were clearly confused by the anti-Snowden onslaught. Several people said Snowden sold secrets to other governments. Some confused him with Julian Assange, the head of Wikileaks, a government transparency website that generally declines to exercise editorial control over documents posted there. In other words, smears and inattentiveness mean that many Americans have either no impression or the wrong impression of who Snowden is and why he disclosed the information he did.

The "is Snowden a traitor" question isn't actually about Snowden. By demonizing Snowden, advocates for massive surveillance can sway public opinion without engaging, or by distracting us from, the real question at hand: is government spying out of control, and if so, what are we going to do about it? As Snowden himself recognized, "I know the media likes to personalize political debates, and I know the government will demonize me."[4]

Rather than talk about Snowden, the public should talk about what he helped reveal: surveillance and government malfeasance. American spies, in conjunction with our global spying partners, are collecting voluminous amounts of information on hundreds of millions of admittedly innocent people, including Americans. The documents Snowden gave to reporters show illegal conduct, the shocking scope of modern surveillance, abuses and other questionable government activity. Without this information, our government would without a doubt still be lying to us.

The public needs to start to understand Snowden, not as a hero or a traitor, but as one of many individuals who discovered that the US government was breaking the law, violating human rights, or secretly conducting surveillance beyond the public's worst fears. Snowden was not the only person that blew the whistle on overbroad surveillance, but he was the one who contributed documents that made it impossible for government officials to continue to ignore all the other conscientious objectors that had come forward. These whistleblowers, acting according to their conscience, revealed classified information to the public, and these disclosures have been and continue to be a critical part of keeping the American government in line. Looking back, the public often decries the disclosure in the moment. But with the benefit of hindsight, leaks that reveal government malfeasance or ill-advised policy become a valued part of American history, a way for us to improve our democracy.

[4] "You can't go home: The uncertain fate of Edward Snowden." *RT.* June 10, 2013. www.rt.com/usa/snowden-nsa-whistleblower-fate-492/

To be very clear, it is not a prerequisite that the government have been acting illegally for whistleblowing to be valuable and justified. There are many things government officials do that are not against the law but which are terrible. There are few laws that regulate national security practices, including surveillance. The legal strictures that might have constrained spying in the aftermath of the Hoover and Watergate eras have been watered down after the attacks of September 11th. The technology has changed such that practices that previously did not impact Americans now very much do. The secrecy surrounding intelligence spying inhibits Congress from realizing where new laws are needed.

The secrecy also creates an echo chamber, where intelligence officials believe they are right because no one else in the room will say otherwise. This is especially true with surveillance. Ethical considerations that constrained American spies have been wiped away by the fear of terrorism. As General Michael Hayden, the former head of the NSA has said, "we're going to play inside the foul lines, but there's going to be chalk dust on our cleats." Anything less, he believed, would be playing it safe, and not doing everything he could to protect the nation. It makes sense that stopping terrorist attacks is Hayden's overwhelming consideration. It was one of his only jobs. But unless there are other people involved in the decision making who are responsible for conducting foreign relations, promoting American economic competitiveness, improving cybersecurity, ensuring information privacy, protecting civil liberties and human rights, and pursuing other US interests, then these countervailing goals are going to get elbowed out of consideration.

The value of whistleblowing under these circumstances is no less real when the disclosures are illegal. In 1971, Daniel Ellsberg leaked the so-called Pentagon Papers, forty-three binders or 7,000 pages worth of information about US mishandling of the Vietnam War. Ellsberg was a former military analyst who worked on the Pentagon Papers while at the RAND Corporation. Nixon demanded that the CIA spy on Ellsberg and that they try to bug his psychiatrist's office. The Department of Justice criminally prosecuted Ellsberg under the Espionage Act. Eventually, the prosecution was so poisoned by misconduct it had to be dismissed. Meanwhile, newspapers sought to publicize the Pentagon Papers. The government scrambled to censor the information before the *New York Times* and other papers could publish it. The Nixon Administration claimed that the publication would irrevocably harm national security. The Supreme Court allowed the newspapers to publish, despite Nixon's national security claims.

That Supreme Court decision is now celebrated for its strong stance in favor of a free press. Nixon's security claims turned out to be false; the Administration was trying to avoid embarrassment, not protect the country. Public opinion about the Vietnam War started to turn, not only because of the Pentagon Papers, but also as reporters discovered and reported on US atrocities like the My Lai massacre. Eventually, the United States got out of Vietnam, and the Department of Justice decided not to retry Ellsberg. Then, he was facing decades in prison. Today, Daniel Ellsberg is viewed as a hero for helping put an end to an ill-advised war.

We have burglars to thank for public exposure of the FBI's extensive COINTELPRO domestic spying program. By breaking into an FBI office, these law breakers helped expose some of the worst political abuses in US history. Antiwar activists knew that the FBI was infiltrating peace and civil rights groups, but without documents, they couldn't conclusively prove it. A small group of activists decided that they would break into an FBI office to acquire evidence. Knowing that the physical security was too great at any main office, the group staked out a small satellite office in Media, Pennsylvania. The break in, compellingly portrayed in the documentary film 1971, netted a number of important papers, but also a routing document, just a slip of paper with the word COINTELPRO on it. No one knew what that word meant at the time, but NBC News reporter Carl Stern demanded more information about COINTELPRO under the Freedom of Information Act. His request eventually revealed that COINTELPRO was a domestic spying program to neutralize political activism from peace groups, civil liberties groups, the American Socialist Party, and more. The Media, PA burglars were never caught. They went underground and waited. In 2014, as part of the film and in support of Edward Snowden, the surviving members came forward and confessed their role.

Snowden wasn't the first and he won't be the last modern surveillance whistleblower. Other brave people have come forward to oppose illegal and massive spying. People are supposed to come forward if they see that something is wrong. But those who have come forward were told to keep their heads down and mind their own business. These people were repeatedly stymied and faced great personal risk – losing their jobs, or worse. Eventually, when other avenues failed, they went public.

In 2004, Mark Klein walked into the offices of the Electronic Frontier Foundation (EFF), a San Francisco–based digital civil liberties organization that I worked for from 2007 to 2010. Klein told EFF attorneys that the NSA had built a secret room in an AT&T facility located in San Francisco.

A fiber optic cable routed an exact duplicate of all the phone and Internet traffic handled by that facility into the secret room, giving the NSA direct access to domestic and international communications handled by the phone company – billions of pieces of sensitive personal information. Klein also reported that similar systems were installed in Seattle, San Jose, Los Angeles, and San Diego, and probably other cities as well.[5] This was surprising not just because it meant that the NSA was altering phone networks for surveillance, but also because the agency, which is supposed to gather intelligence only about foreign affairs, had access to and could scan legally protected domestic calls and emails. Klein's testimony formed the basis for lawsuits against both AT&T and the federal government for illegal wiretapping of Americans.[6]

Modern surveillance is different from traditional surveillance in the extent to which spies gather vast quantities of American data. That is because off-limits information about Americans is intermingled with foreign data to a greater extent on the Internet than on telephone and satellite networks, and the collection techniques the NSA has chosen to use do not precisely discriminate. The intelligence community talks about inadvertent collection as a necessary by-product of critical surveillance that keeps the Nation safe. But what if that over-collection is sloppy or, even worse, opportunistic? Would that change the privacy risks we accept?

That's the debate that a number of NSA engineers came forward to inform the public about after September 11th. These scientists were working to build a tool that would allow analysts to use the data the NSA obtained about foreigners, while hiding data about Americans, who are generally off-limits to the agency. At the same time, the NSA needed to be able to perform sophisticated data analysis to make sense of the flood of information the agency was collecting. Cryptographer William Binney and his colleague Ed Loomis were working on such a tool, which they called ThinThread.[7] Some officials at the NSA

---

[5] Former NSA cryptographer and whistleblower William Binney says that the NSA has built between 80 and 100 surveillance posts in telephone and Internet company offices around the country, of which the Folsom Street office is only one. See A. O'Brien. "Retired NSA technical director explains Snowden docs." *alexaobrien.com.* September 30, 2014. alexaobrien.com/archives/900

[6] D. Kravets. "NSA leak vindicates AT&T whistleblower." June 27, 2013. *Wired.* www.wired.com/2013/06/nsa-whistleblower-klein/

[7] E. Loomis. "Frontline interview: United States of Secrets." *PBS Frontline.* December 12, 2013. www.pbs.org/wgbh/pages/frontline/government-elections-politics/united-states-of-secrets/the-frontline-interview-edward-loomis/

thought Binney was a genius and that ThinThread was amazingly good.[8]

But General Michael Hayden, the NSA Director from March 1999 to April 2005, put the kibosh on ThinThread. Hayden chose to develop a different tool called Trailblazer. Trailblazer lacked the privacy protections Binney and Loomis built into ThinThread. There was internal resistance to Trailblazer, not just because it was unnecessarily privacy invasive, but also because it was not ready for deployment. Meanwhile, Trailblazer was pushed by external government contractors who wanted to charge the NSA for developing the tool.[9]

The terrorist attacks on September 11, 2001 pushed the NSA further toward Trailblazer and more domestic surveillance. The attacks were particularly embarrassing for the NSA, as the agency was charged with making sure US officials have the intelligence to identify and head off such attacks in advance. Ed Loomis, the NSA cryptologist who had worked on ThinThread, took the attacks personally. Later he would tell PBS in tears that if only ThinThread, had been deployed rather than derailed, the NSA might have been able to prevent the September 11th attacks.[10]

Thomas Drake agreed with Loomis. Drake started as a senior NSA executive the very morning of September 11th.[11] The NSA was reeling from the attacks, and Drake was charged with identifying anything and everything that the NSA could do to rise to the challenge. Drake learned about the ThinThread project and championed it internally. But higher-ups rejected it and eventually Drake was told that the NSA had decided to go with a different program. At the same time, he was hearing analysts say that they were being told to use NSA spying tools on internal American networks and conduct surveillance without a warrant.

Drake learned that the agency had decided to strip the privacy-protecting technology out of ThinThread and use the contact chaining functionality built by Binney to find out who Americans were calling. Contact chaining means identifying everyone that a particular phone number or email address is in contact with.

[8] J. Rothman. "Tales: The NSA surveillance programs." *The New Yorker.* June 6, 2013. www.newyorker.com/books/double-take/takes-the-n-s-a-s-surveillance-programs

[9] Ibid.

[10] E. Loomis. "Frontline interview: United States of Secrets." *PBS Frontline.* December 12, 2013. www.pbs.org/wgbh/pages/frontline/government-elections-politics/united-states-of-secrets/the-frontline-interview-edward-loomis/

[11] T. Drake. "Frontline interview: United States of Secrets." *PBS Frontline.* December 10, 2013. www.pbs.org/wgbh/pages/frontline/government-elections-politics/united-states-of-secrets/the-frontline-interview-thomas-drake/

Telephone call analysis was just one part of what Drake learned the NSA was up to. In the days following September 11th, President George W. Bush launched a program codenamed STELLARWIND. Stung that the September 11th terrorists were communicating with people inside the United States and yet the intelligence agencies had failed to stop the attacks, STELLARWIND was designed to keep tabs on Americans. The STELLARWIND program involved four different types of illegal information collection. First, there was the dragnet collection of phone call records, collection that continued through the end of 2015. Second, there was the dragnet collection of Internet metadata – websites you visit, who you email. Third was the warrantless wiretapping of Americans' international calls and emails. Finally, there was the acquisition of financial records. Outraged by what they saw as unnecessary spying on Americans, Binney, Loomis, and their colleague Kirk Wiebe resigned from the NSA.

Drake took the whistleblower path that Secretary Clinton and others have said Snowden should have tried. Drake raised the issue with the NSA's Office of the General Counsel, and was told to stop asking questions. Next, Drake tried Diane Roark, a professional staffer with a top-secret clearance on the House Permanent Subcommittee on Intelligence, who had been overseeing the NSA since 1997. Roark credited Drake's complaints, but she couldn't stop STELLARWIND.

Meanwhile, Binney, Loomis, and Wiebe complained internally to a Department of Defense inspector general about the cancelation of ThinThread and how expensive TrailBlazer was proving to be. Inspectors general are an important resource, investigators who are supposed to identify and stop financial and legal abuses inside the intelligence community. The whistleblowers didn't report the illegal STELLARWIND spying in their complaint to the inspector general. They couldn't. STELLARWIND was top secret, and the inspector general didn't have the necessary security clearance to know about it. So they just raised the issue of financial mismanagement, claiming ThinThread worked and TrailBlazer didn't, and that Trailblazer was proving to be too expensive.

The inspector general instituted an investigation, which went on for years. Meanwhile STELLARWIND continued. Then, in December of 2005, the *New York Times* disclosed the NSA's warrantless domestic wiretapping.[12] Citing anonymous sources, the article revealed that the agency

[12] E. Lichtblau and J. Risen. "Bush lets US spy on callers without courts." *The New York Times.* December 16, 2005. www.nytimes.com/2005/12/16/politics/bush-lets-us-spy-on-callers-without-courts.html

had been capturing Americans' phone calls and emails without a warrant, in violation of FISA and other federal privacy laws.

The story was sparked by information the newspaper received from Thomas Tamm. Tamm was an attorney in the United States Department of Justice (DOJ) Office of Intelligence Policy and Review (OIPR) in 2004. The OIPR is the part of the DOJ responsible for green lighting American surveillance within the executive branch. OIPR attorneys review government surveillance requests and say whether they are legal or not. Tamm learned that the NSA was wiretapping communications inside the United States and that certain of these wiretaps were being hidden from all but one of the eleven judges specially appointed to the FISC, the top-secret surveillance court designed to review surveillance applications. The applications were also being hidden from senior officials in the Department of Justice except Attorney General John Ashcroft himself.[13] Tamm tried to talk to a friend with a top-secret clearance who was working with the Senate Judiciary Committee, the committee charged with overseeing the Department of Justice and OIPR. His friend told him to drop it. So in 2003, Tamm went to the press. Approximately eighteen months later, Tamm's tips to the *New York Times* formed the basis for the paper's December 2005 story revealing the Bush Administration's illegal, warrantless wiretapping program to the nation.

After the *New York Times* story, Tamm was investigated by the FBI and had his house raided. Drake, who had been complaining long and loudly about the NSA's improprieties, was also suspected of the leak to the *New York Times*. But Drake hadn't revealed anything secret. He had, however, leaked unclassified information about contractor fraud related to TrailBlazer to Siobhan Gorman, then a reporter for the *Baltimore Sun*. Gorman wrote a series of stories for the *Sun* detailing government fraud, waste, and abuse. In 2006, she also wrote a story about ThinThread and the cryptographers' view that it both provided superior intelligence and also protected US persons as compared to Trailblazer.

The FBI retaliated. In July 2007, armed FBI agents raided the homes of Drake, Roark, Binney, and Wiebe. One morning Binney got out of the shower to find himself at gunpoint. Drake was charged with five counts under the Espionage Act for giving information to Gorman, even though

---

[13] T. Tamm. "Frontline interview: United States of Secrets." *Frontline.* December 11, 2013. www.pbs.org/wgbh/pages/frontline/government-elections-politics/united-states-of-secrets/the-frontline-interview-thomas-tamm/; M. Isikoff. "The whistleblower who exposed warrantless wiretaps." *Newsweek.* December 12, 2008. www.newsweek.com/whistleblower-who-exposed-warrantless-wiretaps-82805

investigators could not identify any classified information he had disclosed. Drake's charges were dismissed when, instead of risking life in prison, he pleaded guilty to a misdemeanor. Tamm was also under investigation. Only in 2011 did the DOJ inform Tamm that they would not pursue criminal charges against him. Then, in 2016, Tamm learned that as a lawyer, his bar association would pursue ethics charges against him for his role in revealing STELLARWIND. So much for whistleblower protections. Only later did the bar association agree to allow Tamm to keep his license to practice law.

Meanwhile, these whistleblowers' complaints that Trailblazer was a financial fiasco driven by defense contractor greediness were vindicated. In 2005, NSA Director Hayden told the Senate that the Trailblazer program was several hundred million dollars over budget and years behind schedule. In 2006, the NSA shut the Trailblazer program down.

Snowden learned from these whistleblowers' mistakes. He didn't go to the *New York Times*, which at the Bush Administration's request had sat silently on the warrantless wiretapping story for eighteen months, a time period that included George W. Bush's reelection campaign. He went to Laura Poitras, a journalist who had herself experienced government surveillance and harassment following a documentary she made about NSA cryptographer Binney. And, soon after the first leaks, Snowden revealed himself as the whistleblower, knowing that if he didn't, his co-workers would be subject to early morning raids by gun-wielding FBI agents.

Perhaps most importantly, Snowden watched how other whistleblowers, reluctant to disclose classified information, complained about expense rather than illegality. He watched how the government was able to obfuscate the truth about STELLARWIND by renaming it a "terrorist surveillance program" and by only talking about the parts of the program they thought they could defend. So rather than complain verbally, Snowden leaked classified documents. And rather than focus on particular illegal programs, like the section 215 phone dragnet, Snowden obtained documents that broadly described the scope of surveillance the US government was conducting.

As with Ellsberg or the Media, PA burglars, the documents Snowden revealed proved impossible to ignore or spin. Seymour Hersh, the reporter known for uncovering the My Lai massacre, for his Watergate reporting, and for his investigation of the Abu Ghraib prison abuses, summed up the impact of the documents Snowden assembled and disclosed:

> Duncan Campbell [the British investigative journalist who broke the Zircon cover-up story (a SIGINT satellite)], James Bamford [US journalist]

and Julian Assange and me and the *New Yorker*, we've all written the notion there's constant surveillance, but he [Snowden] produced a document and that changed the whole nature of the debate, it's real now.[14]

There's a corollary to my entreaty that the public focus on what Snowden revealed, rather than focus on Edward Snowden as a person. That corollary is that we ought to extend the same courtesy to American spies. We should avoid either demonizing or canonizing the intelligence community officials that have created and sheltered the modern surveillance state in America. This debate isn't personal. I have no doubt that intelligence community officials love this country as much as I do. Nor do I doubt that their primary motivation is to protect our nation from terrorist attacks.[15] This is not a debate over whether intelligence officials are well-meaning or of good character.

Instead, I think the political disagreement over surveillance policy stems from a fundamental philosophical difference about human nature: whether you believe that unchecked power inevitably corrupts, or rather believe that the sincere intentions of well-meaning individuals will protect us. Some Big Surveillance defenders believe that history is made by great individuals standing against evil ones. I believe that brave people can make a difference, but that larger inexorable forces are often more important: history, economics, political and social systems, the environment. I believe that power corrupts and that good people will do bad things when a system is poorly designed, no matter how well-intentioned they may be. American spies are not necessarily bad people, though without question there are bad people among them. Rather, permissive surveillance policies and practices eventually, inevitably, will lead to abuse.

How do good people sit at the witness table before Congress and assure the American public that the government is properly constrained, when in reality officials lie and disregard even the most anemic purported safeguards? A simplistic view is that these are not actually good people. But the easy answer masks the truth about systems of power, a truth we must understand and respect if we are to fix this surveillance nightmare we are just beginning to uncover.

---

[14] L. O'Carroll. "Seymour Hersh on Obama, NSA and the 'pathetic' American media." *The Guardian*. September 27, 2013. www.theguardian.com/media/media-blog/2013/sep/27/seymour-hersh-obama-nsa-american-media

[15] Unfortunately, the same understanding is not always extended to civil libertarians by the intelligence community.

Systemically, we know what will go wrong. History has shown us. There will be mission creep – once you build the mousetrap of surveillance infrastructure, American spies, law enforcement, other countries' governments, and even civil litigants will come for the data. First it was counterterrorism, then it was drug investigations, then it was IRS audits. Next it will be for copyright infringement.

There also will be both "inadvertent" and intentional abuse, inevitable but difficult to discover. Bored analysts will do things like spy on women using surveillance cameras and listen to American soldiers overseas having phone sex with their loved ones back home. Or an FBI agent may investigate strange but not unlawful emails on behalf of a family friend, which is exactly what led to a sex scandal that brought down David Petraeus, former director of the CIA. These surveillance tools and information databases may one day end up in the hands of a Richard Nixon or J. Edgar Hoover. People once believed this could never happen again. But political abuse of private information is not the exception in American history. It has been the rule. For decades, presidents demanded embarrassing information about their political opponents. Only more recently did Congress try to rein in abuse of that information. But today, in our age of modern surveillance, the government most assuredly has salacious news somewhere in its surveillance data treasure trove.

Liberty and security are the hard-won results of democratic process and limited government power. A system of mass surveillance puts innocent people at risk, and is, in itself, an abuse of liberty. Inevitably, it leads to further abuses. When the justification is counterterrorism, and that's your only concern, there is no countervailing interest that justifies slowing you down or stopping you. The good people in the intelligence agencies have run over the Fourth Amendment, government accountability, freedom of expression, rule of law, and so many other equally critical components of the American system out of a good faith belief that it will keep us safe. Actually, they are endangering the economy, security, and political well-being of the United States.

Snowden broke the law by taking and revealing top-secret documents. But in doing so, he helped the American people stand up to government disregard for civil liberties. Today, the US government can no longer ignore public demands to ensure individual freedom and democratic accountability in a modern surveillance world.

4

We Kill People Based on Metadata

It might be surprising in the modern era how easily an outsider could discover what we do every day. In the past, most of our activities went unnoticed and unrecorded. But that is less and less true. Every day, we generate piles of data, just by using cell phones and the Internet. Our location is tracked, our faces are recorded, our digital reading is logged, and our expenditures tallied. Even more surprising is how much someone can learn about us when all this information is aggregated and analyzed by computers. Our most private moments are recorded and subject to exposure, if only someone cares to look.

A Golden Age for Surveillance

It used to be that most of the things we did generated no records. When you read, or pay with cash, or walk down the street, no one takes note. But today, both online and offline behaviors leave a trail.

Online we track things that created no record in real life. For example, reading at a library or bookstore leaves no trace. But online searches, connecting to websites, clicking to the next page, do. If I use a web browser to visit the *New York Times* website, then the *Times* server that hosts the page, as well as the routers between my machine and the news site, have access to the IP address assigned to my computer. The IP address doesn't include my name or address, but it generally can – in conjunction with other information – be tied to my real name and address.

Our web browsing traffic also contains the website address – called a Uniform Resource Locator or URL – of the site I'm visiting and may include the site I just came from. The URL can reveal exactly what I'm reading. For example, if someone visits the opinion piece that law professor Chris Sprigman and I wrote for the *Times* about how the NSA has violated the law, the URL is www.nytimes.com/2013/06/28/opinion/the-criminal-nsa.html. Other browsing data tells anyone with access to that digital traffic – the website host, the Internet Service Provider (ISP), or the government – how long the reader spent on that page, and where she went to next.

This digital effluvia is readily traced back to us. In the early days of the public Internet, people laughed at the joke that no one on the Internet knows if you're a dog. If that was ever true, it's no longer true today. IP addresses are one way that people can be identified online. Police can ask ISPs which of their subscribers was using a particular IP address at a given point in time. But we have even more exact ways now. Internet usage sheds seemingly innocuous little pieces of information, like our computer's default language, time zone setting, operating system version, and "cookies" set on our machines by webpages and advertisers. When aggregated and used together, these bits of data serve as effective digital trackers. They create a "fingerprint" capable of uniquely identifying our computer's web browsing software, and thus us, as we use it to conduct our business online.

It's also true that technology tracks offline activities, and will only do so more in the future. Mobile phones are location trackers. Whenever handsets are turned on, even when they are not in use, they send signals to the nearest cell towers so that the communications network system knows where to route a call, should one come in. These inevitable "pings" can be used to identify the tower or towers closest to the targeted handset. It's necessary for providing cell phone services. But recording pings is also a highly effective way of tracking any particular individual's physical location around the clock.

New technology not only reveals where we go, but whom we know. Mobile phones can be used to figure out who is together at any given place and time. "Tower dumps" give police identifiers for all phones that were connected to a particular cell tower at a particular point in time. Asking for a tower dump from near the scene of a crime can give you a pool of potential suspects. Asking for a tower dump from near the Alcoholics Anonymous meeting gives you a list that includes people managing their addiction. The same records from the tower near a political protest or mosque gives you a list of people exercising their First Amendment right to demonstrate or to practice their religion.

When you make phone calls, email, or text, unless you or your service provider take precautions, you are generating a record of the people with whom you are communicating. The NSA gathers Americans' (and foreigners') phone call records from US companies and abroad. For years, the DEA has had access to records of every call that passes through AT&T switches, even including location information.[1] It is impossible to mask

---

[1] S. Shane and C. Moynihan. "Drug agents use vast phone trove." *The New York Times.* September 1, 2013. www.nytimes.com/2013/09/02/us/drug-agents-use-vast-phone-trove-eclipsing-nsas.html

your physical location when using a telephone because of the nature of how landlines and mobile devices work.

Gus Hunt, former Chief Technology Officer of the CIA, makes this point. Noting that mobile phones and tablets come with cameras, accelerometers, light detectors, and geolocation capabilities, he said, "[Y]ou are aware of the fact that somebody can know where you are at all times, because you carry a mobile device, even if that mobile device is turned off... You know this, I hope? Yes? Well, you should."[2]

If you drive a car in certain cities, cameras are almost constantly recording your travels. Automatic license plate readers are in widespread use. These devices take photographs of every car that drives by, and computers translate the photo of the license plate into a machine-readable, easily searchable database of plate numbers. The portrait that emerges is a comprehensive record of where you go and what you do – church, school, doctor, friends. And it's not just you, it's potentially every driver. These databases are generated by police, toll bridge authorities, and repossession companies. But once they exist, anyone who searches them can find where you went in the past, and even use that information to predict the future.

Automatic license plate readers are supplemented by other kinds of video recorders and cameras taking our picture. Today, these are everywhere, recording and storing our movements. Private businesses frequently install security cameras that record activities at their front door and inside the premises to fight shoplifting or detect employee misconduct. Law enforcement may also install cameras on poles or lampposts in selected neighborhoods. Cameras may be pointed at buildings considered to be high-profile targets for attackers, or may simply be posted around neighborhoods deemed to be "high crime." Increasingly, cameras are mounted on drones, on bike helmets, or on police car dashboards and police officers themselves. Unlike human eyeballs, these cameras create records that are kept and can be searched later. Increasingly, computers will be able to do these searches for little or no cost. Cameras will continue to challenge our ability to maintain a zone of privacy or to conduct our innocent business unnoticed.

Such digital observation of daily life is especially true because new technologies are making it possible for computers to understand photos. Facial recognition technology is getting quite good. So, instead of the

---

[2] M. Sledge. "CIA's Gus Hunt on big data: We 'try to collect everything and hang on to it forever." *Huffington Post*. March 30, 2013. www.huffingtonpost.com/2013/03/20/cia-gus-hunt-big-data_n_2917842.html. It remains technologically unclear how turned-off phones could be tracked.

time-consuming and expensive effort it takes to have a person look at hundreds of photos or watch hours of boring video, now machines can do it at rapid speeds. Tracking is not just an online activity. Technology is making massive offline tracking possible, inexpensive, and useful. These innovations often start on the battlefield or in foreign intelligence.[3] But as the technology gets cheaper, law enforcement and eventually local police departments start to use it for ordinary policing as well.

Of course, there are many more of our activities being digitally tracked – what you read on the web, your credit card transactions, and more. Loyalty cards track your grocery shopping. Apps track your taxi rides and vacations. As Justice Sonya Sotomayor wrote in a recent Supreme Court case involving officers placing a GPS tracking device on a suspect's car:

> People reveal a great deal of information about themselves to third parties in the course of carrying out mundane tasks. People disclose the phone numbers that they dial or text to their cellular providers; the URLs that they visit and the e-mail addresses with which they correspond to their Internet service providers; and the books, groceries, and medications they purchase to online retailers.[4]

Justice Sotomayor's opinion describes the volume and the sensitivity of information individuals provide voluntarily whether they understand this or not. Digital information technology transforms individual experiences that were once secret (like what we read), expensive to track (like where we go), and traditionally ephemeral (whom we talk to or what we buy) and creates durable records that are cheap and easy to find and to aggregate. It makes the past searchable and the future more predictable.

The data shedding is only going to get worse as more of the everyday appliances we use are networked together and connected to the Internet. The business buzzword for this is the "Internet of Things." The term means that hardware devices like your stove, your thermostat, and your car, which were originally stand-alone machines, will be monitored and controlled through the Internet. Like cell phones, social networking, and email, these innovations can be extremely useful. I can preheat the oven before I get home from work. I can get an estimate to fix my car without having to go into the shop. But networked things will inevitably generate information about me from which you can reliably draw meaningful and sensitive

---

[3] J. Risen and L. Poitras. "N.S.A. collecting millions of faces from web images." *New York Times.* June 1, 2014. www.nytimes.com/2014/06/01/us/nsa-collecting-millions-of-faces-from-web-images.html

[4] *United States v. Jones,* 32 S.Ct. 945, 957 (2012) (Sotomayor concurring).

conclusions. The heat was off all weekend; we were probably out of town. I stopped driving my car to the office every day; perhaps I got fired. My Fitbit says I'm not sleeping. Is my insomnia indicative of a health problem?

The NSA is aware of and exploiting these trends. Snowden documents show that the NSA considers offline data like facial images, fingerprints, and other identifiers just as important to its mission of tracking suspected terrorists and other intelligence targets as digital communications data.[5]

Ultimately, we generate more information and it becomes cheaper and cheaper to store it. Government doesn't have to pick and choose who is important enough to tail or wiretap. Private industry keeps data on everyone. American spies can just go to a phone or Internet company and demand all their data. They will get it, unless the law stops the company from turning it over. For these reasons, scholars have said that we are living in a golden age for surveillance.[6]

Public-Private Partnership for Modern Surveillance

Collection of data by private companies is a key part of government surveillance. There are so many great inventions that make our lives easier and more satisfying. Social networks, remote backups, unlimited webmail are extremely popular today because they provide us valuable, even beloved, services. Facebook puts us in touch with our friends, lets us plan and find events, and keeps track of our "Likes" and messages. iPhone owners regularly use Apple's iCloud for replicating data across devices and for backing up precious photos, files, emails, and more. Google's Gmail service provides up to 15GB of free email storage, everything you've ever written to anyone.[7] Moreover, it scans the messages for annoying spam and dangerous malware. Dropbox, a file storage and sharing tool, gives users up to 18 GB of space at no cost.[8] Every draft, authority, and research note for this book is stored and synched through the Evernote tool. Companies collect and keep our information.

---

[5] J. Risen and L. Poitras. "N.S.A. collecting millions of faces from web images." *New York Times.* June 1, 2014. www.nytimes.com/2014/06/01/us/nsa-collecting-millions-of-faces-from-web-images.html

[6] P. Swire. "The golden age of surveillance." *Slate.com.* July 8, 2015. www.slate.com/articles/technology/future_tense/2015/07/encryption_back_doors_aren_t_necessary_we_re_already_in_a_golden_age_of.html

[7] "See your storage limit." *Google.com.* March 2016. goo.gl/JUXe16

[8] "How much does Dropbox cost?" *Dropbox.com.* March 2016. www.dropbox.com/en/help/73

We are all are complicit in generating and sharing this personal information with "third party" companies. In the public debate over consumer privacy, we often see elderly Luddites wagging the naughty finger at young people for using Facebook and other social apps. They argue that it's our own fault if we don't have any privacy. But this blame game only goes so far. What would it take to stop information tracking? People would have to forgo mobile phones, credit cards, and other everyday fixtures of modern life that even self-proclaimed Luddites would have trouble giving up.

On the other hand, innovation libertarians tell us that privacy is dead, and we should "get over it" if we want cool, new innovations. Technology is integrated into our daily lives. Business models and corporate privacy practices are difficult for individuals to influence. There are valuable benefits to be derived from data sharing and collection, including social networking.

But the threat from ubiquitous spying is too great for complacency. Further, data collection is not synonymous with technological innovation. For many services, it's the business model, not the technology, that mandates the collection of data on us.

Free online services pay for themselves by collecting and sharing data about users with their true customers, the advertisers. As technology Bruce Schneier has said, "If you aren't paying, you aren't the customer. You're the product." Our information is used to target advertising that pays for the services we've learned to enjoy for free.

The biggest motivation for information collection is so that digital robots can read our stuff and figure out how to best target advertisements to us. Advertising works better when you already know what the person is interested in. In the past, sellers had to make a rough guess, because ad spaces addressed only mass markets. *Good Housekeeping* has ads that sellers think housewives will be interested in. *Sports Illustrated* has ones that sellers think fans will like. You had to generalize, because tens or hundreds of thousands of people are going to see the same ad.

But online, sellers can be much more targeted. That's because ads are selected and delivered separately from webpage content. When two people visit the *New York Times* website, we'll see the same news stories. But the *New York Times* website "knows" more about us. It probably knows what other *Times* articles we've read. Ad companies on the site may know what other websites we've been to, and even what we shopped for there. That means that the *Times* and its advertising partners can help sellers show each visitor a different ad designed just for their interests. So if the site knows that I'm female, and a lawyer, and my general income bracket, it might show me an ad for a nice pair of heels for the office. It might show my father an ad for a car he wishes he had when he was younger. Advertisers bid for these spaces in a real time auction that takes place in a split second. And they'll pay more to get their ad in front of someone they think will buy. So I'm worth a lot more to the advertiser, and to the *New York Times*, if they know I've been shopping for a washing machine. Then appliance companies will pay more to show me washing machine ads.

So the more they know, the more they can charge for my "eyeballs" – my attention to that ad space. The incentive, then, is to track me all across the web, and to synthesize that data with whatever they can discover about my offline life. As long as we don't pay for online services, as long as providers make money from advertising, the incentives to track, store and correlate data about us will remain huge.

Once private data is collected by service providers, it becomes available to the US and other governments, too. Not only does the data exist, it's readily available from a few reliable key players. AT&T, Google, Yahoo!, Apple, Microsoft are all extremely popular with millions or billions of users. Serving legal process, or hacking, these companies puts amazing amounts and quality of data in both criminal investigators' and spies' hands.

Since surveillance law is complicated and secret, customers are very dependent on platform companies to serve a gatekeeper role. We want a lawyer at the company to check the court orders and government directives with which they are served to see if they are valid. We want someone to make sure that government agents received no more data than that which is absolutely authorized by law. More than that, in the absence of robust legal protections, we do not want the companies to change their networks or their data delivery systems to make it any cheaper or more convenient for the government to come suck that data out.

Certainly, some of the Internet platforms companies have this same pro-privacy streak, and view themselves as a critical check on government power. For example, in 2007, Yahoo! unsuccessfully challenged the Protect America Act (a precursor law to the FISA Amendments Act) before the FISC. All the proceedings took place in secret. Yahoo! did this despite legal fees, government threats of a huge and escalating fine for noncompliance, and the fact that none of their customers would know about the challenge. We only know about the challenge today because Yahoo! pressed the court to declassify the documents, which the FISC did in 2014. The declassification likely happened only because the NSA wanted to tout the court's legal approval of the program so as to blunt public concerns in the wake of the Snowden revelations that the analogous PRISM collection violates the Fourth Amendment. If the US government hadn't decided that it was in the intelligence community's best interests, the public might not have known about this ruling until the sealing order was scheduled to expire, in 2033.

Despite Yahoo!'s efforts, Internet companies generally are in a weak position to rein in government overreaching. The court process and the reasons for surveillance are kept secret from the companies. The cases that interpret the government's powers under the law are secret. And whatever protections the FISA Amendments Act might afford to Americans, it serves no such role for the foreigners that comprise the vast and growing majority of any global company's customers. When the government comes with a lawful but secret court order signed by a judge and demanding data, companies can review the order skeptically. They can judiciously select the responsive information. At the risk of huge fines, they can bring an expensive, secret lawsuit in a court that has proven exceedingly deferential to American spies. But beyond these quixotic efforts, the company's powers to protect their customers from US government surveillance are limited.

Big Data, Big Insights

Modern technology also means that there are new and powerful ways to make sense of the information we have. Modern analysis tools – called "Big Data" tools – can derive important and unexpected conclusions from aggregating and analyzing these kinds of large data sets. The ability to make sense of data means that the data itself is very valuable in unexpected ways. So information that at first glance might not seem so important, like so-called phone metadata, is actually quite revealing and sensitive.

Edward Felten is a Princeton computer science professor currently with the White House Office of Science and Technology Policy as Deputy U.S. Chief Technology Officer. Felten filed a declaration in support of the Electronic Frontier Foundation's legal challenge to the NSA's phone dragnet. Felten's declaration spells out how mere phone call information can reveal exceedingly private facts.

In many cases, just seeing the number you dial reveals private information about you. Investigators can easily find out who the owner of that particular phone number is. There are reverse-lookup directories marketed to law enforcement. Even Internet search engines can often identify the owner of a number.

Once identified, the numbers are quite revealing. It could be a dedicated number for whistleblowing, charitable donations, or health information. Inspectors general at nearly every federal agency have dedicated hotlines through which employees are encouraged to report misconduct, waste, and fraud. One call to this hotline says it all. Hotlines exist for people who suffer from addictions to alcohol, drugs, or gambling; for victims of rape and domestic violence; and for people considering suicide. Contact with a dedicated number can reveal donations to churches, to Planned Parenthood, to the National Rifle Association, or to a particular political candidate. In the hands of the wrong people this information can be used to humiliate, threaten, blackmail, politically target, or ostracize people.

The sensitivity of the data increases as it's collected over time. A call to a bookie means a surveillance target probably made a bet. But, Professor Felten writes, "analysis of metadata over time could reveal that the target has a gambling problem, particularly if the call records also reveal a number of calls made to payday loan services." Similarly, one can figure out the story if:

> A young woman calls her gynecologist; then immediately calls her mother; then a man who, during the past few months, she had repeatedly spoken to on the telephone after 11pm; followed by a call to a family planning center that also offers abortions.[9]

So when Senators Feinstein and Chambliss said that metadata isn't private and isn't anything to worry about, they were wrong.

To illustrate how revealing metadata can be, NPR's national security reporter Larry Abrahmson conducted an experiment. He contacted Cesar Higaldo, a professor at the MIT Media Lab and the designer of a program called Immersion. Immersion is a data analysis tool that looks at the volume and frequency of your email traffic, but only to/from information; it doesn't view the contents of your emails or even the subject line. In other words, it ignores *what* you are writing about and looks only at with whom and when you communicate. In this sense, the data it uses for the experiment is similar to the call detail records in the NSA's phone record database. While the NSA can and does analyze that information in conjunction with other more comprehensive information sources, for the sake of the experiment, let's look at what Professor Hidalgo and Abrahmson found out just by analyzing metadata.

---

[9] *ACLU v. Clapper.* United States District Court for the Southern District of New York. Case No. 13-cv-03994. Declaration of Professor Edward W. Felten, para. 52, p. 18.

Hidalgo's computers mapped everyone Abrahmson wrote to and weighted the connection for frequency over time. This query immediately identified Abrahmson's girlfriend, Anita, and the data visualization tool then drew her as a big blue circle right in the center of Abrahmson's social network map. Hidalgo could see that the couple met four years ago and that things started out slowly, but that as time passed, messages flew back and forth at a faster rate. The couple became closer. Abrahmson reports that the Professor explained, with a wink: " 'It was a little bit timid in the beginning, and then the relationship intensified.' " Hidalgo could also tell that Abrahmson's college-age son was not emailing his father back, and he identified Abrahmson's friendships that had waned over time.

The phone dragnet Snowden revealed is even more insidious than Hidalgo's example since it's more than collection about one person over time; it's collection about *everyone* over time. Data about everyone can reveal surprising things about people that might not be obvious just from those individuals' records. Data scientist Kieran Healy colorfully made this point in an article written to illustrate how revealing metadata can be, especially in bulk. Writing in the voice of a British intelligence agent before the American Revolutionary War, albeit one with access to modern computerized data analysis and visualization tools, Healy started with membership lists of organizations in pre-Revolution Boston, Massachusetts. The data consisted only of whether someone was a member of an organization or not. Echoing common government assurances that bulk collection of metadata was a trivial privacy infringement, Healy wrote, "surely this is but a small encroachment on the freedom of the Crown's subjects."

However, flipping the data tables, Healy could tell not only who belonged to what organization, but also which organizations were linked through the people that belonged to them both. He then visually diagrammed the information as a social network map showing who the links were *between* organizations. This map revealed that out of 254 names on the list, there were two that prominently stood out as connectors between the most groups. Based on minimal information, data science correctly identified Paul Revere as a dangerous man to watch out for, without ever reading a single one of his letters.

The Limits of Encryption

Some look at the problem of surveillance and respond that the answer is to use technology to secure information so that it is impossible for spies to get it. But encryption isn't going to protect most of our sensitive data.

The messages we store with free advertising-based email services like Gmail are not going to be encrypted. Our social networking posts won't be either. Our video viewing habits and books we've read currently cannot be encrypted without impeding the recommendation engines. Our medical records must be able to be encrypted and decrypted by our care providers. If we want to protect private information, we need good laws, too.

When companies need to hold data, the information should be protected from illegitimate access. This is easier said than done. One of the primary tools for protecting data like this is encryption. Encryption is a mathematical technique for scrambling data so that only people with decryption keys can read it. If data is stolen, but encrypted, generally the attackers will not be able to make sense of it.

Generally, services had not prioritized encrypting our data in storage or in transit before 2013. Before 2013, many Internet companies took the view that encryption is too expensive to implement, and consumers don't really want it. But after Snowden, when people realized how much surveillance the NSA is doing and foreigners realized how few privacy protections they have from NSA spying, global Internet companies began rapidly rolling out more encryption. Foreign users whose rights are not robustly protected under US law were demanding it.

Furthermore, the trust between US-based companies and the US government was shattered by the spying revelations. In particular, Internet companies felt stung by news that the NSA had not been using US legal process to ask politely for specific user data. Instead, the agency and the United Kingdom's GCHQ had collaborated to gain access secretly to entire Yahoo! and Google data center information flows. As the companies backed up data on internal networks to improve service performance, spies were there, drinking from the firehose of information. The *Washington Post* published documents obtained from Snowden showing how Google and Yahoo! had been attacked by the GCHQ. One slide included what looked like a yellow Post-It note with a sketch of how Google's internal networks connected to the public Internet. At the point of connection, a notation indicated "SSL added and removed here" with a little smiley face. SSL is encryption for data flows, which at the time was only being used when Google servers communicated over the public Internet. And so the spies tapped the internal network where there was no SSL encryption. As the *Washington Post* explained, by tapping those flows, the NSA can "collect at will from hundreds of millions of user accounts, many of them belonging to Americans." The spying program was called MUSCULAR.

Google employees were shocked by the slides detailing the MUSCULAR program. On the G+ social network, Google network security engineer Brandon Downey detailed the many threats he struggles to protect the Google network from, and his disappointment in learning that one of them was his own government. "Fuck these guys," he wrote. "Even though we suspected this was happening, it still makes me terribly sad. It makes me sad because I believe in America."[10] In his official capacity as Google Chairman, Eric Schmidt told the *Wall Street Journal*, "It's really outrageous that the National Security Agency was looking between the Google data centers, if that's true." The NSA responded:

> The NSA conducts all of its activities in accordance with applicable laws, regulations, and policies and assertions to the contrary do a grave disservice to the nation, its allies and partners, and the men and women who make up the National Security Agency.[11]

The United Kingdom's GCHQ isn't prohibited from hacking American companies and then sharing the data with the NSA. If there are no laws, or we don't even know what the secret regulations and policies are, the NSA's assurance rings hollow.

There were also reports that the NSA had been spoofing Microsoft Windows' crash reporting system to find ways to break into computers and take whatever information was there. A Microsoft spokesperson pointed out that the company complied with valid legal process and handed over data that the US government is entitled under law to get. However, "Microsoft does not provide any government with direct or unfettered access to our customer's data… We would have significant concerns if the allegations about government actions are true."[12]

So Silicon Valley took steps to put customer data out-of-government-reach without asking the companies first. After the MUSCULAR news, Google and Yahoo! started encrypting their data center transfers and email exchanges. Other online publishers and services, including government agencies, moved to secure users' connections with HTTPS, an encrypted protocol for websites. Since June 2013, actions taken by private companies

---

[10] B. Downey. "This is the big story in tech today." *Google+*. October 13, 2013. plus.google. com/+BrandonDowney/posts/SfYy8xbDWGG

[11] "NSA's Activities: Valid Foreign Intelligence Targets Are the Focus." NSA/CSS Press Room. October 31, 2013. www.nsa.gov/news-features/press-room/statements/NSA-Activities-Valid-FI-Targets.shtml

[12] "Microsoft responds to report NSA snooped In Windows." *CBS News*. December 30, 2013. www.cbsnews.com/news/microsoft-responds-to-report-nsa-snooped-in-windows/

to encrypt data have been the most effective step taken to protect innocent persons' private data from massive government spying.

Policy wonks often decry the mistrust that has grown between Silicon Valley and Washington D.C. in the aftermath of the Snowden revelations. But some mistrust is actually healthy. It was a strong bond between AT&T and the US government that was the basis for the illegalities of STELLARWIND. And spying collaboration can go well beyond just unlawful sharing of customer data. One NSA document describes an unnamed corporate partner as "aggressively involved in shaping traffic to run signals of interest past our monitors." In other words, the provider, which carries Internet and phone call traffic on its network, has structured its service so that communications are more likely to flow through spying devices the NSA has installed on various digital networks. There are no laws that require communications providers to conduct traffic shaping at the behest of government. Yet the document reveals that in a single month, this top-secret, voluntary, public-private partnership yielded more than 6 billion records of telephone calls and Internet activity.[13]

Not everything can be encrypted. In order to filter spam, quarantine malware, provide movie recommendations, and show our friends our baby pictures, current technology does not data. That means that the service provider can read the information. If the service provider can read it, so can law enforcement and intelligence agencies. Law enforcement can compel companies to turn over or can wiretap unencrypted data with the proper legal process. But intelligence agencies also have the resources to hack data flows, network switches, telecom gateways, and cell phone providers. These well-funded attackers are capable of accessing unencrypted data in bulk and opportunistically storing as much as possible from everyone.

You ask, "what can they know about me?" The answer is pretty much everything. And there's no point pretending that some categories of data are not revealing and thus there is no need to be worried about government collecting them. With aggregation and Big Data techniques, even Big Surveillance supporters have stopped pretending that metadata collection doesn't violate your privacy. Former NSA General Counsel Stewart Baker has said that, "metadata absolutely tells you everything about somebody's life. If you have enough metadata, you don't really need content." Michael

---

[13] Greenwald, *No Place to Hide*, p. 105.

Hayden, the former NSA and CIA Director, agrees. Referring to the criteria by which the Department of Defense selects targets for assassination by drone – location data, presumed identity, nearby associates – Hayden admits, "we kill people based on metadata."[14]

[14] See "The Johns Hopkins Foreign Affairs Symposium Presents: The Price of Privacy: Re-Evaluating the NSA." Johns Hopkins University. Online video clip. *YouTube*. April 7, 2014. www.youtube.com/watch?v=kV2HDM86XgI

5

The Shadow of September 11th

September 11th made clear that international terrorists could endanger American lives in the United States. Counterterrorism officials point to September 11th as a justification for broad and suspicionless surveillance, and, for the most part, Americans have been sympathetic to that argument. The tragedy may be an honest motivation for massive surveillance. Or counterterrorism may be the most politically palatable explanation for a tool that has other law enforcement, economic, and foreign affairs justifications. But massive surveillance has little or no track record demonstrating its effectiveness in preventing terrorist attacks.

September 11th wasn't the first terrorist attack on American soil. The Oklahoma City federal building bombing in 1995 killed 168 people and injured hundreds more. It wasn't even the first attack by foreign terrorists. In 1993, men affiliated with al-Qaeda detonated a truck bomb at the World Trade Center, killing six. But the September 11th attacks showed that the United States could be seriously hurt by a much weaker opponent.

Americans take this danger personally. A December 2015 poll showed that 47 percent of respondents reported that they are very or somewhat worried that they or someone in their family will be a victim of terrorism, up from 33 percent in 2014.[1] This reaction isn't rational. Vastly more Americans are killed by cars and gun violence than by terrorism. Americans are more likely to be fatally crushed by furniture than killed by a terrorist.[2] More died from gun violence in the United States in 2015 (13,400) than have died in over forty-five years from terrorism across Western Europe (6,411; 1970–2016).[3] But September 11th changed the

---

[1] C. L. Grossman. "Poll: Americans fear terrorism, mass shootings – and often Muslims as well." *USA Today*. December 10, 2015. www.usatoday.com/story/news/2015/12/10/religion-news-service-poll-terrorism-shootings-muslims/77101070/

[2] A. Shaver. "You're more likely to be fatally crushed by furniture than killed by a terrorist." *The Washington Post*. November 23, 2015. www.washingtonpost.com/news/monkey-cage/wp/2015/11/23/youre-more-likely-to-be-fatally-crushed-by-furniture-than-killed-by-a-terrorist/

[3] Numbers via the Global Terrorism Database and the Gun Violence Archive.

way that Americans perceived their risk from terrorism. We have over-reacted ever since.

These asymmetric attacks were particularly scary for intelligence officials, not merely in their surprising scope of damage, but also because the threat remained comparatively hard to ferret out. In the Cold War, the United States spied on the Soviet Union. We could focus our surveillance on known targets and locations. Compared to the Soviet Union, terrorists aren't very powerful. But their strength is in their ability to hide and to strike unexpectedly. Terrorists can be anyone, anywhere. Terrorist groups are small, scattered, moving targets, with no national borders or fixed locations. As Eric Haseltine, the NSA's Director of Research at the time of September 11th, told PBS: "The Russians were easy to find and hard to kill, and terrorists are hard to find and easy to kill."

The lesson the intelligence community took from September 11th was that the United States should conduct much broader spying. The enemy is unknown, and could be anywhere, even inside the United States. So, in theory, there's value in watching everything and everyone. This is the position the Bush Administration adopted following the attacks. It implemented STELLARWIND, a compilation of domestic dragnet programs to collect phone records, Internet data, financial data, and communications with people overseas.

In addition to, and hand in hand with, broader surveillance incentives came an emphasis on an intelligence, rather than enforcement, approach to surveillance. Law enforcement is focused on solving, prosecuting, and punishing crimes. Once something happens, we use searches and seizures to find out who is responsible, and punish them. Intelligence is focused on collecting information that will assist policy makers in understanding the future better. Law enforcement strives to meet a legal standard like "probable cause", or "beyond a reasonable doubt." Intelligence analysis isn't supposed to try to prove anything. It's proactive, seeking to identify potential threats to the public or to gather information that will be useful in trade negotiations, foreign policy planning, and more. As Fred F. Manget, a former Deputy General Counsel of the Central Intelligence Agency, wrote in 2006:

> Intelligence looks forward and provides an estimate of what is happening and will happen. Everyone is guilty until proven innocent, and innocence does not last. Double jeopardy is a fact of life, not a bar to future actions. And plots, betrayal, espionage, hacking, stealing secrets, and deception can be good things.[4]

---

[4] F. F. Manget. "Intelligence and the Criminal Law System." *Stanford Law and Policy Review* 17 (2006): pp. 415–436.

It should be obvious why domestic intelligence could be both a useful and a very dangerous thing. Exploratory intelligence investigations are going to collect information on people who pose no danger to the nation. Intelligence is subtle. At least some of the decisions we make are going to be mistakes, and people will suffer. Once information is obtained, there's a risk that it might be used for all kind of other purposes, from discriminatory or retaliatory enforcement of the law to blackmail. If the US government turns intelligence investigations against US citizens, then the people are at great risk. We haven't yet done the basic work of figuring out how to mitigate those risks.

The United States did not treat the September 11th attacks as a criminal act to be investigated and punished. Instead, President George W. Bush vowed "never again." He made it the mission of the national security agencies – domestic and foreign – to identify planned attacks on American soil in advance and head them off at all costs. Former FBI Director Robert Mueller tells of a meeting with the President soon after September 11th where he began to brief the room on the FBI's efforts to collect evidence against the September 11th perpetrators. President Bush stopped Mueller and asked him what the bureau was doing to stop something like this from happening again.[5]

Mueller saw the need to change the focus of the FBI from a domestic *law enforcement* agency to that of a domestic *intelligence* agency. For most of its history, the FBI had played a domestic intelligence role, going after anarchists, communists, antiwar activists, the civil rights movement, and white supremacists. But congressional investigations during the 1970s revealed that the FBI was spying on antiwar and civil rights groups, breaking the law, and otherwise overreaching its power and infringing on civil liberties. Americans' taste for domestic intelligence operations soured. The FBI temporarily focused on its other mission as the US premier federal law enforcement organization.[6] But now, Mueller and Bush thought the pendulum should swing back. The FBI would reinvest in its domestic intelligence capabilities. The Bureau more than doubled after September 11th, and the technology and human resources were put toward intelligence rather than criminal investigation.[7]

---

[5] February 12, 2014, Mueller Guest Lecture in Modern Surveillance Law class at Stanford Law School taught by Granick and Richard Salgado.

[6] Ibid.

[7] B. Kenber. "Outgoing director Robert S. Mueller III tells how 9/11 reshaped FBI mission." *The Washington Post.* August 22, 2013. www.washingtonpost.com/world/national-security/outgoing-director-robert-s-mueller-iii-tells-how-911-reshaped-fbi-mission/2013/08/22/ee452170-0b54-11e3-9941-6711ed662e71_story.html

The national security justification for intelligence surveillance is not new. Every administration has used this justification for surveillance, from Teddy Roosevelt to Franklin Delano Roosevelt to George W. Bush to Barack Obama. What's new is that the risks such surveillance poses to individual liberties and to political groups are magnified because modern collection is massive, indiscriminate, and can affect billions of innocent people. Since the Cold War, it's also relatively new that there's a shared confidence that a dangerous potential attacker could be anyone, anywhere, and not just a nation state adversary like Russia. We don't know who the enemy is, and we are able to collect data about everyone. These ideas comprise a pro-surveillance ideology premised on the notion that by spying on everyone, we will be able to find "the bad guys." As the CIA's chief technology officer Ira "Gus" Hunt explained, "[t]he value of any piece of information is only known when you can connect it with something else that arrives at a future point in time. Since you can't connect dots you don't have, it drives us into a mode of, we fundamentally try to collect everything and hang on to it forever."[8] The faith is that, as the NSA itself has proclaimed, if we "Collect It All" we will eventually "Know It All."[9]

More surveillance, however, would not necessarily have prevented the September 11th attacks. Independent investigations have concluded that the United States failed to stop the attacks primarily because intelligence agencies didn't understand and share the information they had, a problem that persists today. The problem was not lack of information that an attack was imminent. Rather, intelligence agencies misused or ignored the information they had.

After September 11th, a commission was formed to review the actions of intelligence agencies and make recommendations for improving domestic security. This group, The National Commission on Terrorist Attacks Upon the United States, or 9/11 Commission, has been criticized for failing to fully investigate all the warnings prior to the attacks and for whitewashing its critique of the Bush Administration. But the report it issued is the most comprehensive public review of the state of national security intelligence during that time period.

The 9/11 Commission distinctly did not call for more surveillance. The Commission didn't see more surveillance as a solution because it found

---

[8] M. Sledge. "CIA's Gus Hunt on big data: We 'try to collect everything and hang on to it forever.'" *Huffington Post.* March 30, 2013. www.huffingtonpost.com/2013/03/20/cia-gus-hunt-big-data_n_2917842.html

[9] Greenwald, *No Place to Hide*, p. 97.

that the intelligence community had information in its possession from which it could have identified the September 11th plot. However, analysts mishandled and misunderstood the information they had.

Before September 11th, American spies had multiple indicators that people inside the United States were planning a dramatic attack at the behest of Osama bin Laden. According to the 9/11 Commission, in early 2001, the Bush Administration was receiving frequent but fragmentary information about terrorist threats to US interests around the world.[10] By the Spring, however, the level of reporting increased "dramatically." Reporter Kurt Eichenwald, who has seen classified daily briefings received by President Bush, says that they were full of direct warnings about the possibility of al-Qaeda attack.[11] By May 1, the CIA was aware that "a group presently in the United States" was planning a terrorist operation. Weeks later, on June 22, the daily brief reported that al-Qaeda strikes could be "imminent," although intelligence suggested the time frame was flexible. There were a lot of alarms through the month of July.

The intelligence community was also aware that suspicious al-Qaeda affiliates had recently traveled to the United States. The CIA was tracking two of the September 11th hijackers, Khalid al-Mihdhar and Nawaf al-Hazmi, who they knew had attended an al-Qaeda summit in Malaysia on January 5, 2000. The CIA was aware that one and possibly both of these men had visas to the United States. However, the CIA failed to put either al-Mihdhar or al-Hazmi on an FBI watch list. As a result, immigration and law enforcement officials did not know that they should stop the men when they subsequently entered the United States, which they did under their real names. So ten days after the al-Qaeda meeting in Malaysia, al-Hazmi and al-Mihdhar were allowed to fly to Los Angeles. In other words, the CIA failed to convey this intelligence to the FBI, the agency ultimately responsible for counterterrorism investigations inside the United States.[12] In Los Angeles, the two men would have been easy for the FBI to find. Under their real names, they rented an apartment, got driver's licenses, opened

---

[10] *The 9/11 Commission Report: Final Report of the National Commission on Terrorist Attacks Upon the United States.* National Commission on Terrorist Attacks upon the United States. Washington: GPO 2004, p. 254. govinfo.library.unt.edu/911/report/911Report.pdf [hereinafter *9/11 Commission Report*].

[11] K. Eichenwald. "The deafness before the storm." *The New York Times.* September 10, 2012. www.nytimes.com/2012/09/11/opinion/the-bush-white-house-was-deaf-to-9-11-warnings.html

[12] *The 9/11 Commission Report*, pp. 181–182.

bank accounts, purchased a car, and took flight lessons. Al-Mihdhar was listed in the local phone directory. But no one tried to find them.

The NSA also failed to share its information about al-Hazmi and al-Mihdhar. The NSA was monitoring communications to and from an al-Qaeda safe house in Yemen. The two future hijackers called the Yemen safe house multiple times from Los Angeles. For some reason, the NSA, which was aware of these calls, did not pass on that information to the FBI, which has the authority to act inside the United States. Nor did the NSA tell any other intelligence agency. Only in late August of 2001 did the CIA put al-Hazmi and al-Mihdhar on the watch list. But in response to the watchlisting, the FBI sent out only a "routine" notice requesting further investigation, and nothing came of this request.

As James Bamford, the preeminent NSA historian, told PBS:

> Throughout their whole journey, whether they were in San Diego or they were in New Jersey or they were in Laurel, Maryland, [al-Mihdhar and al-Hazmi] were communicating back and forth to the bin Laden ops center in Yemen. NSA was listening in on the ops center, recording the conversations and then transcribing them. But the NSA never alerted any other agency that the terrorists were in the United States and moving across the country, towards Washington.[13]

A month later, these men were two of the hijackers who flew a passenger plane into the Pentagon. We may never know why the NSA didn't tell the FBI or the CIA about the phone calls. No one from the NSA will discuss it.[14]

Poor information sharing, not lack of information, was a huge problem. The 9/11 Commission report noted the CIA failed to share with the FBI information linking individuals in the USS Cole attack of October 2000 with hijacker al-Mihdhar. A separate investigation by the CIA's inspector general found that up to sixty people in the agency knew that al-Qaeda operatives were in America but didn't tell the FBI.[15]

The Commission also concluded that the NSA was reluctant to search its databases without a direct request from an intelligence

---

[13] "The Spy Factory – Transcript." NOVA/PBS. February 3, 2009. www.pbs.org/wgbh/nova/military/spy-factory.html

[14] United States. Joint House/Senate Intelligence Committee. Joint Inquiry into Intelligence Community Activities Before and After the Terrorist Attacks of September 11, 2001. October 8, 2002. 107th Cong. 2nd sess. Washington: GPO, 2004 (Statement of Eleanor Hill, Joint Inquiry Staff Director).

[15] "OIG Report on CIA Accountability With Respect to the 9/11 Attacks – Executive Summary." Office of the Inspector General (June 2005), p. xiv. www.cia.gov/library/reports/Executive%20Summary_OIG%20Report.pdf

community "customer," i.e. another agency. If analysts had searched these databases, they would have been able to identify and connect al-Hazmi and al-Mihdhar, discover their US visas, and learn they were living in Los Angeles.[16] Wary of pointing fingers, the Commission hedged on whether capitalizing on these opportunities would have prevented the attacks on September 11th. But the Commission was firm that the problem was that the intelligence community needed to "assemble enough of the puzzle pieces gathered by different agencies to make some sense of them and then develop a fully informed joint plan."[17] Notably, the problem wasn't lack of puzzle pieces. It was the failure to fit them together and use them meaningfully.

The Commission also reported that there were instances where the NSA could have obtained surveillance warrants under the existing FISA statute to wiretap people inside the United States who were thought to be connected to al-Qaeda. The NSA failed to do so, however, because it thought that that was the FBI's job, and it didn't want to be seen as targeting people inside the United States.[18]

Another major problem the Commission saw was that intelligence officials misunderstood the so-called wall between criminal and intelligence investigations. The 1978 version of FISA stated that "the purpose" of foreign intelligence investigations had to be to obtain foreign intelligence. For many years, experts inside the government interpreted that provision to limit interaction between intelligence agencies and law enforcement, since the goal of law enforcement is to investigate and prosecute crime or to protect domestic security. In 1995, Attorney General Janet Reno issued guidelines meant to restrict the flow of information from intelligence to criminal prosecution. These restrictions made sense because intelligence collection is generally broader and impacts innocent people. Criminal law and the Fourth Amendment generally require probable cause of criminal activity before a search or seizure can take place. But the Reno guidelines were, according to the Commission, misinterpreted and poorly applied. Over time, the Department of Justice reinterpreted the "wall" as preventing intelligence agents from consulting with criminal investigators at all.

These mistakes helped drive the mishandling of the Zacarias Moussaoui investigation, which might have led to discovery of the September 11th plot. In August of 2001, Moussaoui was arrested on immigration charges

---

[16] *9/11 Commission Report*, pp. 353–354.
[17] Id., p. 355.
[18] Id., p. 87.

in Minnesota after his suspicious behavior at a local flight school. The instructor had found it strange that Moussaoui wanted to learn to fly commercial airliners, but had no intention of getting a pilot's license.[19] According to a later Department of Justice investigation, there were "significant problems" with how the FBI handled the investigation of Moussaoui. Had the FBI searched Moussaoui's property, agents might have found evidence of the September 11th plot.

Since the 9/11 Commission found that information was not appropriately shared between agencies for a variety of reasons, the report planted the seeds of the intelligence community's future efforts to share surveillance information more broadly. The FISA wall was demolished after September 11th by a combination of the USA PATRIOT Act and subsequent FISC rulings.[20] Other minimization rule changes enabled the FBI, the NSA, and the CIA to share unredacted information about Americans. But the longstanding problems of competition and turf-battles between the agencies remain.

The 9/11 Commission report identified a challenge that faced the Nation prior to September 11th. It is a challenge we still face. How do we share, make sense of, and use the information we've got? It wasn't that we needed to "collect the dots to connect the dots," as Secretary of Defense Donald Rumsfeld later said. Rather, we needed to know how to make sense of, and use, the dots we had. Right before September 11th, NSA Director General Mike Hayden said as much. Hayden suggested that access to information isn't a problem. Rather, "there's simply too much out there, and it's too hard to understand."[21]

In other words, too much information is actually a problem, and not a solution, in our counterterrorism efforts. Information is not the same as intelligence, and as we'll see in the next chapter, technology does not change that fact for national security analysts.

In addition, today's surveillance debate raises the important question of whether and when investigators can use the more liberal foreign intelligence rules to conduct surveillance, and when they need to use the traditional criminal authorities that are more privacy protective. There is not necessarily a clear line between intelligence and criminal investigations,

---

[19] Id., p. 247.
[20] §§ 10:5–10:15.
[21] N. Junior. "Spy agency taps into undersea cable." *ZDNet*. May 23, 2001. www.zdnet.com/article/spy-agency-taps-into-undersea-cable

and it often makes sense for investigators to work together. Failure to do so was a major reason that American spies missed the September 11th plot.

Nevertheless, looser foreign intelligence laws can be and have been used as an end-run around privacy protections enshrined in criminal procedure. Senator Ron Wyden (D-OR), who formerly sat on the Senate Select Committee on Intelligence, has drawn public attention to this problem. The government is allowed to collect Americans phone calls with foreigners under section 702 of FISA, but only for certain foreign intelligence purposes and only if the foreigner, not the American, is the target. However, once collected, investigators at the FBI are allowed to search some of the unminimized data for information about specific Americans. Ordinarily, FBI agents wanting to read my email would have to go to a court and get a search warrant based on probable cause. Now, if my communications are part of the PRISM trove, those agents are allowed to read them without a warrant. That means that there is little to stop agents from reading my messages for an inadequate or improper reason. Senator Wyden has called this practice a "backdoor" search because it gets evidence into the hands of law enforcement that it otherwise would not have been able to obtain under criminal laws and the Fourth Amendment.

To date, Americans have relied on usage rules – post-collection regulations on the retention, analysis, and sharing of collected data – to protect privacy, especially when collection is massive. Minimization rules are both underappreciated and underwhelming. There are a host of complex minimization procedures that the intelligence community strives to comply with. Current guidelines include the United States Signals Intelligence Directive SP0018, also known as "USSID-18".[22] There are also "minimization procedures" for the NSA, the FBI, the CIA, and the National Counterterrorism Center, which the FISC approves under section 702 in an effort to balance the impact on Americans with foreign intelligence demands. "Special Procedures Governing Communications Metadata Analysis" or SPGCMA, allow the intelligence community to use US person information collected internationally in mapping Americans connections with foreigners to discover new foreign intelligence targets regardless of nationality.[23] All these procedures are meant to enable use of

---

[22] "United States Signals Intelligence Directive SP0018." National Security Agency. January 11, 2011. www.dni.gov/files/documents/1118/CLEANEDFinal%20USSID%20SP0018.pdf
[23] News reports and congressional testimony confirm the "Special Procedures" are used to map Americans' social networks. See United States Senate Judiciary Committee. *Hearing on FISA: Questions for the Record*, October 2, 2013. 113th Cong. 1st sess. www.judiciary.senate. gov/imo/media/doc/100213QFRs-Alexander.pdf; See also "Documents on N.S.A. efforts

sensitive, private data while reducing the risk of abuse. Minimization rules are going to be necessary, even if not sufficient, for democracies to operate in a Big Data world. Among other reforms, we need to pay far more attention to the crafting and enforcement of minimization rules in the future.

But minimization rules will never protect our civil liberties as well as restrictions on collection of the data in the first place. These databases are too tempting to resist. That's what happened with LOVEINT – insiders used phone calling records to keep tabs on their romantic partners. All the oversight and regulation in the world is only going to prevent so much. Outsiders will also attack the databases to get access to the information. In one instance, it appears that the Chinese government attacked a database of FISA requests sent to Google, in order to determine who the US government is watching.[24]

And what if official policy is to misuse or abuse the data? No set of minimization procedures is going to stop the next J. Edgar Hoover or Richard Nixon. The minimization rules are classified and crafted in secret without input from the public courts, from Congress, or from the public. When a president wants to change the rules to spy on Muslims or political enemies, the rules change. It will be very hard if not impossible to prevent spying when the data is already in the hands of the government.

The 9/11 Commission never called for mass surveillance of innocent people. Nor did the Commission suggest that massive surveillance would have prevented the September 11th attacks. The 9/11 Commission report is no justification for broader SIGINT collection. To the contrary, the Commission expressed concerns about broader spying, specifically referencing authorities (including the controversial section 215 provision) passed as part of the USA PATRIOT Act in the immediate aftermath of September 11th. "Because of concerns regarding the shifting balance of power to the government, we think that a full and informed debate on the Patriot Act would be healthy."[25]

Fifteen years later, we are finally beginning to have that fully informed debate. As we do, the public needs to understand that the failure to properly understand and share information – inability to connect the dots – drove our intelligence failures in 2001. Collecting more information will not resolve the problem and may only make it worse.

to diagram social networks of U.S. citizens." *The New York Times*. www.nytimes.com/interactive/2013/09/29/us/documents-on-nsa-efforts-to-diagram-social-networks-of-us-citizens.html?_r=0

[24] E. Nakashima. "Chinese hackers who breached Google gained access to sensitive data, U.S. officials say." The Washington Post. May 20, 2013. https://www.washingtonpost.com/world/national-security/chinese-hackers-who-breached-google-gained-access-to-sensitive-data-us-officials-say/2013/05/20/51330428-be34-11e2-89c9-3be8095fe767_story.html

[25] *9/11 Commission Report*, p. 394.

6

Modern Surveillance and Counterterrorism

US intelligence agencies continue to face a difficult task. They are supposed to provide meaningful analysis that enables officials to manage serious national security problems such as terrorism, weapons proliferation, network attacks on government infrastructure, and counterintelligence efforts. But today these are diffuse and complex threats. There are newly powerful political actors on the international stage. Organizations that are not governments and have no physical territory can inflict great harm. And individuals and diffuse coalitions are increasingly able to traffic in military technology, digital viruses, and other dangerous, potentially lethal tools. These challenges are real, and overcoming them are legitimate goals of foreign intelligence surveillance.

But the track record of the collection programs Edward Snowden revealed provides little evidence that massive surveillance will help us identify future terrorist attacks or mitigate these new risks. American spies' allegiance to massive surveillance is based on faith, not track record.

The Boston Marathon bombing in April of 2013 illustrates how broad proactive surveillance is no panacea against attacks. The NSA was conducting its massive spying at the time, and the attacks happened anyway. In that case, two brothers allegedly built pressure cooker bombs and placed them near the finish line of the Boston Marathon. The bombings killed three people and injured scores of others. The older brother died and the younger brother was injured in the subsequent manhunt. The younger brother, Dzhokhar Tsarnaev, was sentenced to death in early 2015.[1] Relevant information about the bombers did not come from electronic surveillance. Rather, it came from another government. A few years before the bombing, the Russian government had warned the FBI that the older brother, Tamerlan Tsarnaev, was dangerous. The FBI investigated and found nothing to link either person to terrorism, so they closed the

---

[1] The death sentence has been appealed. As of the date of this publication, the final resolution of the sentencing is unknown.

investigation in June 2011. But later that same year, the Russians sent the same warning to the CIA.

The CIA asked the U.S. National Counterterrorism Center to add Tamerlan and his mother's names to a terrorism watch list. That watchlist is called the Terrorist Identities Datamart Environment, or TIDE. You can be placed on the TIDE list based on an informant pointing the finger at you, your social media posts, or the conduct of your relatives. The list is used to generate other watch lists, like the No Fly list and border security lists. Being on the TIDE list can really complicate your life. But it doesn't necessarily assist the government in identifying true threats among the more than one million people on the list.[2] How could it, when there are so many people on the list for so many different reasons? The Tsarnaev family might have been on the radar, but even with massive NSA collection of phone call and email data, no one identified the plot.

After the bombing, FBI agents looked at nearly 13,000 videos and more than 120,000 photographs taken near the scene of the bombing. They found a video that seemed to show the perpetrators. They were the only people who didn't look surprised when the first bomb went off. The FBI then released the video, asking for the public's assistance in locating the men. Farhad Manjoo, a well-known reporter for the *Wall Street Journal*, the *New York Times*, and NPR, argues that the Boston Marathon bombing makes a good case for broad surveillance. The FBI's access to so many video and still images is what helped them identify and eventually catch the bombers.

But we should not conflate massive surveillance with broad data collection used to investigate crimes that have already occurred. The Boston Marathon investigation photos and videos were made by private parties. The government did not collect, aggregate, or analyze them until after they knew that a crime had happened. This wasn't a fishing expedition. The investigators knew what block of the city to focus on, what time frame, and what they were looking for. While the amount of information collected was large, the targeting was narrow. Officers were investigating a particular crime. They collected only videos and photos that would likely contain evidence of that crime.

That's not to say that there are no problems with broad collection, even in the criminal context. For example, in the same Boston Marathon investigation, FBI agents searched for purchase records for the model of pressure

---

[2] There were over a million people on the TIDE list in 2013.

cooker used to construct the bombs detonated in the attack. They were looking to narrow the field of potential suspects. It turned out, there were only a few dozen of those pressure cookers sold in the year before the attack. But what happened next is worrisome. A woman reported that law enforcement paid her a visit after she had been shopping for pressure cookers and backpacks online.[3] Ultimately the family learned that the investigation was spurred when the husband's former employer reported his Internet searches to local police. FBI agents confronted a Saudi student for carrying a pressure cooker to a student dinner.[4] Interrogating people who purchase pressure cookers is not a good way to find future attackers. Millions of people purchase these devices without using them in a bombing attack.

Targeted surveillance of people known to be connected to terrorism is the best way to find terrorists. Indeed, almost every major terrorist attack on Western soil in the past fifteen years was committed by someone already on the government's radar for one or another reason.[5] In January of 2015, two gunmen shot twelve people dead in the Paris offices of satirical magazine *Charlie Hebdo*. One of the gunmen had already been sent to prison for recruiting jihadist fighters. The other had reportedly studied in Yemen with Umar Farouk Abdulmutallab, who was arrested by the FBI in 2009 after trying and failing while on an airplane to detonate explosives hidden in his underwear. The leader of the July 7, 2005 London suicide bombings had been observed by British intelligence meeting with a suspected terrorist. The men who planned the Mumbai, India attacks in 2008 were already under electronic surveillance by the United States, the United Kingdom, and India.[6] One of the Mumbai plotters had been a DEA informant. Investigators received multiple tips from the informant's family members, friends, and acquaintances, but the officials never effectively followed up on the information.[7]

---

[3] C. Dewey. "Google 'pressure cooker,' get a police visit? maybe not." *The Washington Post*. August 1, 2013. www.washingtonpost.com/news/the-switch/wp/2013/08/01/google-pressure-cooker-get-a-police-visit-maybe-not/

[4] N. Zimmerman. "Saudi student visited by FBI after using pressure cooker." *Gawker*. May 13, 2013. gawker.com/saudi-student-visited-by-fbi-after-using-pressure-cooke-504443418

[5] M. Schwartz. "The whole haystack." *The New Yorker*. January 26, 2015. www.newyorker.com/magazine/2015/01/26/whole-haystack

[6] Ibid.

[7] G. Posner. "Making of a terrorist." *The Daily Beast*. December 8, 2009. www.thedailybeast.com/articles/2009/12/08/making-of-a-terrorist.html; J. Perlez, E. Schmitt, and G. Thompson. "U.S. had warnings on plotter of Mumbai attack." *The New York Times*. October 16, 2010. www.nytimes.com/2010/10/17/world/asia/17headley.html

In another case where the government failed to understand the information it had and act accordingly, Maj. Nidal Hasan, a military psychiatrist, killed thirteen people at Fort Hood, Texas, in 2009. Intelligence agencies had intercepted multiple emails between Hasan and Anwar al-Awlaki, a notoriously militant cleric living in Yemen.[8] In the emails, Hasan asked Awlaki whether a Muslim US soldier who committed fratricide would be considered a martyr in the eyes of Islam. Despite this and other information that could justify discharging Hasan from the military, counterterrorism investigators didn't follow up on these emails. While the Defense Department faulted failures of leadership, the Senate investigated the military's unwillingness to name, detect, or defend against violent Islamist extremism. Scholar Amy Zegart points the finger at the Army's organizational incentives for promoting and disciplining subordinates as well.[9]

There are more examples of intelligence agencies failing to understand counterterrorism information it had in hand. Historian Peter Bergen has assessed the historical record, including the case of Umar Farouk Abdulmutallab, the man who attempted and failed to detonate a bomb in his underwear on Christmas Day 2009. A few weeks before the botched attack, Abdulmutallab's father contacted the US Embassy in Nigeria with concerns that his son had become radicalized and might be planning an attack. This information wasn't further investigated. While the White House concluded that the government did not have sufficient information to determine that Abdulmutallab was likely working for al-Qaeda in Yemen and that the group was looking to expand its attacks beyond Yemen, the man was nevertheless allowed to board a plane bound for the United States without any question despite his father's warning. Bergen concludes by arguing that, "[a]ll of these serious terrorism cases argue not for the gathering of ever vaster troves of information but simply for a better understanding of the information the government has already collected and that are derived from conventional law enforcement and intelligence methods."[10]

***

Massive spying didn't stop these attacks. When they happened, the domestic phone dragnet was ongoing. That dragnet – started in 2001 and

---

[8] Awlaki, an American citizen, was killed by the United States in 2011. His assassination by drone is an extremely controversial Obama Administration decision.

[9] A. Zegart, "Insider threats and organizational root causes: The 2009 Fort Hood terrorist attack," *Parameters* 45 (2015): 35–46.

[10] P Bergen. "Would NSA surveillance have stopped 9/11 plot? *CNN*. December 30, 2013. www.cnn.com/2013/12/30/opinion/bergen-nsa-surveillance-september-11/

continuing through 2015 – failed to identify any terrorist plots against America. The same is true of the Internet dragnet started in 2001 and continuing through 2011.

Nevertheless, the intelligence community seems confident that more information collection will prevent terrorism. Superficially, it just makes sense that in order to "connect the dots" you first have to "collect the dots." The public conversation about the effectiveness of massive surveillance seems to assume this is the case. For example, in her June 6, 2013 press conference seeking to justify the section 215 phone dragnet *The Guardian* had just revealed, Senator Feinstein claimed that the FBI had uncovered approximately 100 terrorist plots since 2009. She couldn't credit the phone dragnet for success in any of those investigations, but it didn't matter to her:

> I do not know to what extent metadata was used or if it was used, but I do know this: That terrorists will come after us if they can and the only thing we have to deter this is good intelligence. To understand that a plot is being hatched and to get there before they get to us.[11]

Feinstein may have revealed more by this statement than she intended. We don't know what works to identify terrorist plots. But surveillance is one thing we know how to do well. So we are going to do that to stop the terrorists. It's a little like looking under the lamppost for your keys, because that's where the light is.

Honestly assessing the value of massive surveillance is hard. How do we know when a counterterrorism program "works"? What does it mean to "work"? Accountability is a challenge where the budget is secret, sources and methods are confidential, and the mission, to learn more about foreign policy matters affecting US interests, is vague. Clearly, a surveillance practice can't be said to "work" merely if the program produces something, anything, of use. Nor should we credit a broad collection tool if a more narrowly tailored kind of collection that impacts fewer people and costs less money would also have done the job just as well.

A major reason we don't know whether bulk surveillance works is because we don't have an agreed-on measure for its effectiveness. The intelligence community does not appear to have any metrics or process for

---

[11] E. O'Keefe. "Transcript Dianne Feinstein, Saxby Chambliss explain, defend NSA phone records program." *The Washington Post.* June 6, 2013. www.washingtonpost.com/news/post-politics/wp/2013/06/06/transcript-dianne-feinstein-saxby-chambliss-explain-defend-nsa-phone-records-program/

assessing the benefits of mass surveillance systems. We know this because when pressed, intelligence officials were unable to provide the public with a reliable assessment of its success. In June 2013, after Snowden revealed the phone call dragnet, lawmakers demanded to know whether the program was working. As part of the public relations campaign to return to spying-as-usual, Big Surveillance supporters told the public that the bulk collection of phone records had thwarted fifty-four terrorist plots against America.[12] But members of Congress disagreed with this assertion and were able to disprove it.

Senator Patrick Leahy, a Democrat from Vermont and currently the longest serving US Senator, questioned NSA Director General Alexander about this claim on the Senate floor. Leahy is one of the leading privacy advocates in Congress and has received the Electronic Privacy Information Center's Champion of Freedom Award for his efforts to promote information privacy and ensure an open and democratic government. Senator Leahy pressed Alexander on whether the phone dragnet and PRISM spy programs Snowden's documents revealed – collection under two laws referred to as section 215 and section 702 – were valuable counterterrorism tools. The exchange went as follows:

LEAHY: For example, we have heard over and over again the assertion that 54 terrorist plots were thwarted by the use of Section 215 and/or Section 702 authorities. ... These weren't all plots, and they weren't all thwarted. The American people are getting left with an inaccurate impression of the effectiveness of NSA programs.
Would you agree that the 54 cases that keep getting cited by the administration were not all plots, and out of the 54, only 13 had some nexus to the U.S. Would you agree with that, yes or no?
DIR. ALEXANDER: Yes.[13]

Of those thirteen, the NSA eventually admitted that the phone records dragnet contributed to only one US case. Basaaly Moalin, a San Diego cab driver, sent $8,500 to Somalia in support of the terrorist group Al-Shabaab. Moalin was convicted of providing material support to terrorism.

Following classified and public hearings, Senator Leahy and other members of Congress concluded that there was no evidence that the phone records collection has ever been important in fighting terrorism. A subsequent review by the Privacy and Civil Liberties Oversight Board

[12] J. Elliott, T. Meyer, and S. Wei. "How the NSA's claim on thwarted terrorist plots has spread." *ProPublica*. October 23, 2013. projects.propublica.org/graphics/nsa-54-cases
[13] "Senate judiciary committee hearing: Continued oversight of the Foreign Intelligence Surveillance Act." *C-SPAN*. Online video clip, October 2, 2013. www.c-span.org/video/?315399-1/foreign-intelligence-surveillance-act

reached the same conclusion.[14] Hundreds of thousands of Americans have had their phone records collected for years, but it hasn't made the country any safer. A 2009 inspector general report says that the section 215 dragnet cost taxpayers $146 million in supplemental counterterrorism funds to buy new hardware and contract support and to make payments to the phone companies for their collaboration.[15] As set out in later chapters, the program was misused and abused for years. America is none the safer for it.

The Internet dragnet – collection of transactional information about activity like emails and website visits – performed no better. No one from either the Bush or the Obama Administrations has ever identified any case where the data was of material assistance. The collection under the FISA Pen Trap statute stopped in 2011. Senators Ron Wyden and Mark Udall have said that the program was both ineffective and highly invasive of people's privacy. Nevertheless, American spies continue to this day to collect Americans' Internet metadata under other legal authorities and less FISC oversight, despite the domestic dragnet's nonexistent record of national security successes.

The Privacy and Civil Liberties Oversight Board, the House Intelligence Committee, and the NSA have offered examples where they say that section 702, the law undergirding the PRISM and Upstream content collection programs, has been useful for both counterterrorism and other foreign intelligence collection. The House Intelligence Committee points to four declassified examples where section 702 and section 215 have stopped terrorist plots.[16] They've put these together to bolster the case for supporting the large-scale domestic surveillance authorities. However, a close look at the examples does not show that these controversial programs should be retained. Baasily Moalin gave money to Al-Shabaab.

In the other three examples, the terrorist either was or should have been under surveillance per narrower and more targeted surveillance that impacts fewer people. According to the PCLOB, the NSA discovered a

---

[14] J. Elliott, T. Meyer, and S. Wei. "How the NSA's claim on thwarted terrorist plots has spread." *ProPublica*. October 23, 2013. projects.propublica.org/graphics/nsa-54-cases

[15] B. Gellman. "U.S. surveillance architecture includes collection of revealing Internet, phone metadata." *The Washington Post*. June 15, 2013. www.washingtonpost.com/investigations/us-surveillance-architecture-includes-collection-of-revealing-internet-phone-metadata/2013/06/15/e9bf004a-d511-11e2-b05f-3ea3f0e7bb5a_story.html

[16] "Four Declassified Examples." www.intelligence.house.gov. US House of Representatives Permanent Select Committee on Intelligence. intelligence.house.gov/1-four-declassified-examples-more-50-attacks-20-countries-thwarted-nsa-collection-under-fisa-section

connection between an extremist based in Yemen that they were monitoring and an unknown person in Kansas City, Missouri. The NSA provided information about this connection to the FBI and the FBI subsequently identified the unknown person and learned that he was in communication with other individuals located in the United States who were "in the very initial stages of devising a plan to bomb the New York Stock Exchange."[17] Neither the phone dragnet nor PRISM appear necessary to identify these people. The FBI could monitor the Yemeni target under traditional, targeted FISA or Executive Order 12333.

Next, take the arrest of David Headley at the Chicago airport.[18] Headley had been involved in planning the deadly 2008 attacks in Mumbai, India that killed 166 people. The NSA tried to claim that Headley's arrest was a section 702 success story.[19] However, the intelligence community's claims have been met with incredulity. There were ample clues that Headley, a DEA informant, was involved in international terrorism. In the year before the attacks, Headley's wife even warned American officials three times that her husband was a terrorist conducting missions in Mumbai. These warnings went unheeded. No surveillance succeeded in thwarting the Mumbai attacks.

Section 702 only played a supporting role in identifying Headley and his plan to go to Denmark to conduct attacks in protest of cartoons mocking the prophet Mohammed. According to Robert J. Holley, the special agent in charge of the FBI's Chicago Division which investigated Headley, the 702 program was "a piece of the investigation" that helped to map out Headley's overseas contacts, but failed to solve the Denmark case or to identify Headley as involved in that plot.[20] According to journalist Sebastian Rotella, there were half a dozen opportunities where US law enforcement could have pursued tips from Headley's associates about his terrorist activity but failed to do so. Rotella pointed to the UK's tracking of the Mumbai plotters, Headley's preexisting relationship with the DEA

---

[17] "Report on the Telephone Records Program Conducted under Section 215 of the USA PATRIOT Act and on the Operations of the Foreign Intelligence Surveillance Court." Privacy and Civil Liberties Oversight Board. January 23, 2014. www.pclob.gov/library/215-Report_on_the_Telephone_Records_Program.pdf

[18] "Four Declassified Examples." www.intelligence.house.gov. U.S. House of Representatives Permanent Select Committee on Intelligence. intelligence.house.gov/1-four-declassified-examples-more-50-attacks-20-countries-thwarted-nsa-collection-under-fisa-section

[19] Ibid.

[20] S. Rotella. "The hidden intelligence breakdowns behind the Mumbai attack." ProPublica, April 21, 2015. www.propublica.org/article/the-hidden-intelligence-breakdowns-behind-the-mumbai-attacks?

as an informant, and other clues that might have stopped the attacks and brought Headley down without large-scale surveillance under either section 702 or section 215.[21]

The House Intelligence Committee website also claims the conviction of Najibullah Zazi in 2009 for plotting to bomb the New York City subway as a section 702 success story. In 2009, the NSA was operating under section 702 when it intercepted emails between Zazi and an associate in Pakistan that contained coded messages concerning the pending attack. These emails were called critical in enabling the FBI to identify Zazi. Taking a closer look, however, there were other leads in the Zazi case that should have resulted in his capture through the narrower and less problematic traditional FISA surveillance procedures. UK investigators were watching a suspected terrorism cell in the north-west of England in 2009. Members of that cell were looking for advice on how to build a bomb. From monitoring them, the United Kingdom and the United States knew that an email address these suspects were in contact with was associated with al-Qaeda. Zazi was also emailing that same address. Since this group were already identified as a potential terrorist cell, the NSA could have obtained a traditional FISA warrant to monitor that email address and would thereby have found Zazi.[22] In fact, defense attorneys in Zazi's criminal prosecution were told that US intelligence officials had been monitoring Zazi under traditional FISA's targeted surveillance as warranted by the FISC, and not section 702.[23] Now, the NSA might have failed to monitor that email address and missed Zazi. But the NSA might also have failed to identify Zazi in the sea of section 702 data the agency grabs. There's no reason to believe that the bulky collection is better.

Until 2015, intelligence agencies continued the dragnet collection and data mining of domestic phone records. Despite the poor track record of that program, some in Congress were loath to end it. As a result, some supporters of Big Surveillance made efforts to invent hypothetical situations that might justify dragnet surveillance. Former NSA General Counsel Stewart Baker offered a hypothetical he says shows how the dragnet might

---

[21] Ibid.

[22] B. Cahill, D. Sterman, E. Schneider, and P. Bergen. "Do NSA's bulk surveillance programs stop terrorists?" *New America Foundation*, January 2014, p. 10.

[23] B. J. Campbell. "Notice of intent to use Foreign Intelligence Surveillance Act information," September 29, 2009, cited in Defendant's Reply in Support of Motion for Notice of FISA Amendments Act Evidence Pursuant to 50 U.S.C. §§ 1881e(a), 1806(c), *United States v. Daoud*, No. 1:12–cr–00723 (N.D. Ill. 2013).

be useful, even invaluable, to finding terrorist plots in the United States.[24] Imagine an al-Qaeda leader in Yemen calls his weapons expert in Yemen and reports that a US-based agent needs assistance constructing a bomb. The NSA picks up that call. (The NSA can tap foreign to foreign communications without any judicial approval.) The al-Qaeda leader continues: "I've told him to use a throwaway cell phone to call you tomorrow at 11 a.m. on your throwaway phone. When you answer, he'll give you nothing other than the number of a second phone. You will buy another phone in the bazaar and call him back on the second number at 2 p.m."

Now, the government knows there is a dangerous operative inside the United States, but doesn't know who it is or what US numbers to tap to capture that call. However, any American who makes a call to Yemen at 11 a.m., Sanaa time, hangs up after a few seconds, and then gets a call from a different Yemeni number three hours later is going to be of high interest. "Finding that person, however, wouldn't be easy, because the government could only identify the suspect by his calling patterns, not by name," says Baker. That's why the NSA needs a dragnet collecting *everyone's* phone numbers.

However, the NSA's phone dragnet wasn't for Americans' calls to countries that are hotbeds of terrorism like Yemen, or even for all international calls. It was for purely domestic calls, Americans calling each other. Further, Baker ignores other, more targeted, avenues that American spies have to get the same information. For example, the NSA could get a court order or issue an emergency request to US telephone providers to save all call detail records from the United States to Yemen and Yemen to the United States for the date and time in question. Then, instead of saving the information for five years, they could quickly get rid of the nonresponsive data. Targeted and time-delineated searches would not track *every person* just to find information about one person under such uncommon circumstances. Baker offers no explanation why timely targeted surveillance would not achieve the investigatory goals.

There is another reason that Baker's hypothetical situation wouldn't justify the phone dragnet program. Oddly, it appears that the phone record database was not comprehensive, as would be required for it to serve the role Baker imagined. In fact, everyone justifying the collection said that for American spies to get value out of the dragnet, it had to be a comprehensive

[24] S. Baker. "Why the NSA needs your phone calls ... and why you (probably) shouldn't worry about it." *Foreign Policy.* June 6, 2013. foreignpolicy.com/2013/06/06/why-the-nsa-needs-your-phone-calls/

collection of records. Multiple officials argued that to find the "needle in the haystack," they need to be able to collect the whole haystack. And the first FISC opinion authorizing the phone dragnet, written in August of 2013 and published with redactions, on September 17 of that year, asserted that it was necessary for the NSA to collect everything.[25] "[I]f production of the information were to wait until the specific identifier connected to an international terrorist group were determined, most of the historical connections (the entire purpose of this authorization) would be lost." Yet, in February of 2014, intelligence community officials told the newspapers that the section 215 dragnet database contained only about 20 percent to 30 percent of Americans calling records. It wasn't clear why this was so, though it appears that the NSA was not getting sets of data from most mobile phone calls. The theory is that the FBI was not permitted to collect geolocation information, which is part of mobile records, and that it did not have the authority to force phone companies to strip that data from their records before turning it over. The public still doesn't have the full story about the NSA's collection of mobile records or why the section 215 database was not comprehensive.

Nevertheless, the 2015 passage of the USA Freedom Act may have rendered the issue moot. That law enables the intelligence community to get phone records directly from providers, rather than collecting them and creating a centralized database in the NSA's computers.[26]

Finally, Baker's hypothetical assumes that there are only a few calls between the United States and Yemen that fit this pattern. Perhaps that's true. But perhaps hundreds or thousands of people in the United States call different numbers in Yemen. If that's the case, then collecting this information may not be enough to identify a suspicious calling pattern. What happens next? Does the FBI visit everyone who called Yemen? Is that an effective use of resources? The false positives may overwhelm investigators.

After the terror attacks in November 2015 in Paris, France, the public learned that ISIS operatives were using burner phones, cheap SIM-card cell phones that they would throw away after only a few uses, in order to plan the attacks. In a Twitter exchange, David Simon, the Director of the popular TV show *The Wire*, opined that this was a reason why the government

---

25 Amended Memorandum Opinion. *In re Application of the Federal Bureau of Investigation for an Order Requiring the Production of Tangible Things from [redacted]*, No. BR 13–109. (FISC, August 29, 2013) www.aclu.org/files/assets/br13-09-primary-order.pdf
26 USA Freedom Act of 2015, Pub. L. No. 114–23, 129 Stat. 268. www.congress.gov/114/plaws/publ23/PLAW-114publ23.pdf

should get access to phone metadata right away, so that it could identify the burner phone and find the caller before plotters threw them away. Edward Snowden responded, saying that phones used in real-world terrorism and intelligence operations are disposed of on a per-action, or per-call basis. The phones are in use for minutes or hours, not for days, making metadata pattern analysis extremely difficult if not impossible. The two men discussed the differences between intelligence investigations in Pakistan and drug operations on the streets of Baltimore. In Baltimore, phones are used for far longer, but there is also access to informants, eye witness testimony, and the like.[27] Despite the fact that some terrorists use burner phones, mass surveillance isn't going to catch them. Such surveillance, however, could be repurposed to monitor the streets of the inner city, without any of the privacy safeguards that are supposed to protect Americans when phone data is properly collected in a targeted way.

Former CIA Director Michael Morrell has admitted that the section 215 program "has not played a significant role in preventing any terrorist attacks to this point." But, Morell added, bulk collection can provide a reassurance that there is no domestic nexus to foreign terrorist plots detected by other NSA efforts.[28] In other words, collecting everything is a good idea, not because the government can find terrorists, but because then the government can feel reassured when it *doesn't* find terrorists.

These kinds of justifications make sense only if you don't look too closely at (1) what the cost and risks of such a practice are or (2) whether the practice even works. There are many things we could do that theoretically would thwart crime but which we do not do because they create other dangers or because they are inconsistent with a free society. We could have a rule that police officers can come into your home anytime to search for drugs. You might not have any drugs, but shouldn't the police be able to confirm that? In the United States, that's not the way we do things, and not just because it would invade personal privacy. Suspicionless spying changes the relationship of people to the police, giving police far more power to harass people, to chill their private behavior, and to dissuade lawful political activity. Arbitrary searches can cause dangerous, even

---

[27] "Snowden talks surveillance with the creator of The Wire." *Twitter.* March 21, 2016. twitter.com/i/moments/711602914796634113
[28] S. Ackerman. "NSA review panel casts doubt on bulk data collection claims." *The Guardian.* January 14, 2014. www.theguardian.com/world/2014/jan/14/nsa-review-panel-senate-phone-data-terrorism

deadly conflicts, for no good reason. What Morrell is saying could only make sense if you think there is zero downside from massive spying. It could only makes sense if you are confident that the money spent creating these programs isn't better spent somewhere else. In other words, it doesn't make sense.

Another argument in favor of bulk surveillance is that it is the only thing that ensures that the government will be able see into the past. In January of 2015, the National Research Council came out with a report examining bulk collection from a technical perspective, as they were requested to do by President Obama. The report asked whether there were technological substitutes for bulk collection. It found that "no software-based technique can fully replace the bulk collection of signals intelligence," specifically for recreating activity trails from the past. If past events or facts become relevant due to changing circumstances, then those past events or facts will be available for analysis only if they have been collected or otherwise preserved beforehand. If you want to find out what names or phone numbers someone used in the past, you need records of the past. Restricting bulk collection, especially in the absence of requiring companies to retain data, may mean that some important information gets lost.[29]

But the National Research Council report did not recommend bulk collection. Nor did it find that bulk collection was useful in predicting or stopping future crimes. It left the political choice of whether bulk collection was more helpful than harmful unanswered, even as it explored ways that software might place controls on the usage of bulk data to help enforce civil liberties interests and individual privacy.[30]

We don't do everything we can for national security – we accept some national security risks. And we don't do everything we could do for civil liberties – we accept some reductions in civil liberties. What is good policy with regards to retaining data? Do we want to ensure that we have data with which we can revive the past, and if so, under what conditions? If the laws change, should investigators be able to look into the past to see who engaged in activity that was legal at the time? If a person's behavior escaped notice, but years later becomes a public figure or a candidate for office, should her past be scrutinized for wrongdoing? Before the United States embraces bulk collection – or even mandates that industry hold

---

[29] "Bulk Collection of Signals Intelligence: Technical Options." National Research Council (Washington, D.C.: National Academies Press, 2015) Chapter 1.
[30] Ibid.

data just in case the government later wants it – the public must confront these scenarios and decide what kind of society we want to live in.

The most persuasive rationale for bulk collection over targeted surveillance is the fact that intelligence agencies do not know who all the potential attackers are. Targeted surveillance is great if you know whom to target. It is relatively simple to track and to eavesdrop on known targets and enemies. But finding previously unknown terrorists and discovering nascent attacks is a different challenge. To accomplish this mission, American spies claim they must collect information on people who may not be terrorists.

Is massive collection going to aid in the discovery of previously unknown terrorists? The claim has superficial appeal. After all, we live in an age where technology can do almost magical things. Analyzing Google searches for queries about cold symptoms can predict influenza outbreaks. Netflix knows exactly what movies I like. Can modern data analysis techniques, so good at drawing inferences from data, also be used to find unknown terrorists, or predict future terroristic behavior? Is collecting massive amounts of information a good strategy to find these unknown terrorists? Big Surveillance advocates' public relations answer is yes. But the scientific answer is no.

Finding terrorists is an inherently different challenge from other data analysis goals. Even if we knew what we were looking for, terrorism is just too rare for useful Big Data analysis. Rather, targeted surveillance starting with known terrorists is the way to go. Other approaches leave analysts buried in false leads.

Big Data is a business buzzword meant to describe the idea that previously unattainable insights into even the most complex phenomenon are available by passing as much information as possible through highly elaborate processing algorithms. Advertising companies analyze massive amounts of data to show Internet users targeted and persuasive ads. Netflix uses its data to make compelling movie recommendations.[31] Financial companies look at millions of transactions to identify characteristics of credit card fraud. Analysis of diverse sets of voluminous and fast moving data can produce quite sensitive and insightful predictions. That's the promise behind Big Data. But Big Data will probably never be useful for identifying unknown terrorists, no matter how much computer science

---

[31] T. Vanderbilt. "The science behind the Netflix algorithms that decide what you'll watch next." *Wired*. August 7, 2013. www.wired.com/2013/08/qq_netflix-algorithm/

advances. The reason is mathematical. And while technology advances, the math won't change.

Pattern matching will never be very accurate at finding rare events. To identify a pattern, you have to have commonalities. But what commonalities do we see in terrorist attacks? Terrorism is rare and distinctive. The Oklahoma City bombing was not like the 1993 World Trade Center bombing, which was different from September 11th, which was nothing like the Boston Marathon bombing. We can't look to the past to identify any common thing or things to look for.

Not only are terrorist attacks rare, but we also cannot entirely agree what constitutes "terrorism," as opposed to just a criminal attack. The political conversation about surveillance is dominated by our perception of the risk of terrorist attacks and by official assurances that the more surveillance we have, the more likely we are to thwart such attacks. But what does it mean to find terrorists or thwart terrorist attacks? What **is** terrorism?

The legal definition of terrorism is dependent on the apparent intention of the dangerous acts. Terrorism appears to be intended (i) to intimidate or coerce a civilian population; (ii) to influence the policy of a government by intimidation or coercion; or (iii) to affect the conduct of a government by mass destruction, assassination, or kidnapping.[32] This legal definition isn't precise and its conclusions are subjective. The ACLU offers an example:

> One recent example is the Vieques Island protests, when many people, including several prominent Americans, participated in civil disobedience on a military installation where the United States government has been engaging in regular military exercises, which these protesters oppose. The protesters illegally entered the military base and tried to obstruct the bombing exercises. This conduct would fall within the definition of domestic terrorism because the protesters broke federal law by unlawfully entering the airbase and their acts were for the purpose of influencing a government policy by intimidation or coercion. The act of trying to disrupt bombing exercises arguably created a danger to human life – their own and those of military personnel.[33]

We can see the risk that the terrorism label will be disproportionately used against certain ideologies. Some killings are terrorism, some are just murder. Is it terrorism when a white Christian shoots children at an elementary school or worshipers in an African American church? Government officials

---

[32] "Definitions of Terrorism in U.S. Code." Federal Bureau of Investigation. www.fbi.gov/about-us/investigate/terrorism/terrorism-definition; See 18 U.S.C. § 2331.
[33] "How The USA PATRIOT Act Redefines 'Domestic Terrorism.'" American Civil Liberties Union. www.aclu.org/how-usa-patriot-act-redefines-domestic-terrorism

did not label as terrorism the Sandy Hook school shooting in which twenty-seven people were killed or the assassination of nine people at a Bible study group at the Emanuel African Methodist Episcopal Church in Charleston, South Carolina. When a man proclaiming himself a defender of the unborn shot three people to death and injured nine at a Colorado Springs Planned Parenthood in November of 2015, he was presumed mentally ill. When a married couple shot and killed fourteen people and injured twenty-two at a work holiday party in San Bernardino a week later, proclaiming themselves followers of ISIS, the media called it the worst terrorist attack on American soil since September 11th.[34]

The concern is that crimes are labeled terrorism as a political judgment, rather than as a judgment of the risk they pose to safety or national interests, and that by granting government greater investigatory powers in the name of counterterrorism, we give it power to squelch disfavored political points of view. Is it terrorism when a Muslim cab driver sends money to an overseas terrorist group? Technically, yes. That classification enabled the FBI and the NSA to trumpet their investigation of cab driver Basaaly Moalin's transmission of $8500 to Al-Shabaab, the Somali militant group, as a counterterrorism victory achieved thanks to the section 215 phone dragnet. The fact that we call the cab driver's conduct terrorism and the white pro-life shooter's conduct a crime is a political decision, not a legal one.

In assessing both the risk Americans face from terrorist plots and the government's success in thwarting them, it matters what is considered terrorism. Calling something terrorism justifies the exercise of government power and legitimizes surveillance and a police force that would otherwise be unacceptable. Applying the term terrorism opens up avenues for governments to use techniques that would otherwise be out of the question. In terrorism cases, the United States does more than just spy. There are a number of cases that feature FBI agents finding young men who express an interest in extremist ideology, goading them into more extreme statements, even providing them with the means to do harm, and then arresting them.[35] FBI agents are the sole co-conspirators in these prosecutions,

---

[34] P. Esquivel. "San Bernardino police are praised for attack response but know not everything went smoothly." *Los Angeles Times.* February 3, 2016. www.latimes.com/local/crime/la-me-sb-police-lessons-20160203-story.html

[35] J. McLaughlin. "U.S. mass surveillance has no record of thwarting large terrorist attacks, regardless of Snowden leaks." *The Intercept.* November 17, 2015. theintercept.com/2015/11/17/u-s-mass-surveillance-has-no-record-of-thwarting-large-terror-attacks-regardless-of-snowden-leaks/

after having egged on hapless or mentally challenged people toward jihad.[36] CIA agents torture and kidnap in the name of counterterrorism.[37] The military uses drones to kill American citizens without a trial.[38] The public would not countenance these techniques if they weren't nominally for fighting terrorism.

There is a lot more that could be said about how language effects public perception of criminal and political acts. But there is a narrower policy point here. We don't have a clear agreement about what terrorism is, and there is no consistent profile of who does it. That means that things that we associate with terrorism are also true not just of criminal conduct but also of regular, run-of-the-mill, innocent behavior. And *that* means that the wrong people will inevitably get caught in the counterterrorism net. It is exceedingly hard to create a reasonably accurate test for terrorism.

Just look at the silly kinds of things that airport security officials are told to look for to spot potential terrorists about to board airplanes. The Transportation Security Administration (TSA) runs a controversial program to identify potential terrorists based on behaviors that it thinks indicate stress or deception. The program is known as the Screening of Passengers by Observation Techniques, or SPOT. The SPOT checklist includes such dubious indicators like a bobbing Adam's apple, trembling, and arriving late for flight. Indeed, the Inspector General of the DHS found in 2013 that TSA had failed to evaluate SPOT, and "cannot ensure that passengers at United States airports are screened objectively, show that the program is cost-effective, or reasonably justify the program's expansion." Nevertheless, we've spent more than $900 million on the SPOT program since it began in 2007, under the theory that it is one tool in a panoply of terrorist identification techniques.[39]

[36] R. Perlstein. "How FBI entrapment is inventing 'terrorists' – and letting bad guys off the hook." *Rolling Stone*. May 15, 2012. www.rollingstone.com/politics/news/how-fbi-entrapment-is-inventing-terrorists-and-letting-bad-guys-off-the-hook-20120515; D. Froomkin. "Another "terror" arrest; another mentally ill man, armed by the FBI." *The Intercept*. July 13, 2015. https://theintercept.com/2015/07/13/another-terror-arrest-another-mentally-ill-man-armed-fbi/

[37] J. Ashkenas et al. "7 key points from the C.I.A. torture report." *New York Times*. December 9, 2014. http://www.nytimes.com/interactive/2014/12/09/world/cia-torture-report-key-points.html

[38] C. Savage and P. Baker. "Obama, in a shift, to limit targets of drone strikes." *New York Times*. May 22, 2013. www.nytimes.com/2013/05/23/us/us-acknowledges-killing-4-americans-in-drone-strikes.html

[39] C. Currier and J. Winter. "Exclusive: TSA's secret behavior checklist to spot terrorists." *The Intercept*. March 27, 2015. firstlook.org/theintercept/2015/03/27/revealed-tsas-closely-held-behavior-checklist-spot-terrorists/

In another embarrassing example, the FBI proposed rolling out an education tool called "Don't Be A Puppet." The website is supposed to educate teachers and students to prevent young people from being drawn into violent extremism. Community leaders criticized the website for its lack of scientific basis and its bias. "The program is based on flawed theories of radicalization, namely that individuals radicalize in the exact same way and it's entirely discernible," said Arjun S. Sethi, an adjunct professor of law at the Georgetown University Law Center. "But it's not." If radicals are all different, if terrorists strike in different ways, then there's no easy answer of what to look for.

Worse, in this case the tool is racially and religiously biased. Community leaders pointed to a question about which Internet posts should spark concern. One choice was a person planning to attend a political event. Another was someone with an Arabic name posting about going on "a mission" overseas. The "correct" answer was the posting with the Arabic name, despite the fact that the word "mission" is often used to describe humanitarian or religious trips.

Once we build an expensive tool that can't meaningfully identify terrorists, it will be used for other things that it **can** do. Do we want massive surveillance for run-of-the-mill crimes like fraud and tax evasion? Because eventually those things are what the techniques will be used for.

The response to these points is usually that as technology improves, it will eventually overcome these obstacles. But that's not true. For the sake of argument, let's assume we agree on the definition of terrorism and we can identify characteristics of terrorism planning. Let us develop a reasonably accurate formula of what to look for in a sea of data. Our search tool is accurate but it's not perfect, because nothing is perfect. That means that you are going to be wrong some of the time. Of course, that means you are going to miss some attacks. But stopping even a few attacks would be far better than missing them all, everything else being equal.

Unfortunately, there is an insurmountable problem, the problem of "false positives." A false positive occurs when the test mistakenly identifies an innocent person as a terrorist. For the innocent person, the consequences can be devastating – from placement on the No Fly or other watchlists, to imprisonment, and even to assassination. In the abstract, that might be a risk our society is willing to take. We have proven tolerant of a disturbing number of false convictions in the criminal justice system already. Except, the rate of false positives isn't just bad for the people who are misidentified. It's also bad for the overall usefulness of the test. Terrorism is rare. So there are going to be far, far more false positives than true positives. After running data through the test, we're going have a huge pool of people tagged as potential terrorists. But for any one of them, we won't be able to have any confidence that they are, in fact, a terrorist.

There are so few terrorists, that you might actually be better off flipping a coin than relying on Big Data analysis to catch them.[40] To find out if a test – say for terrorism – works, statisticians use Bayes' Theorem. Bayes' Theorem requires three estimations:

• The base-rate for terrorists, i.e., what proportion of the population are terrorists;
• The accuracy rate, i.e., the probability that real terrorists will be identified by the NSA;
• The misidentification rate, i.e., the probability that innocent citizens will be misidentified by the NSA as terrorists.

Floyd Rudmin, a professor of social and community psychology at the University of Tromsø in Norway, explains that Bayes' Theorem shows any efforts to develop a data mining tool to identify terrorism will fail. The NSA's accuracy rate will never be 100 percent and their misidentification rate will never be 0 percent. When you combine that fact with the extremely low base-rate for terrorists, it is mathematically impossible for mass surveillance to be an effective way to find terrorists.

Let's do the math. If the probability that someone flagged by the system is a terrorist is zero (p=0.00), then they certainly are not terrorists, and the NSA is wasting resources and damaging the lives of innocent citizens. If the probability is one (p=1.00), then the people definitely are terrorists, and the NSA has saved the day. If the probability is fifty-fifty (p=0.50), that is the same as guessing who is a terrorist by flipping a coin. In any test, there are going to be false positives. How big a problem this is depends on how common the phenomenon you are testing for is in the general population. The more frequent a phenomenon, the more useful the test. But if a phenomenon is rare, false positives end up being a huge problem. It means that the test will inevitably produce many, many wrong results, even when the test itself is very, very accurate.

In practice what this means is that, because terrorism is quite rare in the United States, even an unrealistically accurate system will generate millions of false alarms for every real terrorist plot it uncovers.[41] This statistics

---

[40] B. Schneier. "Terrorists, data mining, and the base rate fallacy." *Schneier on Security.* July 10, 2006. www.schneier.com/blog/archives/2006/07/terrorists_data.html
[41] B. Schneier. "Why data mining won't stop terror." *Schneier on Security.* March 9, 2005. www.schneier.com/essays/archives/2005/03/why_data_mining_wont.html

concept is called the "base rate fallacy." The base rate fallacy means even where there is evidence for a rare phenomenon, people will routinely over-estimate the likelihood that it is true. Here is an illustrative example:

> John is a man who wears gothic inspired clothing, has long black hair, and listens to death metal. How likely is it that he is a Christian and how likely is it that he is a Satanist?
>
> If people were asked this question, they would likely underestimate the probability of him being a Christian, and overestimate the probability of him being a Satanist. This is because they would ignore that the base rate of being a Christian (there are about 2 billion in the world) is vastly higher than that of being a Satanist (estimated to be in the thousands). Therefore, even if such clothing choices indicated an order of magnitude jump in probability of being a Satanist, the probability of being a Christian is still much larger.[42]

Let's apply this understanding to the problem of identifying terrorists. Counterintuitively, the problem is that there are far too few terrorists in the United States. There are about 300 million people in the United States. Let's assume 1,000 are terrorists.[43] That means that for every one terror-ist, there are 300,000 innocent people. Terrorists are 0.00033 percent of the population. Now let's fantasize: we have developed a Big Data tool that is exceedingly good, with an accuracy rate of 90 percent. It catches 90 percent of terrorists. Even better, it isn't wrong very often. It has a misidentification rate of only 0.00001. Wow. This is a fantastic, awesome, impossibly good tool. Nevertheless, out of 3,900 flagged people, 3,000 innocent people are misidentified as terrorists, whereas 900 are correctly identified as terrorists. As applied, the probability that anyone is identified by this amazingly accurate test is a terrorist is less than 25 percent.

The truth is, of course, that the test for terrorists is going to be far less accurate than 90 percent, and it is going to be wrong far more often than 0.00001 percent of the time. There is no fingerprint that all terrorists share, and whatever characteristics terrorists do share, there are hundreds of thousands, if not hundreds of millions, of people, who also share those characteristics, but pose no danger. This is why Keith Devlin, a mathema-tician at Stanford University and funded by the Department of Defense to

---

[42] See http://research.omicsgroup.org/index.php/Base_rate_fallacy

[43] Violent extremism for international causes is vanishingly rare in the United States. For exam-ple, in July of 2015, the FBI said that only 200 Americans have left the country to fight for the extremist Islamic State in Syria (ISIS) against the Assad government. J. Hattem, "FBI: More than 200 Americans have tried to fight for ISIS." *The Hill.* July 8, 2015. thehill.com/policy/national-security/247256-more-than-200-americans-tried-to-fight-for-isis-fbi-says

explore how to extract actionable information from vast amounts of data, has said that it is an impossible goal.[44] "Based on everything I learned in those five years, blanket surveillance is highly unlikely to prevent a terrorist attack and is a dangerous misuse of resources that, if used in other ways, possibly could prevent attacks (such as the 2013 Boston Marathon bombing)."

The danger I've identified here – that "Collecting It All" is generating counterproductive false leads and distracting analysts – is not just a theory. It is the reality inside the NSA today. Top-secret NSA documents – visual presentation aids meant to be shared only inside the intelligence community – reveal that analysts are laboring under exactly this burden of false positives, and that it is interfering with their counterterrorism work. MUSCULAR was a joint US and UK program to intercept entire flows of information from Google, Yahoo! and other privately leased fiber optic cables. The technique gave the NSA and the UK's GCHQ access to oceans of unencrypted communications and metadata for Google and Yahoo! users. But the data was too much, and not good enough for intelligence. The classified slides say, "Numerous [intelligence] analysts have complained of [MUSCULAR's] existence, and the relatively small intelligence value it contains does not justify the sheer volume of collection at MUSCULAR." The slide goes on, "Numerous offices have complained about this collection diluting their workflow."[45]

MUSCULAR slides are just one bit of evidence that "analysis paralysis" is a serious problem at the NSA.[46] A number of internal documents entitled "Data Is Not Intelligence," "The Fallacies Behind the Scenes," "Cognitive Overflow?" "Summit Fever" and "In Praise of Not Knowing" discuss the problem of having so much information, you don't know what to do with it. While authors differed over how well the NSA was managing the problem, the internal angst shows that NSA analysts are suffering from too much, not too little, data.

The internal debate belies the public message the NSA officials push: If you want us to find the needle in the haystack, you need to give us more

[44] K. Devlin. "The NSA: A betrayal of trust." *Notices of the American Mathematical Society* 61 (June/July, 2014): 624–626.

[45] B. Gellman and M. DeLong. "How the NSA's MUSCULAR program collects too much data from Yahoo and Google." *The Washington Post*. March 14, 2013. apps.washingtonpost.com/g/page/world/how-the-nsas-muscular-program-collects-too-much-data-from-yahoo-and-google/543/#document/p2/a129323

[46] P. Maass. "Inside NSA, officials privately criticize 'collect it all' surveillance." *The Intercept*. May 28, 2015. theintercept.com/2015/05/28/nsa-officials-privately-criticize-collect-it-all-surveillance/

haystacks. To the contrary, analysts aren't craving more information to do their jobs well. Professor Devlin emphasizes this. "When the goal is to identify a very small number of key signals in a large ocean of noise, indiscriminately increasing the size of the ocean is self-evidently not the way to go."

A partially redacted intelligence document drives this point home. In a 2011 interview, the Signals Intelligence Division's Deputy Director of Analysis and Production, name blacked out, noted:

> We live in an Information Age when we have massive reserves of information and don't have the capability to exploit it. I was told that there are 2 petabytes of data in the SIGINT System at any given time. How much is that? That's equal to 20 million 4-drawer filing cabinets. How many cabinets per analyst is that?? By the end of this year, we'll have one terabyte of data per second coming in. You can't crank that through the existing processes and be effective. NSA analysts overwhelmed with surveillance data were at a loss to say whether Collecting It All helps them or hurts them more. Without metrics, how do we know that we have improved something or made it worse? There's a running joke … that we'll only know if collection is important by shutting it off and seeing if someone screams.[47]

Nor should we succumb to the attraction of doing something, anything, about terrorism out of fear. The DHS has an annual budget of $60 billion and 225,000 employees. Its chief is Jeh Johnson, a former prosecutor, former Pentagon official, and central figure in the Obama Administration's national security policymaking. Johnson gave a speech in September of 2015 where he reminded the Nation that security efforts should not come "at the cost of who we are as a nation of people who cherish our privacy, our religions, our freedom to speak, travel and associate, and who celebrate our diversity and immigrant heritage."[48] As Director Johnson says, "[i]n the final analysis, these are the things that constitute our greatest strengths as a Nation."[49]

---

[47] P. Maass. "Inside NSA, officials privately criticize 'collect it all' surveillance." *The Intercept.* May 28, 2015. theintercept.com/2015/05/28/nsa-officials-privately-criticize-collect-it-all-surveillance/, *citing* "Is there a sustainable ops tempo in S2? How can analysts deal with the flood of collection? – An interview with [redacted]." *SIDToday.* April 6, 2011. www.eff.org/files/2015/06/15/20150528-intercept-is_there_a_sustainable_ops_tempo_in_s2_how_can_analysts_deal_with_the_flood_of_collection.pdf

[48] S. Harris. "Homeland Security Chief: Everybody stop freaking out." *The Daily Beast.* September 16, 2015. www.thedailybeast.com/articles/2015/09/16/homeland-security-chief-everybody-stop-freaking-out.html

[49] Ibid.

In the last chapter and this one, I've made the case for skepticism about the effectiveness of massive surveillance for national security. Despite the way many people talk about it, security it isn't the opposite of privacy. You can improve security without infringing privacy – for example by locking cockpit doors. And not all invasions of privacy increase security. Collecting a lot of data is harming our ability to find terrorists because it interferes with an analysts' ability to focus on information that actually is useful. In other words, if terrorists are needles in a haystack, the trick isn't to collect more hay.

7

Americans Caught Up in the Foreign Intelligence Net

Americans, including Congress, have not worried much about spying conducted in the name of foreign intelligence or counterterrorism. The large-scale data collection techniques we turn against foreigners are not supposed to touch Americans, and our most sweeping domestic surveillance statutes seem to be carefully limited to counterterrorism investigations. So why should Americans worry about foreign intelligence surveillance?

The truth is that American spies collect vast amounts of American data in the name of foreign intelligence and counterterrorism. The intelligence agencies collected data on Americans via domestic dragnets, and continue to collect via extensive international wiretapping, and large-scale overseas collection. Foreign intelligence officials then share this data with domestic law enforcement at the FBI, the DEA, the IRS, and other agencies. This sharing takes place without judicial oversight, meaning that investigators can trawl through the information looking for dirt on people. The only things that purport to stop investigators from fishing around in the vast repositories of data collected in the name of foreign intelligence are "minimization procedures" – secret internal policies – where such procedures exist.

Domestic Dragnets Aren't Just for Terrorists

Weakening privacy rules in the name of national security is a slippery slope that the United States has repeatedly tumbled down. The result is a legal regime that gives great power to investigators with little to counterbalance it.

After the Snowden disclosures, the Obama Administration repeatedly assured the public that the NSA does not collect the private information of ordinary Americans. The NSA conducts the section 215 telephone call record dragnet to allow agents to identify "leads with respect to folks who might engage in terrorism," President Obama told the country on June 7,

2013.[1] The President's words implied that only Americans who appeared to be engaged in terrorism were under scrutiny.

Any lawyer reading section 215 would likely believe President Obama's claim, but it was not true. US law as written purports to expose only foreigners and terrorists to suspicionless surveillance. But the public now knows that in practice US officials regularly obtains Americans' phone calls, emails, and other communications and uses the information for reasons beyond counterterrorism.

Section 215 was passed as part of the USA PATRIOT Act of 2001. At the time, the provision worried lawmakers and the public because in the name of counterterrorism, investigators would be allowed to access many categories of business records that could reveal information traditionally considered private, like the lending records of a library, which would impinge on intellectual privacy. The provision came to be called the "library records provision," a name that crystallized that concern, even as Congress passed it, and, in the face of reports that it had not been abused, renewed it.

Then in 2013, the public learned from documents revealed by Snowden that section 215 had been reinterpreted in secret to allow bulk collection of Americans' phone records. The statute enabled the FBI to obtain court orders demanding that a person or company produce "tangible things," upon showing reasonable grounds that the things sought are "relevant" to an authorized foreign intelligence investigation. However, the data could not concern a US person unless "relevant" to protecting against international terrorism or clandestine intelligence activities. American spies and the FISC judges decided that section 215's "relevance" provisions, which facially limit collection of American data, actually empowered the NSA to collect *all* American phone data and then data mine it for terrorism connections.

Of course, the intelligence court judges knew that once in government hands, members of the intelligence community were capable of searching the data for anything. Still, the FISC judges allowed dragnet collection, but set usage rules. The rules said that the NSA could only search the data trove for numbers for which it has "reasonable articulable suspicion" to believe it is associated with particular international terrorist groups. Then, for each suspicious number, the agency could conduct "contact chaining." Contact chaining means mapping everyone the number is in contact with, and potentially everyone those numbers are in contact with, and so on.

---

[1] "Statement by the President." White House. Office of the Press Secretary, June 7, 2013. www. whitehouse.gov/the-press-office/2013/06/07/statement-president

The number of "hops" defines how deep the government can dig to create that network. The rules allowed the NSA two or three hops.

At the time the FISC approved the phone dragnet, the existence of the very technique of contact chaining was classified. That's strange because the concept is not unfamiliar. Six Degrees of Kevin Bacon is likely many people's first introduction to this concept (the joke is that everyone can trace a line between almost any actor and the star of *Footloose*), but any social network works along the same lines. On Facebook, you can see whether someone is a friend of a friend. On LinkedIn, you can find out how many people there are between you and someone you want to meet professionally. What the NSA was doing was taking phone numbers presumably associated with a suspected terrorist, then identifying all the numbers in contact with the suspected terrorist, plus all the numbers in contact with those people, plus all the numbers in contact with those people. Then agents would scrutinize this subset of numbers, and not just for counterterrorism purposes.

It was unprecedented to learn that Americans could come under government scrutiny merely for being three hops from a suspected number. One of the serious problems with this extenuated guilt-by-association is that even terrorists call the same businesses that upstanding citizens call. For example, regular people and terrorists both order pizza. So if a suspect calls to order dinner, contact chaining can pull in multiples of people who have no plans to bomb a building or bring down an airliner. At some point, the NSA analysts realized that for this database to be even marginally useful, they had to go through and remove all the pizza parlors, food delivery services, American Idol hotlines, and 1–800 phone numbers.

Despite efforts to reduce irrelevant results, the vast majority of people whose numbers ended up in the NSA's section 215 database were wholly innocent of any wrongdoing. In July 2013, deputy director of the NSA John C. Inglis, told a Senate committee that a year before, the NSA queried the section 215 phone records database (the NSA has other phone number databases) with fewer than 300 unique identifiers. To the careless listener, Inglis' testimony implied that even though the NSA maintains a huge database of domestic calling information, the agency was very selective and discreet when using the resource.

But some basic math shows the opposite. Let's assume that each of those 300 suspected terrorists have 40 unique contacts they call. That is one hop. Then those 12,000 people each call 40 people. That's the second hop. Then each of those 480,000 people call 40 people. That's the third hop: approximately 19 million numbers in 2012 that the NSA got to scrutinize.

That scrutiny was not limited to counterterrorism. While the seed numbers had to be associated with particular terrorist groups, the NSA declared open season on the contact chains. The chain of numbers representing your calling network were moved out of the master dragnet database and into a different database with different rules called the "corporate store." The intelligence community could perform whatever "tradecraft" it wanted on numbers within the "corporate store." It didn't have to be about counterterrorism: all it had to be was about the much broader concept of "foreign intelligence."[2] And while the FISC seemed to place rules limiting other agencies' access to the data, those restrictions were pretty weak, maybe even nonexistent. The NSA could give executive branch authorities, which includes the Department of Justice and the FBI, the results of their intelligence analysis, including information that identifies US persons. This information – if exculpatory or impeaching – could then be used, presumably in pending criminal cases.[3]

In other words, under section 215, the government has the ability to abuse the bulk information it has collected, but we have to trust that it won't. We have to trust that the secret rules adequately protect Americans' civil liberties. We have to trust that the agents will follow the rules, and use the data only for proper purposes. We have to trust that agents will not use that data to spy on their ex-lovers. We have to trust that when something goes wrong, the overseers will be informed. We have to trust that government officials won't lie. We have to trust that the complex, multilayered rules that are supposed to prevent abuse will work.

In response to public outcry about the section 215 program, in 2013 President Obama announced that the NSA would restrict its contact-chain analysis from three hops to two. About two years later, Congress stopped bulk collection and overhauled the program via the USA Freedom Act. The public is waiting to learn whether that effort has been effective, or ignored in secret.

The section 215 phone records dragnet was not the only dragnet spying on Americans purportedly justified by counterterrorism needs. From 2001 to 2011, the NSA also conducted an Internet transactional dragnet under the FISA pen register statute. As with section 215, the FISA pen register statute says that government may only get Internet routing information about Americans if "relevant" to an international counterterrorism

---

[2] *In re Application of the Federal Bureau of Investigation for an Order Requiring the Production of Tangible Things From [redacted]*, No. BR 13–80 (FISC, April 25, 2013) p. 11. https://fas.org/irp/news/2013/07/215_order.pdf

[3] Id., pp. 13–14.

investigation. For years after September 11th, the Bush Administration was collecting this information, but then disagreement inside the Department of Justice over whether the collection was appropriate required the NSA to get FISC approval. The FISC judge created a laughable interpretation of the concept of "relevance." She ruled that "relevant" information is "all" the information based on the Department of Justice's argument that collecting in bulk was a necessary precursor for data mining. But the government isn't entitled to data mine or to conduct any investigative technique it likes. It is supposed to use targeted techniques, not bulk techniques, on Americans. That is what the law says. But it is not how the law was secretly rewritten.

The secret legal history of both section 215 and the FISA pen trap statute illustrate how domestic spying laws have been secretly subverted for massive spying on Americans. These are not the only examples. In Chapter 12, I relate other stories about how the government, sometimes with the complicity of FISC judges, has secretly interpreted intelligence law to legitimize illegal, warrantless wiretapping and domestic dragnet collection.

We also see domestic law enforcement using similar bulk collection techniques to capture Americans' data. In 2015, the public learned that the DEA also conducted a phone dragnet, one that started in 1992. DEA officials collected the phone records without court approval, apparently using subpoenas to obtain logs of virtually all telephone calls from the USA to as many as 116 countries linked to drug trafficking. The destination countries included Canada, Mexico, and most of Central and South America. Agents used the records to track drug cartels' distribution networks. They also used them to help confirm that Timothy McVeigh was not acting on behalf of a foreign power when in 1995 he bombed the Alfred P. Murrah Federal Building in Oklahoma City. After September 11th, the FBI got permission to use the database to investigate Americans suspected of non-drug crimes.[4]

Apparently, this is just one of many phone dragnets constructed with subpoenas – a kind of order you don't even need to go to a court to get – or other scant legal process. "Project Crisscross" began in the early 1990s and involved the DEA, the NSA, the CIA, and the FBI collecting and exchanging billions of phone records. Then there is "Hemisphere," a DEA

---

[4] That collection was sacrificed at the altar of the section 215 dragnet. When the public learned about the section 215 NSA dragnet, Attorney General Eric Holder broke the bad news to the DEA. Since the NSA was going to defend its dragnet on the grounds that sweeping NSA surveillance serves national security interests, and not ordinary policing, it wouldn't look good to have an ongoing ordinary policing dragnet waiting to be exposed.

operation dating back to 1987, where the agency used subpoenas to collect international call records and also location data.[5] A DEA database called DICE contains phone and Internet communication records gathered by the DEA through both subpoenas and search warrants nationwide.[6] We don't know whether these programs are all basically the same program, or how they interact. But the upshot is clear: innocent Americans are getting spied on.

One reason for the lack of public understanding about what these tools do is that the government has been lying about it. For example, law enforcement investigators were trained to hide the source of tips that originated from DEA databases. DEA and IRS agents are told to lie to judges and defense attorneys about their use of NSA data, and about the very existence of the DEA's Special Operations Division (SOD).[7] When agents receive SOD information and rely on it to trigger investigations, they are directed to omit the SOD's involvement from investigative reports, affidavits, discussions with prosecutors, and courtroom testimony. Agents are instructed to then use "normal investigative techniques to recreate the information provided by SOD." They call this "parallel construction." IRS agents receiving SOD data, which presumably can include information from the NSA, have been similarly instructed to create a fake investigative file, and to lie – in particular, to defense lawyers and to judges – about the source of the evidence used in criminal prosecutions. The falsehoods are intended to ensure that no one will know that Americans are being investigated based on evidence from the NSA's top-secret surveillance programs.[8] They have the effect of ensuring not just that people are kept in the dark about these programs, but also of evading potentially meritorious legal challenges, oversight, or even policy changes from Congress.

Today, any number of other government agencies – the DEA, the Secret Service, the Pentagon, and the DHS – are seeking access to NSA data for their own investigations of drug use, tax evasion, and even copyright

[5] S. Shane and C. Moynihan. "Drug agents use vast phone trove eclipsing NSA's." *The New York Times*. September 1, 2013. www.nytimes.com/2013/09/02/us/drug-agents-use-vast-phone-trove-eclipsing-nsas.html
[6] J. Shifman and K. Cooke. "US directs agents to cover up program used to investigate Americans." *Reuters*. August 5, 2013. www.reuters.com/article/us-dea-sod-idUSBRE97409R20130805
[7] Ibid.
[8] J. Granick and C. Sprigman. "NSA, DEA, IRS lie about fact that Americans are routinely spied on by our government: Time for a special prosecutor." *Forbes*. August 14, 2013. www.forbes.com/sites/jennifergranick/2013/08/14/nsa-dea-irs-lie-about-fact-that-americans-are-routinely-spied-on-by-our-government-time-for-a-special-prosecutor-2/

infringement.[9] That's right. In the future, we may well conduct dragnet surveillance on Americans to catch people for smoking marijuana, and downloading music and movies, if we aren't already.

Intelligence Collection Aimed at Foreigners Captures Americans, Too

The NSA is a foreign intelligence agency and therefore generally prohibited from using its vast surveillance powers to spy intentionally on Americans. One exception to this general rule is FISA, which authorizes surveillance of Americans upon a factual showing of complicity with a foreign power. There are ample reasons to be concerned about FISA surveillance, but in the aftermath of September 11th, some in the intelligence community found even that statute's loose rules too constraining. Under the top-secret STELLARWIND program, the Bush Administration started collecting Americans' communications with some foreigners without any factual showing or court order. That practice has morphed into the FISA Amendments Act section 702.

On its face, it is hard for nonexperts to tell that section 702 authorizes suspicionless spying on Americans. Under that provision of law, intelligence authorities need not get a warrant when the target of surveillance is a non-US person outside the country. Under general certifications, investigators can issue directives to Internet and telephone companies, forcing them to turn over the target conversations. Section 702 is the legal basis for the PRISM and Upstream collection programs that Edward Snowden helped shed light on. Snowden's disclosures showed that top Internet companies were disclosing private data to the NSA. In response, President Obama assured that "this [collection] does not apply to U.S. citizens and it does not apply to people living in the United States."[10] But that was not true. Section 702 allows warrantless wiretapping and collection of communications when the foreign target is talking to Americans. That collection – which American spies call "incidental" – turns out to be quite vast. Further, once collected, the NSA, the FBI, and the CIA have access to that data under various conditions. The FBI, the DEA, and even the Treasury

---

[9] E. Lichtblau and M. Schmidt. "Other agencies clamor for data NSA compiles." *The New York Times.* August 3, 2013. www.nytimes.com/2013/08/04/us/other-agencies-clamor-for-data-nsa-compiles.html?pagewanted=all

[10] Ibid.

Department have long had access to emails and other messages obtained via section 702.[11]

To understand how Americans get caught in the nets that the NSA casts for foreigners, you have to understand the broad scope of the NSA's foreign intelligence mission. Foreign intelligence includes counterterrorism and national security, but it also includes the collection information relevant to the conduct of foreign affairs. Intelligence is about helping policy makers be better informed in trade negotiations, economic crises, and foreign affairs. Intelligence is used to inform the government on trends and global players, provide insight on the economy and on enemies' military activity. It's also used for the more nefarious aspects of spycraft, like identifying targets for drone assassination or imprisonment. If there was ever any question about how broad foreign intelligence collection could be, the NSA itself describes the scope of its collection as including information about nuclear proliferation, oil sales, and even "economics."[12] What constitutes a foreign intelligence matter is vast.

What that means is that section 702 authorizes warrantless wiretapping of foreigners talking to Americans about a wide range of topics. Collection similarly happens when spying takes place overseas, but with even fewer restrictions and oversight. While the FISA statute generally says that the NSA cannot eavesdrop on Americans inside the United States without showing that one of the conversationalists is an agent of a foreign power and getting a warrant, FISA does not cover intelligence collection that (1) does not target Americans and (2) takes place outside the United States. In that circumstance, the NSA's collection activities will take place under presidential executive order (EO), specifically EO 12333. EO 12333 collection is vast, multifaceted, top secret, and poorly understood. The FISC does not approve it, and Congress does little or nothing to oversee it.

Historically, EO 12333 collection always has been extensive, but it's growing. The Internet easily connects people with others from around the world, communicating on Facebook, in chat rooms, and via instant messaging applications. When Americans talk with people in other countries and the data is collected overseas in bulk or while targeting foreigners, the

---

[11] C. Savage. "Debate brews over disclosing warrantless spying." *The New York Times.* September 30, 2014. www.nytimes.com/2014/10/01/us/debate-simmers-over-disclosing-warrantless-spying.html

[12] Untitled NSA PowerPoint, The Office of the General Counsel. www.dni.gov/files/documents/1118/CLEANED021.extracts.%20Minimization%20Pr...cted%20from%20file%20021-Sealed.pdf

weaker EO 12333 rules, and not FISA's, apply. American spies increasingly collect data from regular people, and not just heads of state. That's because people increasingly use tools that create a digital record of their words and actions and the data is easier to make sense of today because computers parse written data quite well. Technology is also rapidly getting better at making sense of audio.

With the NSA's monitoring capabilities around the world, it can use its computers to capture everything. Increasingly, "everything" includes some data from Americans. If Americans are talking with people of foreign intelligence interest, a friend who works for the German government, a colleague at an international oil company, a lawyer at Human Rights Watch, then those conversations are going to be collected. The NSA calls this collection "incidental." The information is obtained incident to surveillance of a target. But clearly, there aren't just a few incidents of it taking place.

The proliferation of NSA collection technology means that the agency can make mistakes that grab our information. In one incident, revealed in a 2012 inspector general's report disclosed by Snowden, analysts seeking to wiretap calls to and from Egypt made a mistake. Instead of typing into their powerful machines the country code for that nation, 20, they typed in 202 – the area code for Washington, D.C.[13] This typographical error resulted in over-collection of "a large number" of calls. How on Earth could such a powerful surveillance system be set up without built-in safeguards to prevent unlawful surveillance? However, the NSA decided that it did not need to report the problem to Congress or to the FISC. Supposedly, the mistake only touched Americans' metadata, and the intelligence community does not consider metadata violations as defects that anyone else needs to know about.[14] This was just one of approximately 2,700 incidents of unauthorized collection, storage, access to, or distribution of legally protected communications in the preceding twelve months.

Another risk is that Americans' data will travel overseas where it is subject to broad collection under EO 12333. Given the operation of the modern Internet, sometimes even purely domestic messages that are otherwise off limits to the intelligence agency can be routed or stored overseas. John Napier Tye, former section chief for Internet freedom in the

---

[13] See B. Gellman. "NSA broke privacy rules thousands of times per year, audit finds." *The Washington Post.* August 15, 2013. www.washingtonpost.com/world/national-security/nsa-broke-privacy-rules-thousands-of-times-per-year-audit-finds/2013/08/15/3310e554-05ca-11e3-a07f-49ddc7417125_story.html

[14] Ibid., citing a March 2013 memo stating that the surveillance of the 202 area code was a compliance issue that "pertained to Metadata ONLY so there were no defects to report."

State Department's Bureau of Democracy, Human Rights and Labor from January 2011 to April 2014 has said that this technological tendency exposes American data to indiscriminate collection under executive order.[15] These are just some of the ways that EO 12333 can impact Americans' privacy.

One collection program that illustrates how this happens is MUSCULAR, a collaboration between the NSA and the United Kingdom's GCHQ. Because companies like Google and Yahoo! were encrypting their Internet flows, the spy agencies couldn't see into it. All that intelligence agency machines could see is that a computer was connecting to a Google or Yahoo! server. Then each companies' set of servers was replicating that data to servers around the world to ensure that customers could seamlessly access these services. But the companies made a mistake. Once the data was inside Google or Yahoo!'s internal network, it was no longer encrypted. The GCHQ was able to get access to the fiber optic cables that comprised this internal network and conduct its wiretaps there. The NSA and the GCHQ worked together to grab whole flows of unencrypted Google and Yahoo! data, much of which must have belonged to Americans.[16] In a thirty-month period, the MUSCULAR effort managed to grab 181 million new records, including both content and metadata.

The NSA could have used the PRISM program to ask for information held by Google and Yahoo!. But EO 12333 has far fewer and much looser restrictions and little or no oversight. GCHQ operates freely. So while collecting everything – "full take" – or obtaining information without a particular target – "bulk access" – would be illegal in the United States, the NSA used GCHQ, MUSCULAR and EO 12333 to evade even the anemic section 702 rules. After reporters revealed the existence of MUSCULAR

---

[15] J. Tye. "Meet Executive Order 12333: The Reagan rule that lets the NSA spy on Americans." The Washington Post. July 18, 2014. https://www.washingtonpost.com/opinions/meet-executive-order-12333-the-reagan-rule-that-lets-the-nsa-spy-on-americans/2014/07/18/93d2ac22-0b93-11e4-b8e5-d0de80767fc2_story.html] According to Tye, on the modern Internet, US communications increasingly travel across U.S. borders – or are stored beyond them. Further, the public has learned that some corporate collaborators "shape" Internet traffic so that communications are more likely to flow through spying devices the NSA has installed on various digital networks.

[16] B. Gellman and A. Soltani. "NSA infiltrates links to Yahoo, Google data centers worldwide, Snowden documentary says." The Washington Post. October 30, 2013. www.washingtonpost.com/world/national-security/nsa-infiltrates-links-to-yahoo-google-data-centers-worldwide-snowden-documents-say/2013/10/30/e51d661e-4166-11e3-8b74-d89d714ca4dd_story.html

collection, Google, Yahoo!, and other Internet companies stepped up efforts to encrypt internal data flows, shutting off intelligence access to this private data.

How much data from Americans have spies been able to grab? State Department whistleblower John Tye reported that the NSA was grabbing all Gmail, likely through the MUSCULAR program.

In another revealing incident, a team of NSA analysts in Hawaii asked the DISHFIRE system, which collects financial transactions, SMS text messages, border crossing signals from mobile phones and "pretty much everything it can,"[17] to find any communications that mentioned both the Swedish manufacturer Ericsson and "radio" or "radar." This is not a particularly well-targeted query. Further, American data is in DISHFIRE. So the query could just as easily have collected on Americans as on the purported Pakistani military target.[18]

In the name of foreign intelligence gathering, the NSA has targeted Médecins du Monde and UNICEF,[19] as well as almost every foreign government. Human rights groups like Human Rights Watch and Amnesty International were also targets.[20] The NSA has targeted Petrobras, the Brazilian oil company, and Total, the French oil and gas giant. The NSA collects commercial information or trade secrets for certain noncompetitive purposes. We say, and it is likely true, that our intelligence agencies do not pass such information on to advantage American companies,[21] but this subtle distinction is often lost on or disbelieved by many countries.

[17] J. Ball. "NSA collects millions of text messages in 'untargeted' global sweep." *The Guardian*. January 16, 2014. www.theguardian.com/world/2014/jan/16/nsa-collects-millions-text-messages-daily-untargeted-global-sweep

[18] B. Gellman. "NSA broke privacy rules thousands of times per year, audit finds." *The Washington Post*. August 15, 2013. www.washingtonpost.com/world/national-security/nsa-broke-privacy-rules-thousands-of-times-per-year-audit-finds/2013/08/15/3310e554-05ca-11e3-a07f-49ddc7417125_story.html

[19] J. Gland and A. Lehren. "NSA spied on allies, aid groups, and businesses." *The New York Times*. December 20, 2013. www.nytimes.com/2013/12/21/world/nsa-dragnet-included-allies-aid-groups-and-business-elite.html?pagewanted=2&_r=0

[20] "Snowden: NSA targets communications of human rights workers." *Aljazeera America*. April 8, 2014. america.aljazeera.com/articles/2014/4/8/nsa-human-rights.html

[21] The collection of foreign private commercial information or trade secrets is authorized only to protect the national security of the United States or its partners and allies. It is not an authorized foreign intelligence or counterintelligence purpose to collect such information to afford a competitive advantage to U.S. companies and U.S. business sectors

To undermine certain radical political figures, the agency even collects information about individuals' "online promiscuity." It also collects information showing people "publish articles without checking facts," lead "a glamorous lifestyle," and [engage in] "deceitful use of funds."[22]

But the NSA can do more than just focus on targets under scrutiny. It can conduct searches on network data or stored data for more amorphous goals. Computers might be programmed to save every message in Korean that mentions Sony Pictures. They might pull details sufficient to identify any web browser that someone uses to watch an Islamic State beheading video.

The US government has downplayed the extent of overseas collection on Americans. Robert Litt is General Counsel of the ODNI. Litt regularly comes to conferences to say that Americans' data is a very small percentage of the overall data the NSA collects. But this claim is one of those things that intelligence officers say, but which doesn't necessarily mean anything. As whistleblower John Tye pointed out during a 2015 debate with Litt at Georgetown University, using percentages isn't very revealing.[23] One hundred percent of American Gmail messages might be a small fraction of total Internet traffic – but it is still *every single* message Americans are sending using Gmail.

Attorney Bob Litt also points to post-collection rules meant to regulate how intelligence agencies use messages concerning Americans that are caught in overseas collection. The spying agencies have procedures in place that protect both foreigners and Americans from how messages obtained in overseas spying can be used, Litt says. These rules ensure that Americans' data gets special treatment to protect our privacy. So even if our data happens to be collected, we shouldn't worry.

But that, too, is misleading. The post-collection policies – minimization procedures – set forth what the intelligence agencies are allowed to do with American data, and how they are allowed to share it. The procedures

commercially. Certain economic purposes, such as identifying trade or sanctions violations or government influence or direction, shall not constitute competitive advantage. Obama, Barack. "Presidential Policy Directive 28 – Signals Intelligence Activities." January 17, 2014. Section (1)(c). Hereinafter PPD-28.

[22] Untitled NSA Document (October 3, 2012) cited in G. Greenwald, R. Grim, and R. Gallagher. "Top-Secret document reveals NSA spied on porn habits as part of plan to discredit 'radicalizers.'" *The Huffington Post.* November 26, 2013. www.huffingtonpost.com/ 2013/11/26/nsa-porn-muslims_n_4346128.html

[23] "The NSA, Privacy & the Global Internet: Perspectives on EO 12333." Georgetown University Law Center. Online video clip. September 19, 2014. apps.law.georgetown.edu/ webcasts/eventDetail.cfm?eventID=2430

governing how US person data sucked in from overseas networks may be used by intelligence agencies are contained in EO 12333 and other arcane documents like the Department of Defense Directive 5240.1-R, USSID-18, SPGCMA, and more. Many of the usage policies are totally or partially classified.

To understand what can happen to American data, you have to know and understand the policies for every intelligence agency. That's because each intelligence agency is limited in what it can do by its mission. For example, the CIA is not supposed to have any internal security function within the United States. The NSA is not supposed to conduct surveillance except for foreign intelligence. But the FBI can investigate Americans for both national security and law enforcement. If you only read the NSA and the CIA rules, you have an incomplete picture of government activity concerning Americans. Since these agencies share data with each other, information collected on Americans will be subject to different policies as it flows between these entities and to other agencies like the National Counterterrorism Center, the DEA, and the IRS.

There are problems with relying on the minimization procedures to do the hard work of protecting American privacy and guarding us against government abuses. One problem is that the rules are anemic – sometimes pathetically so. The EO 12333 rules we know about are fraught with discretionary end-runs around limitations. For example, under USSID-18 the general rule is "communications to, from or about U.S. PERSONS that are intercepted ... may be retained in their original or transcribed form only ... for five years unless the Signals Intelligence Director determines in writing that retention for a longer period is required to respond to authorized FOREIGN INTELLIGENCE requirements."[24] Further, the public version of USSID-18, the NSA's main rules for handling American data, is only partially declassified. There are so many redactions in the document that it's unclear what the agency even means when it talks about a "U.S. person." We don't even know who qualifies as an American that may enjoy the special protections that Obama and Litt tell us should give comfort. Even if we could see the rules, we don't know how American spies interpret them. As we've seen, the intelligence community has been adept at pushing fantastical interpretations of seemingly simple legal words like "relevance."

---

[24] "USSID-18: Legal Compliance and U.S. persons Minimization Procedures." National Security Agency. July 25, 2011. Section 6.1.a(1).

Reliance on post-collection procedures to protect civil liberties may be inherently flawed and unfixable. Even if minimization rules were written to be more privacy-protective, they are unreliable. These rules are secret, and can be changed at any time. Only if whistleblowers leak them or officials choose to declassify them do we know what the procedures are. For example, after Snowden revealed the 2009 minimization procedures for the NSA under section 702, the government published the NSA, FBI, and CIA minimization rules from 2014. By early March 2016, reporters discovered that the FBI rules had changed in secret.[25] American spies initially to declassify them. The Privacy and Civil Liberties Oversight Board was allowed to say that the rules addressed some of its complaints about the section 702 PRISM program, but it was not allowed to say anything else.

The procedures are complex. Even experts reading them do not entirely understand what they mean or how unwritten policies impact their effectiveness. Unfortunately, any efforts to figure out what the rules actual are, and what they mean for individual privacy, are blocked from the beginning by official secrecy.

Finally, there are no remedies for people who suffer from violations of those rules. Violations may or may not be reported or cataloged. Victims are not informed. Without the threat of exposure and punishment, there is little incentive for analysts to rigorously follow the rules.

In 2014, President Obama tried to address the public concern. His administration embraced the unproven assertion that bulk collection was necessary for threat identification. "Locating new or emerging threats and other vital national security information is difficult, as such information is often hidden within the large and complex system of modern global communications. The United States must consequently collect signals intelligence in bulk in certain circumstances in order to identify these threats." This assertion is suspect because mass surveillance is not demonstrably effective against terrorism. But the President also sought to reassure the public that there are procedures in place to limit abuse of our information after it is collected. That reassurance came in the form of PPD-28, a presidential directive that for the first time purported to give foreigners some legal protections under US surveillance law.

According to PPD-28, when collected "in bulk," SIGINT may not be used, against Americans or foreigners, except for the following

---

[25] S. Ackerman. "The FBI quietly changes its privacy rules for accessing NSA data on Americans." *The Guardian.* March 10, 2016. www.theguardian.com/us-news/2016/mar/08/fbi-changes-privacy-rules-accessing-nsa-prism-data?CMP=edit_2221

purposes: detecting and countering espionage, terrorism, weapons of mass destruction, cybersecurity threats, transnational criminal threats, or threats to the armed forces. The limits mean that bulk SIGINT information should not be used against Americans for run-of-the-mill criminal prosecutions, for example, and that American spies won't troll through the data to learn embarrassing details about non-Americans' lives unless it is for a good reason.[26]

We don't actually know whether these PPD-28 limitations are in any way meaningful. Remember that "bulk" is a term of art. It doesn't mean large or broad, it means collected without using search terms. The NSA collects information in other countries based on search terms, called "selectors" or "discriminators."[27] We don't know what kind of selectors the NSA uses. They could be exceedingly broad, like "al-Qaeda" or "Yemen." Broad selectors mean an immense quantity of innocent peoples' communications will end up in government hands. Even more tailored selectors, like an email address or phone number, can capture lots of Americans. Think about messages to addresses like "membership@doctorswithoutborders.org" or "mailinglist@greenpeace.net." But because the collection is not "bulk" the PPD-28 limits will not apply.

In sum, there's vast, secret spying on Americans going on. This spying takes place under many different legal authorities. In general, Americans may only be targeted for intelligence surveillance if they are agents of a foreign power under traditional FISA provisions passed in 1978. But there are many other ways for our conversations to end up saved in a government database. For example:

- Talking to a noncitizen in another country about something of foreign intelligence interest (section 702);

---

[26] PPD-28. Section 2. www.whitehouse.gov/the-press-office/2014/01/17/presidential-policy-directive-signals-intelligence-activities. But see EO 12333: The intelligence community should "permanently retain or disseminate such personal information only if the personal information relates to an authorized intelligence requirement, is reasonably believed to be evidence of a crime, or meets one of the other standards for retention or dissemination identified in section 2.3" of EO 12333; "Safeguarding the Personal Information of all People: A Status Report on the Development and Implementation of Procedures under PPD-28." Office of the Director of National Intelligence. July 2014. www.dni.gov/files/documents/1017/PPD-28_Status_Report_Oct_2014.pdf

[27] Intelligence community officials do not like to use the term "search" because it triggers Fourth Amendment concerns. Rather, they use "query" to mean searching through data they have already stored.

- When domestic communications are routed internationally and contain a foreign intelligence selector (section 702 inadvertent collection approved by the FISC in 2011);
- When Americans' communications are obtained while targeted non-Americans or as part of a surveillance program outside the United States (Executive Order 12333);
- When communications are obtained by a spying partner of the United States and given to the US intelligence community.

Under both domestic and foreign rules, American spies have infinite arguments that enable them to do what they want to do, somehow, without ever being revealed to have so clearly broken the rules that someone will get punished.

8

Warrantless Wiretapping of Americans Under Section 702

The NSA started illegally wiretapping Americans after the attacks of September 11th. The public learned of the practice, part of STELLARWIND, in a *New York Times* article published in December of 2005. The disclosure instigated intelligence community efforts in the secret FISC and in Congress to legitimize at least some aspects of the warrantless wiretapping program. Chapter 12 tells the story of the Bush and Obama Administrations' efforts to obtain judicial and legislative blessing for STELLARWIND surveillance in more detail. Ultimately, American spies successfully obtained legislative approval for STELLARWIND-style warrantless wiretapping when Congress passed the Foreign Intelligence Surveillance Act Amendments Act of 2008. In particular, section 702 of that law authorizes warrantless wiretapping of Americans.

For years, American spies were able to deny this was the case by focusing on the legalistic language of section 702. Section 702 hides in plain sight its true function of authorizing spying on Americans under the rhetorical guise of spying on foreigners overseas. Nevertheless, Americans who aren't terrorists are spied on under section 702 because we talk *with* foreign targets, because we talk with foreigners *about* foreign targets, because we are mistaken for *being* foreign, and because our communications are *by-catch* over-collected by NSA surveillance computers. It's particularly important to understand this collection authority and the rules that purportedly govern it because Congress is set to reconsider section 702 at the end of 2017. The law will "sunset" then, and Americans have a choice to make about whether to continue it in its current form, amend it, or end it entirely. It will take a lot of political support to change the law and protect Americans from this warrantless wiretapping.

Section 702 Overview

Traditionally, the FISA allowed the government to conduct electronic surveillance of foreign entities in order to gather foreign intelligence information. FISA required the government to specify to the FISC the individuals to be monitored, and to show probable cause that the target would use the facilities at which the government planned to direct surveillance. These required elements in a FISA surveillance application discouraged indiscriminate collection of communications to and from innocent Americans.

In 2008, in the aftermath of disclosures about the Bush Administration's illegal, warrantless wiretapping, Congress established a new legal regime for wiretapping foreigners from inside the United States and with the help of US-based Internet companies and telecommunications providers. No longer would this kind of surveillance require judicial review, a warrant based on probable cause, or individualized suspicion. Rather, section 702 of the FISA Amendments Act of 2008 (located at 50 U.S.C. §§ 1881 *et seq.*) authorizes the government to broadly collect telephone call, email, instant message, social network, and other communications content where the target is reasonably believed to be a non-US person located outside the United States, for any foreign intelligence purpose.

"Non-US persons" excludes American citizens and people with green cards. It includes foreign entities and individuals. These may be targeted without any suspicion of terrorism, criminal conduct, or any other wrongdoing. The only requirement is that the targeting be for a certified foreign intelligence purpose.

Section 702 allows surveillance of a foreign entity without specifying the people to be monitored or the facilities, places, premises, or property at which surveillance will be directed. The government can direct surveillance at any facility, even without reason to believe that the target is using that facility. That means that under section 702, American spies can not only monitor unspecified Americans' international communications to or from targets, they may also collect our international communications *about* foreign targets. The targets need not be agents of a foreign power or terrorists. They just have to be of foreign intelligence interest. However, the government may not target Americans or intentionally acquire purely domestic communications.

To get a certification, the attorney general and the Director of National Intelligence submit an application to the FISC. Once the FISC issues the certification, under PRISM, the FBI, which is authorized to operate inside the United States, issues directives to Internet companies ordering them to use specified search terms or "selectors" to gather information and turn it over to the government. The selectors must be designed to gather foreign intelligence information. Upstream surveillance involves sending a section 702 directive to compel assistance from providers that control the telecommunications backbone over which communications transit. The FISC doesn't review the directives or the selectors.

The government has not declassified the section 702 certifications, so the public does not in fact know the subject matter of authorized investigations. We do know, however, that certifications are extremely broad. The FISC appears to have accepted surveillance certifications under section 702 for certain categories of foreign intelligence including possibly weapons counterproliferation efforts, cybersecurity, and counterterrorism.[1] There is a section 702 certification for almost all foreign governments (excluding the NSA's closest spying partners, the United Kingdom, New Zealand, Australia, and Canada – together called the Five Eyes).[2]

After a certification is issued, American spies have discretion to decide how to conduct the collection. The statute imposes few restrictions on analysts designing search terms to obtain information relevant to the certifications, and the FISC does not review the terms to ensure that they are not overbroad. Nevertheless, according to the PCLOB, the government first identifies a selector, like an email address, that it reasonably believes is used by the target, whether that target is an individual or an entity. It then acquires only those communications that are related to this identifier. At the time of PCLOB review, selectors could not include names like "Osama bin Laden" or general topics like "Petrobras." Certainly such commonly used terms would capture vast amounts of communications traffic.

Still, collection under section 702 does not resemble traditional domestic surveillance conducted pursuant to individualized court orders based on probable cause. Rather, the FISA court determines whether to approve the surveillance program as a whole, approves broad certifications, and plays some role in overseeing whether the government's approach to collection stays within statutory and constitutional limits.[3]

---

[1] See "FISA Amendments Act of 2008 Section 702 Summary Document." Office of the General Counsel, December 23, 2008. www.eff.org/files/2014/06/30/fisa_amendments_act_summary_document_1.pdf; C. Savage, J. Angwin, J. Larson, and H. Moltke. "Hunting for hackers, N.S.A. secretly expands Internet spying at U.S. border." *The New York Times.* June 4, 2015. www.nytimes.com/2015/06/05/us/hunting-for-hackers-nsa-secretly-expands-internet-spying-at-us-border.html

[2] "FISA judge's order authorizing surveillance of foreign governments and organizations." *The Washington Post.* August 19, 2010. apps.washingtonpost.com/g/page/world/fisa-judges-order-authorizing-surveillance-of-foreign-governments-and-organizations/1132/

[3] "Report on the Surveillance Program Operated Pursuant to Section 702 of the Foreign Intelligence Surveillance Act." Privacy and Civil Liberties Oversight Board. July 2, 2014, p. 111. www.pclob.gov/library/702-Report-2.pdf

The section 702 program may not be indiscriminate, but it is not targeted as traditional FISA or criminal collection is. It is commonly called "programmatic surveillance."

After its passage in 2008, civil libertarians who claimed that section 702 endangered American privacy were ridiculed. Surveillance advocates insisted that the law did not impact Americans. They argued that since the statute requires that the government target a non-US person reasonably believed to be located outside the United States, it didn't authorize wiretapping Americans. At the time section 702 was reauthorized in 2012, Rep. Trey Gowdy (R-SC) assured listeners that "this bill has nothing to do with Americans on American soil. [It] doesn't implicate the Bill of Rights any more than it implicates any other part of our Constitution, unless you think that foreign nationals who are on foreign land fall within the protections of the United States Constitution."[4] House Intelligence Committee Chairman Mike Rogers (R-MI) acknowledged that the law might permit surveillance of Americans, but that this would happen "only very rarely."[5]

For the most part, Americans and Congress were comforted by these claims. As Chair of the Intelligence Committee, Rogers was in a position to know the truth. But the Snowden documents proved Rogers' reassurances wrong.

Collection When We Talk to Foreign Targets

Like EO 12333 spying, section 702 has a huge impact on Americans. There were almost 90,000 targets in 2014.[6] Some of these targets are individuals, but some are organizations or institutions comprised of many people. When Americans talk with these targets, those Americans are wiretapped. In other words, the more we allow wiretapping of foreigners, the more we wiretap the Americans talking to those foreigners. It's no surprise that Americans are spied on when we are talking to valid foreign intelligence

---

[4] T. Gowdy III. "FISA Amendments Act Reauthorization Act of 2012 Floor Speech." September 12, 2012, as cited in J. Sanchez. "Confusion in the House: Misunderstanding spying law, and inverting the lessons of 9/11." Cato Institute. September 14, 2012. www.cato.org/blog/confusion-house-misunderstanding-spying-law-inverting-lessons-911

[5] Rep. M. Rogers. "FISA Amendments Act Reauthorization Act of 2012 Floor Speech." September 12, 2012, as cited in J. Sanchez. "Confusion in the House: Misunderstanding spying law, and inverting the lessons of 9/11." Cato Institute. September 14, 2012. www.cato.org/blog/confusion-house-misunderstanding-spying-law-inverting-lessons-911

[6] "Statistical Transparency Report Regarding use of National Security Authorities." Office of the Director of National Intelligence. June 26, 2014. p. 2. www.dni.gov/files/tp/National_Security_Authorities_Transparency_Report_CY2013.pdf

targets. But when you remove the restrictions on who can be a target – expanding it from agents of a foreign power to any foreigner talking about foreign intelligence matters – the collection is going to suck in more Americans. Because the foreign targets need not be terrorists, or even foreign agents, just foreigners with foreign intelligence information, the collection is likely far more vast than even most experts may have thought.

How broad is section 702 wiretapping? Take the single section 702 certification for almost all foreign governments (excluding the Five Eyes countries). It makes good sense to spy on foreign governments. After all, the conduct of foreign relations is a core purpose of better intelligence. But if the French government is just one of the 90,000 targets, then that could be a huge number of people who are actually placed under surveillance for that one target. When the NSA spies on France, are people who interact with the French government in order to get education benefits or medical care also wiretapped? What about people who are communicating with their aunt who works in the French version of the department of motor vehicles?

Even less well understood is how the NSA uses section 702 for cybersecurity, another likely approved 702 certification. The FISC gave the NSA approval in 2012 to use section 702 to target Internet addresses, malware, and other "cybersignatures" associated with foreign governments. Around the same time, the FBI got approval to target particular foreign Internet addresses for its own cybersecurity investigations.[7] What is the impact of shifting from monitoring people or groups to monitoring Internet traffic with certain characteristics? Generally, security professionals use "threat signatures" to identify efforts to attack computer systems. But how precise are threat signatures in distinguishing between innocent and malicious Internet traffic? Many people are infected by malware, viruses, and Internet worms. Are innocent people's data captured when collection is based on threat signatures than on email address or phone number? Are Americans who contract computer viruses from overseas part of the NSA's cybersecurity collection? Despite congressional hearings and the PCLOB investigation, the public has almost noinformation about the NSA's conduct of cybersecurity surveillance under section 702.

---

[7] See "NSA Staff Processing Form – SSO's Support to the FBI for Implementation of their Cyber FISA Order," 2012. www.nytimes.com/interactive/2015/06/04/us/document-cyber-surveillance-documents.html

Collection When We Talk About or Near Foreign Targets

The major reason section 702 collection includes Americans' written messages is a phenomenon called "about collection." Federal judges assigned to the secretive FISC have secretly interpreted section 702 not only to allow warrantless collection of messages to and from a foreign target, but also to allow spies to collect information *about* that target. That means that multiple people, none of whom is a target, may nevertheless be monitored because of the topic of their conversation, so long as one of the parties to the conversation is a foreigner located overseas. American spies can collect this information inside the United States with few restrictions. They no longer even need to prove that the target is likely using the social network or email service where they are conducting the spying. That increases the chances of monitoring people who are talking about, but not to, targets.

"About collection" is disturbing because it involves monitoring the conversations of nontargets.[8] The scope of the NSA's collection depends on what search terms, or "selectors," the agency chooses to use. Once the government has obtained a broad certification from the FISC, it is up to the NSA what search queries to use to collect data. A search term theoretically could be as broad as "France" or "oil prices." But according to the PCLOB, section 702 selectors are things like email addresses, phone numbers, or Internet protocol addresses. Allegedly, the NSA does not use proper names like "Osama bin Laden" or "Petrobras" to conduct the surveillance. Thus, if the target is Angela Merkel, intelligence officials say you'd need to mention her email address and not just her name in order for your messages to be collected. That's a good thing, because otherwise section 702 collection would be huge as well as mostly irrelevant. Of course, even email addresses can lead to very broad collection if the NSA is acquiring messages sent to or from addresses like "membership@doctorswithoutborders.org" or "mailinglist@greenpeace.net." Internet protocol addresses may be shared by many individuals or entities who are not themselves foreign intelligence targets.

While the PCLOB seemed reassured to learn that the NSA was using email addresses and other selectors designed to avoid capturing massive amounts of irrelevant data, independent journalism investigations tell a far more sobering story. The *Washington Post* did an analysis of a

---

[8] "About collection" does not apply to telephone calls but to written Internet communications.

large cache of section 702 intercepted conversations it obtained from Snowden. The analysis showed that nine out of ten account holders found in the cache were not the targets but were caught in a net the agency had cast for somebody else.[9] If the *Washington Post* analysis is accurate for the entire section 702 database, given that there were 90,000 targets in 2014, that same year 810,000 nontargets were "incidentally" spied on.

The *Washington Post* investigation revealed that some nontargets were monitored because they interacted directly with a target. But many others had more tenuous connections with the target.

> If a target entered an online chat room, the NSA collected the words and identities of every person who posted there, regardless of subject, as well as every person who simply "lurked," reading passively what other people wrote.
>   "1 target, 38 others on there," one analyst wrote. She collected data on them all.[10]

In other cases, the NSA appeared to designate as its target the Internet protocol, or IP, address of a computer server. A single server can be used by hundreds of different people, including the target. Because some people are using the same IP address as a target, the NSA then collects information on them all.

Even more surprising, more than half of the surveillance files contained names, email addresses, or other details that the NSA marked as belonging to US citizens or residents. If the ratio found by the *Washington Post* in its analysis of 160,000 PRISM files holds up across the NSA's entire section 702 collection, then every year hundreds of millions of collected files involve a US person. In other words, the Snowden documents suggest that collecting Americans' international communications is routine under section 702.

Unfortunately, the public still doesn't know how many. In 2012, a number of senators and representatives asked for some idea about how many Americans were being intercepted, but the intelligence community dodged the question. Senator Wyden reported that he was told it is not

[9] B. Gellman, J. Tate, and A. Soltani. "In NSA-intercepted data, those not targeted far outnumber the foreigners who are." *The Washington Post*. July 5, 2014. www. washingtonpost.com/world/national-security/in-nsa-intercepted-data-those-not-targeted-far-outnumber-the-foreigners-who-are/2014/07/05/8139adf8-045a-11e4-8572-4b1b969b6322_story.html

[10] Ibid.

reasonably possible to identify the number of people located inside the United States whose communications may have been reviewed under the FISA Amendments Act. But while an accurate count may be impossible, Wyden and other lawmakers are confident that American spies could give an estimate, if they wanted to do so.[11] To this day, the NSA refuses to tell Congress or the public how many Americans are wiretapped or under surveillance under section 702.

The *Washington Post's* PRISM reporting gives the public an idea of how much more. Section 702's impact on Americans is far beyond what some people expected from its statutory language. It is surprising that, contrary to former Rep. Rogers' and Rep. Gowdy's claims, American data ends up in the NSA's coffers through section 702 all the time.

Fishy Foreignness Determination

The third major reason Americans likely are caught up in section 702 collection is because of the unreliable way that intelligence analysts decide if someone is foreign or not. The *Washington Post* reported that PRISM is designed to produce just 51 percent confidence in the target's "foreignness."[12] As John Oliver, reporting with "The Daily Show," put it, this means "a coin flip plus 1 percent." The NSA subsequently objected to this description, asserting that "foreignness" actually depends on the "totality of the circumstances." If an analyst has any information that suggests a target is an American, it has to be resolved before surveillance can go forward.[13] The PCLOB backed up this representation.[14]

But the Snowden documents suggest the NSA's foreignness determination nevertheless may not be meaningful in practice. NSA documents showing how an analyst gains approval to wiretap a target shows

---

[11] Testimony of Senator Ronald Wyden. "Extending FISA Amendments Act of 2008." C. R. Vol. 158, No 87. June 11, 2012. fas.org/irp/congress/2012_cr/wyden-fisa.html

[12] B. Gellman and L. Poitras. "U.S., British intelligence mining data from nine U.S. Internet companies in broad secret program." *The Washington Post.* June 7, 2013. www.washington-post.com/investigations/us-intelligence-mining-data-from-nine-us-internet-companies-in-broad-secret-program/2013/06/06/3a0c0da8-cebf-11e2-8845-d970ccb04497_story.html

[13] R. De. Testimony at "Public Hearing Regarding the Surveillance Program Operated Pursuant to Section 702 of the Foreign Intelligence Surveillance Act." PCLOB Board. March 19, 2014, p. 175.

[14] "Report on the Surveillance Program Operated Pursuant to Section 702 of the Foreign Intelligence Surveillance Act." Privacy and Civil Liberties Oversight Board. July 2, 2014, p. 44. www.pclob.gov/library/702-Report-2.pdf

a dropdown menu of preapproved reasons to believe that someone isn't an American. Selecting just one of these options can ensure the analyst's surveillance query will be approved by the section 702 computer system. The dropdown menu makes it easy for an analyst to give the system the justification needed for the wiretapping to happen.

Some of the preapproved "foreign factors" could easily be true of Americans. For example, if you are in contact with targets overseas, NSA agents can assume you are foreign unless they have information to the contrary.[15] That may never have been a fair assumption, but it's particularly unfair today, when the Internet makes it free and easy to talk and collaborate with our colleagues in other nations. The *Washington Post* reported that analysts found foreignness based on the fact that the target's emails were written in a foreign language, "a quality shared by tens of millions of Americans."[16] In other cases, analysts assumed anyone on the chat "buddy list" of a known foreign national was also foreign. How often are Americans spied on because they are mistakenly believed to be foreigners?

By-Catch

The fourth major way that Americans get caught in the section 702 net is because the NSA's surveillance technology grabs irrelevant communications along with relevant ones. The NSA has direct access to fiber optic cables that comprise the Internet and phone communications backbone. Inside the United States, the NSA calls this access and the section 702 authorized spying it conducts there Upstream. When conducting Upstream surveillance, the NSA's systems read the content of flows of Internet data, looking for the selector terms. When the NSA computers find a match, they don't always pull in single messages, but the entire Internet flow. In other words, they regularly capture what the agency refers to as "Internet transactions."

An "Internet transaction" may be comprised of a single communication. Intentional collection of domestic messages between Americans is not allowed under section 702, but the NSA acquires them anyway.

---

[15] G. Greenwald. 'XKeyscore: NSA tool collects 'nearly everything a user does on the internet." The Guardian. July 31, 2013. https://www.theguardian.com/world/2013/jul/31/nsa-top-secret-program-online-data

[16] B. Gellman, J. Tate, and A. Soltani. "In NSA-intercepted data, those not targeted far outnumber the foreigners who are." *The Washington Post*. July 5, 2014. www.washingtonpost.com/world/national-security/in-nsa-intercepted-data-those-not-targeted-far-outnumber-the-foreigners-who-are/2014/07/05/8139adf8-045a-11e4-8572-4b1b969b6322_story.html

When these single communication transactions flow internationally, they appear to be international instead of domestic to the NSA's filtering machines. If they also happen to contain one of the foreign intelligence selectors, then the NSA computers copy and collect the messages in Upstream surveillance databases. As explained in Chapter 14, the FISC has allowed the agency to continue to collect and use these domestic messages anyway.

Alternatively, an Internet transaction might contain multiple messages – the agency refers to this bundle of messages as a multi-communications transaction, or "MCT." An MCT could be something like your email inbox, which contains many, many messages. If only one email in your inbox is responsive to the NSA's targeting terms, the NSA devices will nevertheless pull the entire inbox flow into the NSA databases. That means that the NSA is capturing purely domestic messages as well as messages that have nothing to do with foreigners or foreign intelligence. Both categories are supposed to be off-limits but the NSA nevertheless captures them as part of Upstream collection.

In August 2013, the Electronic Frontier Foundation obtained a FISC opinion criticizing the NSA for its collection of MCTs under the Freedom of Information Act. To help explain the opinion, a lawyer from the ODNI gave an illustration of what MCTs might be on a press call:

> One example of this is if you have a webmail email account, like Gmail or Hotmail or something like that, you know that when you go and you open up your email program, you will get a screenshot of some number of emails that are sitting in your inbox. In the case of my server, what I get is the date of the email, the sender, the subject line, and the size of the email message. But I may get 15 of them at one time.
>
> Those are all transmitted across the Internet as one communication, even though there are 15 separate emails mentioned in them. And for technological reasons, NSA was not capable of breaking those down into – and still is not capable – of breaking those down into – their individual components.[17]

While this was the ODNI's official example, the number 15 seems deceptively reassuring. When I receive Gmail on my computer, the server often transmits thousands of messages to me. Similarly, communications between service providers include whole disk backups and batch email

---

[17] "ODNI/NSA conference call 'on background' to NSA surveillance." August 21, 2013. Audio is available at soundcloud.com/bobby-tables/odni-nsa-conference-call-on

routing for speedy service. Are backups and full email inboxes MCTs? When providers send unencrypted data between one data center and another, are those MCTs? If so, the NSA will pull in thousands or tens of thousands of messages, even if the selection criteria are mentioned just once in only a single message.

In 2011, the FISA court first became aware that the NSA was over-collecting MCTs as well as purely domestic single communications that for whatever reason traveled abroad as part of the Internet's routing protocols. Judge John Bates heard the case. The upshot was that, while the court had assumed the NSA was pulling single, relevant, international messages from Upstream surveillance, in reality it was collecting messages that were irrelevant, purely domestic, or both, and had been for years. FISC Judge John Bates wanted to know how bad the problem was. He asked the NSA to make a count of the number of purely domestic communications it was obtaining each year as a result of its practice of collecting transactions and not messages. The NSA was reluctant to count, probably because the agency feared that to do so would give the agency knowledge it did not want to have.

Based on the information the NSA would provide, plus some judicial estimates, Judge Bates estimated that the NSA improperly collected 56,000 or more transactions containing American messages a year. Each of the 10,000 or so MCTs could have contained 15, 100, or 1,000 messages between Americans. The NSA's misrepresentations have hidden, first from the FISA court and then from the public, the fact that every year, the NSA has been collecting messages between innocent Americans who have no foreign connections and are suspected of no crimes.

The information collected under section 702 is very personal. *Washington Post* reporters discovered that the sample data trove included "medical records sent from one family member to another, résumés from job hunters, and academic transcripts of schoolchildren. In one photo, a young girl in religious dress beams at a camera outside a mosque."[18] The data included "scores" of pictures of infants and toddlers in bathtubs, on swings, sprawled on their backs, and being kissed by their mothers. There was also more intimate, risqué content. Men show off their bodies. Women

---

[18] B. Gellman, J. Tate, and A. Soltani. "In NSA-intercepted data, those not targeted far outnumber the foreigners who are." *The Washington Post*. July 5, 2014. www.washingtonpost.com/world/national-security/in-nsa-intercepted-data-those-not-targeted-far-outnumber-the-foreigners-who-are/2014/07/05/8139adf8-045a-11e4-8572-4b1b969b6322_story.html

wearing lingerie or swimsuits pose suggestively for the camera. Many of these people are Americans.

***

To a surprising and disturbing extent, Americans are caught up in section 702 surveillance that is purportedly aimed at collecting data about foreigners. If you are an American, even if you aren't a terrorist, you have a lot to worry about from foreign intelligence spying. You are in the database.

9

Nothing to Hide?: A Short History of Surveillance Abuses

"If you have something that you don't want anyone to know, maybe you shouldn't be doing it in the first place" –

Eric Schmidt, Google CEO[1]

"If one would give me six lines written by the hand of the most honest man, I would find something in them to have him hanged" –

Cardinal Richelieu[2]

"I have nothing to hide." It's one of the most common responses people give to explain why they aren't afraid of modern surveillance. The quotes from Eric Schmidt and Cardinal Richelieu are book-ends for the range of ways that the public feels about surveillance. But Richelieu is right and Schmidt is wrong. If you sit and think for even a moment, you know that everyone has something to hide. We've said things about people we wouldn't want them to hear. We've made mistakes or done embarrassing things we wouldn't want our children, our co-workers, or our mothers to know about. We may even have done something illegal.

The claim "I have nothing to hide" may be a simplistic way of saying something more nuanced. People tend to believe the government would never devote the time or the money to pursuing average citizens like themselves. They are comfortable with the US government knowing things that they wouldn't want their wife or neighbors to know because they assume the US government doesn't care about them.

One in four people in the United States has a criminal record. This information is used to deny access to public benefits, housing, jobs, and

---

[1] "Google CEO on privacy (video): 'If you have something you don't want anyone to know, maybe you shouldn't be doing it in the first place.'" *The Huffington Post*. February 18, 2010. www.huffingtonpost.com/2009/12/07/google-ceo-on-privacy-if_n_383105.html

[2] Cardinal Richelieu to King Louis XII as quoted in J. Freedman. *America Debates Privacy Versus Security*. (New York, NY: Rosen Publishing, 2007) p. 50.

professional licensing. But something closer to 100 percent of Americans have committed crimes other than mere driving infractions. We just haven't been caught. Most Americans participate in activities that are illegal: marijuana use, computer misuse, petty theft, eavesdropping, obstruction of justice, wire fraud. Consider how very different your life could have been had you been caught and convicted for things you have done.[3]

Today, that calculation – that I'll only be investigated if there is good cause to do so – is naïve. It's naïve because modern spying tools have dramatically reduced the cost and trouble associated with investigating someone. Remember, American spies are already collecting vast amounts of information. That means no one has to bother to listen to your calls or read your emails. Instead, machines automatically analyze or search the data, highlighting just the interesting stuff for analysts to read. This is already easy for computers to do with text. It's getting increasingly easy to do with phone calls, as voice recognition software improves.[4] Face and image recognition software is also getting very accurate. It will become trivial, for example, for computers to search a trove of images and find all the pictures of people holding a joint or underage minors holding a can of beer. So if you think whatever you are up to is "not worth it" to the police, what you need to understand is that the cost of going after you is ever diminishing, approaching zero.

Some criminal laws are so broad, you could argue that almost anything is a transgression. US criminal laws can apply to common behaviors like smoking marijuana and loitering, which gives police and other government actors power over millions of individuals. Some laws are so vague that the line between innocent behavior and criminal conduct is unclear. And then there are the regulatory offenses that are so arcane you might be forgiven for not knowing that what you were doing was wrong. For example, it's a federal crime to possess a lobster under a certain size. When there are so many ways that the average person can transgress, prosecutors pick and choose whom to go after.

In his book, *Three Felonies a Day*,[5] Harvey Silverglate documents cases in which federal criminal law was used by overzealous or politically ambitious prosecutors to bring criminal charges against innocent people. Importantly, Silverglate documents the counterintuitive conclusion that the more information prosecutors have about someone, the easier it is

---

[3] See www.weareallcriminals.org/about/
[4] D. Froomkin. "The computers are listening." *The Intercept*. May 11, 2015. theintercept.com/2015/05/11/speech-recognition-nsa-best-kept-secret/
[5] H. Silverglate. *Three Felonies a Day*. (New York: Encounter Books, 2011).

to make a case against them, even if they actually are innocent. Frank
Quattrone was a star banker during the 2000 financial bubble. The SEC
started investigating Quattrone and his employer Credit Suisse First
Boston (CSFB) bank for allegedly receiving illegal kickbacks from clients.
The SEC obtained voluminous numbers of emails from CSFB employees
including Quattrone. After reading thousands of Quattrone's emails, the
government found one message, a single response to an end of the year
email from one of the bank's lawyers. The lawyer wanted Quattrone's permission to remind employees of the bank's document retention policy.
That policy was typical of those at other firms – employees should discard
nonessential documents, as long as they aren't the subject of any probe
or lawsuit. The lawyer made a joke in the request that they should do so
because "Today, it's administrative housekeeping. In January, it could be
improper destruction of evidence." Quattrone replied to the lawyer's email
by saying that he should not "make jokes like that," but that the lawyer
could send the document retention policy reminder email. Quattrone followed up with a message saying he strongly advised the bank employees to
follow CSFB's retention and destruction procedures.

James Comey, now FBI Director, was the lead prosecutor in Manhattan
at the time. Comey's prosecutors used this single email to claim that
Quattrone meant to cause his colleagues to destroy documents that were
responsive to federal subpoenas. A day or two before this exchange,
Quattrone had been told that CSFB received subpoenas related to the
kickback investigation. But the bank's lawyers' office had not yet notified
Quattrone or other bankers that those subpoenas meant they were obligated to preserve documents.[6]

Quattrone's story illustrates the point that government access to large
numbers of emails greatly increase the chances that agents can find some
information on which to base a case. As Silverglate writes – and shows in
his book – citizens from all walks of life have found themselves the targets of federal prosecutions, despite sensibly believing that they have done
nothing wrong.

"I have nothing to hide" is not only naïve, it's a privileged point of view.
Just because you feel safe doesn't mean that other people in the United
States or around the world are. As scholar Michelle Alexander has documented, even though the crime rate in the United States is about the same
as other Western countries, our incarceration rate is much higher. And

---

[6] *United States v. Quattrone*, 149 F.Supp. 240 (D.D.C.1957); see also Silverglate, *Three Felonies
a Day*, p. 110.

those incarcerated are disproportionately poor. Staggeringly more of those are African American. "No other country in the world imprisons so many of its racial or ethnic minorities," writes Alexander. "The United States imprisons a larger percentage of its black population than South Africa did at the height of apartheid."[7]

Many countries do not recognize civil liberties or human rights in their laws. You can be arrested for political organizing, for your religious beliefs, for being gay. The next billion Internet users are going to come from countries that do not have a First Amendment protecting speech and religion, or a Bill of Rights more generally. Digital surveillance poses special dangers for these people, both here in the United States and abroad.

Surveillance History: A Story of Power and Privilege

Surveillance has been misused for political reasons for most of American history. History is replete with examples of government surveillance being used against disfavored groups based on race, political values, and sexual orientation. The FBI has its roots as a domestic spy agency monitoring political groups. The agency was created in 1908, and was initially focused on ferreting out domestic radicals, such as anarchists, communists, and socialists, many of whom were advocating for workplace protections that are common today. The FBI's targeting of American citizens continued into World War I, when the FBI gathered information on those who opposed the draft and American entry into the war. The agency rounded up suspected radicals, wiretapped conversations, and opened mail. The so-called Palmer Raids of 1919 and 1920 resulted in the arrests of up to 10,000 people without warrants or due process, the biggest mass arrests in US history. Most suspects ultimately were released because there was no evidence against them. Hundreds of people were prosecuted under the 1917 Espionage Act and the 1918 Sedition Act for peaceful expression of their opposition to the war. In 1919, J. Edgar Hoover became chief of the Justice Department's Radical Division, when he was only twenty-four years old. Two years later, he was the number two man at the FBI. Soon he would rise to the directorship and lead the agency for the next forty-eight years.

During the J. Edgar Hoover era, peaceful people were under surveillance for First Amendment protected activities, or for no clear reason at all. We don't know why specific people were selected. After all – like the

---

[7] M. Alexander. *The New Jim Crow: Mass Incarceration in the Age of Colorblindness.* (New York: The New Press, 2012) p. 6.

section 702 program today – there was no obligation to create a public record of, or get judicial approval for, targeting decisions. Some opposed the Vietnam War, or supported the civil rights movement. Some were surveilled for no apparent reason. The FBI spied on boxer Muhammad Ali, humorist Art Buchwald, author Norman Mailer, and Senator Howard Baker.[8] Jane Fonda, Joan Baez, Dr. Benjamin Spock, and Black Panther leader Eldridge Cleaver were on the watch lists.[9] At one point, one NSA spy remembers, J. Edgar Hoover gave the order to conduct complete surveillance of all Quakers in the United States. President Richard Nixon was a Quaker. "It gets pretty funny," the spy said.[10]

Particularly frightening for democracy is how the FBI targeted people who were in political power to ensure they didn't cause the agency or the President trouble. Hoover's right-hand man, Cartha DeLoach, proudly reported that the Bureau had learned of a truculent senator caught driving drunk with a "good looking broad." The senator, DeLoach explained, was promptly made "aware that we had the information, and we never had trouble with him on appropriations since."[11] Hoover deliberately sought intelligence embarrassing to senators, and as a result, senators acquiesced to policies that they, and presumably their constituencies, disagreed with. The FBI spied on sitting attorneys general.[12] It spied on people to promote President Nixon's political campaign for reelection.[13] When Adlai Stevenson Jr. won the Democratic ticket nomination for president in 1952, Hoover had a scandalous memo already in hand. He made sure that the allegations it contained, that Stevenson was homosexual and dressed in women's clothing, reached both Nixon and the press.[14]

A common narrative is that J. Edgar Hoover was a particularly power-hungry man, implying that with a different person in office these surveillance abuses would not have happened. But the political spying wasn't a problem unique to Hoover's FBI. Other intelligence agencies were rampantly spying on Americans, too. The Army had its own cadre of spies. One

---

[8]   B. Kaufmann. "MLK, spying, and the 'urgency of the moment.'" *ACLU.* January 20, 2014. www.aclu.org/blog/mlk-spying-and-urgency-moment

[9]   J. Bamford. *The Puzzle Palace: Inside the National Security Agency America's Most Secret Intelligence Organization.* (New York: Penguin Books, 1983) p. 250.

[10] J. Bamford. *Body of Secrets: Anatomy of the Ultra-Secret National Security Agency.* (New York: Anchor Books, 2002) p. 367.

[11] J. Sanchez. "Operation Sex Deviate 2.0." *CATO Institute.* November 27, 2013. www.cato. org/blog/operation-sex-deviate-20

[12] T. Weiner. *Legacy of Ashes: The History of the CIA.* (New York: Anchor Books, 2008) p. 57.

[13] Ibid.

[14] Ibid.

of their targets was Adlai Stevenson III, son of the two-time Democratic presidential candidate in Hoover's sights. Stevenson III had been a state representative and was the State of Illinois treasurer at the time. But because Stevenson had expressed support for Jesse Jackson, who as a civil rights and antiwar activist in Chicago was (falsely) suspected of having ties to violent radicals, he qualified as a surveillance target in the Army's eyes.[15] The Army spy program started with a focus on preparing for civil disturbances, but had metastasized into surveillance on clergymen, politicians, antiwar activists, and civil rights workers.[16]

In 1967, the Central Intelligence Agency, despite being legally prohibited from spying on Americans, nevertheless did so at the behest of President Lyndon Baines Johnson. Johnson was convinced, wrongly, that the civil rights and peace groups agitating for political change were controlled by Soviet communists. At his command, the CIA created a domestic surveillance operation code named Chaos. As part of Chaos, the CIA worked with the NSA to eavesdrop on American citizens and all the major peace groups. Over the seven years of the program, the CIA kept files on 7,200 individuals. Despite these efforts, the intelligence agencies never found any evidence that the American left was linked to foreign powers.[17]

Political spying runs deep through the history of the United States. The absence of political spying, if indeed it has been absent, is the aberration. Americans must be vigilant to ensure that the Nation does not regress.

Blackmailing King

It was only fifty years ago that Dr. Martin Luther King Jr. spoke to a crowd of thousands at the March on Washington. Dr. King talked about racial tolerance and equality. Today, Dr. King is an American hero, and his "I Have a Dream" speech is considered one of the most important political speeches of the modern era.

Yet the US government spied on, and even threatened, this icon and his associates in an effort to dissuade them from their activism. J. Edgar Hoover, the powerful longstanding Director of the FBI, believed that the civil rights movement was a Soviet communist plot intended to destabilize the US government, and that King was himself a communist or at least directed by communists. The FBI had already been tapping the phones of

---

[15] C. Risen "Spies among us." *The American Scholar*. December 1, 2009. theamericanscholar. org/spies-among-us/
[16] Ibid.
[17] Weiner, *Legacy of Ashes*, pp. 329–330.

people who associated with King to gain proof of their theory. The "I Have a Dream" speech particularly frightened Hoover and other FBI agents. "In the light of King's powerful demagogic speech ... We must mark him now, if we have not done so before, as the most dangerous Negro of the future in this Nation from the standpoint of communism, the Negro, and national security," wrote one of these aides in a confidential memo to Hoover. The speech was an impetus to expand surveillance of King and his associates.

Again, people often write this off as misguided abuses perpetrated by a dangerous J. Edgar Hoover. But that conclusion is wrong. Spying on King wasn't just J. Edgar Hoover's doing. Hoover convinced Attorney General Robert Kennedy, John F. Kennedy's brother, to sign off on FBI eavesdropping on King's hotel rooms, apartment, and telephones. It was approved government policy, not just the obsession of one man. And Robert Kennedy authorized the spying even though he and Hoover were political enemies, and the Attorney General didn't trust the FBI director. Hoover and Robert Kennedy collaborated to justify the spying.

Throughout his career, in fact, Hoover had the support of presidents for what he did. Those who might have opposed the spying turned a blind eye and failed to stand up and say "no." Spying on Americans was the officially approved policy of the day, even when it was secret and illegal. They didn't call it an effort to derail civil rights. Rather, the reasons were couched as a more acceptable goal: an investigation of King's alleged connections to communists.

But the results of that spying were put to evil ends. The FBI's surveillance collected King's conversations about the civil rights movement's strategies and tactics – as well as sounds of him having sex with women other than his wife. The FBI then sent King a package of these recordings along with a shocking handwritten warning, a draft of which was found in the FBI files years later. It said, "the American public ... will know you for what you are – an evil, abnormal beast." The note even seems to encourage Dr. King to commit suicide in order to avoid personal embarrassment. "King, there is only one thing left for you to do," the letter concluded. "You know what it is ... You better take it before your filthy, abnormal fraudulent self is bared to the nation."

It's also easy to forget how suspicious the American public likely was about the civil rights movement and its leaders throughout the 1960s. Today, Martin Luther King Jr. is a national hero, and the concept of racial equality before the law is well-accepted if not well-realized. But we forget that many Americans viewed the civil rights movement as controversial and potentially dangerous to US interests. In 1963, a Gallup poll found that 78 percent of white people would move if many black families moved into their neighborhoods. About 60 percent of Americans had an unfavorable view of the March on Washington, stating that they felt it would cause violence and would not accomplish anything. In the height of the Cold War, a majority of Americans either believed or weren't sure whether civil rights groups had been infiltrated by communists.[18] Of course, this false Soviet connection was the FBI's basis for spying on Dr. King. But King's political vision won the day in America, even as people continue to work to try to make it a reality. Our surveillance laws need to protect minority viewpoints of all kinds, even when the public majority is suspicious or concerned.

This story is important. People like to believe that the powerful FBI Director was particularly evil. But Hoover's plans to spy on King had the highest levels of approvals. People like to believe that the spying was based on disavowed racist ideology. But the FBI justified its attention on the civil rights movement by preying on the contemporaneous fears that our greatest enemy, the Soviet communists, had operatives inside the country. The same things are happening today. No one admits that spying on Black Lives Matter, Occupy Wall Street, Tea Party groups, or Amnesty International is ideological. Rather, investigators conduct the spying in the name of counterterrorism, public order, and foreign intelligence. Like the spying on Dr. King, the data eventually will be misused.

Infiltration, Internment, Tax Audits, Deportation

Another misconception is that if you haven't committed a crime, there is little anyone can do to retaliate against you and ruin your life. That presupposes that the US government would never engage in espionage or blackmail. But American spies have done so in the past. In fact, the United States has a history of using surveillance to go after individuals and groups that government officials – at the time – consider politically or religiously suspect.

History shows that American spies use the information they obtained in all kinds of ways, not just to charge people with crimes. For example, in 1964 the FBI planted false documents to persuade the Communist Party that William Albertson, a long-time Communist Party official, was an FBI informant. It appears that in the course of wiretapping thousands

---

[18] "Public Opinion on Civil Rights: Reflections on the Civil Rights Act of 1964." *Roper Center for Public Opinion Research.* Cornell University, July 2, 2014. ropercenter.cornell.edu/public-opinion-on-civil-rights-reflections-on-the-civil-rights-act-of-1964/

of Albertson's phone conversations, intercepting his mail, and monitoring his bank account, agents learned that he was going to lend his car to a friend. The FBI forged documents saying that Albertson was a snitch and an infiltrator and left them in Albertson's car for the friend to find.

> Albertson was expelled from the party, lost all his friends, and was fired from his job. Until his death in an automobile accident in 1972, he tried to prove that he was not a snitch, but the case was not resolved until 1989, when the FBI agreed to pay Albertson's widow $170,000 to settle her lawsuit against the government.[19]

Albertson wasn't doing anything wrong. He had political beliefs outside the mainstream. Those beliefs scared people, but they weren't illegal, and he wasn't violent. The FBI was nonetheless able to use what it knew about him to sabotage him, destroy his life, and try to tear the American Communist Party apart from the inside.

When the US Census Bureau initially proposed collecting demographic data, it faced public resistance, for fear the data would be repurposed for racial profiling. The Census Bureau promised not to do that, and implemented rules to prohibit such usage. Then World War II came along. In 1942, Congress repealed the confidentiality protections of the Census. The rules changed, permitting the US Census Bureau to send block-by-block data on the locations of up Japanese Americans to the War Department.[20] This data enabled officials to round Japanese Americans up and imprison them in internment camps. The Supreme Court approved the Japanese internment in 1944 in a case called *Korematsu v. United States*. The internment of US citizens based on race is widely considered one of the more ignoble periods of US history and *Korematsu* a low point in constitutional law. Mr. Korematsu's conviction for evading internment was overturned only in 1983, after a court found that the government had knowingly submitted false information to the Supreme Court in the *Korematsu* case. The *Korematsu* decision is still on the books, although in 2011 the Department of Justice finally conceded that it was in error.

Another example is the way the FBI went after members of the peace movement during the 1960s and 1970s. In 1969, the FBI learned that one

[19] A. Neier. "Spying on Americans: A very old story." *NYR Daily.* The New York Review of Books. June 18, 2013. www.nybooks.com/blogs/nyrblog/2013/jun/18/spying-americans-very-old-story/

[20] See W. Seltzer and M. Anderson. "After Pearl Harbor: The Proper Role of Population Data Systems in Time of War." (2000). Paper presented at the Population Association of America Annual Meeting, Los Angeles, CA, March 23–25, 2000. pantherfile.uwm.edu/margo/www/govstat/newpaa.pdf

of the sponsors of an antiwar demonstration in Washington, D.C. was a New York City-based organization, the Fifth Avenue Peace Parade Committee. That organization had chartered buses to take protesters to the event. The FBI visited the bank where the organization maintained its account to get photocopies of the checks written to reserve places on the buses and, thereby, to identify participants in the demonstration. The FBI then sent the list of names and the banking information to the Internal Revenue Service.[21]

American spies did not admit that we are spying on these people with the goal of scaring, discrediting, or punishing them. Rather, the government claimed that it had to target these people for national security reasons in case "hot-headed elements within the ranks of demonstrators" got out of hand. No one openly admitted, "we are going to send a message to people that if they vocally oppose the war, we're going to investigate them for tax evasion." But the implicit message was clear. That fear would forever after hang over people's heads.

American spies were demonstrably unable to tell the difference between people who were truly dangerous and those who were not. Thus, the list of targets spied on grew exponentially. During the Vietnam War era, J. Edgar Hoover requested "complete surveillance of all Quakers" because he thought they were shipping food and supplies to Southeast Asia.[22] The FBI collected some 30,000 pages on possible homosexuals in the government. This was not necessarily because Director Hoover was notoriously homophobic.[23] Hoover believed that homosexuals were likely to be communists or spies for communists, particularly because homosexuality was cause for instant dismissal from American government service – and most other categories of employment. Hoover, moreover, believed that all homosexuals (all closeted by necessity) were uniquely susceptible to sexual entrapment and blackmail by foreign intelligence services.[24] More than one million Americans, including half a million so-called "subversives," were under FBI surveillance.[25]

Once American spies had this information, it could be used for all sorts of abuse and improper influence. As head of the FBI, Hoover developed

---

[21] See *Fifth Avenue Peace Parade Committee v. Gray*, 480 F.2d 326 (2d Cir. 1973).

[22] Bamford, *Body of Secrets*, p. 429.

[23] T. Weiner. *Enemies: A History of the FBI*. (New York: Random House, 2013) p. 107.

[24] Id., p. 214.

[25] See "Intelligence Activities and the Rights of Americans: Book II." Final Report of the Select Committee to Study Governmental Operations with Respect to Intelligence Activities. Washington: GPO 1976, pp. 6, 47. www.aarclibrary.org/publib/church/reports/book2/html/ChurchB2_0011b.htm

dossiers on people. The dossiers contained embarrassing information about political figures. Hoover secretly kept these files in his office so that no one could track what he was doing with them. That way, he could use or share them with political friends at his discretion. When the FBI had information on someone who later gained a position of power, Hoover would have the file secretly moved to his office, in case it became useful.

Only one other person has ever seen Hoover's secret files, Judge Laurence Silberman, who was asked to review them when he was Deputy Attorney General of the United States from 1974 to 1975. Judge Silberman says that he will take the secrets he learned from those files to the grave, rather than dishonor any of the victims of Hoover's dirt collecting. The files, he says, were a cesspool.[26]

Abuses Today

Some like to think that oppressive surveillance ended with the death of Hoover and the impeachment of President Nixon. That is not the case. Today, surveillance can be so much more robust and comprehensive than it was in Hoover's day. Just imagine how much more private information the FBI might have collected and used against King, his associates, and the civil rights movement as a whole if they had modern surveillance capabilities. They could know everywhere Dr. King went, everyone he met with, read all the emails and text messages he wrote, judge his taste in television shows and movies, watch his spending, and more, waiting for a misstep they could use against him. Building a case against someone, or learning her most embarrassing secret, is a computer search away. In the words of Edward Snowden:

> You don't have to have done anything wrong, you simply have to eventually fall under suspicion from somebody, even by a wrong call, and then they can use this system to go back in time and scrutinize every decision you've ever made, every friend you've ever discussed something with, and attack you on that basis, to sort of derive suspicion from an innocent life.[27]

---

[26] Comments made at "The Privacy Act @40: A Celebration and Appraisal on the 40th Anniversary of the Privacy Act and the 1974 Amendments to the Freedom of Information Act." Event hosted by Georgetown University Law Center. October 30, 2014.

[27] E. Snowden. Interview with G. Greenwald and L. Poitras. "NSA whistleblower Edward Snowden: 'I don't want to live in a society that does these sort of things' – video." *The Guardian*. Online video clip. June 9, 2013. www.theguardian.com/world/video/2013/jun/09/nsa-whistleblower-edward-snowden-interview-video

The Snowden documents revealed that the NSA has developed plans to discredit people who hold politically radical beliefs. The NSA creates profiles of porn viewing and online sexual activity from its vast database of Internet content and transactional data as part of a plan to discredit those whom the agency believes are radicalizing others through speeches promoting disfavored – but not necessarily violent – political views. These targets were not necessarily criminals, violent, or even foreigners. In the documents, one of the six examples of people ripe for discrediting was an American.

These people's beliefs ranged from the idea that "non-Muslims are a threat to Islam" to the view that "the U.S perpetrated the 9/11 attack."[28] By strategically revealing pornography preferences or sexual search queries, the US government could harm the targets' reputations. Since many of the people have devoutly religious followers, the followers would likely be disgusted and turn away. In other words, we have a contemporary example of the NSA proposing to use personal, private information, gleaned from electronic surveillance, to silence and otherwise marginalize people for advocating "radical" beliefs with which the US government disagrees. Remember, this is exactly what the FBI tried to do to Dr. King. If our plan for dealing with disagreeable or false claims is to discredit or censor the speaker rather than address the substance of the speech, then we are failing to live up to our standards as a free country that respects free expression.

But the failure isn't just that we are not following our principles. It's a failure to understand what true danger looks like. Far more people hold extremist views than commit violence, and espousing even violent views is not the same as recruiting people for terrorist attacks. Empirical studies have proven there is no predictable connection between terrorism and espousing radical views.[29] One report published by the British think-tank Demos in 2010 found that:

> "[c]ertain ideas which are sometimes associated with terrorism were, in fact, held by large numbers of people who renounced terrorism." The authors pointed out that holding radical views and rebelling against the political and social status quo was a normal part of being young, and that

[28] G. Greenwald, R. Grim, and R. Gallagher. "Top-Secret document reveals NSA spied on porn habits as part of plan to discredit 'radicalizers.'" *The Guardian.* November 26, 2013. www.huffingtonpost.com/2013/11/26/nsa-porn-muslims_n_4346128.html

[29] M. German. "Debunked NYPD Radicalization Report Just Won't Die." *ACLU.* February 11, 2013. www.aclu.org/blog/national-security-religion-belief/debunked-nypd-radicalization-report-just-wont-die

"[r]adicalization that does not lead to violence can be a positive thing" when it leads to greater involvement in political and community affairs. It argued that censorship of radical ideas would be ineffective and counter-productive, and the government should ensure "that young people can be radical, dissenting, and make a difference, without it resulting in serious or violent consequences."[30]

Indeed, the views held by the men the NSA singled out as ripe for discrediting were not necessarily very radical. For example, up to 40 percent of Americans think that one or more elements of the US government were responsible for some portion of the death and damage on September 11th.[31]

As always, minority groups are especially at risk of being spied on and retaliated against. The government assures us that it does not collect or use information with the intention of suppressing First Amendment activities or punishing people for their ethnicity or religion. But people are targeted for their political activities, ethnicity, and religion. These spying decisions are easily justified on the grounds of public safety, maintaining order, counterterrorism, situational awareness, and the like. Whatever the motivation, political minorities like Occupy Wall Street and Black Lives Matter are under surveillance, as are ethnic and religious minorities like Muslim Americans. No one admits that's the reason. Anyone who wanted to oppress minority people or viewpoints would be ham-handed indeed to have to openly admit it.

Fusion Centers

Fusion centers are information-sharing offices, many of which were jointly created between 2003 and 2007 under the auspices of the US Department of Homeland Security and the Office of Justice Programs in the US Department of Justice. These centers are designed to promote information sharing at the federal level between the CIA, the FBI, the DOJ, the US military, and state- and local-level governments.

As described in earlier chapters, intelligence collection is vast, collected without strong legal and privacy protections. Further, this collection is designed for situational awareness and not for solving crimes. But fusion centers funnel that massive inchoate trove of information to federal, state,

---

[30] J. Bartlett, J. Birdwell, and M. King. *The Edge of Violence: A Radical Approach to Extremism.* DEMOS. 2010. www.demos.co.uk/files/Edge_of_Violence_-_web.pdf?1271346195

[31] Zogby International 2006 poll. web.archive.org/web/20101119164520/http://www.zogby.com/features/features.cfm?ID=231

and local criminal justice authorities who are looking to discover criminal activity and put people in prison. That means that *via* fusion centers law enforcement officials are being encouraged to initiate investigations, follow, search, seize, or even detain people on the basis of rumors, hearsay, and other unreliable and insufficient evidence. The instinct behind fusion centers makes sense. Don't waste valuable information. But the reality is that police all across the country are flooded with sensitive personal information from which they have to glean who is a criminal threat and who isn't. As Cardinal Richelieu opined, there's more than enough data there to tell a suspicious or damning story about anyone. It's not surprising then that fusion centers' track record is terrible.

A two-year Senate investigation conducted in from 2010 to 2012 found that "the fusion centers often produced irrelevant, useless or inappropriate intelligence reporting to DHS, and many produced no intelligence reporting whatsoever."[32] The investigation found that analysts improperly targeted First Amendment protected activity, creating "homeland information reports" on a Muslim community group's suggested reading list and on a leaflet prepared by a chapter of the Mongols Motorcycle Club, a California-based biker gang. Another fusion center has been involved with spying on antiwar activists and anarchists in Washington State.

Fusion centers designed to promote information sharing for counterterrorism are flooded with so many reports that investigators don't know which ones to take seriously. As a result, FBI agents were sent on wild goose chases, diverting resources from fighting real crimes. For example, in 2009, a Texas fusion center described a purported conspiracy between Muslim civil rights organizations, lobbying groups, antiwar protest groups, a former US Congresswoman, the US Treasury Department, and hip hop bands to spread Sharia law in the United States. In March 2008 a Virginia Fusion Center issued a terrorism threat assessment that described the state's universities and colleges as "nodes for radicalization" and characterized the "diversity" surrounding a Virginia military base and the state's "historically black" colleges as possible threats.[33]

---

[32] "Federal Support for and Involvement in State and Local Fusion Centers." United States Senate Committee on Homeland Security and Governmental Affairs, Permanent Subcommittee on Investigations. October 2, 2012, p. 2. www.hsgac.senate.gov/subcommittees/investigations/media/investigative-report-criticizes-counterterrorism-reporting-waste-at-state-and-local-intelligence-fusion-centers

[33] "More about Fusion Centers." *ACLU.* www.aclu.org/more-about-fusion-centers

Today, almost eighty fusion centers justified by counterterrorism concerns focus on law enforcement policing. Political movements are the target of that policing. Documents show that state and local law enforcement officials used social media and surveillance to keep close tabs on Occupy Wall Street to the tune of about 4,000 pages of unclassified emails and reports.

The Department of Defense is also spying on Americans in the name of keeping military installations safe. In 2004, a group of activists met at a Quaker Meeting House in Lake Worth, Florida, to plan a protest of military recruiting at local high schools. The meeting was recorded in a Defense Department database as a "threat" and one of more than 1,500 "suspicious incidents" across the country over a recent ten-month period.[34] Records of similar instances where people were exercising their First Amendment rights in ways that posed no threat to safety, property, or personnel were similarly maintained by the Department of Defense. The risk is that the military now collects domestic intelligence that goes beyond legitimate concerns about terrorism and overreaches in ways that affect the exercise of political rights. Of course, this surveillance is going to have a disproportionate impact on those who oppose and want to reform current government policy.

Disadvantaged Groups

Who are the innocent people that American spies go after under loosely policed surveillance regimes? They are members of groups pushing for political change as well as members of minority racial or religious groups: Muslim Americans, environmentalists, gun rights activists, the Occupy Wall Street movement, the Tea Party movement, pro-labor groups. People who push to change the status quo, either through political activism or through their very existence, are the groups that American spies put under surveillance.

In the 1980s, the US government listened to service members' phone calls and read their mail in order to identify and dishonorably discharge homosexuals in the armed services. This practice only ended when President Clinton initiated the "Don't Ask, Don't Tell" policy. Today, gay men, lesbians, and bisexuals can openly serve in the military.

Today, Muslim Americans are the suspicious group of choice. After September 11th, Muslims were placed under surveillance, their religion

---

[34] L. Myers, D. Pasternak, and R. Gardella. "Is the Pentagon spying on Americans?" *NBC News.* December 14, 2006. www.nbcnews.com/id/10454316#.VvhKVj_DSPA

suspect, and their loyalty to the United States called into question. Other Americans attacked people believed to be Muslim. The treatment of Muslim Americans in the wake of September 11th provides a concrete set of examples of how surveillance is being abused today.

The popular radio show *This American Life* followed the story of one southern California mosque targeted by the FBI, which sent an undercover informant to ferret out terrorists. The man, Craig Monteilh, was told to pose as a convert to Islam. The FBI told him to gather "as much information on as many people and institutions as possible." Monteilh says that he conducted surreptitious surveillance in about ten Southern California mosques using sophisticated audio and video equipment. At the same time, Monteilh was himself so erratic in trying to find and recruit "terrorists" that the members of the mosque were scared of him and sought help from the FBI, reporting the agency's own informant as a potential danger.[35]

The New York City Police Department (NYPD) conducted a secret surveillance program monitoring American Muslims in New York City and the surrounding area. The surveillance prompted some people to avoid mosques or cut charitable contributions out of fear of that they would be labeled "extremists."[36] In 2011, a significant number of Muslim Americans reported being the targets of name-calling, threats, and harassment by airport security and law enforcement officers. In the poll, conducted by the Pew Research Center, about 21 percent of respondents said they were singled out by airport security, while another 13 percent said they were targeted by other law enforcement officials.

The Snowden documents revealed five Muslim Americans that had been specifically targeted by the NSA. The men included an unsuccessful Republican candidate for office who served in the DHS under President George W. Bush, an attorney who represents people in terrorism-related cases, college professors at Rutgers and California State University, and the executive director of the Council on American-Islamic Relations (CAIR), the largest Muslim civil rights organization in the country.[37]

[35] V. Kim. "Federal judge throws out lawsuit over spying on O.C. Muslims." *Los Angeles Times.* August 15, 2012. articles.latimes.com/2012/aug/15/local/la-me-mosque-spying-20120815

[36] M Apuzzo and A. Goldman. "With CIA help, NYPD moves covertly in Muslim areas." *Associated Press.* August 23, 2011. www.ap.org/Content/AP-In-The-News/2011/With-CIA-help-NYPD-moves-covertly-in-Muslim-areas

[37] G. Greenwald and M. Hussain. "Meet the Muslim-American leaders the FBI and NSA have been spying on." *The Intercept.* July 8, 2014. firstlook.org/theintercept/2014/07/09/under-surveillance/

We don't know the reasons these men were targeted. But in targeting any one of these men, the intelligence agencies now monitor everyone they speak with, from students, to clients, to citizens seeking to assert their human rights. Knowing that talking to advocates gets you monitored will chill mainstream and peaceful Muslim Americans from pursuing their civil rights.

This surveillance and harassment takes place in a general atmosphere of mistrust. Many Americans have a negative view of Muslims. These views are informed by horrible acts committed by a few radicals claiming to act in the name of the Muslim religion, from the Boko Haram kidnapping schoolgirls in Nigeria, to the attacks in France at the *Charlie Hebdo* offices, and less than a year later at multiple sites around Paris. Terrorist videos celebrating beheadings and sex slavery as part of Islam further contribute to anti-Muslim sentiment.[38] But there are about seven million Muslims in the United States who abhor these acts. This community is at greater risk for prejudice-motivated criminal attack by other individuals, as well as government infiltration. There were a number of disturbing hate crimes against Muslims, just in the first six months of 2015, as well as political pandering to Americans' baser instincts by politicians looking for votes.[39]

Surveillance has chilled constitutionally protected rights like religious practice, speech, and political organizing. As one report by a project based at City University of New York (CUNY) School of Law designed to provide legal services to Muslim – and Arab –Americans found, "Every one of our interviewees noted that they were negatively affected by surveillance in some way – whether it was by reducing their political or religious expression, altering the way they exercised those rights (through clarifications, precautions, or avoiding certain interlocutors), or in experiencing social and familial pressures to reduce their activism."[40]

In June 2015, the *Washington Post* published an article reviewing the official mistreatment of Muslim Americans just that year:

---

[38] A. S. Ghazali. "American Muslims 13 years after 9–11: Still scapegoats of the warfare-police state." *Al-Jazeerah*. September 29, 2014. goo.gl/eylQgK

[39] L. Sarsour. "Why this has been the worst year for American Muslims since 9/11." *The Washington Post*. June 17, 2015. www.washingtonpost.com/news/acts-of-faith/wp/2015/06/17/why-this-has-been-the-worst-year-for-american-muslims-since-911/

[40] "Mapping Muslims: NYPD Spying and Its Impact on American Muslims." CUNY School of Law. March 11, 2013. www.cunyclear.org/wp-content/uploads/2013/03/MM-FINAL-4-web.pdf

Recent articles have questioned the shady practices of FBI counterterrorism strategies: Informants have been sought out and coerced through torture;[41] fictitious entrapment scenarios[42] have been created; and in the midst of this there are still many unanswered questions[43] about the shooting of a black Muslim man under surveillance by a joint terrorism task force in Boston.[44]

A sizable subset of Americans were unconcerned about spying on Dr. King, the civil rights movement, or the antiwar movement, in the beginning. Today, a sizable number of Americans are unconcerned about, or even want, spying on Muslim Americans. But that is exactly why we have rules in place to regulate and monitor such spying, to protect minority viewpoints and religions from oppression by the majority.

Political Surveillance

Muslim Americans aren't the only group targeted by American spies. Marginalized groups today come from all across the political spectrum – gun rights advocates and Occupy Wall Street adherents. In 2010, the ACLU did a state-by-state survey and identified 111 incidents of domestic political surveillance in 33 states and the District of Columbia. The report concludes, "Americans have been put under surveillance or harassed by the police just for deciding to organize, march, protest, espouse unusual viewpoints, and engage in normal, innocuous behaviors such as writing notes or taking photographs in public."[45]

A full report of the abusive uses to which modern surveillance has been put since the attacks of September 11th is beyond the scope of this book. But a few examples show both that innocent people are targeted for

---

[41] C. McGreal. "Portland man: I was tortured in UAE for refusing to become an FBI informant." *The Guardian*. March 16, 2015. www.theguardian.com/us-news/2015/mar/16/portland-man-tortured-uae-behest-of-fbi

[42] T. Aaronson. "The Sting: How the FBI created a terrorist." *The Intercept*. March 16, 2015. firstlook.org/theintercept/2015/03/16/howthefbicreatedaterrorist/

[43] J. Bidgood and D. Phillips. "Portrait of suspect in Boston disputed." *The New York Times*. June 4, 2015. www.nytimes.com/2015/06/05/us/portrait-of-boston-suspect-usaamah-rahim-is-disputed.html

[44] L. Sarsour. "Why this has been the worst year for American Muslims since 9/11." *The Washington Post*. June 17, 2015. www.washingtonpost.com/news/acts-of-faith/wp/2015/06/17/why-this-has-been-the-worst-year-for-american-muslims-since-911/

[45] "Policing Free Speech: Police Surveillance and Obstruction of First Amendment-Protected Activity." ACLU. August 11, 2010. www.aclu.org/files/assets/policingfreespeech_20100806.pdf

political reasons and that doing so is a waste of time and energy that ought to go into confronting real threats.

In 2004, a speaker who once worked for People for the Ethical Treatment of Animals (PETA) gave a lecture on the "benefits of a vegan diet" at California State University in Fresno, California. Sixty people came to the talk. Six of them were undercover police officers and county sheriff's deputies – meat eaters with no intention of changing their ways.

A Florida-based reporter was placed on a government watch list as a "credible threat," because, as a Quaker who believes in nonviolence, he had distributed leaflets with "information about conscientious objection to recruiters and interested civilians" at local air shows in 2004 and 2005.

The Maryland State Police spied on more than thirty activist groups, "mostly peace groups and anti-death penalty advocates, and wrongly identified 53 individual activists and about two dozen organizations as terrorists." The state police shared this information with other local, state, and federal law enforcement offices.

A "Prevention Awareness Bulletin" from the North Central Texas Fusion System informed recipients that it was "imperative for law enforcement offices to report" the activities of lobbying groups, Muslim civil rights organizations, and antiwar groups in their areas.[46]

In 2013, the IRS revealed that it had selected political groups applying for tax-exempt status for intensive scrutiny based on their names or political themes. While there was much debate over whether only conservative groups (for example, those with Tea Party in the name) or also liberal groups (ones with "Occupy") were singled out. This practice led to widespread consternation and condemnation of the IRS. The FBI even launched a criminal probe.[47]

Police used military technology to surveil Black Lives Matter events. The full extent of the monitoring is hard to get a handle on because there are so many departments of the federal government, plus local police authorities. But reporters found that the DHS has collected location and other data on Black Lives Matter activities from public social media accounts and has

---

[46] "Fusion Center Encourages Improper Investigations of Lobbying Groups and Anti-war Activists." ACLU Press Release, February 25, 2009. www.aclu.org/news/fusion-center-encourages-improper-investigations-lobbying-groups-and-anti-war-activists
[47] D. Ingram and David. M. Spetalnick. "FBI opens criminal probe of tax agency, audit cites disarray." *Reuters.* May 15, 2013. www.reuters.com/article/us-usa-irs-idUSBRE94E02J20130515

monitored events like silent vigils, a funk music parade, and a walk to end breast cancer.[48]

Spying on Journalists

A free press is a prerequisite for a democratic society, yet US surveillance interferes with journalism. The Obama Administration has been particularly aggressive, going after six current and former government officials suspected of releasing classified material to the press – more leak prosecutions than under all previous administrations combined.

In seeking evidence in these cases, the Obama Administration has spied on journalists it suspects of having talked to government sources. In 2013, Attorney General Eric Holder subpoenaed telephone records of Associated Press (AP) journalists. The AP was not the target of the inquiry. Rather, the Department of Justice was trying to discover who might have leaked information to the AP. But the Department of Justice did not go to the AP for its cooperation in obtaining the records or to narrow its inquiry to more relevant materials. Instead, US attorneys obtained two months' worth of business and personal phone records on particular journalists, editors, and the main AP office.[49] These records not only revealed reporters' personal business to the government, but would also help identify sources in other stories.

In another disturbing effort, the government went after James Rosen, chief Washington correspondent for Fox News. They tracked Rosen's visits to the State Department and attempted to get access to his email in order to establish his connection to a government employee suspected of leaking information about North Korea. Journalists were outraged to learn that the Department of Justice's search warrant application for the email describes the reporter as "at the very least, either as an aider, abettor and/or co-conspirator." In other words, the DOJ accused Rosen of criminal behavior for talking to sources and reporting on current events and government policy.

---

[48] G. Joseph. "Exclusive: Feds regularly monitored Black Lives Matters since Fergusson." *The Intercept.* July 25, 2015. theintercept.com/2015/07/24/documents-show-department-homeland-security-monitoring-black-lives-matter-since-ferguson/

[49] S. Horwitz. "Under sweeping subpoenas, Justice Department obtained AP phone records in leak investigation." *The Washington Post.* May 13, 2013. www.washingtonpost.com/world/national-security/under-sweeping-subpoenas-justice-department-obtained-ap-phone-records-in-leak-investigation/2013/05/13/11d1bb82-bc11-11e2-89c9-3be8095fe767_story.html

In another instance, the Justice Department wanted *New York Times* reporter James Risen to testify at the trial of a former CIA officer who had allegedly revealed details about a botched operation in Iran that was intended to disrupt that country's nuclear program. Risen described the program in his 2006 book, *State of War*. The Bush Administration issued a subpoena to compel Risen to testify against the suspected source, Jeffrey Sterling, but Risen refused to testify, saying to do so would compromise his professional responsibility to keep the sources of his reporting secret. Risen lost the case before the Supreme Court, and it looked as though Attorney General Holder's DOJ was going to ask a court to jail him for contempt for refusing to testify. Eventually, however, the DOJ dropped the subpoena. AG Holder issued new guidelines for federal investigations involving journalists, which the DOJ continues to revise.[50]

These public fights in criminal cases severely damaged the press's trust that federal officials would not spy on, interfere with, or try to imprison or prosecute reporters. The new DOJ guidelines do not go far enough to rebuild that trust. National security reporting relies on access to sources, and sources generally require confidentiality lest they be demoted, fired, or prosecuted. Human Rights Watch (HRW) and the ACLU have issued a report showing that fear of mass surveillance has harmed journalists' ability to monitor and report on US national security policies. That may be the government's desired outcome. The intelligence community has striven mightily to keep national security efforts, including waterboarding, other torture techniques, "extraordinary rendition" (kidnapping), and official deployment of computer viruses and other cyberweapons, out of the news. But interfering with journalists inhibits the public's ability to understand and ultimately to control our government so as to ensure it acts lawfully and in the public interest.

The effects have already been far reaching. The HRW/ACLU report includes accounts by reporters from the *New York Times*, the *Washington Post*, the *Wall Street Journal*, McClatchy News, and many other news organizations on the obstacles they now face doing work that much of the country relies on for information about what our government is doing behind closed doors. As Steve Coll, staff writer for *The New Yorker* and Dean of the Columbia School of Journalism, says: "Every national security reporter I know would say that the atmosphere in which professional

---

[50] "Amending the Department of Justice subpoena guidelines." Reporters Committee for Freedom of the Press. www.rcfp.org/attorney-general-guidelines

reporters seek insight into policy failures [and] bad military decisions is just much tougher and much chillier."[51]

Other Governments

Our personal data also puts us at risk from foreign governments that do not have our best interests at heart. Private data is ripe for espionage. In the summer of 2015, hackers, allegedly working for the Chinese government, were revealed to have stolen highly sensitive background check and other personnel files from the US Office of Personnel and Management. Millions of government workers filled out forms detailing their mental health and illegal drug usage, and now those forms are in the hands of Chinese spies, or worse. This breach puts several generations of federal employees at risk of phishing attacks (computer intrusions assisted by malicious, personalized emails) and blackmail.

In addition to policing disfavored groups, surveillance data may also be shared with foreign governments, putting Americans' relatives in other countries at personal risk. Americans with Arab- and Palestinian-American relatives living in Israel and the Palestinian territories have good reason to be afraid for the well-being and fair treatment of their families. In September of 2014, the public learned that the NSA has been sending Americans' communications and metadata to Israel. Specifically, a division of the Israeli SIGINT National Unit (INSU) called 8200 has been receiving raw surveillance data from the NSA – the contents of messages, as well as bulk metadata. The rules are that when such sensitive information is transferred to another country, it must first be "minimized," meaning that US persons' names and other personally identifiable information would be removed. But the NSA has broken those rules. The data was not minimized before the NSA transferred it to Israel. Forty-three veterans of Unit 8200 sent a letter to their commanders, to Prime Minister Benjamin Netanyahu, and to the head of the Israeli army, charging Israel with using information it collects for "political persecution" of Palestinians. In testimonies and interviews given to the media, the signatories said that Israel was gathering data on Palestinians' sexual orientations, infidelities, money problems, family medical conditions, and other private matters so as to

[51] As quoted in "With liberty to monitor all: How large-scale US surveillance is harming journalism, law, and American democracy." *Human Rights Watch*, 2014. p. 22. www.aclu.org/sites/default/files/field_document/dem14-withlibertytomonitorall-07282014.pdf

coerce Palestinians into becoming collaborators or create divisions in their society.[52]

The intelligence community and law enforcement have do not always know the difference between dangerous people and innocent but different people. For example, a May 2014 document entitled "Countering Violent Extremism: A Guide for Practitioners and Analysts" showcases government efforts to recruit communities and families to report on their loved ones' allegedly suspicious behavior. That behavior includes things like "Expressions of Hopelessness, Futility," "Talk of Harming Self or Others," and "Connection to Group Identity (Race, Nationality, Religion, Ethnicity)." Families are to be assessed on levels of "Parent-Child Bonding" as one factor. In a similar context, White House counterterrorism adviser Lisa Monaco has warned parents and community members to look out for "subtle" signs, like "sudden personality changes in their children at home – becoming confrontational" as signs their child may be becoming radicalized.

There is no scientific basis for the claim that these are useful indicators. In 2013, the Government Accountability Office (GAO) analyzed hundreds of scientific studies and found that there was no evidence to back up the idea that "behavioral indicators ... can be used to identify persons who may pose a risk to aviation security." The GAO concluded that "the human ability to accurately identify deceptive behavior based on behavioral indicators is the same as or slightly better than chance."[53]

When we treat people as potential terrorists for such spurious reasons, we end up putting a lot of innocent people at risk with little to no security benefit. We create an atmosphere of mistrust. We interfere with our ability to focus on the real risks. These decisions aren't just ill advised, they are actually counterproductive. Groups mistrust the government that is supposed to protect them, and become less likely to seek help when someone actually is a danger. Meanwhile money, time, and resources are spent – wasted – on the wrong things.

In policy debates about surveillance, the government will often argue that if it has adequate cause and legal process, then it is entitled to obtain

---

[52] J. Bamford. "Israel's NSA scandal." *The New York Times*. September 14, 2014. www.nytimes.com/2014/09/17/opinion/israels-nsa-scandal.html?_r=0

[53] "TSA Should Limit Future Funding for Behavior Detection Activities." United States Government Accountability Office. November 2013, p. 2. www.gao.gov/products/GAO-14–159

information and individuals have no grounds to withhold it. But these examples show that the issue is more complex than that. Without question, there are times we want the government to have information, and times that the government is not entitled to it. There's a huge gray area, however, where there exists what Alvaro Bedoya has called a "moral lag." Today, the vast majority of Americans oppose the Japanese internment and the discriminatory treatment of immigrants and veterans. But only very recently have we reached moral consensus on these issues. As Bedoya writes, "The American public may never make up its mind about women, gay people, immigrants, minorities, the mentally ill, and the poor – or how they and their data should be treated."[54]

The golden age for surveillance combines dangerously with our current regime of loosely defined federal crimes and extremely high sentences, including for first-time offenders. When so many people could be prosecuted for something, the government can misuse Big Data surveillance technologies to root out categories of wrongdoers, or to selectively investigate unpopular people. Congress might decriminalize illegal but common behaviors. By narrowing and carefully circumscribing the reach of law, it can reduce the chances of discriminatory, malicious, and retaliatory investigation, and of investigations spurred by distaste for an individual's political philosophy.[55] If a free society is one in which it is safe to be unpopular, then we need to consider changing our criminal justice system.

Finally, privacy is not the enemy of security. This chapter tells many stories in which privacy *protects* security. A human rights worker in Syria or a homosexual in India needs privacy, or they may be killed. Americans need a free press to investigate wrongdoing. We need the Muslim Americans who go to school with us, work with us, and live with us to feel safe, to worship freely, and to trust the government. We need political activists to push our country forward. We need to know that even if we are odd or unconventional we will not be isolated, judged, or imprisoned.

We all have something to hide.

---

[54] Comments of Alvaro Bedoya to Federal Trade Commission, Center on Privacy & Technology at Georgetown Law, on "Big Data: A Tool for Inclusion or Exclusion? Workshop, Project No. P145406." goo.gl/QV3tG7

[55] R. J. Reilly. "Aaron Swartz prosecutors weighed 'Guerilla' Manifesto, Justice official tells Congressional Committee." *The Huffington Post.* February 22, 2013. www.huffingtonpost.com/2013/02/22/aaron-swartz-prosecutors_n_2735675.html

10

The Minimal Comfort of Minimization

Intelligence officials regularly tell Americans that we have nothing to fear from overbroad surveillance because after-the-fact minimization procedures are in place to protect our privacy. Minimization procedures are a necessary safeguard, to be sure. But even under the best of circumstances, minimization procedures have limited power to protect people from government overreach.

Current minimization rules are not nearly as effective as they could be at protecting innocent people's privacy and guarding against official misuse. Generally, minimization rules are secret and can be changed at any time. Substantively, they allow broad government discretion in searching, analyzing, and sharing private data. They are complicated and easily manipulated by officials who view their mission as "Collect It All" and "Know It All." Even where judges oversee minimization policies, they are extremely deferential to the demands, factual representations, and promises of American spies.

ODNI attorney Robert Litt inadvertently admitted the limited usefulness this mass of incomprehensible rules has in protecting civil liberties. At a 2015 Georgetown debate with whistleblower and former State Department employee John Tye, Litt was trying to reassure the audience that Tye's concerns about surveillance were misplaced because Tye didn't understand all the safeguards in place that would stop the intelligence community from misusing the massive amount of data it collects. Litt admitted that it took him "years" to learn the rules and policies in place. How can the public trust in a system of rules that is so complicated it takes seasoned intelligence experts years to figure it out? Who will be able to tell when spies are behaving improperly if we can't understand what proper behavior is? How can we trust that the complex system spy agencies have set up to protect Americans actually works? Mistrust is especially appropriate because the NSA repeatedly has violated the rules set for it by federal judges, claiming that the policies were too complicated for the agency to correctly implement, oversee, and report.

Policy makers can and should improve minimization rules. These rules should be public. They should be subject to robust oversight by all branches of government. Their language should be interpreted in accordance with the common definitions of words, and not the tricky intelligence-specific jargon explained in Chapter 2. We should ensure that the procedures enshrine and protect civil liberties principles like freedom of speech, attorney-client privilege, and freedom from unreasonable government invasions of privacy.

But ultimately minimization can only provide so much protection. Collection rules prevent the government from having the *ability* to misuse data. Minimization rules, in contrast, deny government officials *permission* to misuse data in particular ways.

The False Promise of Minimization

As discussed earlier in this book, intelligence surveillance traditionally has been broad and has only expanded over time. Foreign intelligence SIGINT can be massive or even indiscriminate. The risks of privacy, civil liberties, and human rights abuses that massive government collection of data poses today mostly are managed through minimization procedures. These procedures are post-collection usage rules defining how intelligence agencies should manage, share, use, and delete the information they collect.

American spies point to minimization rules to ease fears of official misuse of sensitive data collected in the name of foreign intelligence. For example, Office of the Director of National Intelligence (ODNI) General Counsel Robert Litt has said "tailored minimization procedures are an important way in which we provide appropriate protections for privacy."[1] In responding to reports that the NSA monitors roughly 75 percent of US Internet traffic, an intelligence community spokesperson reassured the public that if American communications are "incidentally collected during NSA's lawful signals intelligence activities," the agency follows "minimization procedures that are approved by the U.S. attorney general and designed to protect the privacy of United States persons."[2]

---

[1] Robert S. Litt. "Privacy, Technology, and National Security: An Overview of Intelligence Collection." Remarks delivered at The Brookings Institution, July 19, 2013. www.dni.gov/index.php/newsroom/speeches-and-interviews/195-speeches-interviews-2013/896-privacy,-technology-and-national-security-an-overview-of-intelligence-collection

[2] S. Gorman and J. Valentino-Devries. "New details show broader NSA surveillance reach." *The Wall Street Journal.* August 20, 2013. www.wsj.com/articles/SB10001424127887324108204579022874091732470

There is little reason, however, to trust minimization procedures to do the hard work of ensuring that government officials cannot misuse private personal data. There will always be employee transgressions, for example. LOVEINT is the tongue-in-cheek name for intelligence employees exploiting their access to databases of phone and email data to stalk their ex-lovers and spouses. It was against the rules to do so, but still it happened.[3] The NSA can take steps to stop these kinds of abuses. The agency needs to ensure data security, employee monitoring, and reliable punishment. Otherwise, the rule alone will not be very effective.

But there is a bigger problem than employee misconduct. Minimization rules may mean that wayward low-level employees who violate internal procedures get their pay docked or are fired. But minimization policies do little to stop officially sanctioned misuse of private data. The policies do little or nothing to constrain a powerful director or the president herself. Official misuse is always a possibility once the data is collected. There is little reason to believe that minimization procedures will stop or even deter it.

Historically, it has been difficult to contravene a president's executive orders. As discussed in Chapter 13, STELLARWIND was illegal. No one, however, stopped it because President Bush had authorized it. Other officials – Attorney General John Ashcroft, the General Counsel of the NSA – went along with the program despite the President's spurious legal justification. The illegal spying programs continued unabated. It wasn't until 2004 that acting Attorney General James Comey refused to reauthorize part of the program. Even then, the FISC's 2004 approval of the Internet dragnet portion of STELLARWIND disregarded federal law requiring that collection of such data be "relevant" to a particular counterterrorism investigation. That program continued under the spurious legal reasoning until 2011, demonstrating the power and persuasion that a president can bring to bear.

If the executive branch could establish STELLARWIND while ignoring the statutes Congress passed, imagine how little restraint internal minimization procedures – which do not have the force of law – impose.

Malleable Secret Rules Are a Lot Like No Rules At All

The limited effect of minimization rules on official surveillance practices is exacerbated by the fact that minimization rules are secret. For most

---

[3] S. Gorman. "NSA officers spy on love interests." *The Wall Street Journal.* August 23, 2013. blogs.wsj.com/washwire/2013/08/23/nsa-officers-sometimes-spy-on-love-interests/

surveillance programs, even judges and Congress are kept in the dark as to what the rules are. When rules are secret, people do not know how their private data may be used, there is less incentive for analysts and officers to follow the rules because no one knows if regulations are being violated, and the rules can be changed at any time.

Minimization policies are generally classified. The public only learns about the procedures that the government selectively decides to declassify, or which someone leaks. For years, the public had no idea what the minimization rules were. Then in 2013, Snowden disclosed the NSA's FISA minimization procedures for section 702 collection. The intelligence community ultimately declassified the FBI and the CIA minimization procedures from 2014 in September of 2015.[4] In November 2015, the procedures for all three agencies were secretly revised. Officials revealed a little bit of information about the new rules, reassuring people that the changes responded to at least some of the recommendations made by the Privacy and Civil Liberties Oversight Board in 2014.[5] But in April of 2016, the Office of the Director of National Intelligence partially declassified a FISC opinion approving aspects of the November 2015 procedures. In approving the new, but still classified, provisions, the FISC revealed that the procedures actually expanded the FBI agents' backdoor search ability, giving agents broader discretion to search the section 702 database for Americans' data. Of course, giving the FBI more discretion to make suspicionless searches is not what the PCLOB recommended.

This story illustrates why there is little reason to have faith that the minimization procedures are doing the hard, necessary work of protecting people from suspicionless government surveillance. While the 2015 section 702 procedures are now partially declassified, the public has no access to the full set of procedures and remains unable assess whether official representations are accurate. The public knows only what American spies want us to know. Whatever they tell us today, whatever actually might be true, the NSA can subsequently change the procedures outside of the public eye.

---

4 See Statement by the Office of the Director of National Intelligence and the Department of Justice on the Declassification of Documents Related to Section 702 of the Foreign Intelligence Surveillance Act. icontherecord.tumblr.com/post/130138039058/statement-by-the-office-of-the-director-of

5 Spencer Ackerman. "FBI quietly changes its privacy rules for accessing NSA data on Americans." *The Guardian.* March 10, 2016. www.theguardian.com/us-news/2016/mar/08/fbi-changes-privacy-rules-accessing-nsa-prism-data

Lack of Oversight

Minimization polices are drafted by the executive branch to police itself. For EO 12333 collection, neither the FISC nor Congress need to approve the provisions. Judges and legislators are cut out of the process. Under traditional FISA, adoption of minimization procedures is a little more strict. The minimization rules governing how analysts may use the large amounts of telephone, microphone, cell phone, and email data must be approved by a FISC judge. But in the section 702 context, the FISC's role in policing minimization is limited. Section 702 minimization procedures only need to "meet the definition of minimization procedures." If so, then the FISC must issue the certification that allows the government to issue directives to companies without further judicial input. The statute denies the FISC authority to sculpt minimization rules beyond the bare minimum, even if the FISC judge thinks there are better ways to protect privacy and avoid abuse.[6]

Complicated and Permissive Policies

Minimization procedures are internal policies and procedures meant to guide the collection, retention, dissemination, or deletion of information about US persons or about foreigners. Depending on the legal authority to which the procedures apply, they may or may not be reviewed or approved by the attorney general or by a FISC judge.

The substance of the minimization rules is simply inadequate in light of the vast power that access to so much personal information provides to intelligence analysts and officials. EO 12333 rules give a nod to protecting the legal rights of US persons[7] and require covert intelligence to be evaluated for "consistency with applicable legal requirements."[8] The United States Signal Intelligence Directive 18 (USSID-18) is a directive that applies to EO 12333 collected data. USSID-18 details policies and procedures designed to ensure that the NSA's missions and functions are conducted as authorized by law and in a manner that is consistent with the Fourth Amendment. The directive sets forth policies and procedures regarding the NSA's SIGINT activities, including the rules for the collection, retention, and dissemination of information about US persons.

---

[6] 50 U.S.C. § 1881a(i)(2)(C). If the rules fit the definition of minimization rules than the FISC must issue the certification.

[7] Executive Order 12333. "United States intelligence activities." § 1.1.

[8] Id. § 1.2.

One would hope that together EO 12333 and USSID-18 could meaningfully limit the government's ability to misuse private information gathered in the name of foreign intelligence. However, portions of USSID-18 are still classified, making it impossible to understand what the directive allows and disallows. For example, many USSID-18 protections do not go into effect until the government has "collected" the data. As discussed in Chapter 2, intelligence lawyers' definition of "collect" is not necessarily the commonly understood meaning of the term. It is possible that under EO 12333 and USSID-18, American spies use "collection" to mean acquisition plus analysis or use, which would enable intelligence agencies to evade at least some of the safeguards detailed in the policies.

Another legal issue is what the intelligence community considers to be a "communication." Through SIGINT, the NSA gets real-time notification of email and instant messaging logins and logouts, basic subscriber information, videos, photos, stored data, and file transfers. The NSA probably also gets task lists, contacts, buddy lists, and address books. Are these considered "communications" to which the USSID-18 rules apply, or does the NSA have leeway with data that is not specifically the content of a message between two or more people? The public simply does not know.

Foreigners get no real comfort from minimization procedures; their privacy concerns aren't directly addressed in USSID-18 or EO 12333. The relatively recent PPD-28 sets forth some limitations on the use of bulk-collected material. Recall from Chapter 7 that PPD-28 says that bulk SIGINT information should not be used against Americans for run-of-the-mill criminal prosecutions, for example, and that American spies won't search EO 12333-collected data for blackmail-worthy tidbits except for a good reason. But we don't know what the limitations are for SIGINT that the intelligence community conducts via selectors, if there are any. We also don't know how the intelligence agencies interpret the permissions given in PPD-28. Those secret interpretations mean that PPD-28 itself could be riddled with loopholes.

Even the judicially approved FISA minimization procedures may not meaningfully constrain the government. Only if information "could not be" foreign intelligence information is it deleted, and evidence of criminal activity which is NOT foreign intelligence activity, nevertheless may be retained and disseminated.[9]

According to statute, FISA-collected information must be used or disclosed in accord with governing minimization procedures and only may

---

[9] 50 U.S.C. §§ 1801(h)(3), 1821(4)(c).

be used or disclosed for lawful purposes.[10] What purposes are lawful? Chapter 9 tells of classified documents proposing that the NSA discredit people with radical religious or political beliefs using data it has collected about their sexual interests and pornography viewing habits. Even such blackmail, and even against Americans, could be a "lawful" use of FISA-collected data. According to David Kris and Douglas Wilson, who wrote the legal bible on SIGINT law, the 1978 Senate Judiciary Committee report on FISA says that the Committee specifically did not want information gathered about a foreign visitor to be used to blackmail him into becoming an agent against his country. However, the House report on FISA was more equivocal. It said that, while the US government should not seek purely personal information about a US person who is a suspected spy, it might be acceptable to seek such embarrassing information about non-US persons "because compromising information about their private lives may itself be foreign intelligence information."[11] Aside from blackmail, we've seen the US government argue in other aspects of the War on Terror, that it may both kidnap and harshly interrogate foreigners, as well as assassinate both foreigners and Americans.[12] What practical effect does language assuring the public that FISA data can only be used for a lawful purpose have when a government has so many arguably "lawful" means of coercively pressuring an individual? Ultimately, the general prohibition on illegal uses in FISA is of minimal comfort.

Back Door Searches

One stark concern with the section 702 minimization rules is that they allow intelligence agencies warrantless access to information about Americans. This permission directs Americans' data to foreign intelligence agencies, albeit for a foreign intelligence purpose. It also allows criminal investigators at the FBI an end-run around the Fourth Amendment and statutory privacy law. In other words, the minimization rules turn warrantless spying on foreign targets – which scoops up information about Americans – into the means for warrantlessly spying on Americans as well. Senator Ron Wyden has confirmed that the NSA is exploiting a loophole potentially allowing "warrantless searches for the phone calls or emails of law-abiding

---

[10] §28:1, p. 206.
[11] Id., §28:3, p. 210.
[12] See, e.g., J. Scahill and G. Greenwald. "The NSA's secret role in the U.S. assassination program." *The Intercept*. February 9, 2014. theintercept.com/2014/02/10/the-nsas-secret-role/

Americans." Wyden has referred to these queries for Americans as the "back door searches loophole."[13]

Via the FBI's back door searches, the vast trove of section 702 data collected in the name of foreign intelligence is repurposed for routine criminal prosecutions.[14] What that means is that information collected in the name of international energy policy, for example, can be searched to identify people growing marijuana. The more the public learns about the FBI's back door searches, the more problematic they become. Initially, we were told that the FBI does not search for American data unless the queries were "reasonably designed" to discover "foreign intelligence" or "evidence of a crime."[15] "Reasonably designed" is far less of a suspicion than the Fourth Amendment's probable cause requirement, but surveillance defenders said that it ensured that the FBI was not permitted to trawl through warrantlessly obtained data out of mere curiosity or in the hopes of finding something scandalous.

Then, the procedures secretly changed in July of 2015.[16] The new FBI minimization procedures no longer require factual justification for a search. The FBI can search section 702 data for US person identifiers in order to initiate an investigation – without a suspicion of wrongdoing. Nor do the procedures require section 702-trained personnel to make them. Any FBI agent can query the data, even for an assessment that requires no underlying factual basis. The agent will not see the relevant data, but a positive hit.[17] Then a FISA-trained agent can rerun the search and get the data.

---

[13] J. Ball and S. Ackerman. "NSA loophole allows warrantless search for US citizens' emails and phone calls." *The Washington Post.* August 9, 2013. www.theguardian.com/world/2013/aug/09/nsa-loophole-warrantless-searches-email-calls

[14] "Report on the Surveillance Program Operated Pursuant to Section 702 of the Foreign Intelligence Surveillance Act." Privacy and Civil Liberties Oversight Board. July 2, 2014, p. 58. www.pclob.gov/library/702-Report-2.pdf. See also "Minimization Procedures Used by the Federal Bureau of Investigation in Connection with Acquisitions of Foreign Intelligence Information Pursuant to Section 702 of the Foreign Intelligence Surveillance Act of 1978, as amended." 2014, p. 3. www.dni.gov/files/documents/ppd-28/2014%20FBI%20702%20Minimization%20Procedures.pdf

[15] "Report on the Surveillance Program Operated Pursuant to Section 702 of the Foreign Intelligence Surveillance Act." Privacy and Civil Liberties Oversight Board. July 2, 2014, p. 58.

[16] "Minimization Procedures Used by the Federal Bureau of Investigation in Connection with Acquisitions of Foreign Intelligence Information Pursuant to Section 702 of the Foreign Intelligence Surveillance Act of 1978, as amended." 2015. See p.11 n.3 ("Examples of such queries include, but are not limited to . . . queries conducted by FBI personnel in making an initial decision to open an assessment concerning . . . the prevention of or protection against a Federal crime."). https://icontherecord.tumblr.com/post/148797010498/release-of-2015-section-702-minimization.

[17] *Memorandum Opinion and Order,* No. [Redacted]. (FISC, November 6, 2015), p. 28. www.dni.gov/files/documents/20151106-702Mem_Opinion_Order_for_Public_Release.pdf

The FISC court considered and approved these loose procedures over the opposition of *amicus* counsel appointed pursuant to the USA Freedom Act. The USA Freedom Act provided that the FISC should appoint an *amicus*, or friend of the court, attorney when it considers new or novel interpretations of law, to try to remedy the problem that only the government gets to appear before the FISC. The appointed *amicus* was Amy Jeffress, a former national security law expert in the Attorney General's Office.

As *amicus*, Jeffress argued that the FBI procedures "go far beyond the purpose for which the Section 702-acquired information is collected in permitting queries that are unrelated to national security."[18] Jeffress argued that the new minimization procedures essentially place no restrictions on the FBI querying section 702 data using US person identifiers. Each query is a search under the Fourth Amendment. That means it should require either probable cause and a warrant or at least be independently reasonable. Because the minimization procedures imposed no limitations on such searches, she argued that the procedures violate the Fourth Amendment.

But the FISC judge, Thomas F. Hogan, approved the new procedures anyway. He concluded that, at the acquisition stage, it was perfectly fine for the government to collect information useful in criminal cases because FISA only requires that gathering foreign intelligence be a *significant* purpose of the collection and not the *sole* purpose.[19] Once in government hands, Judge Hogan said that the subsequent querying of the data need not have any purpose related to foreign intelligence. It was perfectly fine to search for evidence of a crime, or for nothing at all. Judge Hogan said that his job was not to ensure that each query would be reasonable under the Fourth Amendment. Rather, his role was only to assess the reasonableness of the section 702 program overall. He found that by under the totality of the circumstances, considering the national security interests at stake, the program – and the new FBI minimization procedures – passed constitutional muster.

In November 2015, Judge Hogan's opinion, but not the new minimization procedures, was partially declassified. The 2015 procedures themselves were partially declassified in August 2016. They reveal that section 702 enables broad spying on foreign targets. Section 702 incidentally scoops up huge amounts of Americans cross-border and even domestic communications. Further, with the back door searches loophole, it is a route for law enforcement to dig directly into Americans' private conduct without

---

18 Id., p. 30.
19 Id., p. 31.

a warrant, without probable cause, and without reasonable suspicion.[20] In sum, section 702 creates an ocean of data about both foreigners and Americans, and liberally permits government officials to launch fishing expeditions in that ocean. Given how bad this outcome is, one wonders what American spies see fit to still hide from us under the blacked out classification marks.

There is a lot that Congress can do with minimization procedures to improve oversight and to ensure that there are meaningful limitations on American spies' ability to abuse their powers. The procedures must be declassified, sculpted by courts and Congress, and respectful of human rights and civil liberties. But we have to understand that usage rules are inherently limited in their ability to protect people from government over-reach. The rules can be and have been violated. As Chapter 13 details, each official slip up has been a step toward obtaining either judicial or legislative permission for a collection practice that was previously off-limits. To the contrary, there should be punishment for breaking the rules, not a reward. But so far there have been no ramifications for official violations of law or policy in the name of "Collecting It All."

---

[20] At a March 2014 PCLOB hearing, then-NSA General Counsel Rajesh De said that the NSA only conducts searches of collected section 702 data using US person identifiers on PRISM data and not on Upstream data. See R. De. Testimony at "Public Hearing Regarding the Surveillance Program Operated Pursuant to Section 702 of the Foreign Intelligence Surveillance Act." PCLOB Board. March 19, 2014. The public does not know if that has changed.

11

Do Unto Others: Why Americans Should Protect Foreigners' Privacy Rights

One of the most contentious issues in the surveillance debate is how countries, particularly the United States, should treat foreigners under domestic surveillance regimes. Should a nation only concern itself with the rights and interests of its own citizens, or should it respect the human rights and privacy interests of noncitizens? Some people say Americans don't care about foreigners' rights. In 2015, comedian John Oliver of the comedy news show *Last Week Tonight,* flew to Russia to interview Edward Snowden. When Snowden started talking about the rights of non-Americans, Oliver interrupted, telling him that Americans "don't give a shit" about surveillance of foreigners.

For much of this book, I've assumed that the reader is an American not innately committed to other peoples' human rights. Nevertheless, Americans should take foreigners' rights seriously, if only for selfish reasons. Our efforts to broadly spy on foreigners are – for legal and technological reasons – catching Americans' data in the net and putting our civil liberties at risk. First, when intelligence agencies spy on foreigners, they also spy on Americans – a lot. Second, American spies may be using the data they obtain on foreigners to obtain Americans' private information without restriction or limitation, by trading data with other friendly governments. Third, foreign companies and individuals are driven away from doing business with American companies because they know those companies are a conduit for private data and confidential business information to go to the US government. Fourth, as a result of international concern about the scope of US spying, foreign governments are supporting policies that undermine the benefits of the Internet as a global communications network.

US law, coupled with modern Internet services, means that NSA spying has a huge impact on foreigners living their everyday lives. The spying intrudes on the personal lives of people around the globe who pose no conceivable threat to our Nation. American spies are, legally under US laws, grabbing all the data that flows through Belgium, recording all the telephone calls in the Bahamas, and collecting international emails from US services that merely mention foreign intelligence targets. The primary authorization for overseas spying comes from the executive branch, and not from Congress, under EO 12333. Instead of Congress and the courts, the attorney general creates general guidelines for how the CIA, the NSA, and military spies conduct foreign collection activities that are not governed by the FISA statute.[1] The scandal Snowden exposed isn't that American spies are doing all this collection. The scandal is that US law actually allows it.

One reason Congress hasn't regulated surveillance under EO 12333 is the mistaken perception that American rights aren't severely impacted by foreign collection. That may have once been true. For example, in the era of analog telephones, our conversations could be picked up when we were talking to foreign targets overseas and someone would have to listen to our calls. But in the Internet Age, domestic messages may flow overseas, backed up on global computer servers. Today, we communicate in groups using chat rooms and Facebook pages, with no idea that someone in the conversation is not American, providing an avenue for US government interception. EO 12333 has always allowed the NSA to target groups like UNICEF, Doctors Without Borders, or The Pirate Bay. But modern technology makes it cheap and easy to do so. Why not try to "Collect It All?" When that happens, US messages and metadata are also caught in the net.

Another reason to care about the rights of foreigners is so that foreign governments will have less incentive to spy on average Americans – and then trade that information to the NSA in exchange for data on their own people. The NSA is in many spying partnerships, and spy agencies work closely with each other to share and trade information they collect on Americans with information the United States collects on their citizens. The most robust of these partnerships is called the Five Eyes. The relationship is based on a top-secret agreement dating back to the 1940s and initially forged between the United States and United Kingdom, called the UK–USA Agreement or "yoo-koo-sa." Very little is known about Five Eyes relationship beyond the fact that it is a spying alliance between the United States' National Security Agency (NSA), the United Kingdom's Government Communications Headquarters (GCHQ), Canada's Communications Security Establishment Canada (CSEC), the Australian Signals Directorate (ASD), and New Zealand's Government

---

[1] "United States Intelligence Activities." Executive Order 12333, Section 2.4, December 4, 1981. www.archives.gov/federal-register/codification/executive-order/12333.html

Communications Security Bureau (GCSB). The Five Eyes agreement is itself secret.[2] But the idea behind the partnership is that these friendly, English-speaking nations will allow each other to share their interception systems, share the cost, and jointly use the collected information. Many classified documents are marked as shareable with Five Eyes partners.

While the Five Eyes members are not supposed to directly target each others' citizens without permission, a leaked NSA document entitled *Collection, Processing and Dissemination of Allied Communications* and dated 2005 reveals that the NSA prepared policies enabling its staff to spy on Five Eyes citizens even where the partner country refused permission to do so. When Five Eyes countries spy on one another's citizens, the practice is not regulated by domestic law. Given the close relationship between the agencies, how much do they share the take with each other?[3] The NSA and the GCHQ, in particular, have a close working relationship. The GCHQ has boasted that it had "given the NSA 36% of all the raw information the British had intercepted from computers the agency was monitoring."[4] Other GCHQ internal documents explain how the agency "can now interchange 100% of GCHQ End Point Projects with NSA."[5] This relationship was characterized by Sir David Omand, former Director of the GCHQ, as "a collaboration that's worked very well [...] [w]e have the brains; they have the money."[6]

The public has not seen any rules that would protect Americans from Five Eyes spying. Nor have we seen any rules that regulate the way that the NSA, the CIA, or the FBI can use information about Americans that any agency receives from Five Eyes partners. The Five Eyes relationship enables the NSA (and other intelligence agencies) to receive information about our own citizens that we would otherwise not be entitled to have. The Five Eyes collaboration appears to extend the NSA's surveillance capabilities, giving the agency a way to spy on Americans without

---

[2] M. Warner. "An exclusive club: The five countries that don't spy on each other." *PBS.* October 25, 2013. www.pbs.org/newshour/rundown/an-exclusive-club-the-five-countries-that-dont-spy-on-each-other/

[3] J. Ball. "US and UK struck secret deal to allow NSA to 'unmask' Britons' personal data." *The Guardian.* November 20, 2013. www.theguardian.com/world/2013/nov/20/us-uk-secret-deal-surveillance-personal-data

[4] N. Hopkins, J. Borger, and L. Harding. "GCHQ: inside the top secret world of Britain's biggest spy agency." *The Guardian.* August 1, 2013. www.theguardian.com/world/interactive/2013/aug/01/gchq-spy-agency-nsa-edward-snowden#part-one

[5] Ibid.

[6] "UK intelligence work defends freedom, say spy chiefs." *BBC.* November 7, 2013. www.bbc.com/news/uk-politics-24847399

technically breaking US laws that would otherwise prohibit such spying. Edward Snowden described the Five Eyes as a "supra-national intelligence organization that doesn't answer to the laws of its own countries."[7] In other words, if US law doesn't protect the privacy rights of British citizens, and British laws don't protect the rights of Americans, then they can spy on us, we'll spy on them, and our intelligence agencies will just swap information. This evasion of domestic privacy laws would enable essentially unlimited spying unaffected by either collection or usage rules.

Third, rampant spying on foreigners hurts US companies' competitiveness abroad. As described in detail in Chapter 8, under section 702 of the FISA Amendments Act any foreigner can be a target so long as the purpose of surveillance is to collect foreign intelligence information, and the NSA can intercept any international communication, so long as the participants might be talking about a foreign intelligence matter. The PRISM program, built on this legal foundation, was a slap in the face to foreign users of US-based services like Google, Microsoft, Yahoo!, and Apple. With the PRISM revelations, perhaps for the first time foreigners realized that they didn't have to be government officials, criminals, or terrorists to be easy targets. Platform companies' officials based in the United States readily can be served with legal service and be legally compelled to comply with US government demands. Since so many of the most popular Internet companies are in the United States, American spies have hit the jackpot. Just by using some of the Internet's best-loved brands – Google, Microsoft, YouTube, Apple – foreigners are enabling the US government to easily access their Internet communications for any foreign intelligence purpose without warrants or probable cause.

The government's logistical advantage in surveillance is as important as the law. The United States explicitly knows about and tries to capitalize on its home field advantage against foreigners. For example, when Global Crossing, a US-based telecommunications company whose fiber optic network connected twenty-seven nations and four continents, was sold in 2003 to an Asian firm, the US government negotiated with the company to require a "Network Operations Center" on US soil. The Network Operations Center could be visited by government officials with thirty minutes of warning and would ensure that US government surveillance requests got fulfilled quickly and confidentially, despite the foreign ownership. *The Washington Post* reports that the Global Crossing "Network

7 "Snowden-Interview: Transcript." *Norddeutscher Rundfunk.* January 26, 2014. www.ndr.de/ nachrichten/netzwelt/snowden277_page-2.html

Security Agreement" became a model for other deals over the next decade. The government was able to persuade companies to sign up by selectively refusing the Federal Communications Commission's approval of valuable cable licenses. When a foreign telecom wants to buy a US-based one, it appears the Commission holds up approval until government surveillance experts work out an "agreement" for easy future surveillance.

Foreign reaction to PRISM is an example of how rampant spying by the US government has come to hurt the competitiveness of US companies overseas. Foreign companies and individuals have become skittish about doing business with American companies. In the days that followed the PRISM revelations, official government statements only exacerbated foreigners' concerns. For example, on June 7th, the day after the PRISM disclosures, President Obama appeared at a press conference. He responded to reporters by saying that, "with respect to the Internet and e-mails, [PRISM] does not apply to U.S. citizens, and it does not apply to people living in the United States." He promised that "If you're a U.S. person, then NSA is not listening to your phone calls and it's not targeting your emails unless it's getting an individualized court order."

The President's statement was disturbing to non-Americans, the growing majority of US Internet company customers. In 2014, 70 percent of Dropbox's customers were overseas,[8] as were 70 percent of Gmail users.[9] Facebook's next billion customers are most likely to come from Asia. Users who aren't criminals, aren't terrorists, and aren't working for a foreign government are now subject to American spying. Just by using US services, they were giving the US government a clear path to access their Internet communications. That may be why Facebook's founder and Chief Executive Officer (CEO) was unimpressed with the President's defense. As Mark Zuckerberg said at the time, "[s]ome of the government's statements have been particularly unhelpful ... Like, 'Oh, we only spy on non-Americans.'" Zuckerberg continued, "the government blew it."

Foreigners who disagree with the United States' American-centric approach cannot "vote the bastards out" of office. But the extent of their helplessness goes further. Individuals who are subject to NSA surveillance are almost never notified. The proceedings authorizing the surveillance are secret. The orders and directives are classified. The companies that

[8] E. Kim. "Dropbox's new strategy: More Microsoft, less SalesForce." *Business Insider.* August 11, 2015. www.businessinsider.com/dropbox-more-microsoft-less-salesforce-2015-8

[9] M. Yglesias. "PRISM secrecy helps American tech companies." *Slate.* June 7, 2013. www.slate.com/blogs/moneybox/2013/06/07/us_tech_giants_have_many_foreign_customers.html

respond to government demands are under gag orders, or otherwise obligated not to disclose. From the point of view of someone living outside the United States, the company one does business with turns your data over at the request of a foreign government for no better reason than that your business is of foreign intelligence interest. The best that foreigners can hope for is that their private data won't be abused, but there's little cause for these individuals to take comfort. Post-collection minimization rules generally do not apply to foreigners and even where they do, as with PPD-28 and bulk collection, the rules are an exceptionally weak and loophole-fraught mechanism for protecting one's human rights.

The Court of Justice of the European Union (CJEU), which is the highest court for the twenty-eight countries that make up the Union, took a look at this situation in 2015 and found it unacceptable. European Union data protection law requires companies handling European citizens' data to ensure "an adequate level of protection" for privacy and other individual rights before that entity may transfer European citizens' data to another country. The CJEU, however, found that US companies were falling short of that standard when they transferred data to the United States because that transfer made the data subject to PRISM. The court concluded that US companies could not comply with European Union data privacy law because PRISM fails to limit the purposes and circumstances of surveillance, and provides inadequate authorization and oversight processes for the data collection. The CJEU's ruling was a bombshell, putting at risk the ability of US Internet companies to continue to do business with European citizens.

The spying scandal has put the US government and American companies at a severe disadvantage in ongoing discussions with the European Union about upcoming changes to its law enforcement and consumer-privacy-focused data directives, negotiations critical to the Internet industry's ongoing operations in Europe. It also undermines US businesses' ability to make contracts with overseas entities. In June 2014, the German government canceled a contract with Verizon Communications, citing the Snowden revelations. Verizon provided telecom services to many of Germany's federal agencies. European telecoms, including Deutsche Telekom, have been promoting their European roots – and the fact that they comply with Europe's stringent data protection rules – to win domestic business away from American competitors. Companies in the United States will lose business to European firms because of the spying scandal.

In other words, an unintended consequence of mass NSA surveillance may be to diminish the power and profitability of the US Internet economy.

America invented the Internet, and our Internet companies are dominant around the world. American companies – and the domestic economy – have suffered and will suffer as a result of global reaction to overbroad surveillance.[10] People around the world that look to use Internet services or cloud computing storage programs want and need their information to remain private. But American companies cannot promise this privacy, since the NSA's programmatic spying can grab foreigner's information just for being of foreign policy interest. Silicon Valley executives interviewed by the New America Foundation reported that they have been losing global business. The US government, in its rush to spy on everybody, may end up killing our most productive golden goose.

The fourth reason why Americans should care that our government is surveilling foreigners without adequate privacy protections is that foreign governments are using the revelations as an excuse for regulating the Internet in ways that will ultimately hurt innovation, privacy, and human rights. The most basic proposal is that companies should be required to store a country's citizens' data inside the borders of that nation. This practice, if it catches on, could compound US companies' economic losses while forcing expensive and undesirable changes to Internet architecture. Think about what foreign governments' demands would mean for American innovation. As Dropbox general counsel Ramsey Homsany put it, referring to the founders of the Google search engine: "Can you imagine if you are Larry and Sergey and you have to say that number two on the To Do List is to build a data center in Germany?"[11] There would be no Google.

Although Europe has been at the forefront of the push for local data storage, the call for data localization emboldens the so-called cyber sovereignty movement, an effort by many nations for more national control over the Internet within their own borders. But unlike current discussions in Europe, those demands are not motivated by a desire to protect civil liberties. To the contrary, authoritarian countries want data localization in order to censor, spy on, and control Internet access within their own borders. These nations – Russia, China, the United Arab Emirates, Sudan, Saudi Arabia, and others – unsuccessfully pushed for changes to the

[10] See D. Kehl, K. Bankston, R. Morgus, and R. Greene. "Surveillance costs: The NSA's impact on the economy, Internet freedom & cybersecurity." *New America.* July 29, 2014. www.newamerica.org/oti/surveillance-costs-the-nsas-impact-on-the-economy-internet-freedom-cybersecurity/

[11] G. Chapman. "Google's Schmidt fears spying could 'break' Internet." *Yahoo! News.* October 8, 2014. news.yahoo.com/googles-schmidt-fears-spying-could-break-internet-004654968.html

Internet's infrastructure at the International Telecommunications Union meeting December 2012 in Dubai. But now that the US government's fervor for Internet surveillance has been revealed, more repressive regimes have a great new set of talking points. Why should the United States have liberal access to data about their citizens when they do not? The cyber sovereignty effort dovetails nicely with privacy advocates who want to move data out of the United States to protect it from the NSA. In other words, US government's ardor for Internet surveillance has now emboldened the cyber sovereignty nations and given them new privacy-motivated allies.

Further, when it comes to intelligence gathering, European Union countries aren't necessarily going to treat their own citizens' data with any more respect than the United States does. Many European countries have neither written surveillance laws nor judicial review of search warrants. As Europe faces its own security crises, its laws may get even worse. In mid-2015, the French lower parliament passed a radical new surveillance law in the wake of the *Charlie Hebdo* magazine attacks. The proposal, if successful, would authorize bulk collection of metadata and do away with judicial review and inter-branch oversight. In the United Kingdom, the Investigatory Powers Bill, also called the Snooper's Charter, is pending. That proposal would authorize police computer hacking, force companies to save data in case an investigator wants it, and interfere with secure product design. The proposed law may be a sideshow, however. Many observers believe that these invasive investigatory techniques are something the British authorities are already doing, and the Snooper's Charter would merely codify techniques that are already the current practice.

Germany is both a target and a perpetrator of massive surveillance. It is arguably one of the most targeted countries of the twenty-seven members of the European Union. The NSA stores telephone calls, emails, mobile-phone text messages and chat transcripts from around half a billion communications connections in Germany each month.[12] After initially taking the news that the NSA spies on German citizens' calls and emails calmly, German Chancellor Angela Merkel loudly protested that friends shouldn't spy on friends when she learned that the United States was eavesdropping on her personal cell phone. In a meeting with President Obama, Chancellor Merkel compared US surveillance with that of the Stasi, the ubiquitous, all-powerful East German secret police under whose authority she grew

[12] L. Poitras, M. Rosenbach, and H. Stark. "Partner and target: NSA snoops on 500 million German data connections." *Der Spiegel.* June 30, 2013. www.spiegel.de/international/germany/nsa-spies-on-500-million-german-data-connections-a-908648.html

up.[13] After the revelation, President Obama apologized. Senator Feinstein, who had taken such pains to defend bulk collection of Americans' phone records and of PRISM, was quite upset on Merkel's behalf. The Obama White House has said that the United States is not bugging Merkel's personal cell phone, without saying anything about its efforts to surveil millions of other German citizens.[14]

Yet, at the same time, Germany is a huge spying partner for the United States.[15] Despite agreements to the contrary, the German spy agency BND has been broadly monitoring European companies and perhaps individuals at the behest of the NSA. Targets included the European defense company EADS, the helicopter manufacturer Eurocopter, and the interior ministries of European Union member states including Poland, Austria, Denmark, and Croatia.[16] Interestingly, the BND was also spying on the US Department of the Interior and the Vatican, as well as nongovernmental organizations like Care International, Oxfam, and the International Committee of the Red Cross in Geneva. BND gives some subset of this information to the NSA.

Finally, these shifts away from US-based Internet services are a blow to efforts to promote democracy, human rights, and free expression around the world. Certainly, US technology companies have often been complicit with censorship and surveillance by repressive regimes. Yet, foreigners using Internet services based in America is a net plus for democracy abroad. The next billion Internet users will come from countries that have no First Amendment or a Bill of Rights. Many nations don't recognize the right of people to worship, marry, or agitate for political change. Profligate spying and our refusal to recognize foreigners' human rights have played right into these governments' hands. Make no mistake, having US-based

---

[13] I. Traynor and P. Lewis. "Merkel compared NSA to Stasi in heated encounter with Obama." *The Guardian*. December 17, 2013. www.theguardian.com/world/2013/dec/17/merkel-compares-nsa-stasi-obama

[14] D. Jackson. "Obama says NSA not spying on Merkel's cellphone." *USA Today*. October 23, 2013. www.usatoday.com/story/news/nation/2013/10/23/obama-merkel-national-security-agency/3171477/

[15] H. Gude, L. Poitras, and M. Rosenbach. "Mass data: Transfers from Germany aid US surveillance." *Der Spiegel*. August 5, 2013. www.spiegel.de/international/world/german-intelligence-sends-massive-amounts-of-data-to-the-nsa-a-914821.html

[16] "Government and NGOs: Germany spied on friends and Vatican." *Der Spiegel*. November 7, 2015. www.spiegel.de/international/germany/german-bnd-intelligence-spied-on-friends-and-vatican-a-1061588.html; H. Gude, L. Poitras, and M. Rosenbach. "Mass data: Transfers from Germany aid US surveillance." *Spiegel Online*. August 5, 2013. www.spiegel.de/international/world/german-intelligence-sends-massive-amounts-of-data-to- the-nsa-a-914821.html

companies operating globally promotes American values. For example, having Twitter in the United States helped when the US Department of State asked it in 2009 to delay its regularly scheduled maintenance to ensure activists could communicate during the Iranian elections.[17] All else being equal, US-based companies are more likely to build technologies and adopt policies that protect users from being investigated for political activism, religious beliefs, homosexuality, or other exercises of human rights, at least as compared to companies based in China, Russia, or Saudi Arabia.

***

President Obama has chided Americans concerned with government spying, saying, "You can't have 100 percent security and also then have 100 percent privacy." But this rhetoric is shortsighted. In fact, rampant surveillance harms our long-term security. We can't have secret warrantless mass surveillance of Americans or foreigners and also enjoy Internet-fueled economic, democratic, and political empowerment.

Respecting rights globally makes for a more peaceful world and a more influential United States. The US Department of State pushes for Internet access as a democratizing force because it fosters a free press and pro-democracy activism. If using the Internet exposes people to surveillance risks, we undermine those goals. In addition, when the United States takes a stand in favor of human rights, it has greater moral authority on the world stage. Disregarding foreigners' rights here at home undermines US credibility abroad and gives legitimacy to other governments' denial of human rights and suppression of democratic change.

[17] M. Landler and B. Stelter. "Washington taps into a potent new force in diplomacy." *The New York Times*. June 16, 2009. www.nytimes.com/2009/06/17/world/middleeast/17media.html?_r=1&scp=2&sq=Twitter&st=cse

12

US Surveillance Law Before September 11th

The history of surveillance law is a complicated dance between technological advances, revelations of surveillance abuses, changing political values, congressional enactments, and judicial rulings. In the course of this legal history, two things are clear. First, sometimes the Supreme Court of the United States took the lead in establishing new privacy rights and sometimes it was Congress. In both cases however, changes have usually come after surveillance abuses sparked a huge public outcry. Second, the executive branch – the president and the intelligence community agencies – rarely has been a force for surveillance limitations. In the course of this give and take, push and shove, the law has made slow, arduous, stumbling progress toward recognizing stronger privacy interests and more personal freedom.

People often talk about "the right to privacy" as if it were an established legal entitlement. But under US law, privacy is more complicated than that. In the United States, privacy is *sectoral.* That means that legislatures pass statutes that give us some privacy rights against certain actors, for some categories of data, and not for others. So we have rules governing the way that medical providers can use our health information and schools can use our education data, but we do not have generally applicable rules limiting corporations from sharing our online browsing behaviors with advertisers or limiting private parties from taking photographs of us on the public street. We have no generalized "right to privacy" in America.

The Fourth Amendment

The Fourth Amendment to the US Constitution is the fundamental law that protects our privacy against government actors. The purpose of the Fourth Amendment was to abolish indiscriminate exercise of government investigatory power against innocent individuals. It was enacted in response to general warrants and writs of assistance, which were tools that gave British customs officials in pre-Revolutionary America the power to enter private homes and business to search for smuggled or untaxed goods.[1] These legal orders authorized suspicionless fishing expeditions rather than targeted searches based on justifiable suspicion. Colonists hated these devices, calling them instruments of arbitrary power, and offenses to their notions of liberty. The Founding Fathers wanted to outlaw these devices in their new Republic and so they guaranteed in the Fourth Amendment that:

> The right of the people to be secure in their persons, houses, papers, and effects, against unreasonable searches and seizures, shall not be violated, and no Warrants shall issue, but upon probable cause, supported by Oath or affirmation, and particularly describing the place to be searched, and the persons or things to be seized.

This language is the fundamental privacy protection in the US legal system against government actors. The Fourth Amendment is a baseline. However, Congress and state legislatures are free to grant additional privacy protections beyond what the Constitution demands. This is fortunate because the scope of the Fourth Amendment is quite narrow. It only applies to certain kinds of government action. It's fair to say that the history of US surveillance law is the effort of courts to sculpt Fourth Amendment protections as technology and social priorities evolve, and of legislators to fill in the gaps and provide additional safeguards.

One of the first things you'll notice about the Fourth Amendment is that it does not mention the word "privacy." Nor does the word "privacy" appear anywhere in the US Constitution. The Fourth Amendment is not a privacy catch-all. Rather, it is a regulation of certain kinds of intrusive governmental conduct. It does this by requiring that searches be reasonable. It also requires warrants, meaning that a judge approves access to private matters in advance and ensures there is a good reason for that access. Searches may not be arbitrary. Warrants also target and narrow the scope of what may searched. This is important. A warrant requirement is not only a limitation on arbitrary police action, it is also inherently a limit on massive and indiscriminate surveillance.

Lawyers know that the spare and open-ended language of the Fourth Amendment raises more questions than it answers. Who are "the people"? What is "unreasonable"? What government conduct constitutes a "search" or a "seizure"? When is a warrant required? How much evidence constitutes "probable cause"? The question of when the Fourth Amendment

---

[1] Officials could "enter and go into any House, Warehouse, Shop, Cellar, or other Place" to seize goods. Section X, Revenue Act of 1767 (7 Geo. III ch. 46) as cited in M. H. Smith. *The Writs of Assistance.* (University of Berkeley Press, 1978) p. 1.

applies and what it requires is the subject of every court battle in which a defendant invokes these constitutional protections. Our shared notion of privacy as a right has evolved not only through the legislative process but also through hundreds of court decisions interpreting what these sentences mean.

These decisions now structure our rights in the digital age, even when technology has altered the balance between privacy and power. For example, the Supreme Court has decided that foreigners outside the United States are not among "the people" that the Fourth Amendment protects. That formulation has left Americans who communicate with foreigners in other countries without constitutional safeguards. That's because the operating principle appears to be that if the US government is targeting foreigners, or even if it is simply *not* targeting Americans, then the Fourth Amendment doesn't apply, regardless of whether the government thereby obtains information about Americans. For Americans living before the digital age, this loophole in the Fourth Amendment would have been of little consequence. However, with the advent of the Internet and ubiquitous global connectivity, more of us communicate more often and easily with people overseas. Today, all those messages are susceptible to warrantless access by the US government. The impact of the foreigner exclusion rule on American privacy today is greater than it was twelve years ago before social networking.

The Fourth Amendment also applies only to "searches" and "seizures." Government activity that is not a search or seizure is unregulated by the Fourth Amendment. Early judicial interpretation of the amendment defined searches and seizures in terms of interference with property. Specifically, physical trespasses against the four named (and in modern times narrow) categories –"persons, houses, papers, and effects" – were the sum and substance of searches and seizures. If the police took your property, that was a seizure. If the police came into your house or opened your luggage, that was a search. During colonial times, there weren't many situations where investigators could invade your privacy without also physically trespassing on your physical person, house, papers, or property.

But over time, this property-based conception left out a lot of clearly invasive government activity. One major issue was wiretapping. As telephones became widely used, so did recording devices to capture the contents of private conversations. Eavesdropping no longer required entering into someone's home. Early telephone networks carried calls over copper wires. All police needed was physical access to the wire as it ran to the suspects' home or office. Wiretapping was the new eavesdropping, but it happened without a trespass on personal or real property. Did the Fourth Amendment apply?

Federal Surveillance Power

In 1901, anarchists assassinated US President William McKinley. Adherents to this political philosophy had already killed the president of France in 1894, the prime minister of Spain in 1897, the empress of Austria in 1898, and the king of Italy in 1900.[2] In the wake of the assassination, Theodore Roosevelt became president and went to Congress for approval to start a federal law enforcement agency to fight anarchists and other national threats. His proposal was rejected. So Roosevelt secretly started the FBI in 1908 and told Congress about it several months later.

From the beginning, the FBI was focused on ferreting out anarchists and Communists, pitting the agency against labor rights activists in the early 1900s. When World War I started in 1914, the FBI gathered information on citizens opposing US entry into the war and the draft. Hundreds of people were prosecuted during that period under the 1917 Espionage Act and the 1918 Sedition Act for peaceful expression of their opposition to the war.

Around this time, J. Edgar Hoover entered the picture. He became chief of the Justice Department's Radical Division in 1919, when he was twenty-four years old. Two years later, he was second in command at the FBI. In 1924, he was made Acting Director and would go on to head the FBI for the next forty-eight years.

In 1923, after President Warren Harding died, Calvin Coolidge became President and appointed Harlan Fiske Stone as attorney general. The two men were serious about cleaning up the scandals of the Harding era. As part of this, Stone attempted to return the Bureau to its prewar role, directing that its activities be "limited strictly to investigations of violations of the law."[3] But this limitation was short-lived. By the 1930s, President Roosevelt allegedly had given Hoover license to collect domestic intelligence about subversive activities, especially the actions of fascists and communists.

Federal law enforcement was also the FBI's responsibility, and Prohibition was a major endeavor. In 1928, the Supreme Court considered the case of *United States v. Olmstead*. In *Olmstead*, federal agents had listened to the defendant's phone calls to gather evidence against him for

[2] Weiner, *Enemies*, p. 8.
[3] Id., p. 59.

violating Prohibition era laws against liquor sales. The wiretapping violated statutory protections passed by the legislatures of the state Olmstead was in. But no federal statute prohibited the government from using the evidence obtained during the calls to put Olmstead in prison. In other words, even if the wiretapping was illegal under *state* law, officers could still use the calls as evidence against Olmstead in a *federal* prosecution unless they violated baseline Fourth Amendment protections. Only then would the illegally obtained evidence be thrown out of court.

The question before the Supreme Court, then, was whether listening to someone's calls was either a search or a seizure. The Supreme Court's majority said "no." Federal agents had never trespassed on Olmstead's property to conduct their wiretapping. Rather, officers used alligator clips and a recording device to tap wires in the street outside his house. Since they did not trespass on Olmstead's "person, house, papers, or effects," as the Fourth Amendment says, there was no search, and so no search warrant was required. The Supreme Court did not think about the Fourth Amendment as protecting "privacy" or any other intangible right. Rather, it saw the Amendment as protecting tangible property from certain kinds of government interference.

Based on the *Olmstead* case, the FBI and other law enforcement agencies found ways to eavesdrop on phone calls without probable cause for at least the next fifty-nine years. This wasn't popular. As more people started to use telephones, public opinion moved against such spying and more states adopted laws against it. Even Congress tried to stop warrantless wiretapping. The Communications Act of 1934[4] prohibited service providers from intercepting communications and divulging their contents to others. Congress made no exceptions for foreign intelligence gathering or for national security. Three years later, the Supreme Court held that the provision applied to federal agents and said that federal authorities could not use evidence obtained from wiretaps in court.[5]

But the executive branch nevertheless continued the practice of warrantless wiretapping. In 1940, with World War II imminent, President Franklin Delano Roosevelt authorized his attorney general to approve wiretapping for defense of the Nation. Roosevelt understood that the Supreme Court had prohibited introduction of this evidence against criminal defendants in federal courts, but believed that the Justices did not intend to limit his

[4] 47 U.S.C. § 605, 48 Stat. 103.
[5] *Nardone v. United States*, 302 U.S. 379 (1937).

ability to defend the country. His statutory argument was that because the Communications Act talked about interception *and* disclosure, the federal government could wiretap, so long as it didn't *also* disclose the intercepted communications in a court of law. So the DOJ interpreted the statute to mean that the FBI could not use information obtained from unwarranted eavesdropping in court, but were otherwise free to listen in.

Roosevelt also had an expansive notion of the president's national security powers under Article II of the Constitution. In his view, the executive branch has a right to conduct electronic surveillance for national security purposes regardless of what Congress might do to try to regulate it. Nevertheless, in an effort to keep Congress informed, in 1941, the Attorney General went to Congress to explain Roosevelt's decision. With this information in hand, Congress did nothing to amend the Communications Act. This failure to act was considered to be an approval of President Roosevelt's approach to wiretapping. In his book *The Terror Presidency*, Harvard Law Professor Jack Goldsmith explains the wisdom behind the methods that Roosevelt used to assert and expand presidential power:

> Roosevelt was obviously not romantic or naïve about congressional relations. He was a manipulative, often secretive, sometimes deceitful, and very skilled politician. He was motivated to consult and garner consent not only because it was the right thing to do but also because it was good politics, even though it was painful and ran the risk of rejection.

Consultation and consent, Professor Goldsmith argues, "forced other institutions, especially Congress, to accept partial responsibility for the country's important decisions, thereby ensuring that the President had the country's backing when he took steps that involved the country's fate."[6]

In retrospect, however, Congress's unwillingness to counter Roosevelt's assertion of power in wartime eventually enabled the executive branch to expand surveillance to abusive levels. In part, it was a "slippery slope" problem: what begins as a little bit of sensible eavesdropping becomes a lot of abusive spying. Roosevelt's directive authorized the installation of listening devices during wartime but limited the surveillance to noncitizens. When the next Attorney General asked the next President, Harry Truman, to affirm Roosevelt's directive, he failed to inform Truman of these limitations.[7] So the kinds of situations in which the attorneys general approved warrantless eavesdropping expanded and continued to expand.

---

6 Goldsmith, *The Terror Presidency*, p. 204.
7 Kris and Wilson, *National Security Investigations and Prosecutions*, 3:3, p. 95.

This is an example of why secret policies are not reliable limitations on government power, especially when the details are not written down.

The Fourth Amendment imposed the only clear legal limitation on warrantless eavesdropping in that it prohibited breaking into people's houses to install listening equipment. Nevertheless, FBI agents would conduct break-ins – "black bag jobs" – to install microphones and recording devices. A low-level operative would conduct a "black bag job" to install the bug. Then, a higher up in the office would sign an order activating the device. The order did not mention the fact that the device was installed by illegal break-in.[8] So long as the information wasn't used in a court, no one had a reason to ask any questions. To further hide this technique, if investigators found good information, they would develop a legitimate source for the same evidence, and use that in any prosecution. This is called "parallel construction" and is still used today to hide massive intelligence and novel enforcement surveillance.

From the 1940s through the 1970s, federal surveillance expanded. Attorneys general approved spying on American citizens, including Dr. Martin Luther King, Jr., and on journalists, in the name of investigating leaks of government information. Wiretaps could last for years based on a single authorization from the attorney general, and FBI agents often would not go back and check with, or even inform, his successor. Over this same period, the NSA read nearly every telegram sent to or from Americans in the United States, and the CIA opened and photographed international letters.[9]

Courts and Congress, Working Together

Then, starting in the late 1960s, the legal presumptions that explicitly or implicitly enabled warrantless surveillance got struck down. The public's use of telephones – and its expectations of privacy in that use – had changed since *Olmstead*. In 1929, less than 42 percent of Americans had a telephone in the home. But by 1967, the rate had more than doubled to 87 percent. That saturation likely effected the public's perception of what an appropriate limit on government investigations should be.

In the *Katz* case, decided in 1967, investigators placed a listening device on the glass wall of a public phone booth and were able to eavesdrop on the defendant's phone calls. Mr. Katz argued that his Fourth Amendment

---

[8] Weiner, *Enemies*, p. 338.
[9] Kris and Wilson, *National Security Investigations and Prosecutions*, 3:4, pp. 98–99.

rights were violated. But the government asserted that because they did not commit a physical trespass in any way – the phone booth didn't belong to Mr. Katz and even if it did, the listening device was on the outside – there was no search or seizure. The government's argument was in line with the way the Supreme Court had ruled in *Olmstead*.

But now the Supreme Court changed the rule. In *Katz*, the Supreme Court created the "reasonable expectation of privacy" test. If police invade someone's reasonable expectation of privacy, an expectation society thinks is legitimate, then that is a search regulated by the Fourth Amendment. No longer would searches be defined solely by physical trespass. Because people have an expectation that their calls are private, the Justices reasoned, a wiretap is a search. Thus, the Supreme Court reversed its ruling in *Olmstead* and held wiretapping requires a warrant.

The Supreme Court's change of heart was based on ideas contained in Justice Louis Brandeis' dissent almost forty years prior in the *Olmstead* case. In objecting to the outcome of that case, Brandeis had written that the Fourth Amendment was adopted at a time when force and violence – trespasses – were the only means by which a government could interfere with intellectual privacy. But, Brandeis warned in his dissent, those days were over:

> Subtler and more far-reaching means of invading privacy have become available to the Government. Discovery and invention have made it possible for the Government, by means far more effective than stretching upon the rack, to obtain disclosure in court of what is whispered in the closet.[10]

Brandeis anticipated that technology would keep changing, further expanding the reach of government surveillance:

> Ways may someday be developed by which the Government, without removing papers from secret drawers, can reproduce them in court, and by which it will be enabled to expose to a jury the most intimate occurrences of the home. Advances in the psychic and related sciences may bring means of exploring unexpressed beliefs, thoughts and emotions.[11]

To Brandeis, the Fourth Amendment wasn't there just to protect private property. It was there to protect privacy, intimacy, and the freedom of the mind. In its 1967 ruling in *Katz*, the Supreme Court recognized what Brandeis had known forty years earlier. Physical trespass is just one of

---

[10] *Olmstead v. United States*, 277 U.S. 438, 473 (1928).
[11] Id. at 474.

many ways that a government might intrude on fundamental personal and political freedoms.

Nevertheless, *Katz* left some important questions unanswered. In a footnote, the Supreme Court stated that it was not considering the question of whether there was a national security exception to the Fourth Amendment. So the Supreme Court didn't grapple with the question raised by President Roosevelt's wartime wiretapping – does either Congress or the Supreme Court have any say over executive branch exercise of its surveillance powers when used for national security purposes?

After *Katz* and *Berger v. New York*, another 1967 case that struck down New York's wiretapping law as insufficiently protective of constitutional interests, Congress passed the Omnibus Crime Control and Safe Streets Act of 1968 to provide more clarity to investigators about what they needed to do to lawfully wiretap. This legislation included the Wiretap Act, also known as Title III. Title III, in conjunction with traditional Fourth Amendment law, requires investigators to get a warrant based on probable cause that a crime has been committed before eavesdropping or conducting a search or seizure. Because wiretaps are so invasive, it also imposed additional safeguards. Wiretaps could only be used for investigating certain serious crimes and could only be used if other "necessary," less intrusive investigative techniques had been tried and failed. Wiretaps had to be "minimized," meaning that investigators could neither listen to nor record calls that were unrelated to the offense under investigation. Essentially, if Grandma called, then police had to hang up. People intercepted had to be notified at some point after the investigation was over. Evidence illegally obtained could not be used in court. The Department of Justice had to count wiretaps and issue a public report on their usage. And, most fundamentally, the government normally must demonstrate to a court that it has probable cause to believe that the person targeted is involved in criminal activity before it can get a warrant to conduct wiretapping.

Because of all these safeguards, a Title III warrant is sometimes called a "super warrant." Nevertheless, in the years since Title III was enacted, there has been mission creep. For example, today, the list of predicate crimes for which wiretapping is allowed is so expansive that the limitation is essentially meaningless. A surveillance technique developed or justified by national security needs to expand to reach serious crime and then eventually is used in everyday policing.

While Title III provided a methodology for surveillance in criminal cases, it didn't address national security cases. The statute explicitly left

national security outside of its scope. This left only constitutional protections to constrain national security and foreign intelligence investigations.

But what are those constitutional protections? Still unknown was
whether the president enjoyed inherent constitutional power to spy in the
interests of national security or foreign intelligence. Through the 1960s,
this seemingly academic legal question went unanswered. But in secret
and behind the scenes, in the absence of clear doctrine to the contrary,
the executive branch engaged in questionable or improper surveillance.
The FBI wiretapped civil rights groups, journalists, and antiwar activists
based only on Director Hoover's personal beliefs that these individuals or
entities might be controlled by foreign nationals or conspiring against the
Nation.

Eventually, the warrantless wiretapping was so extensive that a case
challenging the practice finally reached the Supreme Court. In 1971,
the Court considered a case involving a plot to bomb a CIA office. The
defendants had asked the trial court to disclose to them all wiretapping
that the government had conducted without a warrant. This discovery
motion was a precursor to challenging the admissibility of incriminating
evidence on the grounds that the FBI should have obtained a warrant to
wiretap their conversations. (This was a constitutional argument under
the Fourth Amendment, and not a statutory argument under the Wiretap
Act, because Title III by its own terms did not apply to a national security
case such as this one.)

In the litigation, the Attorney General submitted an affidavit saying that
he – and not a judge – had authorized the wiretapping. There was no warrant. However, the Attorney General asserted that he was authorized to do
so as a reasonable exercise of power by an agent of the President to protect national security. In other words, the Department of Justice defended
the wiretapping as part of the President's inherent national security power
under Article II of the Constitution. The Department of Justice argued
that the Fourth Amendment didn't apply at all to this national security
surveillance and, even if the Fourth Amendment did apply, national security cases deserved a special rule. If national security was at stake, the government should not need to get a search warrant or have probable cause
as in law enforcement investigations. Instead, the Department of Justice
argued that the Fourth Amendment was satisfied so long as the search was
reasonable overall.

The Supreme Court disagreed with the DOJ on all counts. The case is
United States v. United States District Court, commonly called the *Keith*

case after the presiding judge. In *Keith*, the Supreme Court said that investigations of domestic threats to national security could not be conducted in the sole discretion of the executive branch and its intelligence agencies. Inter-branch approval was constitutionally required. A judge needed to review for probable cause and issue a warrant. The Justices concluded that the Fourth Amendment applied to government surveillance of domestic groups, *even when national security was at stake.*

Still, the *Keith* decision left two important questions unanswered. First, the opinion raised the question of whether "probable cause" means something different for domestic security investigations, because they involve different policy and practical considerations. Today, there is still no definitive answer to that question. The second open question was whether the executive branch needs to get a warrant when it is conducting *foreign* intelligence searches or seizures. In *Keith*, the Supreme Court suggested but didn't decide whether foreign intelligence surveillance might be different enough that the Constitution would not require a warrant. As we'll see, both the lower federal courts and Congress have worked to answer this second question but have not definitively answered it.

In the years following *Keith*, scandalous revelations of domestic spying by federal intelligence agencies in the name of national security and foreign intelligence came to light. Burglars tied to President Richard M. Nixon's reelection campaign were arrested for breaking into the Democratic National Committee headquarters at the Watergate office complex in Washington, D.C. Based on documents stolen from the FBI's Media, PA office, in 1973 reporters exposed the COINTELPRO program, domestic spying aimed at peace and civil liberties groups. Reporting by Seymour Hersh revealed that the CIA was spying on thousands of American citizens. These revelations led to the formation of congressional committees to investigate and report on surveillance abuses, The Church Committee was the popular name for the United States Senate Select Committee to Study Governmental Operations with Respect to Intelligence Activities, a US Senate committee chaired by Senator Frank Church in 1975. The House of Representatives corollary was the Pike Committee, or United States House Permanent Select Committee on Intelligence chaired by Democratic Representative Otis G. Pike of New York. In 1975, these committees investigated illegal intelligence gathering by the NSA, the CIA, and the FBI.

The congressional and journalistic investigations revealed the vast, disturbing scope of domestic surveillance. President Nixon spied on his political enemies. The FBI spied on and threatened Dr. Martin Luther King,

Jr., along with tens of thousands of other peaceful people. The FBI had developed over 500,000 domestic intelligence files.[12] People were targeted for their political beliefs, and not because they were violent, dangerous, or controlled by hostile foreign governments.

These revelations impelled Congress to constrain American spies. The Church Committee had recommended that Congress pass a law limiting the FBI's authority, much as Attorney General Harlan Fiske Stone had tried to do in the 1920s. Congress ultimately did not pass the legislation recommended by the Church Committee, seemingly relying on a voluntary initiative by President Ford's Attorney General Edward Levi. Levi issued the first set of Attorney General's Guidelines, known as the Levi Guidelines, to govern the FBI's domestic intelligence activities. Like the Stone initiative, the Levi Guidelines included meaningful limits on the FBI's intelligence gathering capabilities. Like the Stone initiative, eventually the Levi Guidelines were discarded – repeatedly watered down over time until what was left was a much broader surveillance mandate enabling the FBI to gather information far afield from evidence of criminal wrongdoing.[13] In 1995, Attorney General Janet Reno amended the existing guidelines in the aftermath of the Oklahoma City bombing, allowing the FBI to investigate domestic groups that advocate violence, so long as those groups had the ability to carry out illegal violent acts. In 2001, after the September 11th attacks, Attorney General John Ashcroft changed the "central mission" of the FBI from investigating federal crimes to "preventing the commission of terrorist acts against the United States and its people" and issued classified guidelines expanding the FBI's ability to spy on domestic groups that might pose a threat to national security. In 2008, Attorney General Michael Mukasey again expanded what the FBI could do under internal guidelines, giving the agency more discretion to investigate US individuals and groups while also limiting oversight requirements.[14]

Stone and Levi were rare examples of the executive branch willingly limiting its surveillance authority. In both cases, the steps were taken in response to public outrage about government conduct – the scandals of the Harding Administration and COINTELPRO, respectively. But they were careful to do so in ways that would not need congressional approval to change. Over time, the executive branch expanded its power, often, but

---

[12] M. Halperin et al. *The Lawless State: The Crimes of the U.S. Intelligence Agencies.* (New York: Penguin Books, 1977) p. 3.

[13] E. Berman. "Domestic Intelligence: New Powers, New Risk." *Brennan Center for Justice.* New York University School of Law, 2011, pp. 13–15.

[14] Id., p. 21.

not always, in response to perceived national threats like terrorist attacks and war. At the same time, attorneys general under both Democratic and Republican Presidents have taken steps to limit oversight by doing away with supervisory approval and reporting requirements, and even classifying the procedures themselves.

This history mandates skepticism of American spies' claims that improvements to intelligence minimization rules ever will suffice to protect civil liberties interests. Voluntary internal rules are disregarded, repeatedly watered down, and ultimately unenforceable.

Congress finally took decisive action in 1978, passing the Foreign Intelligence Surveillance Act (FISA). FISA is the principal foreign intelligence collection law today and the only significant legislation to result from the Watergate-era revelations of the FBI's, the CIA's, and the NSA's illegal surveillance and other abuses.

FISA addressed a question left open by *Keith* – whether to treat national security investigations differently from law enforcement ones – by setting up a different standard of probable cause for *some* domestic intelligence investigations. FISA is an extraordinarily complex statute. In short, it defines four kinds of foreign intelligence information collection as "electronic surveillance" or ELSUR. The categories are complicated.[15] They generally involve some investigative activity connected either to US persons or to US territory, where the target has a reasonable expectation of privacy, and for which the government would normally need a search warrant.

---

[15] Just to illustrate how complicated surveillance law can be, for many years the rules for pen register collection – gathering dialing, routing, signaling, or addressing information – were different depending on whether it was a criminal investigation or a foreign intelligence one – with traditionally more liberal foreign intelligence collection actually imposing more strict limitations. That's because while the Supreme Court found no constitutional protection for phone numbers under the Fourth Amendment, there was nevertheless statutory protection for phone numbers dialed in FISA. FISA defines "wire communications" differently than the Wiretap Act does. FISA's definition of "wire communications" includes information that reveals the identity of the people communicating. Dialed phone numbers do this. And, if the collection takes place in the United States and involves a US person, then under traditional FISA it was regulated electronic surveillance, even if there is no reasonable expectation of privacy in the information. So, while law enforcement officers didn't need to have probable cause to find out who Americans were calling, for the first twenty years of FISA, foreign intelligence agencies were nevertheless required to obtain a warrant with a showing of probable cause to believe that the target was an agent of a foreign power. This is just one of many strange outcomes resulting from the interplay between complicated and developing constitutional and statutory law. It explains why in this book, and so much other writing about surveillance law, the authors rely so heavily on hedge words like "generally."

The agents can get a warrant if they have probable cause showing that the target of the surveillance is an agent of a foreign power, regardless of whether the activity engaged in is a crime. FISA's scheme maintains judicial supervision of electronic surveillance, while allowing more freedom to gather intelligence. Judicial supervision is critical because involving and empowering another branch of government is one of the only tools we have to ensure that the exercise of power doesn't get out of control – the checks and balances that we learn about as school children.

FISA also introduced the "agent of a foreign power" test. Foreign powers include other governments as well as international terrorist groups. For Americans to be agents of a foreign power, we have to be engaged in clandestine intelligence gathering activities, sabotage, or international terrorism, or entering the country under a false or fraudulent identity. There is a broader definition of "agent" for foreign citizens as compared to US persons. Foreigners can be spied upon also for lawful, nonfraudulent activity so long as they are acting as agents of foreign powers. FISA does not apply to surveillance that takes place outside the United States and which targets foreigners.

In the FISA Amendments Act of 2008, Congress added provision to FISA that put some procedures in place when analysts target Americans located overseas. Congress also added section 702, allowing surveillance from US soil targeting foreigners overseas even if they are not agents of foreign powers.

In sum, surveillance of noncitizens outside the United States is unregulated by the Fourth Amendment or by Congress. Foreign intelligence surveillance originating from inside the United States – for example gathering data from domestic telephone interchanges – or targeting US persons generally requires some kind of FISA process, typically either probable cause that the target is an agent of a foreign power or a section 702 certification. Under the original version of FISA, investigative activity that was not "primarily" for foreign intelligence gathering but for criminal law enforcement had to proceed under criminal procedures. (Today, after the USA PATRIOT Act, the intelligence purpose need only be significant, and the law enforcement interest could be primary.) Otherwise, searches, seizures, and eavesdropping required a traditional warrant or wiretap order under Federal Rule of Criminal Procedure 41, the Fourth Amendment, and the Wiretap Act.

Today, there are other rules enabling both intelligence gathering and criminal investigations including section 215, the pen register and trap and trace statutes, and "national security letters" that may be issued by FBI agents without judicial review. But in 1978, the upshot of Congress having passed FISA was that if you didn't have some evidence that Dr. King is an agent of the Soviet Union, and you didn't have some evidence that Dr. King is breaking the law, then you couldn't wiretap Dr. King.

***

Why did legislation about foreign intelligence surveillance evolve so much more slowly than the law regulating criminal investigations? One answer might be political. American voters didn't see foreign intelligence as impacting their civil liberties, while it was clear that police conduct could do so. Without public investment in the issue, legislators saw no need to do anything. Lawmakers do not feel an urgent need to spend time worrying about the civil liberties of nonvoting foreigners and domestic terrorists. Perhaps Americans also feared communism and supported surveillance of adherents of an unpopular political viewpoint. It wasn't until the public was confronted with the evidence that the government was using national security and foreign intelligence justifications to spy on law abiding people that the courts and Congress got involved.

The delay was also a response to legal complexity. As the Supreme Court recognized, there may be different considerations in conducting domestic intelligence investigations than criminal ones. But what are they, and does it matter? Second, the Supreme Court suggested that there might not be a constitutional warrant requirement at all for foreign intelligence surveillance. This remains unresolved today. If there is no warrant requirement, what standard should Congress set? Finally, regulating in the national security and foreign affairs space implicates complicated constitutional questions about what branch – Congress or the president – has the authority to act. The Constitution divides foreign policy powers between the president and Congress but not in a definitive or exclusive manner. The Constitution is "cryptic and ambiguous" in its allocation between Congress and the Executive of powers affecting foreign policy.[16] So there has long been tension about what each branch can do, or stop the other from doing. This tension exploded during the Bush Administration, when Vice President Cheney and others asserted that, even where Congress has explicitly set rules, the president is free to ignore those rules if they would infringe on his power to conduct wartime activities or foreign affairs.

[16] A. Schlesinger Jr. "Congress and the making of American foreign policy." *Foreign Affairs*, October 1972. www.foreignaffairs.com/articles/united-states/1972-10-01/congress-and-making-american-foreign-policy

Data in the Hands of Others

Over time, new communications technologies and new law enforcement techniques continued to raise interesting challenges for Congress and the courts. The challenge is to protect people from overzealous government agents while allowing reasonable investigations to take place. Consider, for example, the question of what it takes for the government to collect the phone numbers someone dials from the telephone company. Arriving at an answer is a complicated dance between constitutional theory, statutory law, and technical realities.

In the years following the 1967 *Katz* ruling, police officers and FBI agents were not sure whether the Fourth Amendment protects phone numbers dialed. The Wiretap Act protects "wire communications," defined as communications you could hear, and so its warrant procedures do not extend to phone numbers dialed. But the Fourth Amendment might have independently imposed a warrant requirement. If not, the only obstacle to obtaining phone records would be an officer's and a phone company's natural disinclination to waste their time with fishing expeditions.

During this era, officers would ask telephone companies to voluntarily disclose the information, and take the risk that the data would be excluded from evidence. Phone companies would sometimes comply. Even if the government was violating the Fourth Amendment, there was no clear legal risk or penalty to the phone companies.

But some telephone companies would balk at assisting the government. These companies presumed that "pen registers" – devices that collect phone numbers dialed from phone company networks – were governed by the Fourth Amendment. They also expressed concern about potential liability under federal privacy statutes and state laws. They did not want to be compelled to spend too much time, too much money, or change too much about their network architectures to assist the government. Courts struggled with what they could or could not order phone companies to do in the absence of clear guidance from Congress regarding their ability to command the assistance of law-abiding third parties not before the court.[17]

Then, in 1979, the Supreme Court got the chance to consider the Fourth Amendment question. In *Smith v. Maryland,* local police suspected Mr. Smith of stalking a woman by calling her repeatedly. So they went to

---

[17] See R. B. Parish. "Circumventing Title Three – The Use of Pen Register Surveillance in Law Enforcement." *Duke Law Journal.* (1977): 751–774.

the telephone company to find out what numbers Smith was dialing. They did not get a warrant or a court order. Sure enough, the victim's phone numbers were there in Smith's dialing history. Smith argued that the information was private, protected by the Fourth Amendment. If he was right, the police should have gotten a search warrant before obtaining his phone calling information from the telephone company. Their failure to do so would mean that the prosecution would have been prohibited from using the information in the case against Smith. If not, however, then the evidence was admissible and Smith was going to prison.

The Supreme Court held that Smith had no "reasonable expectation of privacy" in the phone numbers he was dialing, so they weren't protected by the Fourth Amendment. To arrive at that conclusion, the Supreme Court harkened back to the days when callers would talk to a live operator and place calls by asking for Mayfield-555, meaning information was knowingly and voluntarily disclosed to the phone company. Because the numbers aren't private, when police ask for them from the phone company, the request does not constitute a Fourth Amendment search.

The Supreme Court also reasoned that phone numbers dialed were the business records of the phone company and did not belong to the customer. Here, the Supreme Court was relying on the reasoning of a 1976 case, *United States v. Miller*. In *Miller*, police had obtained a suspect's bank records. The defendant challenged the investigation, arguing that he had an expectation of privacy in his banking records, and so the government shouldn't have obtained them without a search warrant. But the Supreme Court held that the records belonged to the bank, *not* the customer, so Miller had no expectation of privacy in them. Similarly, in *Smith*, the Supreme Court pointed out that the phone company was generating and storing calling records for its own billing purposes. So again, the customer had no protected expectation of privacy in the call data.

This reasoning, however, has proven over time to be a dangerous slippery slope. The Department of Justice came to argue that *Smith* and *Miller*, together apply well beyond phone numbers and bank records – effectively creating a loophole in Fourth Amendment protection of Internet communications. The DOJ believes that if your information is exposed to *any* third party, then you do not have an expectation of privacy in it and the government can get it without a warrant. In other words, if it isn't secret, then it isn't private, and if it isn't private, then the Fourth Amendment doesn't apply. This notion has come to be known as the "third party doctrine."

The third party doctrine today works to create a huge uncertainty in constitutional protection for digital communications. The 1980s saw the beginning of the Internet and centralized data processing services. Given *Smith, Miller,* and the third party doctrine, the growing tech world was unclear how the Fourth Amendment might apply to personal and private digital data, especially when stored on remote computers. After all, email companies or remote storage providers are technically capable of accessing your data, meaning that under the DOJ's reasoning, you lost any expectation of privacy in it.

To help answer this question, Congress passed the Electronic Communications Privacy Act of 1986 (ECPA). Congress intended ECPA to protect citizen privacy in digital communications. To this end, Congress updated Title III to prohibit government agents not only from wiretapping phone calls (wire communications) and installing bugs (oral communications) but also from intercepting digital messages – "electronic communications." It then added another provision, the Stored Communications Act (SCA), which prohibited access to the content of messages stored with service providers, to customer records, and to transactional data without proper legal process.

ECPA's Pen Register/Trap and Trace statute enables law enforcement acquisition of transactional data like phone numbers dialed with less of an evidentiary showing that a search warrant would require, as permitted by *Smith v. Maryland.* If the attorney for the Government has certified to the court that the information likely to be obtained by such installation and use is relevant to an ongoing criminal investigation, the court must issue the order.

The statute also sought to resolve the problem of whether courts could force companies to help the government spy. The "provider assistance" provision of the statute requires companies to assist as "necessary to accomplish the installation of the pen register unobtrusively and with a minimum of interference with the services."[18] [In 1998, Congress amended FISA to allow the government to obtain foreign intelligence pen/trap orders under a similar set of standards.[19] Then in 2001, the USA PATRIOT Act amended both pen/trap statutes to indicate that they should also apply to Internet routing information and not just calling records.]

ECPA also attempted to answer the question of whether email and other remotely stored content is protected by the Fourth Amendment or falls outside of it due to the third party doctrine. Under ECPA, access to stored email and other content requires a warrant only if the information is less

---

[18] 18 U.S.C. § 3124(a)(b).
[19] Kris and Wilson, *National Security Investigations and Prosecutions,* § 4:2.

than 180 days old. That's because at the time of ECPA, Congress thought that information you stored with a third party for more than six months was likely unimportant, or even abandoned. At 181 days, government can obtain emails with an intermediary showing of "specific and articulable facts," which is less than probable cause.

Eventually, targets of investigations raised the question of whether ECPA provisions allowing warrantless access to transactional data and to email content comply with the Fourth Amendment. Based on the third party doctrine, the DOJ has argued that it can seize your web browsing records and your email without getting a search warrant. Today, neither of these issues is completely settled. The DOJ has generally succeeded in arguing that you have no expectation of privacy in web browsing and other transactional electronic data. But some federal courts have held that while obtaining Mr. Smith's phone records does not implicate the Fourth Amendment, acquiring *everyone's* phone records in the section 215 dragnet does. Similarly, some judges have held that obtaining cellular telephone transactional data that reveals your location inside your home or office requires a search warrant. The DOJ has so far failed to convince courts that people have no reasonable expectation of privacy in cloud stored email content. But only one federal appellate court has ruled directly on the issue and the matter is technically still up-in-the-air outside of that judicial Circuit.

The "expectation of privacy" test not only is fundamental for Fourth Amendment protection but also for privacy-protecting rules set forth under FISA. In general, FISA's ELSUR definition depends on there being an expectation of privacy for which a warrant would be required. Without an expectation of privacy, the information gathering will not be ELSUR and thus unregulated by FISA. That enables government agents to warrantlessly collect, sometimes in bulk, phone records, library lending data, hotel stays, travel plans, and financial records, all without any reason to believe that criminal activity is afoot.

In sum, there is much uncertainty in surveillance law. Does the Fourth Amendment protect data stored on the Internet? Is massive spying constitutionally different from the collection of one person's data? How do FISA and ECPA apply to information for which the expectation of privacy is not legally settled given the third party doctrine? If the Fourth Amendment doesn't apply to foreigners abroad what does that mean for foreigners living in the United States and for the Americans that talk with them? Today we live under a confusing, convoluted, and technologically outdated legal regime that has left American privacy with uncertain legal protection. The uncertainty is exacerbated by the fact that so much surveillance – both law enforcement and intelligence – is secretly authorized via sealed and *ex parte* court proceedings.

As memory of the horrors of the J. Edgar Hoover era faded, American spies increasingly took advantage of these legal uncertainties in favor of greater surveillance. Intelligence and law enforcement agency heads are graded on whether they've provided valuable insight into foreign affairs, stopped terrorist attacks, thwarted criminal plots, or arrested perpetrators. So the incentives to collect more information are strong. Over time, limitations adopted after the Watergate-era were watered down or abandoned at the same time that technological advances strengthened investigators' capabilities and incentivized private collection of data, which could then be funneled to the government. But after the attacks of September 11th, Congress and American spies threw lingering concerns about human rights and privacy out the window.

13

American Spies After September 11th:
Illegality and Legalism

One response to critiques of modern surveillance has been to argue that American spies are acting lawfully, so public outrage is misplaced. While some important and controversial surveillance developments took place in public, many more important decisions were made by the president and intelligence officials in secret.[1] Modern surveillance in the United States was birthed illegally. Legal justifications came after-the-fact. Sometimes a federal judge issued a deeply flawed, secret reinterpretation of law in order to give a stamp of approval, but not always. Even when the intelligence community was able to paint a veneer of legitimacy on its massive spying techniques, that mask appears quite shabby in the light of day. The secrecy didn't just make it impossible for citizens to know whether the government needed the new powers it was requesting. It impeded Congress in exercising its responsibility to make laws and oversee intelligence officials. It also greatly increased the likelihood of abuse.

American spies have tried to counter public outcry about modern surveillance under a blanket of legalities, invoking convoluted executive branch policies, after-the-fact statutory enactments, and aging court rulings. But the upshot is that Congress and the public did not know and did not approve of what is going on.

STELLARWIND

After the attacks of September 11th, the Nation watched as Congress passed controversial expansions of government investigatory powers in the USA PATRIOT Act. Meanwhile, behind closed doors, the Bush

---

[1] C. Savage. "N.S.A timeline of surveillance law developments." *The New York Times*. March 11, 2014. www.nytimes.com/interactive/2014/03/12/us/nsa-timeline.html; C. Savage and L. Poitras. "How a court secretly evolved, extending U.S. spies' reach." *The New York Times*. March 11, 2014. www.nytimes.com/2014/03/12/us/how-a-courts-secret-evolution-extended-spies-reach.html

Administration was launching surveillance programs well beyond existing law and what Congress was in the process of authorizing.

The Bush Administration initiated illegal spying practices code named STELLARWIND. STELLARWIND included wiretapping Americans' international calls, dragnet collection of phone call and Internet metadata, and acquisition of financial transaction data. The warrantless wiretapping of Americans' calls with people overseas violated the Wiretap Act and FISA. Phone and Internet dragnets transgressed the pen register/trap and trace statutes and the new Patriot Act section 215, as well as the NSA's preclusion from domestic spying. Congress never voted for or approved STELLARWIND.

Part of the impetus for STELLARWIND was the (unfounded) belief that massive surveillance would give intelligence agencies a better chance of stopping the next September 11th. But if this were true, why didn't the Bush White House go to Congress and ask it to pass new laws to give spies this ability? One reason is that they may have been afraid Congress would say no. Better to ask for forgiveness than for permission. Another reason might be that the Bush Administration did ask, but failed. In 2003, the Bush Administration offered another surveillance law revision dubbed Patriot Act II, which included dangerous and unacceptable proposals for things like classifying the identity of American citizens detained in terrorism prosecutions – "disappearing" people. Patriot Act II also included proposals to expand government wiretapping and subpoena power, as well as information sharing between intelligence and law enforcement.[2] Civil libertarians may have felt relief when Congress refused to enact these proposals into law. But these proposals were actually signs of what the government was already secretly doing.

More recently, some Big Surveillance advocates have said that if the intelligence community had asked Congress to pass certain surveillance laws, the terrorists would be better informed about American spies' methodologies and be better prepared to evade them. But this argument proves too much. On this theory, all details of government investigatory capabilities should be kept secret without oversight or public debate. If we can't be an honest democracy, then the terrorists have already won. America can fight and has fought terrorism in the past without secret spying laws. But more fundamentally, the kind of surveillance that STELLARWIND entailed wasn't something terrorists could readily escape: Authority to

---

[2] See Domestic Security Enhancement Act of 2003, Draft, January 9, 2003. w2.eff.org/Privacy/Surveillance/Terrorism/patriot2draft.html

collect **all** domestic and international phone records, all Internet records, all financial transactions. The only way to avoid it would be not to use the phone, the Internet, or the banks. These evasions would seriously hinder nefarious plotters. Given the difficulty of identifying meaningful information in the noise of data we collect, driving would-be terrorists to inefficient means of communications may well be a feature, and not a bug.

There may have been an ideological reason as well. Vice President Dick Cheney and his aide David Addington had an ideological mission. They wanted to expand the power of the executive branch. They believed that in the name of national security, the President could do anything he wanted, regardless of what Congress said. In their national security policy making, whether approving massive surveillance, torture, kidnappings, or other controversial measures, they pushed the Executive Power argument to the limit. The Administration's justification was that, because the nation was at war with al-Qaeda following the attacks of September 11th, the President as Commander-in-Chief had complete authority to conduct any kind of surveillance he saw fit in furtherance of the military effort.

Whatever the reason, Congress was left out, as were important officials. People were informed about STELLARWIND only on a need-to-know basis. Attorney General John Ashcroft, the highest law enforcement officer in the land and the chief of the department responsible for federal interpretations of laws, only learned about domestic warrantless wiretapping, bulk collection, and other aspects of STELLARWIND after Bush had already okayed it and the spying had begun.[3] Attorney General Ashcroft conducted no legal research to verify the President's conclusion that the domestic dragnets were acceptable. The President had "just shoved [the order] in front of me and told me to sign it."[4] Ashcroft didn't rock the boat, and he didn't delay to do any research on the legality of this expansive and novel order. He just signed it.[5]

At the same time, it was too risky not to develop a certain amount of legal cover for the spying. Not everyone in the executive branch agreed with Cheney and Addington. Even some who favored a strong national security posture and powerful President did not necessarily agree with their categorical approach. Further, surveillance cannot be conducted

---

[3] "Unclassified Report on the President's Surveillance Program." Inspectors General of the DoD, DoJ, CIA, NSA, and ODNI. July 10, 2009, p. 11. fas.org/irp/eprint/psp.pdf

[4] E. Lichtblau. "Debate and protest at spy program's inception." *The New York Times*. March 30, 2008. www.nytimes.com/2008/03/30/washington/30nsa.html

[5] K. Eichenwald. *500 Days: Secrets and Lies in the Terror Wars*. (New York, NY: Simon & Schuster, 2012) p. 106.

efficiently alone. The intelligence agencies needed cooperation from communications companies like AT&T. Getting that cooperation sometimes required convincing the companies that they weren't going to be sued later by their customers for going along with the government's demands.

Eventually, the Department of Justice's Office of Legal Counsel (OLC) performed a legal analysis of STELLARWIND. OLC is responsible for providing legal advice to the executive branch on all constitutional questions, and for assessing complicated and important legal questions, especially where there are likely to be interagency or inter-branch disagreements.

Many people don't realize how powerful the OLC is, and thus how careful it should be in crafting its advice. The OLC is particularly powerful because its opinions have the practical effect of immunizing government officials from criminal and civil liability. Only officials who are "plainly incompetent or who knowingly violate the law" are liable.[6] Relying in good faith on an OLC opinion is something close to a "get out of jail free" card.[7] If the OLC is wrong, even if it only paid lip service to the law, the OLC opinion will protect officials from future prosecution.

Cheney and Addington knew this. The pair hand-picked a junior OLC attorney to write opinions justifying massive surveillance as well as other controversial government escapades in the name of national security. The lawyer's name was John Yoo. Today, Yoo is a professor at the University of California Berkeley School of Law.

The White House knew Yoo, knew his political beliefs, and knew he would write the kind of opinion they wanted. With that opinion in hand, the Bush Administration could comfort officials afraid they were being asked to break the law. It is unclear how much Attorney General Ashcroft, purportedly Yoo's boss, knew about the sloppy and ideologically driven memos Yoo was drafting.[8] Instead, Yoo seemed to answer directly to the White House. Nor was anyone at the NSA allowed to see the STELLARWIND opinion he wrote. The memo was classified along with other OLC memos approving kidnapping, detention, torture, and later, under the Obama Administration, drone strikes on alleged terrorists.[9]

---

[6] *Malley v. Briggs*, 475 U.S. 335, 341 (1986).
[7] D. L. Pines. "Are Even Torturers Immune from Suit?: How Attorney General Opinions Shield Government Employees from Civil Litigation and Criminal Prosecution." *Wake Forest Law Review* 43 (2008): 122–131.
[8] "Unclassified Report on the President's Surveillance Program." Inspectors General of the DoD, DoJ, CIA, NSA, and ODNI. July 10, 2009, p. 14. fas.org/irp/eprint/psp.pdf
[9] D. Nguyen and C. Weaver. "The missing memos." *ProPublica*. April 16, 2009. www.propublica.org/special/missing-memos

With the approval of junior attorney Yoo in hand, the White House then went to the lawyers at the NSA. The NSA is a foreign intelligence agency. It was supposed to be baked into the agency's DNA that you do not spy on Americans. But Cheney and Addington assured the NSA lawyers that there was a legal basis for the domestic dragnets approved by the OLC. Apparently, no one wanted to disagree with the White House. So, rather than do their own legal analysis, the NSA attorneys decided to accept the White House's assurance on faith and go along. STELLARWIND was up and running. The NSA legal counsel was not even allowed to see the OLC memo. Addington just read the parts he thought were relevant over the phone to the NSA lawyers.[10] Over the next several months, more people were informed about STELLARWIND, but the information was kept close. People who were "read in" to the program – informed – were legally obligated to keep the matter secret. This strict obligation also limited people who were "read in" from talking and debating among themselves the legality, legitimacy, or usefulness of the program.

Playing Fast and Loose with the Patriot Act

Not all of the Bush Administration surveillance efforts took place in secret. After September 11th, President Bush went to Congress to ask for expansion of the FBI's surveillance powers. These efforts culminated in passage of the USA PATRIOT Act in October of 2001, within weeks of the September 11th attacks. But with the Patriot Act in hand, the Bush Administration was able to garner legal cover for spying well beyond what Congress debated and approved. They did this via internal OLC interpretation of Patriot Act provisions, and by going to the FISC for its stamp of approval.

In May 2002 however, the FISC rejected the government's request to dismantle a "wall" believed to limit how criminal prosecutors and intelligence investigators could work together. Recall from Chapter 5 that this wall was premised on FISA language that said that the primary purpose of FISA surveillance had to be the collection of foreign intelligence and not criminal evidence. The "wall" was initially meant to ensure that criminal authorities did not circumvent the warrant requirement by colluding with intelligence operatives who had access to private data through the less rigorous FISA surveillance standards. In time, the Department of Justice

---

[10] R. Lizza. "State of deception." *The New Yorker Magazine*. December 16, 2013. www.newyorker.com/magazine/2013/12/16/state-of-deception

reinterpreted the "wall" as preventing intelligence agents from consulting with criminal investigators at all.

After September 11th, some intelligence experts argued that adhering to that norm had interfered with government officials sharing valuable information about Zacarias Moussaoui, the "20th hijacker" who was arrested by the FBI in August of 2001. Moussaoui drew official attention for his interest in learning how to fly the relatively advanced Boeing 747 commercial jet, despite his lack of familiarity with the smaller planes that hobbyists generally aim to rent and command. His behavior was suspicious and he held jihadist beliefs. He was also in the country illegally, having overstayed his visa as a French citizen. The FBI wanted to search Moussaoui's laptop, but did not believe they had probable cause that he was involved in criminal activity. They then considered obtaining a FISA warrant, but that would have required probable cause that he was acting as an agent of a foreign power. The failures to search Moussaoui's property and to fully share information about his activities with the Federal Aviation Administration and with other intelligence agencies have been blamed for contributing to our failure to learn about and stop the September 11th attacks.[11]

In response to this perceived failure, the Bush Administration sought to tear down the wall, altering the relationship between intelligence agencies and law enforcement. The view was that the two should work together more and share information more freely. The Department of Justice looked first to the Patriot Act. The Patriot Act had changed FISA to allow the powerful intelligence authorities to be used so long as a *significant* purpose, instead of *the* purpose, of the surveillance was to gather foreign intelligence (including but not limited to counterterrorism).[12] It also explicitly authorized law enforcement investigators to share foreign intelligence information they gathered with intelligence analysts,[13] a less controversial provision since the FBI presumably would be following the more stringent rules that apply in criminal investigations.

With these Patriot Act amendments in hand, the Bush lawyers went to the surveillance court. A FISC judge rejected the argument and upheld the wall between regulated law enforcement surveillance and less-limited intelligence spying. Then, in the first-ever appeal from a FISC judge decision to the Foreign Intelligence Surveillance Court of Review, or FISCR, that FISC judge's opinion was overturned. In Fall of 2002, the FISCR said that

[11] *9/11 Commission Report*, pp. 273–276.
[12] USA PATRIOT Act, Pub. L. No. 107–56, § 217, 115 Stat. 272 (2001) amending 50 U.S.C. § 1804(a)(7)(B) and 50 U.S.C. § 1823(a)(7)(B).
[13] USA PATRIOT Act, Pub. L. No. 107–56, § 203, 115 Stat. 272 (2001).

the original formulation of the wall, especially after the USA PATRIOT Act amendments, meant that intelligence and law enforcement officials could work together to determine surveillance targets.

Did the FISCR understand that by tearing down the wall, it wasn't allowing criminal surveillance to go forward with FISA warrants but rather with no warrants at all? After all, the FISCR opinion contemplates surveillance within the confines of FISA. But did the FISCR know about the warrantless surveillance under STELLARWIND? While the Chief of the FISC, who signed the order to maintain the wall, knew about STELLARWIND, it does not appear that any of the three judges sitting on the FISCR and who overturned the wall had been informed about the STELLARWIND program.[14] Context matters. Without any knowledge of STELLARWIND, these judges would likely think that they were approving a situation where criminal investigators would help identify people to spy on who were also agents of foreign powers. If the FISCR had known that intelligence authorities were engaged in massive collection of Americans' calls and emails with foreigners, it might have opposed allowing intelligence and law enforcement to collaborate since that would mean that the FBI could take advantage of the fact that Americans were subject to massive, warrantless intelligence surveillance. Did the FISCR know that the Bush Administration meant to allow intelligence agencies to give criminal investigators private information obtained from warrantless surveillance to use to identify and prosecute Americans? We just don't know.

While the "wall" decisions were public, there were other Bush Administration petitions before the FISC that were not. In July 2002, a FISC judge issued a "Raw Take" sharing order. This order allowed the FBI to share raw data containing the names of Americans with the CIA and the NSA. Previously, the FBI had to obscure nonrelevant names of Americans in FISA wiretaps to protect citizens from intelligence spies,[15] a process called minimization. But after 2002, the FBI no longer had to mask Americans' identities before sharing intelligence data. (Slippery slope alert: Over time, the FISC expanded the Raw Take order, allowing the three

---

[14] From the IG's report on who had been briefed. Over 500 people knew. The report specifically mentions Judge Lamberth's replacement, Judge Kollar-Kotelly, but no other federal judges. See "NSA Inspector General report on the President's Surveillance Program." Office of the Inspector General. March 24, 2009, p. 24 and "Unclassified Report on the President's Surveillance Program." Inspectors General of the DoD, DoJ, CIA, NSA, and ODNI. July 10, 2009, p. 27.

[15] C. Savage. *Power Wars: Inside Obama's Post-9/11 Presidency.* (New York, NY: Little, Brown and Company, 2015) p. 189.

agencies to share unminimized data about Americans obtained through other legal surveillance tools as well.) Without rigorous minimization,[16] FBI criminal investigators can get floods of information about Americans that would otherwise have been off limits without a search warrant. What did the combination of the fall of the "wall" and the Raw Take order mean for criminal authorities' general obligation under the Fourth Amendment and the Wiretap Act to use warrants? Did they just have a legal end run around that obligation, and how often did they take advantage of this legal end run around those obligations? Again, we don't know. But by tearing down barriers to data exchanges about Americans, the FISC enables both robust investigations of Americans without search warrants and the use of intelligence tradecraft techniques on citizens.

Domestic Dragnets

At least with the "wall," one could argue that Congress intended to enable more information sharing. But there is nothing in the Patriot Act that suggests Congress meant to initiate dragnet domestic spying. Congress never authorized it. The dragnets were initiated by the Bush Administration illegally and in secret, and later papered over with a spurious, nearly shameful, legal argument concocted to protect officials after the program was well underway.[17]

Since at least 1996, phone call records have had federal privacy protections. The Communications Act prohibits companies from voluntarily giving them to the government without legal process. Federal law says phone companies must keep "customer proprietary network information" (CPNI) confidential except under certain circumstances.[18] CPNI includes information relating to how the caller uses the phone number, as well as billing information. The pen register and trap and trace statute passed in 1986 prohibited the government from installing or using devices that would collect calling records, Internet transactional records, and similar "dialing, routing, addressing, and signaling information."

[16] Earlier, I argued that minimization procedures are inadequate to protect civil liberties. But minimization is nevertheless extremely important because it is one of the few tools standing between broad, suspicionless intelligence surveillance and targeted, cause-based law enforcement access. Usage rules contained in minimization procedures are a necessary safeguard in the face of really broad intelligence surveillance.

[17] Ultimately, Congress chose to end the government collection of phone records via the USA Freedom Act of 2015. But the USA Freedom Act expanded government access to this information even as it remained in the custody and control of telecoms.

[18] 47 U.S.C. § 222(c).

For the government to get a hold of this kind of information, it needs to go to a court and get an order. But it didn't. As part and parcel of STELLARWIND, even though it was illegal, AT&T, Verizon, and Bellsouth agreed to turn over their call records to the government. After all, who was going to prosecute them? Certainly not the very same DOJ that was overseeing the unlawful bulk collection. Only a few phone companies resisted.

For years, massive collection continued, but, in 2004, the political calculus changed. High-level DOJ official James Comey was filling in for a bedridden Attorney General John Ashcroft. (Comey is now the Director of the FBI, appointed by President Obama in 2013.) Comey had recently learned about the STELLARWIND project and didn't believe that it was entirely legal. We don't know exactly what his objections were, but it seems that Comey was concerned about the Internet surveillance under STELLARWIND. Unlike phone numbers dialed, certain Internet transactions reveal the *content* of communications, as discussed in Chapter 4.

Under the Fourth Amendment, listening to telephone requires a search warrant. But in the case of *Smith v. Maryland*, the Supreme Court held that gathering telephone numbers does not. One reason the Supreme Court gave to treat dialed phone conversations differently from dialed numbers is that conversations are the *content* of communications and phone numbers are not. The Department of Justice jumped on this reasoning, taking *Smith* as a relatively bright line rule that the Fourth Amendment does not protect metadata, only content. But while the content/noncontent distinction is relatively clear in the telephone context, it is not so on the Internet. Website addresses reveal what you are reading. Email addresses reveal what you are talking about. So, STELLARWIND collection of Americans' URLs, email metadata, and more was not only in violation of statutory law. It likely was unconstitutional as well. So Comey talked to Ashcroft, who had initially signed off on STELLARWIND without reading the Yoo memos, and convinced him that that approval had been a mistake.

Later that same day, Ashcroft fell seriously ill and ended up in the hospital.[19] Comey became Acting Attorney General just as STELLARWIND needed the attorney general's signature to renew it. Comey wouldn't do it, and Ashcroft was in the hospital. Without a signature from the highest acting law enforcement officer in the land, the Internet metadata dragnet would have to come to a screeching halt, or continue without legal cover, potentially exposing officials to personal liability.

[19] T. Weiner. *Enemies: A History of the FBI.* (New York, NY: Random House Publishing Group, 2012) p. 433.

At this point begins one of the more dramatic confrontations in surveillance history. White House counsel Alberto Gonzales set off for the hospital where the ailing Ashcroft lay abed, to get his approval. Gonzales had called Mrs. Ashcroft, who was at her husband's bedside, to say he was coming. Mrs. Ashcroft immediately called Comey. She said she was concerned that her husband was in no shape for this meeting. When Comey got word of Gonzales' intentions, he grabbed FBI Director Robert S. Mueller. Mueller and Comey raced to hospital in a police car, sirens blaring. They barely beat Gonzales, who came with Andrew H. Card Jr., President Bush's chief of staff. Gonzales and Card refused to acknowledge that Comey was even in the room. According to Comey, "Ashcroft, summoning the strength to lift his head and speak, refused to sign the papers they had brought."[20] According to Jack Goldsmith, a relatively new addition to the Office of Legal Counsel who was present, as Gonzales and Card turned and left, "Mrs. Ashcroft sticks out her tongue" to express her "strong disapproval."[21]

Without Ashcroft's or Comey's signature, the White House had to decide whether to end the program or go ahead with it without attorney general approval. Comey, Mueller, Goldsmith, and others were prepared to resign if Bush let the Internet dragnet go forward. Comey, who the *New York Times* described as "an imposing former prosecutor and self-described conservative who stands 6-foot-8," was one of the only people willing to disagree with Cheney and Addington. According to the *Times*, at one testy 2004 White House meeting, Mr. Comey stated that "no lawyer" would endorse Yoo's justification for the NSA program. Addington said that he was a lawyer and found it convincing. Mr. Comey shot back: "No good lawyer," according to someone present.[22]

In the end, the White House satisfied the dissenters by going to the FISC for approval. FISC presiding judge Colleen Kollar-Kotelly was persuaded by the White House's argument that the NSA could collect Americans' Internet traffic data in bulk under the FISA pen register/trap and trace statute. To obtain phone call data or pen trap data, the FISA pen register/trap and trace statute requires an authorizing judge to find that the

[20] D. Eggen and P. Kane. "Gonzales hospital episode detailed." *The Washington Post*. May 16, 2007. www.washingtonpost.com/wp-dyn/content/article/2007/05/15/AR2007051500864. html

[21] D. Eggen and P. Baker. "New book details Cheney lawyer's efforts to expand executive power." *The Washington Post*. September 5, 2007. www.washingtonpost.com/wp-dyn/content/article/2007/09/04/AR2007090402292.html

[22] S. Shane, D. Johnston, and J. Risen. "Secret U.S. endorsement of severe interrogations." *The New York Times*. October 4, 2007. www.nytimes.com/2007/10/04/washington/04interrogate.html

information sought is *relevant* to a legitimate counterterrorism investigation. Relevance means that there is a connection between the desired information and a specific investigation. It does not mean collecting everything when there is no particular reason to believe that any but a tiny fraction of the data collected might possibly be suspicious.

Nevertheless, Judge Kollar-Kotelly accepted the White House's redefinition of "relevance" and allowed bulk acquisition of communications metadata. She wrote in her opinion that dragnet collection could go on, but she set up some post-collection rules meant to limit abuse of the data. This opinion was called the FISA PR/TT opinion and the Internet dragnet aspect of STELLARWIND was renamed as the FISA PR/ TT program, for FISA's "pen register/trap and trace." Bulk Internet data collection didn't stop, but now it had a veneer of legality. That was enough to satisfy Comey and his crew of dissenters.

Comey's "revolt" failed to lead to substantive reform. It also laid the foundation for how officials would deal with controversial Bush era national security policies in the future. Surveillance scholars would see the same dynamic time and again, even if without the hospital room drama. Objectors complain. Proponents push for congressional or judicial buy-in. The controversial practice continues.

Some might find it surprising that Comey, Mueller, and others were willing to quit their jobs, but ultimately stayed even though nothing changed. But the way that some lawyers looked at the surveillance problem, it never was a matter of civil liberties. It was the principle of the rule of law. Once President Bush had the legal imprimatur of a court order, the rule of law was (at least partially) satisfied and the crisis was over.

Reporter Charlie Savage notes this dynamic in his 2015 book, *Power Wars*. Savage identifies two main categories of objections to the Bush Administration's conduct of the War on Terror. One was substantive: the policies were illegal, immoral, or detrimental to privacy. The other was procedural: the executive branch agencies failed to follow legal procedures for getting approval of the practices. While there was strong opposition to Bush policies from the incoming Obama Administration, Obama's DOJ mostly addressed these concerns by obtaining additional legal approvals. The substance of the controversial national security policies, including surveillance but with the notable exception of torture, remained the same.

How could lawyers, professionally responsible for the advice they give their client, be satisfied by a FISC judge signature? The statutes were abused. The judges were handpicked. The public and Congress were in the dark. The civil liberties risks were obvious. And yet, they were satisfied because a process had been followed.

Secrecy Cracks

In December of 2005, the *New York Times* reported on some aspects of the illegal, warrantless wiretapping. Then, in February 2006, *USA Today* reported that the phone companies were handing over records on tens or hundreds of thousands of people.[23] The stories caused great concern within the telecoms, which didn't want to get burned by customer lawsuits for helping out the government in violation of the law.

Five years after September 11th, and with the breaking news about illegal surveillance, the political calculus was changing. American spies needed to find additional legal cover for what they were doing. Officials again looked to the USA PATRIOT Act passed in 2001 immediately following the attacks of September 11th. Part of the Patriot Act, section 215, says that the FBI can compel a person or company to produce "tangible things" upon showing reasonable grounds that the things sought are "relevant" to "an authorized foreign intelligence investigation." If the records concern a US person, then the information must be relevant to a counterterrorism or counterespionage investigation.

Section 215 was quite controversial when it was proposed as part of the USA PATRIOT Act following September 11th. While there was already a statute on the books that allowed the FBI access to some tangible things, section 215 lowered the burden of proof and increased the categories of things available to the government.

Civil libertarians were concerned that the FBI would use section 215 to obtain peoples' library records and thereby learn what they were reading. By 2001, people were sensitized to the idea that one's reading records, like one's video rentals, should be confidential, and that they could be sought and potentially abused in a kind of smear campaign. Years before, the public had already seen efforts to bring down a public figure by digging into his media consumption. In 1987, an enterprising reporter had obtained Supreme Court judicial nominee Robert Bork's video rental records in an effort to find something embarrassing that could derail his nomination.

---

[23] L. Cauley and J. Diamond. "Telecoms let NSA spy on coms." *USA Today.* February 6, 2006. www.usatoday.com/news/washington/2006-02-05-nsa-telecoms_x.htm. It wasn't until Snowden's revelations that we had proof that the data collection affected hundreds of thousands of people, potentially everyone in the nation.

Bork's viewing habits were unremarkable, but Congress could see the writing on the wall. Reporters would now routinely seek video rental records in an effort to find embarrassing details about politicians and public figures. So Congress passed a law prohibiting video stores from voluntarily disclosing their rental records.

Given the controversy over whether section 215 would enable investigators to obtain peoples' library records, Congress put a provision in the Patriot Act saying that section 215 would automatically sunset, or die, unless Congress reauthorized it. That way the FBI could have the powers it said it needed to fight terrorists in the aftermath of the World Trade Center attacks, but Congress could revisit how the provision was being used at a later time. What no one was talking about was the possibility that section 215 could be used for bulk collection on everyone.

Nevertheless, American spies were able to torture the statute to serve their ends. In 2006, FISC Judge Malcolm Howard relied on Judge Kollar-Kotelly's 2004 FISA PR/TT opinion to opine that bulk domestic phone records collection was allowed under section 215 of the Patriot Act. Howard didn't even bother to write an opinion explaining his reasoning. Indeed, no judge would until after Snowden documents revealed the program to the public. Nevertheless, Judge Howard's signature on a FISC order was enough for the phone companies to allow the collection to continue.[24]

Section 215 had required that investigators show that Americans' records they sought under that provision be "relevant" to an authorized counterterrorism investigation. Judge Howard, like Judge Kollar-Kotelly, reinterpreted the meaning of the word "relevant" to mean "all." Further, instead of the data going to the agency named in the statute, the FBI, which is allowed to investigate Americans but under traditional, more robust privacy rules, it would go to the foreign intelligence spies at the NSA. So long as American spies had a counterterrorism justification, Judge Howard authorized the NSA to get *all* phone call records.

Even in the fearful time when the Patriot Act was enacted, one month after the attack on the World Trade Center, lawmakers never contemplated that section 215 would be used for bulk collection of phone data, or for a dragnet of any sort. It is impossible to read that statutory language and think that Congress intended to authorize bulk collection when it passed the USA PATRIOT Act. If it had, why would it employ the concept of "relevance" in the first place? Why not explicitly authorize bulk collection and subsequent data mining?

[24] Savage, *Power Wars*, pp. 203–204.

The substandard legal work by FISC judges is just one more reason to radically change the role of the FISC. FISC judges didn't bother to explain their reasoning, even from the outset. The few who did, did a sloppy, credulous job. In the public courts, in contrast, three Second Circuit judges wrote almost 100 pages assessing the statutory basis for the phone dragnet and unanimously concluded that section 215 did not authorize the NSA's bulk collection of Americans' phone records. In fact, every single one of the public courts, even those that have agreed with the FISC's ultimate conclusion, has given the issues more informed and careful consideration than the FISC judges have.

Through disregard and sloppy legal work, the FISC resolved a political crisis. But this was also the slippery slope at work. The 2004 FISA PR/TT opinion was the basis for the 2006 section 215 "business records" order authorizing the phone dragnet. The judicial acquiescence during this time continued in secret. The orders cumulatively sanctioned the US government's collection and use of more and more data about Americans without meeting statutory or constitutional standards.

Warrantless Wiretapping

Today's warrantless international wiretapping and content collection under PRISM and Upstream was illegally born as part of STELLARWIND. Just as it did with phone records and Internet records, in the months following the terrorist attacks of September 11, 2001, the Bush Administration approached telecommunications companies seeking access to calls and messages flowing over fiber optic cables carrying customers' calls and emails. The contents of these kinds of communications are highly protected under both the Fourth Amendment and the Wiretap Act. Traditionally, collecting these would entail a super warrant for government wiretaps. So this request was plainly illegal. Regardless, AT&T had long been a trusted surveillance partner. The company, and other telecoms, allowed Bush Administration spies to conduct eavesdropping on company property without any warrants or court orders at all.

The public still lacks full technical details about how this wiretapping was accomplished, whether the NSA has direct access to fiber optic cables, and what the provider's involvement in either building the technology or collecting the data may have been. However, thanks to whistleblower Mark Klein, we have information about how AT&T helped the NSA install a network monitoring system in its San Francisco switching center. In the summer of 2002 and into 2003, Mark Klein, then an AT&T engineer who later quit the company and went public with what he knew, learned that the agency was splitting the fiber optic cable signals carrying telephone and Internet traffic and directing a copy of the data stream into a secret room. The NSA's system was capable of monitoring billions of bits of Internet traffic a second, including the playback of telephone calls routed on the Internet, and pulling specific pieces of data out of the stream for further analysis. In other words, AT&T and the NSA could access everyone's communications that ran through that switch. According to Klein, the NSA installed similar systems in AT&T offices in Seattle, San Jose, Los Angeles, and San Diego.

In 2006, Klein became the primary source for a lawsuit by the Electronic Frontier Foundation (EFF) against AT&T. EFF is a civil liberties group based in San Francisco, and which I worked for as Director of Civil Liberties from 2007 to 2010. But Klein was not alone in blowing the whistle. In 2004, Thomas Tamm, formerly an attorney at the DOJ's Office of Intelligence Policy and Review (OIPR), confidentially told the New York Times that Bush Administration officials had installed eavesdropping equipment at various telephone company facilities across the United States.[25] Tamm was in a position to know. OIPR, like the OLC, was part of the executive branch effort to come up with a legal justification for STELLARWIND. Tamm said that the NSA was using wiretapping facilities inside phone company offices to eavesdrop on Internet messages and phone calls without first obtaining a warrant as the law required.

At the behest of the Bush Administration, the Times sat on the story for eighteen months – through a presidential election season – until December 2005. The Administration claimed that publishing the story would help al-Qaeda evade surveillance. But once revealed, there was public consternation that the Times had hidden illegal activity, especially during an election season. The paper's delay in publishing would prove to be an important factor in Snowden's decision to reach out to Laura Poitras and Glenn Greenwald instead of the Times. Snowden was afraid the Times would make the same mistake of sitting on the story at a time when it could have a policy impact.

In response to the Times article quoting confidential sources, President Bush publicly acknowledged the government's warrantless wiretapping. But, the President said, the government was only listening in when

---

[25] J. Risen and E. Lichtblau. "Bush lets U.S. spy on callers without courts." *The New York Times.* December 16, 2005. www.nytimes.com/2005/12/16/politics/bush-lets-us-spy-on-callers-without-courts.html

terrorists called. Rather than admitting that the tapping was part of a broader domestic spying program, the Bush Administration gave it a more media relations friendly name, the "Terrorist Surveillance Program."

Behind the public relations, the Bush Administration had no sound statutory basis for the warrantless wiretapping. Instead, the Bush Administration used this opportunity to push its pet theory – a very expansive view of presidential power. The Administration, spearheaded by Cheney and his aide Addington, argued that the executive branch didn't have to follow the Wiretap Act or FISA (and get a court warrant) to conduct the eavesdropping. Rather, presidents have unlimited power under Article II of the US Constitution to protect the nation, they argued, and that's what this eavesdropping was for. Congress didn't have the constitutional authority to limit the President's national security power by passing statutes that required court review. According to Jack Goldsmith, the former OLC attorney who disapproved of the John Yoo memos and who threatened to quit over STELLARWIND, Addington repeatedly opposed efforts by other administration lawyers to soften counterterrorism policies or to include outsiders in considering and approving them. Bush, Cheney, and Addington, especially in the first few years following the September 11th attacks, basically thought that the President could do *anything* he wanted in the name of national security, and there was nothing Congress could do to stop it.

As a backup argument, in case this power grab didn't win the day, Bush claimed that the 2001 Authorization for the Use of Military Force (AUMF) passed by Congress one week after the September 11, 2001 attacks necessarily included the authorization to monitor Americans' communications with foreign terrorists.

Bush's legal argument was weak. The AUMF only applied to certain terrorist groups, so if the warrantless wiretapping was broader than that – something the Administration would not reveal – then the AUMF could not apply. Nor did the AUMF make any mention of conducting electronic surveillance. Finally, the same laws that require warrants for wiretapping have special procedures for wiretapping during hostilities. So, there *were already* laws that said what kind of surveillance was acceptable when there's an AUMF in place. Those laws say that the government – after a short period of time – needs a warrant to continue tapping communications lines. Obviously, STELLARWIND did not comply with that rule.

Members of Congress weren't going along with the story that they had authorized the spying when they issued the AUMF, either. Then-Chairman of the Senate Judiciary Committee, Senator Arlen Specter (R-PA), said that he would call the phone companies to the Senate floor to get to the bottom of the issue.[26] Senator Patrick Leahy (D-VT) was incredulous. "Are you telling me that tens of millions of Americans are involved with al Qaeda?" Leahy asked. "These are tens of millions of Americans who are not suspected of anything ... Where does it stop?"[27]

In 2005, the full extent of Bush's power grab and of the illegal spying was not publicly known. With the Administration saying they were only spying on terrorists as the AUMF contemplated, Klein knew that his testimony was more important than ever. The NSA had all of AT&T messages running through its surveillance machines, not just messages from terrorists. So, a few weeks after the *Times* reported Bush's warrantless wiretapping, in early 2006, Klein gave his information to attorneys at the EFF. Klein's documents showed that the NSA had access to all communications running through AT&T, not just international ones and not just ones where terrorists were on the other end of the line. The EFF sued AT&T in January of 2006 for violating the wiretap laws which prohibited companies from voluntarily disclosing private customer communications without proper legal process. Soon other organizations followed with lawsuits of their own against both AT&T and the government.

By this point, the pressure was on AT&T and on American spies. Though the details were still unknown, the public was now aware of the warrantless wiretapping and that the NSA had been collecting Americans' calling records in bulk. This scared journalists who depend upon keeping the identity of their sources confidential. It scared lawyers who interview spooked witnesses and try to convince them to come forward with their stories. It scared advocacy groups that organize political minorities, disadvantaged, and disenfranchised people into effective political organizations. These groups, including the California Association of Federal Firearms Licensees, the ACLU, Students for Sensible Drug Policy, the Council on American Islamic Relations, and Free Press, feared being eavesdropped upon because they were actively engaged in (lawfully) challenging government policy.

To ensure continued access to data, the Bush Administration had assured the companies that had participated in the spying that they would not suffer if they continued to cooperate. That meant protecting them

---

[26] L Cauley. "NSA has massive database of Americans' phone calls." *USA Today.* May 11, 2006. usatoday30.usatoday.com/news/washington/2006-05-10-nsa_x.htm
[27] Ibid.

from the lawsuits that had been filed and putting warrantless wiretapping on firmer legal ground for the future.

In the short term, the Bush Administration decided to seek help from the FISC, just as it did in 2004 with respect to the metadata dragnet. To understand what the Administration asked of the FISC, you have to understand what surveillance tools the NSA already had. During the Reagan Administration, the NSA had started building the relationships and technological means for conducting massive surveillance on communications networks inside the United States. The legal basis for creating this infrastructure was *transit authority*. The Reagan era intelligence community came up with transit authority out of concern that they were losing spying capabilities due to technological progress. The NSA was capable of and competent at tapping copper wires and using satellites to grab radio signals. Copper wires were easily tappable on the sea floor – unregulated by FISA. But to intercept messages from newer fiber optic lines, it was easier to collect them at one end or the other – where the cable head emerged from the ocean and plugged into a network hub. That tap, on land at the network hub, might require a FISA warrant because it took place inside the United States. Plus, the government would need a telecom's cooperation to conduct such a tap.[28]

So in the 1980s, the intelligence community developed the theory – not disclosed to the public – that collecting foreign-to-foreign communications while they were traversing the United States was not "electronic surveillance" under FISA and therefore was only regulated by the looser EO 12333 rules. Transit authority meant that the NSA was allowed to build, on US soil, tools capable of grabbing whole streams of phone calls and messages, but just for foreign-to-foreign communications. Transit authority also supported cooperation between American spies and the telephone companies. Once phone companies – highly regulated industries with a lot to lose from rejecting government requests – said "yes" to transit authority, a beautiful friendship was born. The NSA was able to build technologies for mass surveillance. Technologically, there were challenges. Some fiber optic switches commingled both purely foreign messages and some international messages that terminated inside the United States. So these wiretapping technologies were initially designed to screen out domestic and international messages. But by the time of September 11th, the NSA fox was now in the telecom henhouse.[29] As part of STELLARWIND, it

---

[28] Savage, *Power Wars*, p. 173.
[29] Id., p. 176.

seems likely that all American spies had to do was to stop screening international messages out of the transit authority data it was already gathering.

After the warrantless wiretapping program was revealed by the *New York Times* in 2005, the Bush intelligence community sought to expand "transit authority" to get legal approval for collection of Americans' international messages.[30] Under existing law, to collect communications traveling on fiber optic cables to the United States and from inside the country, FISA required intelligence agencies to have probable cause to believe that a particular "facility" was being used by an agent of a foreign power. "Facility" traditionally meant email addresses or phone numbers. The NSA had to develop and present probable cause that the email address or phone number was going to be used by a legitimate target. This meant the NSA had to know with some precision how the terrorists were communicating. But the NSA was no longer targeting known terrorists. It was fishing in the sea of incoming messages for unknown terrorists who might be talking to Americans.

To deal with the legal issue, Bush's DOJ secretly came up with a new meaning for the word "facility." The government went to the FISC and asked for "facility" to be redefined more broadly than just email addresses and telephone numbers. In late 2006, the Bush Administration petitioned that the FISC define "facility" to mean international switches and gateways, essentially connection points in the global communications network that connect the United States and other countries around the world. In early 2007, a FISC judge, Malcolm Howard, agreed to adopt the new and broader definition. This enabled the STELLARWIND's warrantless wiretapping to continue, though Judge Howard did impose some restrictions for surveillance targeting Americans.[31] The agency called this legal maneuver "Large Content FISA."[32]

Judge Howard was the same judge who had signed off on the domestic phone records dragnet under section 215 in 2006 – without so much as a legal opinion explaining his reasoning. This was not a coincidence. The Department of Justice lawyers had advance notice of which judges would be sitting when, and surveillance advocates had pushed internally to file the papers in time for Judge Howard to be the one to rule on them. This

---

[30] Id., pp. 177, 181, 186.
[31] Id., p. 203.
[32] C. Savage and L. Poitras. "How a court secretly evolved, extending U.S. spies' reach." *The New York Times*. March 11, 2014. www.nytimes.com/2014/03/12/us/how-a-courts-secret-evolution-extended-spies-reach.html

forum shopping ensured a happy outcome, at least initially, for the warrantless wiretapping aspect of STELLARWIND.[33]

Once the FISC adopted this new definition of "facility," it was quite easy to show that al-Qaeda or other foreign targets were "probably" using those switches – thereby satisfying the probable cause requirement. They would have to be using those switches if they were making *any* calls or sending *any* messages to the United States. But this redefinition also put the NSA in the position of spying on innocent people. Worse, there was no obvious limit to what the Administration claimed the law allowed it to do. As David Kris and Douglas Wilson write about Large Content FISA in their cannonical treatise on national security surveillance:

> The problem, of course, is that thousands of other persons, with no connection to al Qaeda or terrorism, are also making international calls and using the switches. The broader the definition of "facility," the more likely it is that al Qaeda is using the facility, but the less likely it is that any given communication on the facility relates to al Qaeda. If a FISA "facility" can be a gateway switch, why can it not be something even broader, like all of AOL or Google, or even the entire U.S. telecommunications grid, or the Internet? There is no doubt that foreign powers are using (some part of) the Internet; does that justify surveillance of the entire Internet? This line of questions leads to the heart of the Fourth Amendment's Particularity Clause and proscription on general warrants.[34]

The Bush Administration's answer was that privacy protections would be applied after information was collected, via post-collection minimization procedures. In the criminal wiretap context, minimization means that police aren't allowed to listen to conversations that aren't about the crime. But in the intelligence gathering context, minimization is quite different. It means that after-the-fact rules kick into place after broad collection of almost certainly irrelevant data about innocent people. Minimization rules regulate intelligence agencies' storage, analysis, and sharing of the data they collect. Minimization procedures require the NSA to delete data after a certain period of time, or to black out Americans' names before sharing data with certain other agencies, or with foreign governments. They are rules that the intelligence community drafts and, to some extent, the FISC oversees, but which were, and still are, predominantly classified.

When, under great political pressure and in secret, a FISC judge reinterprets the long-standing meaning of words like "relevance" or "facility" to

---

[33] Savage, *Power Wars*, p. 202.
[34] Kris and Wilson, National Security Investigations and Prosecutions, §§ 16:12.A.

allow a president to continue surveillance that he has already commenced and that the public does not know about, the signatures may be mere gestures toward maintaining the rule of law.

Protecting privacy by stopping the government from collecting information on innocent people is pretty effective. Protecting privacy by issuing secret, internal rules about the different ways different agencies can use or analyze data already collected about innocent people is hard. For the rules to have any effect, they must be rigorously interpreted, people must be properly trained, and violations must be punished. Technology has to be designed so that it is impossible to wiretap Washington D.C. when you mean to wiretap Egypt. Only then will internal agency procedures help, and only to prevent low-level misconduct. Even protective, well-enforced usage rules will be thrown out of the window if the president or the attorney general or the director of the FBI is the person who comes asking for the data in the name of national security. No one wants to refuse such an august official. And in any case, they can just quietly change the usage rules to permit the data gathering they seek.

When the Large Content FISA orders came up for renewal four months later, a different surveillance court judge balked at the broad scope of surveillance. This judge was not handpicked by the DOJ lawyers for his sympathetic ear. After the Department of Justice successfully gamed the system to get Judge Howard, Chief Justice Kollar-Kotelly abruptly stopped the practice of sending the advance roster of judges' duty weeks to the agency.[35]

Instead, the DOJ lawyers pulled Judge Roger Vinson. Vinson thought Judge Howard's and the DOJ's redefinition of "facility" was all wrong. Judge Vinson thought that the Bush Administration would have to go to Congress to get authorization for STELLARWIND.

Even so, Judge Vinson didn't shut down STELLARWIND surveillance. As DOJ lawyers begged for more time, he found ways to let them continue. He let them go back to Judge Howard to get signatures that Vinson could not in good faith provide. He then allowed DOJ lawyers to reinterpret a provision of the USA PATRIOT Act, the roving wiretap provision, to allow the NSA to target any email address it believed was related to al-Qaeda without making a probable cause showing to the FISC.

While Vinson gave the Bush Administration more time on the clock, American spies pursued a longer-term plan. In 2007, the Bush Administration pushed through the Protect America Act, a short-lived

[35] Savage. *Power Wars.* p. 202.

stop-gap statute that was meant to give Congress and the Administration time to figure out what it wanted to do about STELLARWIND – surveillance of Americans' international calls and messages. The Protect America Act led to the Foreign Intelligence Surveillance Act Amendments Act of 2008 and section 702.

FISA Amendments Act

One of the most important parts of the Foreign Intelligence Surveillance Act Amendments Act (FISAAA) was a provision that gave retroactive immunity to the telephone companies that had participated in the warrantless and illegal spying. At the time, there were about forty different lawsuits pending, including the lawsuit the EFF filed with the help of retired AT&T technician Mark Klein. Congress enabled the Department of Justice to kill them all without resolution.[36] It let the telecoms get away with breaking the law. It also sent a message: If the president asks you to break the law, you can, and it will be OK. That was a major victory for the White House, and took care of one of the Bush Administration's big problems: How to comfort the companies that had been complicit in illegal spying, and encourage companies to cooperate in the future.

Next, section 702 of the FISAAA set up new rules that departed from traditional FISA. Under traditional FISA, the NSA could generally spy on foreigners abroad without any court oversight, but couldn't collect their emails, text messages, chats, or other electronic messages from American soil without getting a warrant from the court. The new rules added a way for the NSA to collect these kinds of messages from inside the country without any warrant. Section 702 also removed the requirement that domestic spying target agents of foreign powers, and not average, run-of-the-mill foreigners. Under section 702, if the target is a foreigner in another country, American spies don't have to show probable cause that the target is either an agent of a foreign power or doing anything wrong. They don't have to have probable cause to monitor any particular email address or phone number. Nor do they need to stop listening if the foreigner is talking to Americans. All they need is a FISC judge's broad certification that the topic under investigation is legitimate. Then the court gives a general approval of the rules for selecting targets and minimizing the collected data. Once a judge signs off on those rules, so long as the target is

---

[36] E. Lichtblau. "Deal reached in Congress to rewrite rules on wiretapping." *The New York Times.* June 20, 2008. www.nytimes.com/2008/06/20/washington/20fisacnd.html

a foreigner overseas, and the subjective purpose of the monitoring is not to investigate Americans, the eavesdropping is allowed.

To conduct the surveillance, the government gives "directives" to service providers. These directives compel the providers to assist in the acquisition of communications. The directives identify or "task" certain "selectors" believed to be associated with targets. Electronic communications service providers use these selectors to acquire the data to turn over to the government.

Another way to understand section 702 is as a policy that allows the NSA to listen to Americans when we talk to foreigners overseas about matters of foreign intelligence interest. Foreigners are the *targets* but Americans are eavesdropped upon in the process. There are two forms of content collection under section 702: PRISM and domestic Upstream. PRISM is the collection of communications from service providers like Google, Apple, and Yahoo!. Upstream collection comes directly from the fiber optic cables that the NSA has tapped inside AT&T and potentially other phone company offices as well. The legal justification is the same (section 702), but the technological means are different (provider assistance versus direct access wiretaps). This happens without probable cause and with very little judicial oversight or intervention.

The NSA argues that its approach to section 702 has done nothing more than it had traditionally been allowed to do as part of its foreign-based international tapping of copper wire cables. FISA did not regulate this broad spying when it took place in international waters on the sea floor. Intelligence agencies had longstanding authority to conduct warrantless surveillance on suspects overseas, so why should the law require a court order to surveil these suspects' communications when intercepted in the United States? This argument makes it appear as if, from the perspective of an American, there is nothing particularly new or worrisome about section 702.

In truth, section 702 surveillance appears frighteningly broad. Independent analysis suggests that moving international surveillance inside the country has made it far more invasive than Congress or the public have understood. Based on a sample of data that the *Washington Post* obtained from Snowden, we can suspect the following: Nine out of ten times, the information collected is about an innocent person, not the target. Further, nearly half of the surveillance files contain US citizens' or residents' names, email addresses or other details, even though the statute purports to prohibit collecting information about Americans. And the information can include intimate moments. There are photos of mothers kissing their infants and of men posing without shirts. There are medical records. Even though this information is admittedly irrelevant to foreign intelligence, the NSA keeps the data. Then the FBI can use it to look for evidence of crime or otherwise investigate Americans.

According to the intelligence community, there were about 90,000 section 702 targets in 2014.[37] That might seem reassuring in a world of 4 billion people. But if one of those targets is "the French government" or "the United Nations," then it starts to get frightening because lots of people talk about those entities for all kinds of innocent reasons. Messages referencing these topics are chosen for acquisition using search terms or "selectors." Selectors can include telephone numbers or email addresses. Government officials commonly mention these as examples, and people intuitively think of these categories of data as associated with a particular individual. But selectors could also include broader categories of data than these two examples. Selectors could include IP addresses, which many websites or users share, cybersecurity threat indicators, which can emanate from the systems of both attackers and victims, and communications signatures like web browser language and geolocation. These kinds of selectors can sweep in a lot of people who aren't even talking with targets. Using just one IP address as a selector could draw in everyone working from a foreign cybercafé, as well as any Americans they email or instant message.

Despite hearings and an investigation by the Privacy and Civil Liberties Oversight Board (PCLOB), the public still doesn't know exactly what categories of selectors American spies use. The statutory language doesn't limit the government's use of broad selectors. And the FISC doesn't review selectors used to make sure they are well-designed for the intended target and don't cause collateral damage to privacy or civil liberties.

Since the attacks of September 11th, the conversation about intelligence gathering and the development of surveillance law have been secretive and dishonest. Domestic surveillance started as a top-secret and illegal program under the Bush Administration. Over time, FISC judges, sometimes hand-selected by the intelligence community, signed off on highly questionable legal legitimizations for the spying that was already being done. Congress never approved bulk domestic collection, and indeed after the practice was revealed to the public, ended the phone dragnet in 2015

---

[37] "Statistical Transparency Report Regarding use of National Security Authorities." Office of the Director of National Intelligence. June 26, 2014, p. 2. www.dni.gov/files/tp/National_Security_Authorities_Transparency_Report_CY2013.pdf

with the USA Freedom Act. In only one case did Congress ever validate a STELLARWIND program, with the section 702 warrantless wiretapping statute. Surveillance advocates repeatedly claimed that section 702 "only rarely" impacted Americans or "had nothing to do" with us.[38] In truth, as Chapter 8 details, the little we know about section 702 shows it is far-reaching and invasive, that under its authority the government routinely collects vast quantities of American data. Recently adopted, legal procedures have done little to constrain American spies. Instead, the rules have either been ignored, or been manipulated to justify shadowy, controversial, and even illegal programs.

[38] Rep. M. Rogers. "FISA Amendments Act Reauthorization Act of 2012 Floor Speech." September 12, 2012 and Rep. Trey Gowdy, "FISA Amendments Act Reauthorization Act of 2012 Floor Speech." September 12, 2012, cited in J. Sanchez. "Confusion in the House: Misunderstanding spying law, and inverting the lessons of 9/11." Cato Institute. September 14, 2012. www.cato.org/blog/confusion-house-misunderstanding-spying-law-inverting-lessons-911

14

Modern Surveillance and the Fourth Amendment

The question that animates this chapter is whether the Fourth Amendment protects Americans from suspicionless spying. There should be a simple answer: yes. I believe that one day that will be the answer. But for now, the Fourth Amendment has been left in the dust by rapid technological change and by the secret expansion of spying. As a result, there are huge gray areas where the protections of the Fourth Amendment are either in doubt or absent. Government officials are exploiting these gray areas to justify massive data collection.

This situation is changing as I write, however. The United States frequently scales back surveillance via congressional action. As the public becomes aware of new kinds of privacy infringement, people start to worry. Selfish or not, it helps when a significant percentage of the population understands that they, too, could be the subject of this surveillance technique. As public opposition coheres, politicians take up the cause. If reform is successful, written laws will structure and limit the collection activity to situations democratically deemed appropriate.

Frequently this cycle happens with some influence from the Supreme Court. It was the Supreme Court's failure in *Olmstead* that led to the Communications Act of 1934, which attempted (unsuccessfully) to limit warrantless wiretapping. It was the Supreme Court's leadership in *Katz* and *Berger* that led to the Wiretap Act in 1968. Congress took the lead with the Electronic Communications Privacy Act (ECPA) in 1986. The question today is whether the Supreme Court is ready to take the lead in formulating case law that imposes limits on modern surveillance. There are signs that the Justices are willing, even eager, to do so.

The Fourth Amendment was written to do away with writs of assistance and general warrants. These were tools that gave customs officials in pre-Revolutionary America the power to enter private homes and business to search for smuggled or untaxed goods.[1] In 1760, James Otis quit his job

---

[1] Officials could "enter and go into any House, Warehouse, Shop, Cellar, or other Place" to seize goods. Section X, Revenue Act of 1767 (7 Geo. III ch. 46) as cited in M. H. Smith, *The Writs of Assistance*. (University of Berkeley Press, 1978) p. 1.

as Advocate General of the Admiralty Court, a tribunal with jurisdiction over ships containing import goods, because he objected so strongly to these intrusive decrees.[2] General warrants, he said, constituted "a power that places the liberty of every man in the hands of every petty officer."[3] Otis offered his legal services for free to anyone who wanted to challenge the writs. In one such challenge, Otis railed for five straight hours against the practice.

Otis lost the case, but won the war. Seated in the audience that day was John Adams, who would go on to become the second president of the not-yet-formed United States of America. Otis' speech had a huge effect on Adams, who later wrote that "the child independence was then and there born, [for] every man of an immense crowded audience appeared to me to go away as I did, ready to take arms against writs of assistance." Thus the Fourth Amendment, born from Otis' ideas, embodied the hostility of America's founders to arbitrary general searches in their new Republic.

This particularly American tradition informs many constitutional experts who believe the Fourth Amendment prohibits massive surveillance. There should be no fishing expeditions, no broad, untargeted exercise of government power. Instead, searches and seizures should be predicated on a reasonable belief that a wrongdoing of some kind has occurred and that the search or seizure is likely to turn up evidence of a crime. Moreover, the government should have to specifically describe what agents are looking for and where the search will be conducted.

It sounds pretty straightforward, but new technologies introduce new complications. Recall from Chapter 11 that the Supreme Court grappled for years with the question of whether listening to telephone calls was a search or seizure. For decades, warrantless wiretapping under the Fourth Amendment was the rule.[4] It wasn't until the *Katz* case in 1967 that investigators around the country were required to get a search warrant for eavesdropping, an outcome that we take for granted today.

---

[2] R. Balko. "General warrants, NSA spying, and America's unappreciated founding father, James Otis, Jr." *The Huffington Post.* July 4, 2013. www.huffingtonpost.com/2013/07/04/james-otis_n_3547302.html

[3] J. Otis. "Speech on Writs of Assistance, 1764" as quoted in H. Gillman, M. A. Graber, and K. E. Whittington. *The Complete American Constitutionalism: Introduction and the Colonial Era* (New York: Oxford University Press, 2015) vol. I, p. 491.

[4] Legislatures were free to pass more protective laws. States did so, but federal authorities ignored those laws in federal prosecutions. Congress also did so, in 1934, but the Department of Justice interpreted the law only as limiting the use of warrantless wiretap data in court.

Now think about email. Are emails protected by the Fourth Amendment? The lawyer's approach to resolving a legal question like this one would be to appeal to judicial precedent. But selecting the right precedent depends on the way a court frames the question. Are emails like letters and phone calls? Or are they more like post cards, which are not constitutionally protected because anyone with access to the card can read them?

Certainly, the kinds of things people say in emails are more like the private conversations we have in letters or over the phone, and not the casual reports that characterize post cards. Millions of Americans use email every day for practically every type of personal business. Private messages and conversations that once would have been communicated via postal mail or telephone now occur through email. Love letters, family photos, requests for (and offerings of) personal advice, personal financial documents, trade secrets, privileged legal and medical information are all exchanged over email, and often stored with email providers after they are sent or received. These myriad private uses of email demonstrate society's expectation that the personal emails sent and received over the Internet and stored with email providers are as private as a sealed letter, a telephone call, or even papers that are kept in the home.

But technologically, unencrypted emails are like a postcard, which is readable by your email provider and any operator of an Internet router that carries the message from one place to another on the network. When you use the Internet, your messages, at various points between sender and receiver, are temporarily stored on intermediate computer servers. Not only that, with webmail and hosted backups or data storage, our information may permanently reside on computer servers owned by someone else. We don't think that anyone but the recipient is going to read our messages, but she could.

And digital messages are far more searchable than those written on paper, at least with today's technology. Part of our expectation of privacy in letters and phone calls comes not from legal theory or normative conviction, but from reality. It is an insurmountable challenge for police officers or intelligence agents to read all the US Mail or listen to all our phone calls. That would take far longer and be far more expensive than any country could accomplish. Not so with digital messages. Computers already scan all our messages in order to serve us context-specific advertising or identify spam. We know that a simple search query can trigger examination of all the documents on our computer, or retrieve information from any document on the World Wide Web.

Does this mean that digital communications should be less private than analog ones? Do algorithms reading data invade our privacy, or only humans reading data? What happens when we develop computers – as we are very close to doing, or have done – which can read letters and listen to phone calls just as easily as search a hard drive? How do these facts impact our expectations of privacy in our digital messages?

Today, the Department of Justice argues that the fact that your email can be read by intermediaries as it makes its way to you across the Internet means that you have no legitimate expectation of privacy in those messages other any other unencrypted Internet communications – instant messages, social networking, backups, and more. Third parties have access to them. Robots controlled by these third parties may analyze them. So under *Smith* and *Miller* – the third party doctrine – those communications therefore are not protected by the Fourth Amendment.

The DOJ's argument is unlikely to win the day. The Supreme Court has never considered whether the public has a Fourth Amendment interest in email. Despite the fact that the public Internet is over twenty years old, it wasn't until 2006 that any civilian appellate court decided whether police need a search warrant to read your email. In *United States v. Warshak*, the defendant was suspected of unlawful business practices in the course of selling herbal supplements over the Internet. Using a subpoena, and then a court order authorized under ECPA, investigators obtained approximately 27,000 of the defendant's emails from one of his service providers. Mr. Warshak claimed that investigators should not have been able to get this information without first obtaining a search warrant and demonstrating probable cause to believe he was committing a crime.

Over the DOJ's objections, the Sixth Circuit Court of Appeals agreed with the defendant. Previous cases held that various kinds of communications were protected by the Fourth Amendment, including phone calls (in *Katz v. United States* (1967)) and letters (*United States v. Jacobsen* (1984)). Entrusting a letter to the mail carrier doesn't defeat a reasonable expectation that the letter will remain private. We know that phone calls may be wiretapped or monitored by the phone company, but we have a reasonable expectation of privacy in those, too. As the Supreme Court found in *Katz*, the wiretapping case, "what [a person] seeks to preserve as private, even in an area accessible to the public, may be constitutionally protected." It would defy common sense to have a different rule for email. "Email requires strong protection under the Fourth Amendment; otherwise, the Fourth Amendment would prove an ineffective guardian of private communication, an essential purpose it has long been recognized to serve," said the Sixth Circuit opinion.

In other words, the *Warshak* court understood something that the DOJ did not. The Fourth Amendment isn't about whether something is a secret. It's about our social conception of, and need for, privacy. Email may not be kept secret from service providers. But that doesn't mean the messages aren't and shouldn't be private.

Even though no other federal circuit court nor the Supreme Court has squarely ruled on the question of email and the Fourth Amendment, the *Warshak* case has had national impact. Thanks to the ruling, almost all of the major online messaging providers now refuse to turn over emails to law enforcement without a warrant.

For the layperson, it initially might be hard to fully understand the legal impact of applying the Fourth Amendment, or even a statutory warrant requirement, to the collection of data. If the law requires a warrant, it doesn't just mean that there are hoops for the government to jump through. A warrant requirement means that a judge reviews government access, so that there has to be a good reason; searches can't be arbitrary. It also means that the search has to be targeted, because a warrant has to specifically describe what is going to be searched. So the warrant requirement is not only a limitation on arbitrary police action, but it should also limit mass surveillance.

The Fourth Amendment has not successfully played this role in foreign intelligence surveillance law. Because noncitizens outside the United States don't enjoy Fourth Amendment rights, mass surveillance takes place overseas. And, even inside the United States, the DOJ argues that so long as the target is a foreigner without Fourth Amendments rights, the surveillance is constitutional, even when the target is talking to an American. This is the basis for the government's argument that section 702 collection is constitutional, for example. And what of the "inadvertent" over-collection of even purely domestic messages, information subsequently shared even with the FBI? If otherwise lawful collection has "unwanted" side effects, those do not make the it unlawful, says the DOJ.

How will the Fourth Amendment apply to other technological advances? The Fourth Amendment protects your home from police entry, but does it stop the police from using machines that can sense heat or radio waves escaping from your house, thereby revealing private things that are going on inside to law enforcement? Today, the Supreme Court says that the Fourth Amendment does stop this kind of surveillance. But in that same legal opinion, the Justices suggested that when such surveillance technology is "in general use," citizens might lose their reasonable expectation that their homes will not be scanned.[5]

Is there a constitutional difference between following one person down the street and going to the phone company to obtain everyone's cell phone location data? May police implement widespread video and facial recognition technology to identify and track individuals as we walk down the street? Can the government grab Internet metadata – URLs, email addresses, IP addresses – to find out what we are reading and with whom we communicate?

Today, tracking everyone is nearly as easily or sometimes easier than tracking just a few suspects. Does the Fourth Amendment have anything to say about this new reality? Technology has moved so far beyond existing Fourth Amendment law that these questions do not have clear-cut answers, but these are the questions that will shape the scope of our Fourth Amendment rights.

We aren't likely to get any answers soon because of the way the federal government has managed to insulate its practices from legal challenge. The few public lawsuits challenging massive spying on constitutional grounds have been dismissed without deciding the issues. The chief reason for this is a legal doctrine called "standing." Standing means litigants must prove they were actually harmed by the law they are challenging before the dispute can proceed in court.

Requiring standing for lawsuits makes a lot of sense if you want someone who actually has a vested interest to litigate a case and you want courts to resolve real disputes, not issue advisory opinions. But the standing requirement has become a real barrier to people seeking redress through the courts, especially for privacy violations.

Section 702 of the FISA Amendments Act expanded intelligence agents' authority to read Americans' emails without first having to show some proof that they were doing something wrong or acting on behalf of a foreign power. As soon as the law passed in 2008, ACLU attorney Jameel Jaffer and his colleagues filed a lawsuit on behalf of Amnesty International and several journalists and human rights activists who believed that they had been illegally subjected to spying under section 702. The plaintiffs in the case, *Amnesty Intl. v. Clapper*, were lawyers for suspected terrorists and journalists investigating terrorism and US counterterrorism efforts. As a result, they were highly likely to be subjected to suspicionless surveillance

[5] *Kyllo v. United States*, 533 U.S. 27, 34 (2001).

when communicating with their clients and sources. The lawsuit argued that these Americans had a constitutionally protected interest in their telephone and Internet conversations, even though they were talking with foreigners. Because section 702 allowed them to be spied on without any probable cause, the ACLU attorneys argued section 702 violated the Fourth Amendment.

But the Supreme Court refused to decide that substantive issue. Rather, it dismissed the ACLU's case on procedural grounds, saying that the plaintiffs could not *prove* they had been spied on. And even if they were spied on, they couldn't prove that it was under section 702. They might be subject to wiretapping under another provision of FISA, for example. The Supreme Court said that the ACLU could only speculate that its clients were spied on under section 702 as opposed to some other legal authority. And you can't ask the government to confirm you were a target or ask what legal authority the government relied on, because that is a secret. Inability to overcome this Catch-22 meant the case was dismissed.

Similarly, lawsuits challenging our government's kidnapping,[6] torture,[7] and other disturbing practices undertaken in the name of the War on Terror have been dismissed. The US government is able to repeatedly use a combination of standing requirements and state secrets rules to get cases dismissed before judges can rule on the merits. Without judicial oversight, the national security agencies can continue the practices.

Another avenue for judicial review would be for criminal defendants to challenge modern surveillance techniques when used in their cases. But such challenges are very risky. Criminal defendants are routinely offered plea deals that go like this: If you plead guilty now, we'll agree to a sentence of X years. But if you challenge anything in the case, then we will file a superseding indictment and add all kinds of charges, which will make you eligible for 3X years in prison, and we will argue for the maximum. This approach hugely discourages even meritorious constitutional claims.

The other reason we aren't seeing challenges in criminal cases is that for years the Department of Justice has kept defendants uninformed about where the evidence against them comes from. Investigators find other, more targeted, ways to explain how they obtained information about the defendant. For example, after obtaining data using massive spying tools, investigators will serve a subpoena on a telecom for the defendant's

---

[6] *El-Masri v. Tenet*, 479 F.Supp.2d 530 (E.D. Va. 2006).
[7] *Meshal v. Higgenbotham*, 47 F.Supp.3d 115 (D.D.C. 2014), *affirmed* 804 F.3d 417 (D.C.Cir. 2015) *rehearing en banc denied* February 2, 2016.

records, which investigators already have. Then they will tell the defendant, her counsel, and the court that the subpoena was how they got the information, not the spying program. This kind of parallel construction has been a technique used by the FBI and the DEA for years to insulate massive spying programs from legal challenge. What defendants don't know, they can't complain about.

While it may seem surprising that we have so little surveillance law precedent, it's not because we have so little surveillance. To the contrary, there are troubling reasons for the judicial silence. The government has found many ways to avoid court review despite the prevalence of modern surveillance practices.

∗∗

In the next few sections of this chapter, we'll look at the Fourth Amendment implications of the phone dragnet, the section 702 warrantless wiretapping, and finally the overseas surveillance happening pursuant to EO 12333.

The Phone Dragnet

To understand the phone dragnet and the Fourth Amendment, it helps to go back to *Smith v. Maryland* in 1979. In that case, Smith argued that a phone operator could listen in to phone calls, but the calls should nevertheless be considered private under the Fourth Amendment. The Supreme Court rejected this argument. It said that Smith knew the phone company was collecting this information – it was included on his bills – so he assumed the risk that the company would disclose the data to the government. The same, however, also could have been said of phone calls, where the operator was capable of listening in. But the Supreme Court didn't take this point of view with respect to the phone calls. Instead, in *Katz* it said that phone calls were protected. The Court's opinion in *Smith* distinguished phone numbers dialed from phone calls by noting that calls are the *content* of communications, and dialed phone numbers are not: "a pen register differs significantly from the listening device employed in Katz, for pen registers do not acquire the contents of communications."[8]

That allegedly "significant" distinction has been the cause of much official mischief. *Smith* has provided the government's legal justification for its phone and Internet dragnets. When asked to assess the legality of collecting everyone's phone numbers, the Department of Justice just did a little

---

[8] *Smith v. Maryland*, 442 U. S. 735, 741 (1979).

math. If obtaining phone number records on one user is not a search (as *Smith v. Maryland* held), then obtaining a more detailed version of that kind of information for hundreds of millions of users is not a search either. Zero plus zero plus zero times three hundred million still equals zero.

When it came time to get domestic dragnets approved, American spies turned to *Smith, Miller*, and the so-called third party doctrine. In 2004, to resolve the hospital bedside dispute that left James Comey and other officials ready to resign, the Bush Administration went to FISC Judge Kollar-Kotelly. In the face of the official showdown that officials claimed would shut down valuable counterterrorism spying unless someone found a legal justification, Judge Kollar-Kotelly was asked to give judicial approval to the notion that the government could indiscriminately collect Internet transactional data.

To justify this, the DOJ extrapolated from that claim in *Smith* that "pen registers do not acquire the contents of communications." Rather than examining why the Supreme Court concluded that telephone pen registers are very different from telephone calls, the DOJ decided to read *Smith* simply to mean that the Fourth Amendment only protects content and nothing else. Internet transactional data like URLs and email addresses are *analogous* to telephone numbers, and telephone numbers are not content. So therefore, Internet data is not protected by the Fourth Amendment.

But this conclusion goes far beyond what the Supreme Court said in *Smith*. The *Smith* case did not say that all metadata falls outside the Fourth Amendment's umbrella of protection. *Smith* said that collecting a list of phone numbers one man has dialed does not infringe a reasonable expectation of privacy, and for particular reasons. *Smith* did not draw a bright line between constitutionally protected content and unprotected "metadata." The case never uses the term "metadata." Rather, the case drew a line between information knowingly conveyed to a particular entity so that it can provide a service to you and which is contained in that entities' business and billing records. Dialed numbers transmitted to the phone company and the financial transactions you enter into at your bank are two examples. But email and other information carried by a communications network are not – to the knowledge of the user, at least – routinely accessed and retained by that entity, even if it may have the technical capability to do so (such as the words spoken in a phone call).

Smith had nothing to say about Internet transactions – which didn't exist then – or about any other kinds of metadata. Internet data shares little in common with the phone numbers in *Smith*. It is not included on any bills; no humans routinely look at it. URLs and email addresses can be far more revealing than phone numbers dialed. As discussed in Chapter 4, these reveal what you are interested in, who in your life is important to you, what political groups you are allied with and more.

These distinctions between phone numbers and Internet metadata were not helpful to the NSA's mission to "Collect It All." Nor was it helpful to criminal prosecutors who did not want to have to get a warrant for Internet investigations. So it is unsurprising that the DOJ would like to rely on a so-called third party doctrine to justify treating everything but phone call content as equivalent to phone numbers unprotected by the Fourth Amendment. Recall that the DOJ's position is that email messages, even though they are content, are nevertheless unprotected by the Fourth Amendment because they are stored on Internet company servers. The DOJ lost that argument in *Warshak*, but has never disavowed it, and we do not fully know how the government uses this argument in attempting to legitimize other forms of content spying.

But it is surprising that Judge Kollar-Kotelly agreed, rather perfunctorily and in a top-secret opinion, with the government that Internet information acquired in bulk "like other forms of meta data [sic]" is not protected by the Fourth Amendment. She wrote summarily that "users of e-mail [redacted] voluntarily expose addressing information for communications they send and receive to communications service providers."

If you know a bit about how email works, you know that phone numbers and email transactional data are quite different. Internet service providers generally need not, and often do not, look at anything in the message beyond the destination IP address. The routers where the NSA does its Upstream surveillance and collects transactional data do not take note of the sender's IP address. They do not review or process the website addresses (URLs) that someone is browsing. The servers do not examine "to" or "from" email addresses. Nor do they process any other of a number of computer communication attributes like packet size, number of packets, or browser attributes. The Internet router simply moves the message packets one step closer to their final destination IP address. Only once the message arrives at its destination computer – the webserver or the email provider – does a computer figure out what the message consists of (e.g. email, video, chat), where it goes, the email address of the sender and recipient, and other revealing things Judge Kollar-Kotelly called "metadata." Again, the provider may make no record of this information. Thus, it is technologically inaccurate to say that people voluntarily expose email routing information to providers in the same way that we do phone numbers. What's more, most people have no idea how this process functions, so the idea that Internet metadata is voluntarily disclosed like phone numbers dialed are defies common sense.

Similarly, URLs (the addresses of websites you visit like cyberlaw.stanford.edu or nytimes.com) are not like telephone numbers. Nor are IP addresses (the numbers that indicate machines and devices connected to the Internet like 8.8.8.8). Unlike the phone numbers in *Smith*, URLs and IP addresses do not appear on bills. Unlike the phone numbers in *Smith*, users probably have no idea whether their Internet service provider is tracking and storing the URLs and IP addresses they visit. In fact most ISPs do not keep records of such things, unlike phone companies that record dialed phone numbers for billing purposes.

Moreover, on the Internet, there is no clear line between content and noncontent. If someone sends a message to a substance abuse help list, like subscribe@alcoholicsanonymous.org, that tells you everything the message is supposed to be about.[9] Or think about a website address. URLs usually start like this: cyberlaw.stanford.edu or www.google.com. Then they continue to point to where on a webserver a particular piece of information resides, and the title of that informative page. So if you look in your browsing history, you'll see URLs that looks like this:

http://www.amazon.com/Divorce-Financially-Emotionally-Securing-Financial/dp/1937458490/

or

http://www.mayoclinic.com/health/cancer/DS01076/DSECTION= coping-and-support.

As these examples illustrate, URLs can communicate important aspects of the content of the articles that someone visiting those websites is reading. There is no bright line between content and metadata in the world of the Internet.

The content/noncontent distinction is legally important because the Supreme Court said in *Smith v. Maryland* that content is protected by the Fourth Amendment, while phone numbers dialed are not. But this distinction has gotten less clear over time. Think about the reality show So You Think You Can Dance. When you call the SYTYCD hotline, after dialing the toll free number, fans enter numbers to vote for their favorite dancers. Are those numbers transactional information, or are they the content of

⁹ Julian Sanchez, CATO Institute, as quoted in A. Greenberg. "Court says tracking web histories can violate Wiretap Act." *Wired*. November 10, 2015. www.wired.com/2015/11/ court-says-tracking-web-histories-can-violate-wiretap-act/

the call? When you call your bank, and then enter your account number, are those numbers content? For years, law enforcement agents were asking for this kind of information as if it were merely transactional, and telephone services were turning the data over. It wasn't until some magistrate judges started publishing opinions questioning whether these "post cut through dialed digits" were metadata or content and asking for civil liberties groups to weigh in on the issue that the practice of warrantless disclosure changed.

In short, the quality, detail, and processing of modern phone and Internet data is quite different from the phone numbers dialed in *Smith*. Internet data is only superficially like dialed phone numbers. The Fourth Amendment rules for phone numbers do not clearly, if at all, map onto Internet records. And yet for years, the Department of Justice has asserted, and FISC judges have accepted, that they do. The truth is more complex. As Michael Morell, the former deputy CIA director, has said, "[t]here is quite a bit of content in metadata. There's not a sharp distinction between metadata and content. It's more of a continuum."[10]

There is another reason that *Smith* shouldn't apply to dragnet collection – even of phone calling records. The Fourth Amendment was written for the very purpose of ending suspicionless surveillance. The Fourth Amendment is meant to constrain arbitrary and invasive government conduct. Collecting narrow information about a single person is not constitutionally equivalent to mass surveillance of all available data about every person.

This is what District Court Judge Richard J. Leon held in one of the first challenges to the phone dragnet, *Klayman v. Obama*. In 2013, Larry Klayman sued the government after the phone dragnet was made public and argued that it violated the Fourth Amendment. Judge Leon wrote that *Smith v. Maryland* did not legitimize the bulk collection and storage of five years of telephony metadata for purposes of high-tech data analysis without any case-by-case judicial approval. Judge Leon described the phone dragnet as "almost Orwellian," referring Orwell's novel *1984* and its depiction of omnipresent government surveillance. Judge Leon distinguished the use of telephony metadata in *Smith v. Maryland* from the dragnet. *Smith* involved targeted, short-term, and forward-looking capture. The phone dragnet is suspicionless, long-term, and retrospective.

---

[10] L. Martinez. "NSA review panel defends its recommendations." *ABC News.* January 14, 2014. abcnews.go.com/blogs/politics/2014/01/nsa-review-panel-defends-its-recommendations

I cannot imagine a more "indiscriminate" and "arbitrary" invasion than this systematic and high-tech collection and retention of personal data on virtually every single citizen for purposes of querying and analyzing it without prior judicial approval ... Surely, such a program infringes on "that degree of privacy" that the founders enshrined in the Fourth Amendment.[11]

Just as the Supreme Court changed its mind about the privacy of phone calls when that technology became important in modern society, Judge Leon said that *Smith* didn't apply in an era where modern surveillance tools enabled dragnet spying and Big Data analysis.

Just a few days after Judge Leon's decision, Judge William H. Pauley of the Southern District of New York upheld the phone dragnet.[12] In its phone dragnet challenge, the ACLU was able to prove it had standing because the organization is a Verizon business customer, journalist Greenwald had published a FISC order commanding that Verizon business disclose its phone call records, and the intelligence community had admitted that the order was accurate. Judge Pauley held that *Smith v. Maryland* controls the case. Mainly, Judge Pauley seemed to believe that calling records belong to the phone company – not to the caller. Therefore, phone customers don't have a reasonable expectation of privacy in the records. This was Pauley's ruling despite the fact that the Telecommunications Act of 1996 defines telephone numbers dialed, information contained in phone bills, and similar information as "*customer* proprietary network information" and prohibits phone companies from disclosing or using it in statutorily unapproved ways.

Judge Pauley was also unmoved by the argument that mass surveillance is constitutionally different in kind than targeted collection. He wrote that if one man's dialed phone numbers (the defendant in *Smith*) are not private, then neither are everyone's. "The collection of breathtaking amounts of information unprotected by the Fourth Amendment does not transform that sweep into a Fourth Amendment search." The ACLU appealed Judge Pauley's ruling to the Second Circuit Court of Appeals and received a ruling that the phone dragnet, as discussed in the last chapter, violates section 215 of the USA PATRIOT Act.[13] As a result, the Court of Appeals did not have to consider the Fourth Amendment arguments. So we still do not know whether the appellate justices would have approved of Judge Pauley's Fourth Amendment analysis. In a third phone dragnet case, an

---

[11] *Klayman v. Obama*, 957 F.Supp.2d 1, 42 (D.D.C. 2013), *vacated and remanded by* 800 F.3d 559 (D.C.Cir. 2015).
[12] *ACLU v. Clapper*, 959 F.Supp.2d 724 (SDNY 2013), *affirmed in part, vacated in part, remanded by* 785 F.3d 787 (2d Cir. 2015).
[13] 785 F.3d 787 (2d Cir. 2015).

Idaho nurse and Verizon customer sued, also arguing that the program violated the customer's Fourth Amendment rights by amassing private details about her familial, political, professional, religious, and intimate associations. The District Court there ruled against the plaintiff.[14]

Despite these legal challenges, the phone dragnet continued until mid-December of 2015. The FISC continued to authorize it. Until Snowden revealed the existence of the program, no judge, including NSA-friendly Malcolm Howard who first approved the program under section 215 of the USA PATRIOT Act, bothered to write an opinion explaining either a statutory or constitutional reason why the collection might be lawful.

In the months following the Snowden revelations, President Obama selected a group of experts, which included former national security officials Richard Clarke and Michael Morell, to form a President's Review Group on Intelligence and Communications Technologies. The President's Review Group report examined the section 215 dragnet program and concluded that it had not been effective. The committee recommended that the NSA stop collecting phone records. A few months after Judge Eagan's opinion came out, the PCLOB also reviewed the phone dragnet. It, too, recommended that the NSA stop storing phone call records, saying that it could not identify any success stories.[15]

Nor did Judge Eagan cite relevant Supreme Court precedent in her opinion. In 2012, the year before her ruling, the Supreme Court issued an opinion in which the majority of Justices called into question the reasoning underlying *Smith*, *Miller*, and the third party doctrine. In the case, *United States v. Jones*, the Supreme Court considered long-term recording and aggregation of location information from a GPS device that police warrantlessly installed on a suspect's car. The government had argued that use of the device was not a search because it only revealed information the defendant already disclosed to others – the location of his vehicle on the public roads.

The Supreme Court unanimously rejected this argument, though the Justices did so for different reasons. The majority held that attaching a GPS-tracking device to a vehicle and using the device to monitor the car's movements over a period of twenty-eight days was a Fourth Amendment "search" because it interfered with the defendant's property interest in the

[14] *Smith v. Obama*, 24 F.Supp.3d 1005 (D. Idaho 2014), *vacated and remanded by* 816 F.3d 1239 (9th Cir. 2016).

[15] "Report on the Telephone Records Program Conducted under Section 215 of the USA PATRIOT Act and on the Operations of the Foreign Intelligence Surveillance Court." Privacy and Civil Liberties Oversight Board. January 23, 2014. www.pclob.gov/library/215-Report_on_the_Telephone_Records_Program.pdf

car. This was interesting reasoning because it echoed the trespass theory of the Fourth Amendment enshrined in the *Olmstead* case. But the Justices didn't entirely forget about *Katz* and the reasonable expectation of privacy test. In two concurring opinions, five of the Justices agreed that the surveillance impinged on expectations of privacy. Justice Sotomayor, who also signed on to the majority opinion, explained:

> GPS monitoring generates a precise, comprehensive record of a person's public movements that reflects a wealth of detail about her familial, political, professional, religious, and sexual associations. The Government can store such records and efficiently mine them for information years into the future. And because GPS monitoring is cheap in comparison to conventional surveillance techniques and, by design, proceeds surreptitiously, it evades the ordinary checks that constrain abusive law enforcement practices: limited police resources and community hostility.[16]

In other words, five Supreme Court justices rejected the idea that just because information was revealed to others – the location of the defendant's car on the public streets was visible to anyone who looked – it was no longer constitutionally protected.

This reasoning in *Jones* undermines the DOJ's conception of the third party doctrine. The DOJ argues you have no expectation of privacy in records exposed to another person, just like it argued you have no expectation of privacy in your movements exposed to the public. *Jones* rejected this. Yet Judge Eagan, one year later, utterly ignored *Jones*, failing to even mention it.

After serious public critique from scholars and Fourth Amendment experts, another FISC Judge, Mary McLaughlin, wrote a follow-up opinion justifying her subsequent reauthorization of the ongoing phone dragnet, on October 11, 2013. Judge McLaughlin at least mentions *Jones*. But McLaughlin's opinion simply reiterates a simplistic version of *Smith v. Maryland*: the Fourth Amendment does not protect phone call records because they are held by third parties. It is true that the *Jones* majority opinion does not renounce the third party doctrine. Five concurring judges just called that theory into question. So, according to Judge McLaughlin's holding, the NSA's phone records collection program can lawfully continue until the Supreme Court directly rejects the third party doctrine.

Congress eventually took action. In June 2015, it passed the USA Freedom Act, which purports to end dragnet government collection of

---

[16] *United States v. Jones*, 132 S.Ct. 945, 956 (2012) (J. Sotomayor concurring).

Americans' phone records. Instead, intelligence agencies can go directly to the telephone companies to get the records. The legislation gave the intelligence community six months to prepare for the change, and the dragnet under section 215 officially stopped in December of that year.

No one knows exactly what will happen to the US government's ability to data mine Americans' phone records. One view is that any analysis will be more complete, because the phone company records include cell phone data that the NSA was not previously collecting. Another view is that the analysis will stop, because the phone companies aren't required to retain any records for longer than eighteen months,[17] and because the intelligence community cannot meaningfully use federated datasets held by three or more different parties. It's not clear whether or how the public will find out for sure which is the case, never mind whether the practice is abused.

Now that the section 215 phone dragnet has ceased, the NSA continues its massive metadata collection, albeit overseas and through other means.

Warrantless Wiretapping Under Section 702

The NSA's wiretapping under section 702 of the FISA Amendments Act scoops up huge amounts of Americans' emails and phone calls, potentially reaching to the hundreds of thousands. These communications are Fourth Amendment protected thanks to *Katz* and *Warshak*, meaning that the government has to get a warrant that is tailored to the particular target. But section 702 wiretapping is warrantless. Warrantless wiretapping may be constitutional when performed overseas and targeting foreigners, who have no Fourth Amendment rights. But does the Constitution apply when surveillance targeting foreigners takes place inside the United States and sweeps up the communications of Americans, who do have such rights? However the program is phrased, since the program is designed to wiretap Americans' international communications, Americans' constitutional rights are directly implicated.

Civil libertarians have challenged the constitutionality of section 702 surveillance. So far, all the challenges have failed on procedural grounds. The DOJ has successfully argued that the litigants have failed to show that they were spied on – something difficult to do when the spying is secret and only a chosen few are notified that they have been surveilled. Even when it's likely that someone has been spied on because they are reporters or attorneys who

---

[17] Billing records must be retained for eighteen months. See 47 U.S.C. § 42.6 (1986).

have spoken to suspected terrorists, the DOJ has argued that litigants must show both that they were spied on and also that the spying happened under section 702 and not pursuant to some other legal authority.[18]

The US government responds that its incidental surveillance of Americans under section 702 is unremarkable. After all, if the police have a warrant based on probable cause to believe that your roommate is dealing drugs, they can search any place in your apartment that your roommate has access to. The same is true if they have your roommate's permission to search your shared rooms. So long as the government has legal authority to search one person, the other people who get caught up in that investigation aren't entitled to any additional privacy protections. And, say American spies, we protect American rights with post-collection rules on how information from or about Americans can be stored, used, or shared – the minimization rules.

The weakness in the government's argument is in the analogy: the two situations are not similar. In criminal wiretaps, surveillance is targeted at a criminal suspect. Under section 702, surveillance is "targeted" only as the intelligence community uses that word; NSA systems ingest data based on selectors. But the surveillance is programmatic and the rationale for data collection is exceedingly broad; it only has to relate to some matter of foreign intelligence interest. The targets can be individuals, but they can also be groups and organizations, like UNICEF, Petrobras, an IP address that is used by thousands of people, or the government of Germany.

In the wiretap context, collection is limited to targets talking to others about the criminal activity. Under section 702, nontargets talking about targets are intercepted. That's the difference between listening to Jimmy Hoffa plan a crime and listening to my friend in Germany and me talk about the Mafia.

The DOJ deploys other legal arguments, as well, to evade the warrant requirement for collecting US persons' international communications. As discussed earlier, for example, the US Department of Justice has argued in the past that *no* Internet messages – not instant messages, emails, social networking, nor backups – are protected by the Fourth Amendment. Because these messages traverse and are stored on computers owned by third parties, and because third parties have the technical ability to read these messages, the DOJ could assert, as it argued unsuccessfully in the *Warshak* case, that there is no reasonable expectation of privacy, and the Fourth Amendment does not apply. Since the precedents of the

---

[18]   *Clapper v. Amnesty Int'l*, 133 S. Ct. 1138, 1149 (2013).

Sixth Circuit, which decided the *Warshak* case, only bind courts in Ohio, where the *Warshak* prosecution took place, plus Tennessee, Kentucky, and Michigan, the DOJ may continue to argue in other Circuits, including before the FISC, that Internet messages are unprotected.[19]

Some declassified FISC opinions show that American spies are currently arguing for – and getting – an exception to the Fourth Amendment warrant requirement for national security matters. Generally, if a government action invades a reasonable expectation of privacy, the Fourth Amendment applies. If the Fourth Amendment applies, then government agents generally need a warrant. However, there are some situations where the Fourth Amendment applies, but there is an *exception* to the warrant requirement. These established exceptions to the warrant requirement are situations where an individual has a reasonable expectation of privacy, but the police can act without a warrant so long as their overall conduct is reasonable. For example, when police are in "hot pursuit" of a suspect, they can chase her into a home without a warrant. When officers hear drugs getting flushed down the toilet, they can rush in under "exigent circumstances."

The Supreme Court also has carved out an exception to the Fourth Amendment's requirement of a warrant based on "special needs." The special needs exception applies when a government search or seizure has some legitimate objective beyond ordinary crime control. Examples of the special needs doctrine at work are drug testing student athletes or drunk driving checkpoints. The government doesn't need a warrant for those kinds of searches, though other legal safeguards apply.

While the Supreme Court has never decided the question, other courts have said that foreign intelligence collection can qualify as a special needs exception to the warrant requirement. How does the special needs exception apply to foreign intelligence surveillance? We don't really know. Few public courts have reached the question, and the legal decisions of the FISC are classified. But in one top-secret FISC case, only unsealed in 2014, the FISC considered whether the special needs doctrine could insulate programmatic spying similar to that under section 702 from the warrant requirement.

---

[19] Generally, communications providers – Google, Yahoo!, Apple, and more – will not disclose email content to law enforcement without a warrant or similar legal process from another country based on the *Warshak* case. This means a de facto national practice that government entities have to get a warrant for communications content. To keep track of which providers have the most privacy friendly policies, people can check out the Electronic Frontier Foundation's annual report, Who Has Your Back? www.eff.org/who-has-your-back-2014

Yahoo! brought the case in 2007, challenging the precursor statute to the FISA Amendments Act and section 702. Congress passed the precursor statute, the Protect America Act or PAA, at the Bush Administration's behest after the public discovered content surveillance under STELLARWIND, AT&T got sued for violating the Electronic Communications Privacy Act, and Judge Vinson balked at Large Content FISA orders that would have allowed STELLARWIND to be approved under the existing FISA statute.

In the litigation, Yahoo! claimed that the PAA's version of programmatic collection violated Americans' Fourth Amendment rights because it took place without a warrant. The FISC, and ultimately the secret court that hears appeals from the FISC, the Foreign Intelligence Surveillance Court of Review, or FISCR, denied Yahoo!'s challenge. The FISCR wrote that the surveillance didn't need a warrant because the purpose of the wiretapping wasn't regular law enforcement, but foreign intelligence for national security purposes.[20] This, it said, was a "special need" that justified doing away with the warrant requirement.[21]

In making this ruling, the FISCR was (secretly) making a giant leap. It said, for the first time and unbeknownst to almost everyone, that the Fourth Amendment permits programmatic surveillance of Americans with no connection to a crime or terrorism, so long as the targets are not Americans. If the FISC is looking to an exception to the warrant requirement to justify section 702's warrantless wiretapping, that might explain why there are so few certifications, and only (allegedly) for relatively serious topics like counterterrorism and weapons proliferation.

Regardless, a national security exception to the warrant requirement is a strange and highly debatable legal conclusion. To see why, we have to go back to the history of how national security surveillance and the Fourth Amendment doctrine grew up together. Remember that in 1972, the Supreme Court held in the *Keith* case that investigators need to get a warrant even in domestic national security related investigations. Until that point in time, wiretapping justified as "national security" took place at the attorney general's discretion. But not after *Keith*. Noting the First Amendment implications of excessive surveillance, the Supreme Court explained:

> History abundantly documents the tendency of Government – however benevolent and benign its motive – to view with suspicion those who most

---

[20] *In re: Directives [REDACTED] Pursuant to Section 105B of the Foreign Intelligence Surveillance Act*, 551 F.3d 1004 (FISCR 2008), p.15. fas.org/irp/agency/doj/fisa/fiscr082208.pdf

[21] Ibid.

fervently dispute its policies. Fourth Amendment protections become the more necessary when the targets of official surveillance may be those suspected of unorthodoxy in their political beliefs. The danger to political dissent is acute where the Government attempts to act under so vague a concept as the power to protect "domestic security." Given the difficulty of defining the domestic security interest, the danger of abuse in acting to protect that interest becomes apparent.[22]

Moreover, said the Court, the Fourth Amendment requires a warrant, not just that the search be "reasonable." The potential for abuse in domestic security wiretaps is too high. The Supreme Court acknowledged the ways that domestic security investigations raised different policy and practical considerations than investigations of ordinary crime. The list of possible differences is entirely familiar to those engaged in the debates since September 11: the gathering of security intelligence often takes place over a long term; it involves "the interrelation of various sources and types of information"; the "exact targets of such surveillance may be more difficult to identify"; and there is an emphasis on "the prevention of unlawful activity." Nevertheless, in the eyes of the Supreme Court, the dangers from doing away with the warrant requirement were simply too great.[23] However, the Supreme Court in Keith, like Congress in the Wiretap Act, left open the question of whether the Fourth Amendment requires a warrant for foreign intelligence surveillance.[24]

Warrantless foreign intelligence surveillance inside the United States continued until the passage of FISA in 1978. In the years following Keith, but before the enactment of FISA, three appellate courts upheld this warrantless foreign intelligence surveillance in limited circumstances.[25] The most legally important of these cases was United States v. Truong in the Fourth Circuit Court of Appeals. Mr. Truong had come to the United States in 1965 to study at Stanford University. While in the United States, his father, an opposition leader, was jailed by South Vietnam's American-backed

---

[22] United States v. U.S. District Court, 407 U.S. 297, 314 (1972).
[23] However, while a warrant and judicial oversight are constitutionally required for domestic security searches, the Court said that there might be a different kind of probable cause acceptable for such searches. Traditionally, police need probable cause to believe that they will discover information about a crime. But: [A] [d]ifferent standard[] [of probable cause] may be compatible with the Fourth Amendment if [it is] reasonable both in relation to the legitimate need of Government for intelligence information and the protected rights of our citizens. For the warrant application may vary according to the governmental interest to be enforced and the nature of citizen rights deserving protection.
[24] United States v. U.S. District Court, 407 U.S. at 321–322 (1972).
[25] United States v. Truong Dinh Hung, 629 F.2d 908 (4th Cir. 1980); United States v. Butenko, 494 F.2d 593 (3d Cir. 1974) (en banc); United States v. Brown, 484 F.2d 418 (5th Cir. 1973).

government. Rather than return home and risk imprisonment himself, Mr. Truong became an antiwar activist and lobbyist in the United States. The US government wiretapped him without a warrant. Those wiretaps revealed that Mr. Truong gave documents – low-level diplomatic cables including some that were classified – to a United States Information Agency officer who served in Vietnam as part of an alleged plot to pass the sensitive documents to Vietnamese diplomats in Paris. Civil libertarians argued that the government was going after antiwar activists but the Carter Administration defended the investigation.[26] The DOJ argued before the Fourth Circuit that the government didn't need a warrant. Rather, there is foreign intelligence exception to the Fourth Amendment warrant requirement which applies in "carefully limited" situations "in which the interests of the executive are paramount." The Fourth Circuit agreed with the Administration and required that the object of the search or surveillance be "a foreign power, its agent or collaborators," and that the surveillance was conducted "primarily" for foreign intelligence reasons. Finally, the *Truong* court said that the warrant exception was justified by the "practical difficulties of obtaining a warrant for foreign intelligence surveillance … at the time [the underlying] surveillance was conducted." The issues raised in the *Truong* case informed Congress' passage of FISA in 1978.

The details of the *Truong* decision are crucial to the contemporary question of whether modern surveillance under section 702 violates the Fourth Amendment. In rejecting Yahoo!'s challenge to the PAA – which allowed the government to conduct warrantless foreign intelligence surveillance on targets (including United States persons) "reasonably believed" to be located outside the United States – the FISCR relied on the *Truong* foreign intelligence exception to find that warrantless PAA surveillance was legal. In the Yahoo! case, the FISC judges found that PAA surveillance presented a "carefully limited" situation where "the interests of the executive are paramount." The FISCR said getting any warrant takes some time, and speculated that it might possibly be an undue burden, contravening *Truong*.[27]

But things have changed with respect to the burden purportedly posed by requiring a search warrant. Today, we have FISA and the FISC, an established way for the government to obtain a warrant for foreign intelligence surveillance. The operation of the FISC eliminates one of *Truong's*

---

26 P. Vitello. "David Truong, figure in U.S. wiretap case, dies at 68." *The New York Times*. July 6, 2014. www.nytimes.com/2014/07/07/us/david-truong-figure-in-us-wiretap-case-dies-at-68.html?_r=0

27 *In re Directives to Yahoo! Pursuant to Section 105B of the Foreign Intelligence Surveillance Act*, 551 F.3d 1004, 1011. (FISCR 2008).

justifications for a special needs/foreign intelligence exception. All warrants take time, but the situation was entirely different when *Truong* was decided.

The PAA was also different from the surveillance defended in *Truong* in that it was not "carefully limited." To the contrary, the PAA authorized extremely broad surveillance for any matter of foreign intelligence interest. In the future, public courts may well reject the FISCR's reading of *Truong*.

But for now, the FISC has probably extended, in further secret rulings, the FISCR's endorsement of a special needs exception warrant requirement to reach spying under section 702 of the FISAAA, which Congress enacted after the PAA expired.

One public court has considered whether section 702 surveillance violates the Fourth Amendment for failing to require a search warrant. The pending case involves terrorism charges against Jamshid Muhtorov, a permanent resident who was legally living in Colorado. As a lawfully documented permanent resident, Mr. Muhtorov is a US person under FISA. Mr. Muhtorov stands accused of planning to travel abroad to join an Islamist terrorist group. Section 702 surveillance produced some of the evidence used against Mr. Muhtorov.

In November of 2015, Judge Kane of the District of Colorado dismissed Mr. Muhtorov's motion to suppress the evidence against him as illegally seized. Judge Kane looked at the overall structure of section 702, found the procedures "reasonable" and held, therefore, that the search was legal. Judge Kane did not engage in a legal analysis of whether national security considerations in this international wiretap overrode the traditional warrant requirement.[28] Judge Kane did not accept the government's argument that anyone talking with foreigners deserved less Fourth Amendment protection ("The government contends defendants have little or 'severely diminished' expectations of privacy in their communications with non-U.S. persons overseas.") The searches were reasonable he said, simply because the data came from the Internet. Citing *Smith v. Maryland*, Judge Kane wrote, "expectations of privacy are diminished the more information one puts out into the ether, especially the ether of the global telecommunications network."

---

[28] *United States v. Muhtorov*, D. Colo. 1:12-cr-00033-JLK-1; See also S. Vladeck. "Section 702, the Fourth Amendment, and Article III: The Muhtorov (Non-) Decision." *Just Security*. November 20, 2016. www.justsecurity.org/27784/section-702-fourth-amendment-article-iii-muhtorov-non-decision

There is an absence of public law on whether a foreign intelligence exception to the warrant requirement survived the passage of FISA and if so how far it extends. There is little law on whether the Fourth Amendment protects Americans using email or other Internet services. There is little law on whether people have a reasonable expectation of privacy when they talk with friends abroad. In this vacuum, the DOJ has many secret arguments in defense of massive surveillance.

One reason there is so little public law about section 702 is because so few people have been notified that evidence against them has come from section 702 surveillance. The story behind the lack of notice is both odd and upsetting. Recall that in *Amnesty Int'l v. Clapper*, a challenge to the constitutionality of section 702 by journalists and human rights lawyers, the Supreme Court never decided the substantive issue. Rather, it dismissed the case on standing grounds. During oral argument, ACLU attorney Jaffer had told the Justices that if they dismissed his case for these reasons, no court could ever review the constitutionality of section 702, or any other secret surveillance law. No one would ever be able to prove she had standing because if she were spied on, she'd never know.

Justice Sonia Sotomayor asked the august Solicitor General Donald Verrilli, who argued the case for the government, whether Jaffer was right. Would anyone have standing to challenge section 702, or would the ruling he was asking the Supreme Court to make essentially insulate the statute from judicial review altogether? Of course, said Mr. Verrilli, as he stood before the Justices in his traditional striped trousers, gray ascot, waistcoat, and a cutaway morning coat. If the government wants to use information gathered under the surveillance program in a criminal prosecution, the source of the information would have to be disclosed. The subjects of such surveillance, Verrilli continued, would have standing to challenge the program.

In reality, it was the policy of the DOJ's National Security Division to use parallel construction techniques to hide the fact that evidence had been derived from warrantless surveillance. It was Senator Feinstein who leaked this tidbit to the press. Under pressure to identify cases in which section 702 surveillance had been effective, the Senator referred to a pending criminal case against a Chicago teenager accused of planning to bomb a bar. That teenager's lawyer was surprised, because the government had told him the evidence against his client – including that he had been reading the online al-Qaeda publication *Inspire* magazine – came from traditional FISA surveillance. After Solicitor General Verrilli raised questions with his government colleagues, he learned of the policy, and realized that the National Security Division had led him to inadvertently misrepresent the facts to the Supreme Court.

In response, the Department of Justice allegedly changed its practice. So far, however, the government has issued only five notices in criminal cases – including to the Chicago teenager and to Mr. Muhtorov. In April 2014 the notices stopped and no one knows why.[29]

The Future of Modern Surveillance and the Fourth Amendment

The Supreme Court hasn't had much opportunity to judge the constitutionality of modern surveillance. But in the few cases where it has, it has suggested that it understands that as technology changes, so must constitutional rules, in order to more broadly honor the original rationale behind the Fourth Amendment.

United States v. Jones questions the whole idea that the Fourth Amendment does not protect privacy in public.[30] The case held that attaching a GPS-tracking device to a vehicle and using the device to monitor the car's movements was a trespass that violated the Fourth Amendment because it interfered with the defendant's property interest in the car. In concurring opinions, however, Justice Sonia Sotomayor and four other justices added that the GPS surveillance "impinge[d] on expectations of privacy" because it allowed authorities to monitor every place a suspect traveled and infer many things about a suspect's private life based on that information. This was true even though the defendant was just driving about on public roads.

Relying on the *Jones* concurrences, a panel of the Eleventh Circuit initially concluded that under the "reasonable expectation of privacy" test, cell phone location data is also protected under the Fourth Amendment, since this data can reveal private matters such as "being near the home of a lover, or a dispensary of medication, or a place of worship, or a house of ill repute."[31]

In that case, *United States v. Davis*, the appellate judges also dismissed the argument used in *Smith v. Maryland* that people lose their privacy interests

---

[29] P. C. Toomey. "Why aren't criminal defendants getting notice of section 702 surveillance – again?" *Just Security*. December 11, 2015. www.justsecurity.org/28256/arent-criminal-defendants-notice-section-702-surveillance-again

[30] *Jones v. United States*, 132 S.Ct. 935 (2012).

[31] *United States v. Davis*, 754 F.3d 1205 (11th Cir. 2014) *reversed en banc* 785 F.3d 498 (11th Cir. 2015).

in data submitted to businesses. The panel reasoned that people do not know in any meaningful way that by using their cell phones they are sending their location information to their provider. By refusing to apply *Smith* to a case involving mobile phone company records, the Eleventh Circuit undermined the legal justification propping up many of the government's targeted and bulk metadata collection practices. The panel opinion was subsequently overturned when the case was reheard *en banc* a few months later. Still, the panel opinion suggests that some appellate level judges are beginning to see privacy differently based on evolving Supreme Court precedent.

A different appellate court has also disagreed with one of the grounds for the dismissal of Mr. Muhtorov's motion to suppress. In Mr. Muhtorov's case, the Colorado District Court had said that once information was reasonably seized for foreign intelligence purposes under section 702, the defendant could not challenge the NSA's practice of sharing that information with the FBI for criminal investigations. Judge Kane wrote that "[a]ccessing stored records in a database legitimately acquired is not a search in the context of the Fourth Amendment because there is no reasonable expectation of privacy in that information." In other words, once the government legally gets its hands on information, it can do whatever it wants with it.

But a panel of the Second Circuit Court of Appeals in *United States v. Ganias* has disagreed. In *Ganias*, government investigators had a warrant to make a mirror image of relevant computer hard drives for off-site review. Two-and-a-half years later the government obtained a second warrant to search the same files, which it already had in its physical possession, for evidence of additional crimes by a different person. It found incriminating evidence and filed new charges. The new defendant claimed that this second search – even though it took place pursuant to a warrant – violated the Fourth Amendment.

The Second Circuit panel agreed. Just because the information was in government hands didn't mean agents could repurpose it for different investigations of different people. Nor could they retain information for too long. If the government seizes more information than it needs for an investigation, it can't take unfair advantage of that overseizure to indefinitely store and search private information. On appeal, the *Ganias* panel decision was overturned, but not because the judges were wrong about the Fourth Amendment. Rather, the Court said that it would not reach that question, because the government relied in good faith on the search warrant. But if the reasoning original is upheld, it will give people Fourth Amendment rights in how data is used, analyzed, stored, shared, and ultimately deleted.

In June 2014, the Supreme Court invalidated warrantless searches of cell phones in *Riley v. California*. At issue was whether the traditional rule allowing police in the course of an arrest to conduct warrantless searches of things you are carrying also applied to modern smartphones. The Supreme Court said no – and did so unanimously. The opinion is exceedingly important, and not just because nowadays almost everyone carries a cell phone replete with photos, messages, and other personal data. The Supreme Court's reasoning affirms several principles that may inform future cases involving the Fourth Amendment.

The first and most important is that Digital Is Different. The DOJ argued by analogy that searching an arrestee's cell phone is basically the same as searching inside her purse, or examining a cigarette pack found in her pocket. But the Supreme Court was unequivocal, even colorful, in its rejection of that equation. "[T]hat is like saying a ride on horseback is materially indistinguishable from a flight to the moon."[32]

The government also sought to extend *Smith v. Maryland*'s third party doctrine in *Riley* by arguing that the defendant's cell phone call log was just like the numbers dialed in *Smith*, so the officer didn't need a warrant to look at it. But the Court rejected that argument as well:

> There is no dispute here that the officers engaged in a search of [the defendant's] cell phone. Moreover, call logs typically contain more than just phone numbers; they include any identifying information that an individual might add, such as the label "my house" in [the defendant's] case.[33]

What might the *Riley* ruling mean for the NSA's bulk collection of call detail records and other so-called metadata? Privacy advocates have long been saying that the volume, detail, and quality of digital information means that analogies to predigital world data are misleading. In *Riley*, the Supreme Court appears to have unanimously agreed with them. Privacy advocates have also said that the assertion that metadata categorically gets no Fourth Amendment protection is wrong. Again, the Supreme Court agreed, finding that metadata that reveals location was protected by the Constitution. *Riley* shows there may no longer be such thing as a "metadata" exception to the Fourth Amendment, if there ever was one.

Finally, the *Riley* opinion raises a serious question about whether bulk collection or mass surveillance ever can meet Fourth Amendment requirements. Remember, much foreign intelligence surveillance is

---

[32] *Riley v. California*, 134 S.Ct. 2473, 2488 (2014).
[33] Id. at 2492.

extremely broad. Spy agencies regularly assert that broad collection is not unreasonably invasive by pointing to the existence of formal minimization procedures or other after-the-fact rules and policies meant to address the privacy interests of US persons who are spied on. Can post-collection minimization procedures make a massive surveillance program "reasonable?" The government asked the Supreme Court in *Riley* to approve a similar approach in criminal case – broad collection of all information on the phone, with privacy rights protected by post-seizure usage rules. As with   •
section 702, the government wanted permission to conduct warrantless searches incident to arrest and then use post-search protocols to weed out private information and protect privacy interests.

The Supreme Court's response was derisive and decisive, utterly rejecting the idea that mere post-collection protocols were a substitute for advance judicial authorization via the warrant procedure. In response to the government's assertion that it would develop "protocols" to minimize the privacy problems that its cell phone searches would create. The Court was emphatic. "Probably a good idea," wrote Chief Justice John Roberts, "but the Founders did not fight a revolution to gain the right to government agency protocols." The Supreme Court seemed to be taking a stand. Minimization procedures just aren't going to convert otherwise unconstitutional government intrusions into lawful practices.

Modern surveillance is fundamentally different from traditional surveillance. The rules that made sense for things like dialed phone numbers, searches incident to arrest, and bank records, just don't make sense in the modern world. Yet, the constitutional questions raised by modern surveillance are as yet unanswered. But it seems that the Supreme Court is prepared to take these issues on. The Justices are demonstrating the kind of leadership that earlier generations on the Court showed in cases like *Katz* and *Berger*. The public courts could percolate these issues up to the Supreme Court, getting some much needed guidance on the role of the Fourth Amendment in the digital age. That is, the courts could address these issues if a litigant can get past lack of standing, state secrets, parallel construction, congressional grants of immunity, and the other tools that American spies use to insulate themselves from meaningful judicial review.

15

The Failures of External Oversight

Many government officials involved with mass spying have tried to reassure the public that suspicionless surveillance is closely controlled to make sure that spies don't abuse the power. The claim that spying under the Obama Administration is subject to an immense amount of paperwork is certainly true. In reaction to the lawlessness of the Bush Administration, Obama's intelligence officials have insisted on legal justifications for each of the STELLARWIND surveillance programs. But this approach to intelligence is not a normative one. Instead of asking "Is this what we should be doing?" it asks "Are we complying with the rules and regulations when we do this, and if not, how can we proceed?"[1] The relationship between American spies and their overseers inside the executive branch, in Congress, and in the courts makes it difficult, if not impossible, to ask the normative questions and to answer them correctly.

Oversight is a critical but insufficient part of ensuring that surveillance doesn't get out of control. Most of current oversight is insufficient because it is internal to the executive branch. But without public scrutiny and pressure, even oversight by the other branches of government does not work.

NSA officials have assured the public that "all three branches of government are involved" in approving and overseeing domestic spying.[2] ODNI General Counsel Robert Litt says that there is extensive oversight and meaningful limitations on how information about Americans can be used. The Civil Liberties Protection Officer in the ODNI, Alex Joel, says that "oversight is extensive and multi-layered." Joel identifies various legal offices, inspectors general, and civil liberties committees that allegedly ensure that the intelligence agencies do not run amok.

Listening to these officials, one can see why intelligence agencies feel policed. There is a staggering amount of training, bureaucracy, and red

---

[1] M. Schlanger. "Intelligence Legalism and the National Security Agency's Civil Liberties Gap." *Harvard National Security Journal*, 112 (2015): 112–205.

[2] M. J. Glennon. "National Security and Double Government." *Harvard National Security Journal* 1 (2014): 69.

tape in the conduct of intelligence on US soil. At least today under the Obama Administration, the intelligence community seems to take its obligation to adhere to the rule of law seriously.

The offices that officials like Joel and Litt point to as conducting oversight are mostly part of the executive branch, the same branch that American spies belong to. Internal oversight by its very nature has limited capacity to keep the executive branch itself in line. Internal oversight might be a good way to catch most people who break the rules to spy on their former spouses. For example, documenting database queries will expose agents who are improperly stalking their ex-lovers or spouses. But internal oversight is not an effective tool to ensure that the rules do not allow the president, the FBI, the CIA, or the NSA to decide on high to abuse surveillance powers. Internal oversight is inherently compromised because it is provided from within the executive branch by people who ultimately report to the very same bosses who are ordering and conducting the surveillance activities they are supposed to oversee.

It wasn't that long ago that the Bush Administration got away with STELLARWIND, which was illegal, despite the fact that such a large-scale program required cooperation between various executive branch agencies. When President Bush said, this is how we are going to spy, even though its illegal, everyone just fell into line. After all, he was the President. Specifically, the people who were supposed to play a watchdog role, ensuring compliance with the law, fell down on the job. In giving the green light to bulk collection of Americans Internet metadata under STELLARWIND, the NSA leadership, including DOJ Office of General Counsel lawyers and the Inspector General had ratified the program as lawful based on the argument that "NSA did not actually 'acquire' communications until specific communications were selected" for analysis.[3]

In other words, internal oversight alone is unlikely to stop another STELLARWIND or J. Edgar Hoover.

While intelligence analysts may rightfully feel that they have to answer to lawyers and legal concerns a lot, the lawyers are not necessarily playing any independent policing role. Instead, interviews with the NSA's top lawyers suggest that legal higher ups believe they have little if any independent power to question or change an administration's interpretation of the NSA's legal authority to spy.[4]

---

[3] NSA Draft Inspector General Report at 38.
[4] C. Sprigman. "The NSA's culture of 'legal compliance' still breaks the law." *Just Security.* February 24, 2014. www.justsecurity.org/7485/nsas-culture-legal-compliance-breaks-law/

Obama Administration officials have demonstrated their legalistic approach to surveillance oversight, an approach which means little when there are no applicable rules, or only vague, easily manipulated ones. When James Comey and others threatened to resign in mass over aspects of STELLARWIND, President Bush resolved the impasse by getting a FISC judge to sign an order reaching the erroneous conclusion that mass domestic collection of Internet data could be justified under the FISA pen register statute. There was more paperwork. There was a laughable legal conclusion. But the massive surveillance didn't stop or change and the rule breakers were not punished. Nominal compliance with the law, even a ridiculously attenuated interpretation of the law, was paramount.

Further, internal oversight alone is a poor way to figure out whether surveillance programs are a good idea.

An emphasis on compliance rather than crafting balanced policies is a real problem in an area like surveillance where our technological capabilities have so outpaced the development of legal doctrine. Law is lagging behind, and surveillance overseers can let spying practices expand in the gaps without violating the "rule of law."

Our democratic approach to ensuring that government policies are well-advised and serve the nuanced needs of the general public is to ensure that people with different values and points of view are able to debate and decide policy. The place where this happens is in legislatures, specifically at the federal level in Congress. This kind of review is essential to ensure, not just that our policies are nominally lawful, but also that they are effective, nondiscriminatory, and otherwise well-advised.

Unfortunately, our elected officials in Congress have little ability or incentive to keep surveillance in check. Looming in the backs of many Congress members' minds is the perpetual fear of casting a career-endangering vote. What if you voted against surveillance, or waterboarding, or drone attacks, and a cataclysmic national security breakdown followed? For these reasons, Congress' ability to stand up to even useless and dangerous surveillance remains limited. Elected officials have little ability or incentive to counter the terror narrative. As political scientist Michael Glennon writes:

> While the public may not care strongly or even know about many of the Bush policies that Obama has continued, the public could and would likely know all about any policy change – and who voted for and against it – in the event Congress bungled the protection of the nation. No member wishes to confront the "if only" argument: the argument that a devastating attack would not have occurred if only a national security letter had been sent, if

only the state secrets privilege had been invoked, if only that detainee had not been released.[5]

In June 2013, when senior NSA officials invited all the senators to a classified briefing to educate them about controversial surveillance programs, fewer than half attended.[6]

Congress' institutional fear of challenging the intelligence community is at its most crippling when it comes to spying that takes place overseas. Foreign spying takes place under EO 12333. There's ample evidence that American privacy and security is directly affected by EO 12333 surveillance. But Congress doesn't get involved. The Senate Intelligence Committee – the lead committee on foreign intelligence and national security policy – has not been conducting oversight of EO 12333 collection.[7] Senate Intelligence Committee Chair Dianne Feinstein admitted last August that her committee had never really examined foreign collection under EO 12333, and then initiated an effort to get the intelligence community to create a classified list for the Committee of all its top-secret programs. Feinstein went on to say that the Senate Intelligence Committee "has not been able to 'sufficiently' oversee the programs run under the executive order…[because 'Twelve-triple-three programs are under the executive branch entirely.']"[8]

Because the president's constitutional powers are at their greatest when conducting foreign spying, it seems that when EO 12333 comes up for funding, Congress mostly keeps its head down and doesn't ask too many questions so as not to fuel a constitutional conflict.

When they do ask questions, lawmakers may feel it's impossible to get a straight answer. In a hearing where NSA Director Alexander and ODNI Director Clapper were testifying, Senator Patrick Leahy told the room that even when lawmakers attend briefings, they often get more and more

---

[5] M. J. Glennon. "National Security and Double Government." *Harvard National Security Journal* 1 (2014): 64.

[6] A. Bolton. "Senators skip classified briefing on NSA snooping to catch flights home." *The Hill.* June 15, 2013. http://thehill.com/homenews/senate/305765-senators-skip-classified-briefing-on-nsa-snooping-to-catch-flights-home

[7] B. Gellman and A. Soltani. "NSA collects millions of e-mail address books globally." *The Washington Post.* October 14, 2013, www.washingtonpost.com/world/national-security/nsa-collects-millions-of-e-mail-address-books-globally/2013/10/14/8e58b5be-34f9-11e3-80c6-7e6dd8d22d8f_print.html

[8] A. Watkins. "Most of NSA's data collection authorized by order Ronald Reagan issued." *McClatchy DC.* November 21, 2013. www.mcclatchydc.com/2013/11/21/209167/most-of-nsas-data-collection-authorized.html#storylink=cpy

accurate information from newspapers.[9] Senator Richard J. Durbin of Illinois, the Senate's No. 2 Democrat, has said that when intelligence officials hold briefings, Congress doesn't always attend or get the full story. "You can count on two hands the number of people in Congress who really know," he told the *New York Times*.[10] In the power vacuum, surveillance programs that hurt Americans continue unchecked.

While Congress may not have the time, inclination, or resources for actual oversight, the problem is compounded by the fact that American spies stonewall congressional efforts at oversight. The National Security Act of 1947 requires that Congress be kept "fully and currently informed" about "significant" intelligence activities. But American spies themselves are the ones who decide what "fully and currently informed" means and what details to share with Congress.[11]

Domestic surveillance, on the other hand, *is* subject to many rules – and the intelligence community acknowledges that both courts and Congress have a right to conduct some oversight. But that doesn't mean that American spies are subject to meaningful constraints. Somewhat counterintuitively, the rules governing spying are so complex and so numerous that they actually get in the way of real oversight and democratic accountability. This stuff is hard to understand in its own right, not to mention all the misdirection, jargon, alternative definitions of common words, and legalese the government comes up with to make it even more difficult to grasp. Congress doesn't understand it and very few average citizens get it. These are the main obstacles to transparency and accountability.

Even judicial oversight, the main means of ensuring that criminal surveillance is properly conducted, is working less well in the intelligence context. Serious problems can – and have – gone on for years before the oversight authorities found out. In fact, for each of the controversial bulk spying programs we know about, the FISC judges discovered major legal abuses only years after they occurred, when someone at the NSA voluntarily came forward. There are no examples of the FISC discovering abuses on its own initiative.

---

[9] "Patrick Leahy at NSA hearing: 'We get more in the newspapers than in classified briefings." *The Huffington Post*. October 2, 2013. www.huffingtonpost.com/2013/10/02/patrick-leahy-nsa_n_4030514.html

[10] *National Security Act, 1947*, Pub. L. No. 235, 61 Stat. 495 (1947).

[11] A. Watkins, "Most of NSA's data collection authorized by order Ronald Reagan issued." *McClatchy DC*. November 21, 2013. www.mcclatchydc.com/news/nation-world/national/national-security/article24759289.html

The Foreign Intelligence Surveillance Court, or FISC, was created in 1978. In the wake of the Church Committee report documenting COINTELPRO, NSA surveillance of telegrams, and decades of other government abuses, Congress passed FISA, a set of rules for foreign intelligence collection with a domestic impact. FISA established the FISC to conduct classified judicial review of the factual basis for foreign intelligence surveillance.

In that role, it makes sense that the FISC's processes were secret, as are almost all of its rulings. The bread and butter of the FISC was deciding whether the government had probable cause to believe that a particular person or entity was an agent of a foreign power and was likely to use a particular communications facility such that it was acceptable to spy on that person or facility to get foreign intelligence information. This generally isn't something the public needs to know.

But today, the FISC is playing a completely new and much wider role: authorizing mass surveillance programs and assessing constitutional protections under dubious legal authority, without the benefit of an adversarial process or open debate. Today, FISC judges, and their *ex parte*, secret practices, are the main authority that establishes surveillance law. It is secretly interpreting the law, essentially developing a body of secret law, which is anathema in a democracy.

The FISC is also the main authority we would expect to oversee spies' power – but it never reliably works out that way. Without fear of public or professional rebuke, the FISC judges repeatedly cave in to pressure to find a legal basis for secret, broad, and even lawless surveillance. Instead, the FISC has, even in the face of spying abuses, generally gone out of its way to give the NSA and FBI more power.

Remember that in 2004 Judge Kollar-Kotelly found out that the NSA had been illegally collecting Internet metadata about Americans for the past four years as part of STELLARWIND. There was no law on the books that would allow it, but American spies were looking for her help in defusing the stand-off between Attorney General John Ashcroft and Deputy Attorney General James Comey, and the Bush White House. Rather than send the spies away empty handed, Kollar-Kotelly for the first time interpreted a US statute as allowing bulk collection of Americans' data. Knowing that this was a dangerous power, Judge Kollar-Kotelly issued "minimization" rules, limits on what categories of data American spies were allowed to collect in bulk and what they could subsequently do with the information.

This interpretation was odd under the statute. Not only did the law require "relevance," and relevant doesn't mean "everything," but also the pen register statute doesn't allow an authorizing court to look beyond whether the attorney general has checked all the boxes and made the required certifications. The pen register statute has no provisions for the court to supervise how spies use the data they collect. In other words, the Bush Administration asked Kollar-Kotelly to authorize spying on everyone's Internet usage based on a mere certification and no evidence, and then keep out of whatever American spies ultimately would do with the data they obtained.

This should have been a sign that it is simply crazy to obtain everyone's Internet records under this statute, that Kollar-Kotelly was misconstruing the pen register statute to authorize illegal surveillance that the law was never intended to permit. But instead she allowed the dragnet. Knowing it could be abused and misused, Kollar-Kotelly wanted to set up rules for how American spies could collect and use the data. The NSA argued vigorously against any restrictions, asking the judge basically to "trust them" with this novel surveillance power.

The history of the FISC's involvement in STELLARWIND follows exactly this pattern. Rather than oversee and limit illegal surveillance, judges repeatedly issue unlikely, even revolutionary orders in order to cure executive branch illegality and bolster surveillance legitimacy, even where there is no legal authority to do so.

In 2006, the Bush Administration was faced with news reports shedding light on still secret and illegal aspects of STELLARWIND, including the phone record collection, reported by *USA Today*, and the content surveillance, reported by the *New York Times*. Bush officials decided to seek FISC authorization, as they had done to appease Comey in 2004 regarding surveillance involving Internet transactional data. The Administration filed an application asking the FISC to approve domestic phone record collection under section 215. Judge Malcolm Howard of the Eastern District of North Carolina ordered the phone companies to give the NSA the data. He didn't issue an opinion explaining his reasoning, even though the conclusion that section 215 could authorize bulk collection is criminally weak.[12] He also ensured that when the program needed to be renewed, that he, Howard, would be the judge to hear the application. Of course, he reissued the orders. When the application finally came before a different judge, the

---

[12] Savage, *Power Wars*, pp. 197–198.

program had been in place for almost six months. That judge reapproved the orders, also without writing an opinion or explaining his reasoning.[13]

It was only in August 2013, after a public outcry, that a FISC judge bothered to write an opinion explaining the thinking behind approving domestic dragnet collection.[14] The opinion, by Judge Claire Eagan, was both short and substandard. The phone records surveillance was taking place under section 215 of the USA PATRIOT Act. But Judge Eagan's opinion changed the words of that statute to fit the conclusion she wanted to draw. Eagan's statutory analysis is less than four pages. She omitted section 215's critical admonition that the information the government seeks must be "relevant to an authorized investigation." Instead, she rephrased the statute as follows: "The government may meet the standard under Section 215 if it can demonstrate reasonable grounds to believe that the information sought to be produced has *some bearing on its investigations* of the identified international terrorist organizations."

Judge Eagan then wrote that collection of virtually all Americans' call metadata is "necessary" in order to permit the NSA to do the sorts of searches that allow the agency to determine "connections between known and unknown international terrorist operatives." Because collecting all of the data is "necessary" to facilitate such data mining, the data are "relevant" to an investigation.

But Judge Eagan assumed that collecting the data was "necessary," both technologically and as a means of identifying terrorists. She never considered whether the same kinds of searches could be performed another way, for example by phone companies, with only the relevant data turned over to the government.

Nor did she consider available information showing that the phone dragnet, far from being "necessary," is actually ineffective at identifying connections with terrorists. Senator Patrick Leahy had examined the evidence presented by NSA Director Alexander and found that the section 215 program was not effective against terrorism.[15] Nor could the press identify any phone dragnet counterterrorism success stories. Judge Eagan

---

[13] Id., p. 198.
[14] Amended Memorandum Opinion. *In re Application of the Federal Bureau of Investigation for an Order Requiring the Production of Tangible Things from [redacted]*, No. BR 13–109. (FISC, August 29, 2013) www.aclu.org/files/assets/br13-09-primary-order.pdf
[15] See, e.g., United States Congress. Senate. Committee on the Judiciary. *Strengthening privacy rights and national security: oversight of FISA surveillance programs: Hearing, July 31, 2013.* 113th Cong. 1st Sess. Washington: GPO, 2014.

did not mention this or other testimony before Congress[16] that the phone dragnet was not useful.

The record shows that the FISC is not in the business of saying "no." It is in the business of getting to "yes." Further, once the FISC gets involved, radical surveillance programs are not only on firmer legal footing, but they also expand. For example, when the FISC approved the domestic phone call records dragnet from STELLARWIND, it expanded the collection to include local calls and to authorize database queries for the information of people not associated with al-Qaeda.[17]

Thanks to reporting by Charlie Savage we know that this pattern happened again with the FISC's involvement in the content surveillance aspect of STELLARWIND. After the *New York Times* revealed the surveillance, President Bush admitted it, but claimed that officials were only listening to Americans' calls with al-Qaeda, and started using the press-friendly moniker "Terrorist Surveillance Program" for the spying activity. The practice was illegal under FISA, but in January of 2007, Attorney General Alberto Gonzalez reported that that little problem was solved. A FISC judge had issued "innovative" and "complex" orders to bring the Terrorist Surveillance Program under the authority of FISA and the court's supervision.[18]

That innovation was the 2007 redefinition of the term "facility" to mean international switches and gateways that connect global communications networks instead of just email addresses or phone numbers. This "Large Content FISA" order was signed by Judge Malcolm Howard, the same judge who had signed off on the domestic phone records dragnet under section 215 in 2006 – without so much as a legal opinion.

According to Savage's reporting, this was not a coincidence. The Department of Justice lawyers had advance notice of which judges would be sitting when, and surveillance advocates had pushed internally to file the papers in time for Judge Howard to be the one to rule on them. This forum shopping ensured a happy outcome, at least initially, for the warrantless wiretapping aspect of STELLARWIND.

After Chief Justice Kollar-Kotelly stopped the practice of sending the advance roster of judges' duty weeks to the agency, DOJ lawyers ended up in front of FISC Judge Roger Vinson. Vinson did not believe that

---

[16] *The NSA Report: Liberty and Security in a Changing World.* The President's Review Group on Intelligence and Communications Technology (Princeton University Press, 2014). www.whitehouse.gov/sites/default/files/docs/2013-12-12_rg_final_report.pdf
[17] Savage, *Power Wars*, p. 198.
[18] Id., p. 200.

Judge Howard's and the DOJ's redefinition of "facility" was legitimate. Nevertheless, Vinson scrambled to find a way to let the surveillance continue, first allowing Judge Howard to sign the authorizations that Vinson would not provide and then accepting the DOJ lawyers' argument that it could use the Patriot Act's roving wiretap provision, to allow the NSA to target any email address it believed was related to al-Qaeda without making a probable cause showing to the FISC.

As Charlie Savage writes, these shenanigans "showed how hard it is to be responsible for turning off a counterterrorism program – to accept the risk that if there is an attack, people will say the blood is on your hands …"[19] What Savage's insight means in practice is that the surveillance dynamic is a one-way ratchet, even when a court is involved. The incentive is to always get broader, because authorities are too afraid to stop spying in progress, just in case.

Even years later, when the FISC learned that the NSA had violated court rules for the Internet data collection, the phone record dragnet and the content surveillance, judges let the programs continue. In 2010, FISC judges learned that the NSA disobeyed Kollar-Kotelly's restrictions on Internet data collection from the get-go. The agency was collecting categories of information, potentially including Fourth Amendment protected communications *content*. Not only that, it was sharing that data with domestic law enforcement and other intelligence agencies without proper authorization. The NSA also ignored the rule that said it was supposed to create a record of what it was collecting so that a FISC judge could ensure that it was following the law. Despite the radical new power, despite the fact that this grant of authority was expanded in 2006 to legalize the phone dragnet, it appears no judges bothered to check during all that time on what the NSA was actually doing (nor did anyone inside the intelligence community appear to figure it out until 2009).

Surely, once they heard about how the NSA had been skirting the rules, the FISC cracked down? Actually, no. When two FISC judges – Judge John Bates and Judge Reggie Walton – asked the NSA to explain why the dissemination rule had been disregarded, the government, as they put it, "provided no comprehensive explanation." As far as Bates and Walton could see, Kollar-Kotelly's requirements were simply ignored.

How could this have happened? Judge Bates does not know, since the NSA refused to provide the FISC with a meaningful explanation, but he

---

[19] Id., p. 205.

seemed willing to chalk it up to something less than deliberate wrongdoing. Instead, he blamed complexity. In his 2011 written opinion explaining what happened, Judge Bates said, "It seems likely that widespread ignorance of the rules was a contributing factor."

That may be charitable on the Judge's part, but it doesn't exactly inspire confidence if the nation's leading spy agency doesn't even understand its own operating rules. And it certainly doesn't excuse the FISC for not stepping in and policing the situation. As Professor Margo Schlanger writes, despite Judge Walton and Judge Bates finding that the NSA was acting illegally, they both allowed not just the surveillance – but also the illegalities – to continue.[20]

No one was punished. The FISC agreed to let the domestic Internet dragnet go forward, even after the NSA failed so spectacularly to comply with the rules. Not only that, the FISC changed the rules to make the NSA's rule violations permissible. Before 2010, when contact chaining, if analysts encountered a US number, they had to stop. But in November 2010, the FISC adopted new procedures that would allow the intelligence agencies to find out who Americans were in contact with, so long as a foreigner was the purported target of the search.[21] The public was never told how the laws were being manipulated and abused. Congress didn't act.

Eventually, in 2011, the NSA discontinued the collection, at least under the pen register statute. Senator Ron Wyden and former Utah Senator Mark Udall said that it was because there were no examples of counterterrorism successes. However, an NSA inspector general's report that was obtained by the *New York Times* through a lawsuit under the Freedom of Information Act gives some insight into the evolution of the Internet dragnet and what it may look like today. The report lists four reasons that

---

[20] M. Schlanger. "Intelligence Legalism and the National Security Agency's Civil Liberties Gap." *Harvard National Security Journal* 6 (2015): p. 129 note 61, pointing out that in 2009 Judge Reggie B. Walton allowed the government to continue using "defeat lists" in its handling of PR/TT metadata, even though those defeat lists "deviated, at least in part," from court-approved procedures. See Supplemental Order, No. PR/TT [Redacted], at 2 (FISC June 22, 2009, released March 28, 2014) (J. Walton), www.clearinghouse.net/chDocs/public/NS-DC-0013-0001.pdf. Also, in 2012, Judge Bates permitted "upstream" collection of Internet communications under Section 702 to continue, even though he had previously found the collection violated court-ordered minimization. See Memorandum Opinion, No. PR/TT [Redacted] (FISC 2012). These violations were absolved not by stopping the practices, but by changing the orders to reflect the practice. www.clearinghouse.net/chDocs/public/NS-DC- 0057-0008.pdf

[21] C. Savage. "File says N.S.A. found way to replace email program." *The New York Times.* November 19, 2015. www.nytimes.com/2015/11/20/us/politics/records-show-email-analysis-continued-after-nsa-program-ended.html

the NSA decided to end the dragnet in 2011. Three of those reasons were blacked out and remain classified. The only reason made public was that "other authorities can satisfy certain foreign intelligence requirements" that the Internet dragnet program was intended for.[22]

In other words, the NSA almost certainly still collects voluminous Internet data about Americans, but via other legal authorities and techniques. First, the NSA is able to collect bulk data in other countries, where surveillance is generally free from regulation as well as oversight from courts and Congress. Because of the way the Internet operates, domestic data travels over foreign fiber optic cables. Second, the NSA may have replaced the Internet dragnet with metadata it now gleans from Upstream surveillance under section 702.[23]

By combining these two sources of information, the NSA would have access to similar data as under the controversial and disaster-plagued Internet dragnet. So it willingly stopped the collection under domestic law but may have pursued it under EO 12333.[24] Surveillance doesn't seem to stop, it just shifts around, as do the rules under which it operates.

Given that the two domestic dragnet programs revealed by Snowden had their legal roots in the same Kollar-Kotelly 2004 opinion, perhaps it comes as no surprise to find that the FISC was no better at keeping tabs on the phone dragnet than it was on the Internet transactional dragnet. Right from the start, the NSA disobeyed the few limitations imposed on its use of Americans' telephone call records. Remember, the agency was only supposed to search for telephone numbers for which it had a "reasonable articulable suspicion" (RAS) of being connected to a particular terrorist group – and requests for those searches were supposed to be approved by officials within the intelligence community. That didn't happen. Instead, the FISC eventually learned that over time 89 percent of the numbers the NSA searched for did not meet the RAS requirement. And this illegal practice continued from 2006 until 2009, at which point the NSA finally informed the FISC about it.

22 Ibid., citing an NSA Inspector General report.
23 "Report on the Surveillance Program Pursuant to Section 702 of the Foreign Intelligence Surveillance Act," Privacy and Civil Liberties Oversight Board, July 2, 2014, pp. 62, 64, 140. www.pclob.gov/library/702-Report.pdf
24 J. N. Tye. "Meet Executive Order 1233: The Reagan rule that allows the NSA to spy on Americans." The Washington Post. July 18, 2014. www.washingtonpost.com/opinions/meet-executive-order-12333-the-reagan-rule-that-lets-the-nsa-spy-on-americans/2014/07/18/93d2ac22-0b93-11e4-b8e5-d0de80767fc2_story.html

Judge John Bates was also the recipient of this unfortunate piece of news. He said that the FISC's approval of the phone dragnet program was premised on "a flawed depiction" of how the NSA uses metadata. "Contrary to the government's repeated assurances, the NSA had been routinely running queries of the metadata using querying terms that did not meet the required standard for querying." The FISC concluded that this requirement had been " 'so frequently and systemically violated that it can fairly be said that this critical element of the overall... regime has never functioned effectively.' "[25]

Again, the problem seems to have been either ignorance or bad faith on the part of American spies. Director of the NSA General Keith Alexander explained to Judge Bates that key personnel did not understand what the analysts were doing.

And again, the problem was exacerbated by the fact that the oversight was primarily internal, so no one caught the mistakes. American spies were responsible for documenting their own compliance with the rules, documentation that ended up being both inaccurate and ignored. NSA Chief Alexander told presiding Judge Walton that the NSA not only violated FISC rules but that the agency also kept making false reports to the FISC. That's because key personnel did not know what analysts were doing, even when key people became aware of what was going on, they nevertheless remained unaware that false reports were still going to FISC judges.

Again, overly complicated rules were an excuse for noncompliance and interfered with the ability of other branches to conduct oversight. And again, despite the abuses and law breaking, the FISC judges allowed the NSA's bulk collection program to continue to this day.

Third, the NSA also misled the FISC in its content surveillance. Remember, under these two programs, the NSA was authorized under section 702 of the FISA Amendments Act to warrantlessly collect Americans' communications with foreigners abroad about topics relating to foreign intelligence matters. PRISM collection comes from US-based service providers while the NSA conducts Upstream collection via devices connected directly to the fiber optic wires comprising the Internet. Until 2011, FISC judges and Congress (and the American people) were told that the agency's content surveillance system was quite accurate in both capturing only relevant messages and in avoiding forbidden, purely domestic

---

[25] Foreign Intelligence Surveillance Court Memorandum Opinion, No. [Redacted] (FISC September 25, 2012) (J. Bates). www.dni.gov/files/documents/September%202012%20 Bates%20Opinion%20and%20Order.pdf

communications between American citizens. That also was not true. The NSA regularly collects Americans' domestic messages. And although the FISC was initially outraged at this practice, it now allows it.

To understand how this happens, and how the NSA misled FISC judges for so long, you have to understand the technology of Upstream surveillance. The NSA chose to build its facilities to spy on fiber optic communications traffic at telecommunications offices that handle both domestic and international traffic. The search process is supposed to leave off-limits domestic traffic alone. But the NSA's Upstream systems capture Internet transactions. These transactions could be single message transactions or a bundle of messages, MCTs.

Recall from Chapter 8 that an email inbox is an example of an MCT. If you have a webmail email account, like Gmail or Hotmail, when you open up your email program, you will receive some number of emails sitting in your inbox. There isn't just one message in there, there are multiple messages, and these are transmitted across the Internet as one communication transaction – the inbox – even though there are multiple separate emails in there.

In 2011 for the first time, the NSA told the FISC that even if only one message in an MCT is responsive to the NSA's targeting terms, the NSA devices nonetheless pull the entire package of messages into the NSA databases. MCTs can contain any number of communications, including purely domestic messages that have nothing to do with foreign intelligence.

The inbox example was one that an ODNI official gave at a press conference. But the number 15 is a suggestion, not an upper limit. When I log into Gmail on my computer, the server will transmit thousands of messages to my browser. How many of these comprise a single transaction? Similarly, when I sync my data across devices using Apple's iCloud, all my contacts, emails, and photographs might be communicated as a single transaction with multiple communications. What about when I back my computer or phone up to the cloud?

Potentially worse, does the NSA pull in service providers' transmissions as MCTs? If so, when providers send unencrypted data between one data center and another, the NSA will pull in the entire transaction even if only one message meets its selection criteria. That could mean that if any legitimate target is using a Google service like Gmail, and that target's messages are transmitted to another server overseas as part of a huge data back up or to improve quality of service, hundreds of thousands of other Google customers will get pulled in to the NSA coffers as part of that MCT. The public does not fully understand what an MCT is or how they are handled.

The NSA claims it is not capable of breaking MCTs down into individual messages.[26] That claim was a major reason Judge Bates let the collection continue. He did not want to interfere with a surveillance program that the intelligence community claimed was protecting the nation. But after Bates' judicial opinion was made public, almost fifty renowned technologists who are experts in Internet routing and digital communications wrote to the Director of National Intelligence Review Group on Intelligence and Communications Technologies to express their doubts that this was in fact true. "As technologists," their letter reads, "it strikes us as highly unlikely that no reasonable solution exists to overcome the technical hurdle in this example."[27]

The experts went on: "It is deeply problematic that the court has no way to verify these types of assertions, and that the court is not provided an independent technologist or adviser outside of the intelligence community." Indeed, FISC Chief Judge Reggie Walton has admitted that "the FISC is forced to rely upon the accuracy of the information that is provided to the Court."[28]

Is NSA's over-collection of MCTs truly unavoidable? We don't know.

Further, the NSA systems do not adequately distinguish messages that are purely domestic messages but routed internationally, from those where an American is actually communicating with someone overseas. Domestic messages are legally off limits, but NSA machines grab them when they are *about* a foreign intelligence target. And remember, targets can be countries or organizations. The broadness of the collection depends on the selectors the NSA uses, which are not subject to judicial oversight.

Judge Bates asked the NSA to make a count of the number of purely domestic communications it was obtaining each year as a result of its practice of collecting single communications transaction that were for whatever reason internationally routed, as well as MCTs. The NSA refused to count. The spies may have been worried that counting would give the NSA legal knowledge that its collection violated the statute – knowledge that's a prerequisite for criminal and civil liability. By refusing to count, the NSA avoids knowing the truth and thus escapes liability.

---

[26] ODNI press conference. August 21, 2013. Audio file. www.eff.org/sites/default/files/odni-call-excerpt.mp3

[27] Technologists' Comment to the Director of National Intelligence Review Group on Intelligence and Communications Technology. October 4, 2013. www.cdt.org/files/pdfs/nsa-review-panel-tech-comment.pdf

[28] Ibid.

So Judge Bates tried to make the calculation on his own. He determined that the NSA was collecting at least 56,000 emails – and possibly many more – between innocent Americans who have no foreign connections and are suspected of no crimes.

This was the third serious NSA violation that the FISC had learned about. Judge Bates excoriated the agency: "[t]he court is troubled that the government's revelations... mark the third instance in less than three years in which the government has disclosed a substantial misrepresentation regarding the scope of a major collection program." These misrepresentations, Bates concluded, had utterly subverted the court-mandated oversight for that program.

Based on the new information, Judge Bates concluded that the previous FISC judges should not have authorized section 702 collection to begin with. Given that the scale of the NSA's incidental acquisition was objectively large and, in many cases, not justified by national security, he found that section 702 was in violation of the Fourth Amendment. He ordered the government to remedy the problem immediately or cease the program altogether.

But again, Judge Bates did not stop the program. Nor did he stop the most problematic aspects of the program, the NSA's Upstream collection of MCTs and other purely domestic messages. Instead, the NSA proposed post-collection usage rules, called minimization procedures, which simply means rules governing what the NSA would be allowed to do with the data once it's got it. To address the MCT problem, the NSA adopted rules for Upstream surveillance that require it to treat MCTs as a special category. MCTs were to be screened for irrelevant information, which must be deleted. No agency but the NSA is supposed to have access to MCTs, not the CIA or the FBI. The NSA put special procedures in place designed to identify when a communication within an MCT is between American citizens.[29]

The NSA continued to collect and share the single communication domestic messages obtained via Upstream surveillance, even though domestic messages are explicitly off limits under the statute. Section 702 says that the court is supposed to ensure that the NSA's targeting procedures don't knowingly and intentionally collect purely domestic communications. But Bates found that the Upstream single communication

---

[29] "Minimization Procedures Used by the National Security Agency in Connection with Acquisitions of Foreign Intelligence Information Pursuant to Section 702 of the Foreign Intelligence Surveillance Act of 1978, as amended." October 2011, § 3(b)(5)(a)(1)(a).

domestic collection was acceptable. He reasoned that the NSA analysts do not know at the time of acquisition that such messages are domestic. Only after they are already collected can the NSA analysts tell that some single communications transactions are domestic. So, Judge Bates decided that because this overbroad collection was not intentional, the NSA shouldn't be punished by being prohibited from using and sharing the messages it captured.

Let's review what happened here. There is a law that the public was told only targets foreigners overseas. Domestic messages are off limits. And there are minimization procedures to protect American privacy. Despite all of that, the NSA, with FISC approval, routinely collected and shared domestic messages under section 702. Section 215 requires that business records be "relevant" to a counterterrorism investigation, but that law was used for dragnet domestic collection. To paraphrase *The Princess Bride*, these laws don't mean what you think they mean.[30] There is a pattern here. Spies want to "Collect It All" for counterterrorism purposes. Judges are legitimately worried about overreaching, so they create complicated rules to try to allow the spying but prevent potential abuses. But the spies break the rules, intentionally or not. Courts don't know about it until they are told, because they aren't conducting and perhaps do not have the technical and other resources to conduct, any meaningful oversight. Instead, the main way judges discover that abuses have occurred is when the spies themselves decide, for one reason or other, to come clean. Maybe the officials who started breaking the rules are gone, so the spies can confess now that there is no one to be punished or blamed.

Once the judges find out about crazy legal arguments or outright abuses, they make some angry noises. But they remain reluctant to penalize the government officials who finally are telling them the truth. They also don't want to stop the spying because they're told that if they do, some people could die. So they expand the NSA's authority, issue more complex rules, and let the surveillance go forward.

Until Edward Snowden, judicial oversight was entirely in the secret FISC. No public courts reviewed these programs because of standing doctrine, state secrets claims, and "parallel construction." Even after the programs started to become known and lawsuits were filed, Congress enabled the attorney general to immunize providers who had cooperated with STELLARWIND in the FISAAA of 2008. As a result, the federal

---

[30] "You keep using that word." *YouTube*. Online video clip. February 4, 2007. www.youtube.com/watch?v=G2y8Sx4B2Sk

courts are way, way behind in playing a policing role, and unlikely to catch up soon.

You might say that Congress doesn't understand intelligence spying, and has, at least until the recent public outcry, abrogated its responsibility to learn. The FISC seems entirely dependent on the NSA to self-report its own abuses, since the judges lack the power to force the NSA to disclose information and are apparently afraid to shut down or say no even to patently illegal programs. Regular courts are out of the game. And executive branch oversight, even when well meaning, is simply spies overseeing themselves. It's not a tool to prevent another STELLARWIND.

Professor Michael Glennon offers a pessimistic view of the future of democratic oversight:

> The public believes that the constitutionally-established institutions control national security policy, but that view is mistaken. Judicial review is negligible; congressional oversight is dysfunctional; and presidential control is nominal. Absent a more informed and engaged electorate, little possibility exists for restoring accountability in the formulation and execution of national security policy.[31]

Glennon's diagnosis of the problem is terrifying. Yet, we don't have the luxury of throwing our hands in the air and letting the patient die. This is our democracy on the operating table, and oversight is one of the only things we have going for us. We need to make the patient healthy, and like real health, it's not going to be just diet, or just exercise, or just good genes. Oversight is not a single effective thing, it is a complex web that includes public transparency, record-keeping, investigator generals and other watchdogs, internal and external accountability, strong rules, a culture of compliance, a normative agreement about what's right and what's wrong, whistleblower protections, and the threat of liability or imprisonment when the rules are broken.

At a 2015 event co-hosted by *Just Security* and NYU's Brennan Center for Justice, the NSA's Civil Liberties and Privacy Director Rebecca Richards was asked whether the rules the NSA has in place are adequate to withstand a dangerous president. Richards' answer noted the "layers of accountability" provided by the Office of the Director of National Intelligence, the Justice Department, the Privacy and Civil Liberties Oversight Board, and Congress. We've seen that those are wholly inadequate. History tells us that

---

[31] M. J. Glennon. "National Security and Double Government." *Harvard National Security Journal* 1 (2014): 1–2.

up against a determined adversary from within the most powerful office in the world, America's surveillance safeguards are anemic, barely bumps in the road. What about oversight has changed since 2001 that would stop another president from starting another STELLARWIND?

Surveillance law should be president-proof, exactly because someone like Richard Nixon could be president again. Our laws are nowhere near ready for what might come next.

16

The National *In*Security Agency

The NSA's surveillance fervor is making all of us less secure. In order to ensure access the world's communications, the NSA is actively hacking computers and networks, stealing encryption keys, and otherwise compromising the security of networks that people rely on every day.

These NSA hacking efforts expose the public to all kinds of attackers: not just the US government, but other governments, spies, corporate espionage, thieves, and hackers. Security vulnerabilities are agnostic. They don't work for American spies and stop working when a foreign hand is at the keyboard. A back door that the US government can walk through may also be used by others. If the NSA can break in or decrypt, then so can China. Sooner or later, the same attacks will be discovered and adopted by criminals as well.

When there are choices about whether to secure networks (thereby preventing crimes and protecting privacy) or to hack them (thereby enabling surveillance), the NSA has a major role in making those decisions. That's because the NSA is supposed to spy on foreign threats, and insecure information technology makes that possible. But the NSA has another important mission. It is also responsible for securing US government information from foreign threats. In other words, the NSA has two missions, information assurance and signals intelligence collection.

These missions are complementary in that the expertise that makes for a great spy is also useful in fending off spying by others. But the missions also clash. Governments around the world use the Internet to communicate, as do private parties. Attacking, or failing to secure, the same technology that the US government and the American people use jeopardizes security in the interests of more surveillance.

Conversely, because the NSA has a spying mission, private industry justifiably views its information assurance services with strong suspicion. Government officials and military contractors share classified information over privately owned facilities. The security of some private networks – critical infrastructure like energy and transportation – is of national

263

interest. But if the NSA has access to, or even gives advice about, private sector security more generally, it might not be a trustworthy partner, preferring surveillance over customer security.

Unsurprisingly, the NSA's information assurance efforts have a twisted history.[1] The policy question then and now is what role the NSA should play in securing private networks, given their importance in government communications, critical infrastructure operation, and the national economy. Historically, Congress has given the Department of Commerce jurisdiction over US communications networks and anticipated the NSA playing only an advisory role.

Nevertheless, the NSA has had repeated – sometimes public, sometimes classified – battles with the private sector over encryption. Encryption is a mathematical way to scramble, and thus ensure the confidentiality of, data. That is not, however, its only useful function. It can also mathematically attest to the validity of the source of information (I am who I say I am), as well as to the integrity of data sent (this information has not been tampered with). Starting in the 1970s, private sector cryptography was getting good enough to pose a real challenge to the NSA's abilities to descramble and spy. As Professor Susan Landau explains, during this critical period the government had no problem with the authentication and integrity checking function of encryption, but strongly opposed its use outside the government for confidentiality purposes.

The NSA waged an ultimately unsuccessful battle against broad public opposition to limit the spread of encryption technology.[2] In the 1970s, the hallmark of that battle was export control, an effort to limit the spread of difficult-to-crack encryption to the foreign governments that the NSA wanted to spy on. By the 1990s, those efforts included proposals for "key escrow" systems for cellular phones – a "Clipper Chip" that would enable the government to decrypt and wiretap phone calls. As part of its political efforts in the 1990s, the NSA convinced FBI Director Louis Freeh that widespread crypto would seriously impact his agency's investigative abilities. Freeh became a strong ally fighting for surveillance-friendly communications systems.

But by the mid-1990s that it became obvious that financial transactions on the Internet and mobile communications services would need to be secured from eavesdroppers, and that would mean implementing strong

---

[1] For a history of NSA's conduct of its information assurance mission, see S. Landau. "Under the Radar: NSA's Efforts to Secure Private-Sector Telecommunications Infrastructure." *Journal of National Security Law & Policy* 7 (2014): 411–442.
[2] Id., p. 424.

crypto. Congress rejected proposals that would create technological obligations to ensure wiretappability of handheld devices, computers, and the Internet. In other words, Congress rejected mandatory "back doors" for government agents to access digital systems. Congress did, however, mandate technology to maintain the current wiretappability of telephone networks, as well as export controls that would track the sale of specialty software to certain governments. But otherwise, the proliferation of encryption in commercial off-the-shelf software was allowed. Industry was happy because they could sell the same desirable product around the world. The NSA was comfortable with this outcome because it preserved controls on equipment sold to governments and communications providers in other countries where it focuses its attention. The FBI, however, was not happy because the proposals allowed broad use of encryption domestically inside the United States, exactly where the FBI had hoped to maintain and extend its surveillance capabilities. (This disparity between the NSA and the FBI on crypto policy persists today.) Meanwhile, civil libertarians and industry rejoiced. They believed they had won the Crypto Wars.

In some ways, the NSA's views on encryption changed, too. There are several examples where the NSA's information assurance division shared knowledge with industry in an effort to promote strong encryption and ensure communications security.

But on the SIGINT side, the NSA's efforts tell a different story. With the proliferation of strong crypto, the agency appears to have put a huge amount of time, effort, and money toward attacking or undermining encryption. The NSA wants to "Collect It All," not "Protect It All." And when these decisions are being made – whether to undermine encryption algorithms, whether to pay companies to adopt backdoored encryption, whether to hoard information about security vulnerabilities, or share it so the flaws may be patched – the decision is a in the hands of the intelligence community. Does any federal agency charged with consumer privacy, security, economic development, foreign affairs, or human rights have a part in the decision-making process? The Federal Trade Commission – which fights for consumer privacy and security – should be in the room. The State Department – invested in promoting Internet freedom – should be in the room. The Department of Commerce should be in the room. Without countervailing political pressure from agencies charged with upholding a range of public values, internal decision making may give the NSA officials a lot of "process" and "compliance" to worry about – contributing to that feeling of overregulation. But the upshot is that national security interests will overrun economic interests and civil liberties.

The problem is, vulnerabilities in our communications systems are indifferent to who exploits them, so if the NSA can access our private communications, so can foreign governments, spies, corporate competitors, thieves, and hackers. If the NSA can use security vulnerabilities to access our private communications, so can others. You can't hack the network to ensure surveillance and at the same time secure the network to prevent hacking.

The NSA's policies promote insecurity in two ways. First, there are the security flaws, or bugs, that already exist, that the NSA discovers and fails to take steps to fix. If the agency finds a bug in an operating system or a web browser, it could tell Microsoft or Google. Then those providers could issue a software update, or patch, which fixes the problem for everyone. As part of its information assurance mission, the NSA likely notifies companies of the vulnerabilities it discovers, at least some of the time.

But in at least some cases, the NSA is keeping the information secret, exactly so that the vulnerable parties do not fix it. Then, the NSA waits for a good opportunity to use what it knows to accomplish surveillance or in a system attack. This approach creates security risks because other skilled attackers may have discovered the same flaw and exploited it themselves. The security flaws don't exist only in machines targeted by the NSA, either. When vulnerabilities are found in commercial software, the general public is exposed. The NSA and its spying partners in the United Kingdom and Canada also scan the Internet for vulnerable computers to attack. These vulnerable machines aren't operated by targets. They are innocent third parties. Nevertheless, the spies will use them as intermediaries through which they route their own hacking attacks. The goal is to hide the fact that the source of a hack is actually the NSA or the GCHQ.

Second, there are vulnerabilities that the NSA itself creates. The NSA has subverted the development of encryption standards to get the world to adopt encryption that the agency can descramble. The NSA has stolen millions of phone encryption keys so that it can decrypt cell phone conversations around the world. The NSA hacks into the computers of system administrators, and then into the systems they are charged with securing, to gain access to communications bottlenecks where the agency can efficiently spy on hundreds of millions of people at a time.

It's like the NSA is picking the lock on your front door so it can come on in, search your house, and rifle through your underwear drawer. Now, your door is unlocked. While the NSA and the FBI think that they are going to be the only ones able to walk through the door, computer scientists almost uniformly agree that unlocked doors mean that other burglars can get into your home, too. So the NSA is picking locks, or it's discovering that peoples' doors are unlocked, and it's exploiting the situation, rather than helping the homeowner fix them. The intelligence community is valuing surveillance over security.

Because this is the Internet, the NSA's hacking is dangerous in a way that real-world burglaries never could be. The NSA hacks communications routers and gateways, the places on the network through which billions of messages travel. Conducting massive spying on hundreds of millions of innocent people, the NSA also leaves hundreds of millions of innocent people simultaneously susceptible to network attacks. In short, the NSA views itself as breaking one kind of security in favor of another. It's breaking network security, which protects people from theft, stalking, attacks on their free speech and political organizing, intellectual property theft and more, in favor of the phantom claims of increased counterterrorism capabilities that it says will result from a massive "Collect It All" program.

As it turns out, the NSA is filled with some of the most talented hackers on the planet, capable of amazing things. A recently leaked document reveals an NSA catalog of hacks, called the TAO or Tailored Access Organization catalog. The catalog reveals that the TAO team is both skilled and equipped with powerful attack software. Step one is hacking into the targets' computers. Step two is installing software "implants" – computer code that gives spies the ability to steal information from or manipulate a compromised machine. One implant is codenamed CAPTIVATEDAUDIENCE. That tool takes over a targeted computer's microphone and records conversations taking place near the device. Another implant, GUMFISH, can covertly take over a computer's webcam and snap photographs. The software makes sure that the webcam light doesn't go on so that the target has no way of knowing the camera is on and recording. FOGGYBOTTOM records the users' Internet browsing history and collects login details and passwords used to access websites and email accounts, then sends those login credentials to the NSA. GROK is used to log keystrokes, basically creating a record of everything you type. SALVAGERABBIT steals data from removable flash drives that connect to an infected computer.[3] But while these "implants" have cool names and sound scary, they aren't the scariest things the NSA is doing. Many of these NSA super-hacker techniques are

[3] R. Gallagher and G. Greenwald. "How the NSA plans to infect 'millions' of computers with malware." *The Intercept*. March 12, 2014.

"targeted." In other words, American spies have very effective tools they can use to break into the machines that a terrorist or a government worker uses.

But the serious, terrifying problem isn't targeted surveillance, it's mass surveillance. American spies don't just want to spy on specific targets. They want to control the network so they can spy on everyone and anyone. In 2004, the NSA's plans to infect networks affected only a few hundred targets. But over the next six to eight years, the number of TAO implants installed on networked machines soared to tens of thousands.[4] According to former NSA cryptographer William Binney, the NSA currently has access to over 50,000 implants in the switches and servers around the world on the Internet.[5]

The NSA has a surveillance initiative named "Owning the Net." The agency sought $67.6 million in taxpayer funding for its Owning the Net program last year. One part of Owning the Net is an automated system codenamed TURBINE. TURBINE will be a system that expands the NSA capacity so that it can send "millions of implants." In other words, the NSA is building the capacity to hack into hundreds of thousands or millions of computers at a time.[6]

Obviously, all of the users of infected computers are not threats. Perhaps less obviously, this technique opens up the victims to attacks by others. Vulnerabilities can beget other vulnerabilities, and the failure to inform someone that they are open to attack means that others can exploit the same weakness.

The NSA's goal isn't just to spy on the people who own these compromised machines, but to control the machines the public uses to communicate, so the NSA can "Collect It All." In order to "Collect It All," American spies need access to major network switches or gateways – network points through which lots of digital traffic flows. Getting access to the treasure trove that flows through communications gateways works well when the entity that operates the gateway cooperates with the spies. In the United States, the majority of the communications network is privately owned.

---

[4] Ibid.

[5] "NSA Whistleblower William Binney Private Presentation/Q&A on Snowden Files/ THINTHREAD." Presentation by W. Binney, *Leak Source*, October 3, 2014. leaksource.info/ 2014/10/03/nsa-whistleblower-william-binney-private-presentation-qa-on-snowden-files-thinthread/

[6] R. Gallagher and G. Greenwald. "How the NSA plans to infect 'millions' of computers with malware." *The Intercept.* March 12, 2014. firstlook.org/theintercept/2014/03/12/ nsa-plans-infect-millions-computers-malware/

Some private companies are quite willing to help out the government that regulates them. So after September 11th, AT&T helped the NSA to build secret spying rooms at its offices, even though President Bush's warrantless wiretapping was illegal at the time. Verizon and other providers gave over call records without legal process even though the information was protected by federal statute.

Other companies may or may not have the legal right to resist spies who want access to the infrastructure. Fiber optic provider Level 3 appears to have cooperated with the GCHQ when it tapped Google and Yahoo! data center transmissions. That cooperation was probably pursuant to a legal demand under UK law. (We do not know for sure, as this process was secret.) Under US law, the NSA likely needs to get a FISC judge order to target US corporations overseas.[7] A FISC judge might have balked at an application for an order such as this. But if the United Kingdom took the lead, then that country's liberal rules for targeting noncitizens (such as "American" company Google) would apply. Further, the United Kingdom generally doesn't have court oversight for its intelligence spying. Rather, the Secretary of State, a Cabinet minister position, signs such surveillance orders.[8] It's possible that Level 3 decided to comply with this legal process, which would not be sufficient under US law. Once the data was acquired, in an end run around US laws meant to protect American citizens overseas, the GCHQ could share that data with the NSA.

But what happens when the entity controlling the communications network won't cooperate with American spies or our Five Eyes partners, either because the spying is illegal, they aren't subject to US legal process, or they can't be trusted to keep the spying secret? That's when the spies resort to network hacking. Hacking hubs and gateways often will start with hacking the system administrators who work at foreign phone and Internet service providers. Hacking an administrator's computer can give American spies trade secrets that they can use to find vulnerabilities. "Sys admins are a means to an end," an NSA operative wrote on an internal message board. Compromising a systems administrator, the operative notes, makes it easier to get to other targets of interest, including any "government official that happens to be using the network some admin takes care of." In other words, the system administrator's compromised computer is a vehicle

---

[7] FISA Amendments Act sections 703, 704, enacted at 50 U.S.C. §§ 1881b, 1881c.

[8] "Foreign Intelligence Gathering Laws: United Kingdom." *Library of Congress*. United States Library of Congress. June 9, 2015. www.loc.gov/law/help/foreign-intelligence-gathering/united-kingdom.php

for learning about potential network weaknesses, finding passwords or encryption keys, discovering router access interfaces, and more.

Once the NSA knows how to hack the routers and machines that make up the Internet backbone, it can get access to every phone call and digital message that goes through that switch. It's a big deal to exploit vulnerabilities in an entire telecommunications switch. The attacker can compromise the privacy and security of everyone who uses that part of the network. But also, by either creating vulnerabilities or not repairing the ones it uncovers, the attacker leaves everyone whose messages flow through that switch at risk of attacks from others. Other spies or criminals can walk through the same doors the NSA used.

The public has learned that the NSA nevertheless exploits telecoms, including ones that handle traffic from countries presumed to be our close allies. For example, Belgacom – Belgium's largest telecom – was broken into by the GCHQ. Belgacom services are used by millions of people across Europe. Its customers include the European Commission, the European Council, and the European Parliament. Hacking the Belgacom network also allows spying on and meddling with not only Belgacom customers but also anyone whose calls were handled by that central router.

The GCHQ infected Belgacom with a highly sophisticated piece of attack software, or malware, developed by the NSA. The malware looked like legitimate Microsoft software but was actually stealing customer data from Belgacom. Security researchers think the malware the GCHQ used on Belgacom is one of the most advanced spy tools ever identified, and have codenamed it "Regin." Regin was able to grab encrypted and unencrypted streams of cell phone calls and other private communications handled by Belgacom and forward it all to the GCHQ.

The GCHQ's goal was to access the central cell phone roaming router in Belgium. That router processes and directs international cell phone calls. With that access, the GCHQ could not only get unencrypted messages, it also could conduct "man-in-the-middle" attacks on smartphone users. A man-in-the-middle attack occurs when an outsider is able to intercept and change messages flowing back and forth between two or more people talking to each other. Man-in-the-middle attacks enable wiretapping, as well as corrupting or falsifying data streams between entities. Remember when the FBI planted false information in the car of a member of the American Communist Party to convince his colleagues that he was an FBI informant? Corrupting data streams would be the digital version of that kind of attack.

Having access to the central router would also enable the GCHQ to attack cell phone users directly. Spies could falsify traffic to install malware on some smartphone users' devices. (These malicious updates would not work on all devices. For example, because Apple's iPhone requires its software to be cryptographically signed by Apple, malware that has not been signed will not work. The government would have to force Apple to sign its attack software, as it most recently tried to do in an investigation involving the cell phone of one of the 2015 San Bernardino shooters.) If successful in using router access to compromise user handsets, spies can implant software that would force the phone to reveal its GPS location, to covertly take pictures or video, and to record calls or even ambient conversations.[9] This kind of software exists. There are spyware companies that sell this kind of software to governments and others around the world.[10]

Regin malware was also behind an attack on computer systems belonging to the European Commission, the European Council, and to a prominent Belgian cryptographer. Researchers also discovered the malware on networks in Algeria, Afghanistan, Belgium, Brazil, Fiji, Germany, Iran, India, Malaysia, Syria, Pakistan, and Russia.[11] In one undisclosed middle-eastern country, the targets tend to be telecoms, government agencies, and research institutes. One security company has also found hotels infected, likely to gain access to the traveling schedules of foreign government officials. It's likely that all these entities were hacked by the same entity, the NSA's best spying partner, the GCHQ.

NSA hacking also extends to the physical hardware that runs the Internet. The NSA puts software backdoors in the laptops, mobile devices, and other machines sold to the public. The NSA intercepts shipments of Internet routers, the hardware devices that process network traffic. Agents grab the boxes from the US mails, open them, install computer chips with malware that reports traffic back to the NSA in the machine, repackage it, and send it on its way. One of the Snowden documents contained a photograph of NSA operatives tampering with a Cisco brand router. Reports say that the NSA has had agents in China, Germany, and South Korea working

---

9   P. Langlois. Interview with Christian Stocker. "Passively 'sniffing data: How mobile network spying works." *Der Spiegel*. November 15, 2015. www.spiegel.de/international/europe/interview-telecom-security-expert-philippe-langlois-on-gchq-spying-a-933870.html
10 FinFisher: en.wikipedia.org/wiki/FinFisher
11 K. Zetter. "Researchers discover government spy tool used to hack telecoms and Belgian cryptographer." *Wired*. November 24, 2014. www.wired.com/2014/11/mysteries-of-the-malware-regin

on programs that use "'physical subversion' to infiltrate and compromise networks and devices."[12] When this happens, the hacks can leave anyone who uses the hacked software, protocol, tools, or networks subject to attack.

In response to the news reports, Cisco first wrote a letter to President Obama. The company told the White House "if these allegations are true, these actions will undermine confidence in our industry and in the ability of technology companies to deliver products globally."[13] The company asked Obama to develop rules of the road that would serve national security objectives without harming industry. After almost a year without an answer, Cisco reported that it started shipping its boxes to vacant addresses in a bid to foil the NSA. If the NSA doesn't know who the customer is, then it doesn't know which boxes it wants to intercept.[14] It's unfortunate that an American company has to come up with this kind of strategy to avoid the American government subverting its products.

The NSA's "Owning the Net" initiative also means being able to deny Internet access to adversaries. One way American spies do this is through denial of service, or DoS, attacks. The most common type of DoS attack occurs when the attacker "floods" a network with too many requests for information. Since a targeted server can only process a certain number of requests at once, flooding the server with requests will overload it until it grinds to a halt. To accomplish DoS attacks, the NSA has control over swarms of computers – botnets – capable of bombarding websites and computer systems with traffic from many different computers until they collapse.[15] Denying an enemy access to communications can be a critical tool in warfare, but it is a dangerous capability in peacetime. Meanwhile, the botnet computers remain infected with malware that the NSA knows about, but chooses not to disclose to affected users. That malware can leave the zombie computer open to attacks from people other than the NSA.

The NSA's activities have undermined users' trust in the Internet. Well-founded trust is an important part of security. If customers can't trust US products, then they won't buy them. If businesses can't trust that they can operate safely online – whether it's conducting credit card transactions or

[12] P. Maass and L. Poitras. "Core secrets: NSA saboteurs in China and Germany." *The Intercept.* October 10, 2014. theintercept.com/2014/10/10/core-secrets/

[13] Letter to President Obama from Cisco Systems, Inc., May 15, 2014. goo.gl/wv4gmD

[14] D. Pauli. "Cisco posts kit to empty houses to dodge NSA chop shops." *The Register.* March 18, 2015. www.theregister.co.uk/2015/03/18/want_to_dodge_nsa_supply_chain_taps_ask_cisco_for_a_dead_drop/

[15] K. Poulsen. "NSA has been hijacking the botnets of other hackers." *Wired.* February 12, 2014. www.wired.com/2014/03/nsa-botnet/

providing legitimate access to health care data – then they will either stay in the analog world or put their customers at risk. If the Department of Commerce were involved in the NSA's decision making process, it is hard to imagine that the NSA would be sabotaging American products.

To understand how serious the trust problem is, consider the NSA's FLAME hack, which exploited software updates to create, rather than fix, vulnerabilities. A user would think she was simply downloading a legitimate update from Microsoft, but would actually be installing FLAME software instead. Once there, the software could activate computer microphones and cameras, log keyboard strokes, take screen shots, and attack nearby Bluetooth devices.[16] The fact that FLAME's attack vector was the subversion of Microsoft software update procedures is notable. It creates a situation in which people will not – and should not – trust updates.

Security professionals uniformly agree that we need to regularly update the software on our machines, a process called patching. Patches can include software improvements and system updates that improve the security of the machine, that fix known vulnerabilities, and more. SANS, a research and education organization, advises, "you should install *ANY AND ALL* patches that apply to your system hardware and software, whether or not they are security related. If a program that has a patch resides on your system, APPLY THE PATCH. To repeat, if a program that has a patch resides on your system, APPLY THE PATCH."[17] The FBI gives the public the same advice: "Keep Your Operating System Up to Date: Computer operating systems are periodically updated to stay in tune with technology requirements and to fix security holes. Be sure to install the updates to ensure your computer has the latest protection."[18]

But people need to trust patches to install them, and that is precisely what FLAME undermined.

Access is only one part of spying. Once the NSA gets access to the data, analysts can't read it if it's encrypted. So a related spying goal is to be able to

---

[16] E. Nakashima, G. Miller, and J. Tate. "U.S., Israel developed Flame computer virus to slow Iranian nuclear efforts, officials say." *The Washington Post.* June 19, 2012. www.washington-post.com/world/national-security/us-israel-developed-computer-virus-to-slow-iranian-nuclear-efforts-officials-say/2012/06/19/gJQA6xBPoV_story.html

[17] L. Zirkle. "IDFAQ: Do I 'really' need to install patches to my system? I don't run the services/products that patches were issued for." *SANS.* www.sans.org/security-resources/idfaq/patches.php

[18] "How to Protect Your Computer." *FBI.* https://www2.fbi.gov/cyberinvest/protect_online.htm

break or evade encryption. Encryption is a critical tool for protecting people online. Encryption today involves using mathematical algorithms to scramble data so that outsiders cannot readily understand or interfere with communications. Encryption can protect the contents of messages as they travel across the network. Encryption can also protect information stored on email servers, social networking platforms, or other online services.

Encryption protects communications from spies and thieves alike. Without encryption, anyone with a radio receiver can listen to your cell phone calls. Without encryption, anyone with access to the fiber optic cables, the routers, or the network switches that comprise the Internet can copy or read all the traffic that flows across the compromised hardware. The interloper can also change the traffic to corrupt it, misdirect it, or otherwise alter it.

Spies wanting to read communications have to either figure out how to decrypt them, or grab them before they are scrambled. The GCHQ hacked Belgacom to get access to phone calls that, while encrypted elsewhere in the network, were unencrypted within Belgacom's systems. The MUSCULAR program grabbed raw Google and Yahoo! data from a point in the network where it was unencrypted.

Edward Snowden has said that, as a general matter, the mathematics of encryption is sound, but the NSA is effective at subverting the implementation of cryptography and at stealing keys. For example, the NSA has hacked phone chip manufacturers to get encryption keys that enable it to listen to cell phone calls and other mobile communications. For example, Gemalto is a company in the Netherlands that manufactures chips for cell phones, tablets, and the like. The NSA hacked into the Gemalto computers and stole encryption keys by the hundreds of thousands that the company stored there.[19] Having these keys allows the NSA to decrypt and listen to the calls of whoever happens to have a Gemalto-produced chip in their device.

Another NSA anti-crypto project was BULLRUN, an effort to get the world to start using cryptographic protocols vulnerable to the NSA's attacks.[20] The National Institute of Standards and Technology (NIST) has a public process to identify and adopt encryption standards. The NSA subverted the process, encouraging NIST to adopt a standard that had a mathematical back door in it. Encryption algorithms use random large

[19] J. Scahill. "Gemalto doesn't know what it doesn't know." *The Intercept*. February 25, 2015. www.theintercept.com/2015/02/25/gemalto-doesnt-know-doesnt-know/

[20] J. Ball, J. Borger, and G. Greenwald. "Revealed: How US and UK spy agencies defeat Internet privacy and security." *The Guardian*. September 6, 2013. www.theguardian.com/world/2013/sep/05/nsa-gchq-encryption-codes-security

numbers to generate encryption keys that are hard to guess. The NSA-backed standard, Dual EC-DRBG, was far more likely to use a particular large number to create encryption keys than to use any other large number. The NSA knew what the commonly occurring large number was. That gave the NSA a statistically enhanced chance of decrypting messages encrypted with Dual EC-DRBG.

BULLRUN undermined global trust in NIST. NIST was supposed to promulgate strong cryptography through an open consultative process. Public faith in NIST helped industry, both domestically and internationally, to adopt compatible standards. Today, international companies are less inclined to trust NIST standards because the US government influences them for US purposes – which are often at odds with the interests of foreign nations and corporations.

BULLRUN was not the only trick up the NSA's sleeve. Snowden documents obtained by *The Guardian* show that sometime around 2010, the NSA successfully developed the know-how to break some widely used Internet encryption: "For the past decade, NSA has lead [sic] an aggressive, multi-pronged effort to break widely used internet encryption technologies. ... Vast amounts of encrypted Internet data which have up till now been discarded [because it had previously been impossible to decrypt] are now exploitable."

The details of the NSA's new capability were not detailed in the documents, but the success gave the NSA and the GCHQ the ability to "monitor 'large amounts' of data flowing through the world's fiber-optic cables." The capability was so impressive that, according to an internal agency memo, that British analysts shown a presentation on the NSA's progress were "gobsmacked!"[21]

The NSA reported that its efforts to defeat online encryption would enable it to obtain "data flowing through a hub for a major communications provider" and a "major internet peer-to-peer voice and text communications system." From 2011 to 2013, the agency spent $800 million on that project.

In light of how important encryption is to online security, the NSA's and the GCHQ's programs to defeat encryption are disturbing. According to reports from *The Guardian*,[22] *ProPublica*,[23] and the

---

[21] Ibid.
[22] Ibid.
[23] J. Larson, N. Perlroth, and S. Shane. "Revealed: The NSA's secret campaign to crack, undermine Internet security." *ProPublica*. September 5, 2013. www.propublica.org/article/the-nsas-secret-campaign-to-crack-undermine-internet-encryption

New York Times,[24] some of the NSA's most intensive efforts have focused on defeating SSL, an encryption protocol used to protect information as it travels over the Internet, virtual private networks (VPNs), and the protection used on fourth generation (4G) smartphones. As Matthew Green, a cryptography expert and research professor at Johns Hopkins University said in September of 2013 in response to the BULLRUN revelations, he was "totally unprepared for today's bombshell revelations describing the NSA's efforts to defeat encryption." Professor Green found that his worst case scenario was not only true, but was "true on a scale [he] couldn't even imagine."[25]

American spies acknowledge no hacking, but their actions leave ample evidence as to how they would defend it: they like to remind the public that encryption not only protects regular people, it also helps legitimate targets hide, even when the spies have a very good reason to conduct surveillance.

But do we want to sacrifice public safety in the name of spying on potential terrorists (as well as other surveillance targets)? If we lock our doors, then we are keeping out cops and criminals. But if the police have a search warrant, they can come and kick down the door. Modern encryption algorithms are so strong that the digital version of a battering ram – supercomputers trying to decode at a trillion guesses a minute – will regularly fail to gain access to data in a useful time period.

This level of protection scares law enforcement and intelligence officials alike. What will they do if a kidnapper grabs a child? What if they seize a terrorists' laptop and can't decrypt it, but the documents would help them stop another September 11th?

Thanks to Edward Snowden, we know what intelligence agencies' plan is. In secret, the NSA and its spying partners like the GCHQ have been finding ways around encryption, building up the TAO hacking team, breaking into telecoms like Belgacom, and introducing security vulnerabilities to ensure access for surveillance. One of the NSA's "core secrets" is the fact that American spies work with US and foreign companies to weaken their encryption systems and that the agency spends "hundreds of millions of dollars" on technology to defeat commercial encryption.[26]

[24] N. Perlroth, J. Larson, and S. Shane. "NSA able to foil basic safeguards of privacy on the web." *The New York Times*. September 5, 2013. www.nytimes.com/2013/09/06/us/nsa-foils-much-internet-encryption.html

[25] M. Green. "A few thoughts on cryptographic engineering." *cryptographyengineering.com*. September 6, 2013. www. blog.cryptographyengineering.com/2013/09/on-nsa.html

[26] P. Maass and L. Poitras. "Core secrets: NSA saboteurs in China and Germany." *The Intercept*. October 10, 2014. theintercept.com/2014/10/10/core-secrets/

The FBI has done similarly, developing law enforcement malware that agents can use to infect target computers and conduct spying on laptops and computers.

In public, the FBI has embarked on a public relations campaign. This campaign is built on the idea that criminals will effectively use encryption technology in ways the FBI can't break, making crime solving impossible. FBI officials use the term "going dark" as a short hand reference for this scenario:

> Those charged with protecting our people aren't always able to access the evidence we need to prosecute crime and prevent terrorism even with lawful authority. We have the legal authority to intercept and access communications and information pursuant to court order, but we often lack the technical ability to do so.[27]

The latest iteration of the "going dark" campaign is a battle between the FBI, Google, and Apple. In line with their foreign customers' interests, both Apple and Google announced that their smartphones' operating system software would be architected to encrypt much more of the data on them. Because smartphone decryption keys are stored on the phone and require someone who knows the passphrase to decrypt, the new architecture means that the manufacturer will not be able to decrypt the phones, even if law enforcement produces a search warrant and asks the provider to do so. The only person who can decrypt the data on the phone is the phone's owner. This feature protects overseas customers from oppressive governments and from the US.

This announcement prompted FBI Director James B. Comey to publicly upbraid the companies, saying he could not understand why they would "market something expressly to allow people to place themselves beyond the law." The FBI appears committed to the "going dark" campaign and to forcing companies to change their networks to make surveillance easy.

The NSA's support for the FBI in undermining domestic communications security has been equivocal. In the 1990s, the NSA drew the FBI into the Crypto Wars as an ally in its effort to push for legal limits on strong encryption. But the NSA supported proposals that would limit special strong encryption tools for foreign governments and telecoms. As a foreign intelligence agency, it was not particularly opposed to domestic proliferation of encryption. The FBI disagreed. It seems that's because, unlike

---

[27] Remarks by Director James B. Comey at the Brookings Institute, October 16, 2014. www.fbi.gov/news/speeches/going-dark-are-technology-privacy-and-public-safety-on-a-collision-course

the NSA, the FBI doesn't have a big off-the-record budget for subverting encryption. Nor does it have legal and political carte blanche the same way the NSA does. The FBI needs the law to force the hands of companies like Apple, Google, Facebook, and Microsoft.

But the "going dark" campaign is dangerous. Notice how government spies use narrow cases – the kidnapper, the terrorists' laptop – as a justification for attacking security measures that protect hundreds of millions or even billions of people. They never say, "we want to defeat encryption so we can conduct mass surveillance just in case there is something fishy in the flood of global communications traffic." In other words, they highlight the need for targeted surveillance – something that most people desire in at least some circumstances – to justify massive surveillance capabilities – where that consensus markedly breaks down.

Today's Internet is primarily a civilian resource, and US companies' customers are increasingly likely to be from countries other than the United States. Google and Apple are competing domestically with South Korea-headquartered Samsung and LG, and Taiwan-based HTC. All these players are battling globally for market share, and competition is fierce. China's Xiaomi is suddenly fifth[28] in the world, and there are fourteen other Asian manufacturers hoping to crush leaders Samsung and Apple.[29]

Global customers do not want backdoored products any more than Americans do, and with very good reason. Authoritarian countries like Russia, China, the United Arab Emirates, Sudan, and Saudi Arabia want to censor, spy on, and control their citizens' communications. These nations are just as able to make demands that Apple and Google decrypt devices as the FBI is, and to back up those demands with effective threats. These nations also have spy agencies that can exploit weak security architectures. Backdoors expose confidential information to identity thieves, business competitors, American law enforcement, and oppressive governments on an equal opportunity basis. Protecting data from unauthorized access is not lawless behavior – it's preventing lawless behavior. On balance, the public is more secure, not less secure, with the wide use of strong cryptography – including cryptography without back doors or centrally accessible decryption keys. (As the NSA's break-in at Gemalto showed, centrally stored keys can be stolen.)

Demanding key escrow from Apple and Google isn't just bad for business. It's not going to work. As a customer, if Apple and Google don't

[28]   A. Moscaritolo. "Xiaomi cracks list of top 5 smartphone makers." *PC Magazine.* July 31, 2014. www.pcmag.com/article2/0,2817,2461691,00.asp

[29]   S. Millward. "14 new Asian smartphone makes hoping to crush Samsung and Apple." *Tech in Asia.* April 22, 2015. www.techinasia.com/new-asian-homegrown-smartphone-brands

make secure devices, people will buy a more secure phone or tablet from another company, including one headquartered overseas. Once I've got my device, I'm more or less in control of the software on it. I can install stronger crypto on my phone. Apps make doing this easier and easier, as protesters in Hong Kong are showing with FireChat, a secure chat software that works without an Internet connection or cellular phone coverage.[30] I use Signal from Whisper Systems to secure my communications on my Android device in a manner that law enforcement cannot readily decrypt. Downloading, installing, and learning to use this software took me less than five minutes. So, for people who care, secure encryption is out there.

If properly implemented and used, these security tools will protect human rights workers, journalists, and terrorists alike from certain kinds of surveillance. The US government wants access that could be used to investigate or even stop some serious crimes. But because a system that is insecure against the US government will also be insecure against other attackers, there's no way to be sure that other governments will not have the same capability to conduct mass surveillance and to spy on – and then undermine, attack, or imprison – petty criminals, journalists, religious minorities, homosexuals, human rights workers, and physicians working for Doctors Without Borders. Nor can we be sure that the US government will not abuse weak cryptographic implementations to engage in mass surveillance for reasons unrelated to the investigation of serious crimes. Not only that, weak crypto creates security vulnerabilities that criminals, identity thieves, stalkers, abusive spouses, and corporate spies can use. American spies don't talk much about how encryption also stops people from breaking the law. Without strong encryption, data breaches expose millions of social security numbers, trade secrets are stolen, and information cannot be trusted. Nor do they talk about how encryption also protects civil liberties. It protects attorney–client communications, human rights workers, journalists and their sources, religious and political minorities, and more. So there is a trade-off here. The trade-off isn't between privacy and security. It's between catching criminals and preventing crimes. Compromising encryption might help the NSA and FBI identify some criminals, but only at the cost of enabling other attacks.

The trade-off is even less appealing because there are often other ways to get the same information in targeted investigations. Far from "going dark," modern communications have illuminated our activities like never

---

[30] P. Mozur and A. Wong. "Hong Kong protesters flock to off-grid messaging app." *The New York Times*. September 29, 2014. nyti.ms/1sK23cz

before, producing a vast quantity of new information about everyone as we use the Internet, carry mobile phones, and connect our bodies and our homes to networked devices. Digital networks have brought the FBI far *more* information than it had at its disposal in the past. Cell phones can be used for location tracking. People who used email instead of the telephone leave a trail of messages that would otherwise have been ephemeral. Computerized data storage makes searching and analyzing old records a lot easier than when things were kept on paper and archived in banker's boxes. As we discussed in Chapter 1, there is more information available about us than ever before.

The "going dark" campaign, and in particular the criticisms from FBI Director Comey, have provoked a personal response from Apple CEO Tim Cook. In February of 2015, Cook stood before an audience at the White House's Stanford-based "CyberSummit." Cook explained in passionate and personal terms why Apple gives its users strong encryption that the company itself can't decrypt, even when asked by investigators who have legal authority. Encryption and privacy, he said, can mean the difference between life and death:

> We still live in a world where all people are not treated equally. Too many people do not feel free to practice their religion or express their opinion or love who they choose.... A world in which that information can make a difference between life and death. If those of us in positions of responsibility fail to do everything in our power to protect the right of privacy, we risk something far more valuable than money. We risk our way of life. ... Fortunately, technology gives us the tools to avoid these risks.[31]

American spies respond that our government's hacking only makes people insecure with regard to the American government. They believe that America is so far ahead of other nations in our hacking and surveillance capabilities that other nations can't take advantage of the same flaws that we've found or created. Spies call this NOBUS – intelligence community jargon for "nobody but us." Former NSA Director Michael Hayden says that the NSA, when it comes across security vulnerabilities, makes a judgment call on whether to fix the problem or to use it. "NOBUS" represents

---

[31] D. Rushe. "Apple CEO Tim Cook challenges Obama with impassioned stand on privacy." *The Guardian.* February 13, 2015. www.theguardian.com/technology/2015/feb/13/apple-ceo-tim-cook-challenges-obama-privacy

the NSA's assessment that only the United States could exploit the hole. Says Hayden:

> You look at a vulnerability through a different lens if even with the vulnerability it requires substantial computational power or substantial other attributes and you have to make the judgment who else can do this? If there's a vulnerability here that weakens encryption but you still need four acres of Cray computers in the basement in order to work it you kind of think "NOBUS" and that's a vulnerability we are not ethically or legally compelled to try to patch – it's one that ethically and legally we could try to exploit in order to keep Americans safe from others.[32]

We can't trust the NSA to make NOBUS decisions accurately. Just look at the debate over encryption back doors. The intelligence community wants Google, Facebook, Apple, and other companies to make products that the NSA and FBI can spy on, using encryption that escrows keys either with the US government or a neutral third party. The idea is that only if the NSA has legal authority, it will get the key and be able to decrypt.

But computer scientists and encryption experts outside the intelligence community almost uniformly agree that key escrow is a surveillance "back door" that creates serious security concerns, not the least of which is how to secure the valuable and vast repository of keys from being stolen (again, recall the NSA's break-in at Gemalto). Deploying secure products is hard, and key escrow makes it much, much harder. In fact, researchers were able to show that key escrow architectures pushed by the government in the past didn't work and weren't secure.

The Obama Administration also misunderstands the position that US companies are in with regard to demands for key escrow from other governments, including ones that do not respect civil liberties or human rights. At an event in early 2015, the Chief Security Officer for Yahoo!, Alex Stamos,[33] asked the head of the NSA which other countries Yahoo! should build back doors for, other than the United States. NSA Director Mike Rogers could only answer, "I think we can work our way through this."[34]

Hayden, Rogers, and others almost certainly underestimate the ability of other governments (China and Russia, for example) or criminals to

---

[32] A. Peterson. "Why everyone is left less secure when the NSA doesn't help fix security flaws." *The Washington Post.* October 3, 2013. www.washingtonpost.com/ blogs/ the- switch/ wp/ 2013/10/04/ why-everyone-is-left-less-secure-when-the-nsa-doesnt-help-fix-security-flaws/
[33] Stamos is now Chief Security Officer at Facebook.
[34] J. Reed. "Transcript – NSA Director Mike Rogers vs. Yahoo! on encryption backdoors." *Just Security.* February 23, 2015. www.justsecurity.org/20304/ transcript-nsa-director-mike-rogers-vs-yahoo-encryption-doors/

exploit the NSA's prized vulnerabilities. Academic and real-world cryptographers are almost unanimous on this point. If the NSA has figured out how to defeat widely used encryption technologies, the odds are high that other governments, crime syndicates, and hackers have also figured it out. It is conventional wisdom among computer security practitioners that there is no such thing as "security through obscurity."[35]

In other words, someone other than the researcher can take advantage of the back door. They could hack the system and steal the keys or otherwise subvert the encryption implementation. Other governments will force companies via domestic law to provide them with the same decryption capabilities the company has provided to the NSA.

We have real-world examples of how unpatched security vulnerabilities can and will be abused. Consider the "Stuxnet" malware. It was designed to target Iranian uranium facilities and cause damage to the Iranian factories that process plutonium, the first real-world example of a computer attack causing physical damage. Stuxnet is widely believed to have been a joint American-Israeli intelligence community development. Today, Stuxnet has spread to infect other industrial systems and companies.[36] And criminals later exploited some of the flaws used in Stuxnet to attack other kinds of computer systems running vulnerable Microsoft software.[37]

Packet-injection attacks used by American spies and listed in the TAO catalog are also used by the Chinese government, and the software for conducting such an attack is part of surveillance tools private researchers sell to foreign governments. The same is true of vulnerabilities in phone switching networks. The NSA uses these flaws for location tracking. So do third world governments. Private hackers have learned how to accomplish the same thing and have published the attacks.

Another example comes from the United States' past effort at requiring surveillance-friendly communications networks, the 1992

---

[35] The principle comes from the work of Auguste Kerckhoffs. See A. Kerckhoffs. "La Cryptographie Militaire." *Journal Des Sciences Militaires* 49 (1883): 5–38. www.petitcolas. net/fabien/kerckhoffs/

[36] See Symantec summary from 2013: www.symantec.com/security_response/ writeup.jsp?docid=2010-071400-3123-99; hypothesis that Stuxnet didn't start in Iran but spread from elsewhere into the Iranian facilities: www.symantec.com/connect/blogs/ countdown-zero-day-did-stuxnet-escape-natanz

[37] Statement by Chris Soghoian cited in A. Peterson. "Why everyone is left less secure when the NSA doesn't help fix security flaws." *The Washington Post.* October 3, 2013. www.washingtonpost.com/blogs/the-switch/wp/2013/10/04/why-everyone-is-left-less-secure-when-the-nsa-doesnt-help-fix-security-flaws/

Communications Assistance to Law Enforcement Act or CALEA. CALEA requires telephone networks to be wiretappable with the assistance of the provider – something euphemistically called "lawful intercept." But CALEA makes wiretapping easier for everyone, not just law enforcement.

Take the "Athens Affair," a wiretapping scandal in Greece. In 2004 and 2005 a still-unknown person or group was able to use a Greek phone company's built-in lawful intercept mechanism to listen to the cell phone calls of scores of important Greek officials, including the Prime Minister and the head of the Ministry of Defense. Essentially, the unknown attackers secretly turned on a CALEA-type interception functionality in the phone company computers and used that functionality to eavesdrop.[38]

This wasn't a one-time attack. In 2010, a researcher at IBM disclosed that he had discovered that the law enforcement interception capabilities in a Cisco-developed Internet networking system could be exploited for unauthorized wiretapping. The system was based on European-approved technical standards and was already in global use.

Security implementation problems plague CALEA-compliant telephone equipment – and create security risks even for the US government. Communications switches used by the US Department of Defense must be submitted to the NSA for security testing before they can be deployed. As Richard George, Former Technical Director for Information Assurance with the National Security Agency, told computer scientist Susan Landau, when several large manufacturers submitted CALEA-compliant switches to the NSA for testing, the NSA found security problems with the CALEA-compliant implementation on every single one of them.

The NSA's own documents show that other nations are catching up to us in exploiting network vulnerabilities that the NSA has either developed or maintained. As *First Look* reported, one of the NSA's primary concerns appears to be that foreign rivals are adopting its clandestine tactics:

> "Hacking routers has been good business for us and our 5-eyes partners for some time," notes one NSA analyst in a top-secret document dated

---

[38] Reporting suggests that the eavesdroppers were from the NSA. See J. Bamford. "A death in Athens: Did a rogue NSA operation cause the death of a Greek telecom employee?" *The Intercept.* September 28, 2015. theintercept.com/2015/09/28/death-athens-rogue-nsa-operation/

December 2012. "But it is becoming more apparent that other nation states
are honing their skillz [sic] and joining the scene."[39]

The NSA says that its officers are capable of making a subtle technological analysis of whether and when NOBUS is true. But there is so much at
risk, the decisions are complicated, and, inevitably, the intelligence community has incomplete information. Just take a look at the factors that
American spies say they would like to consider when trying to decide
whether to fix a security hole or to save it and exploit it later:

- How much is the vulnerable system used in the core Internet infrastruc-
  ture, in other critical infrastructure systems, in the US economy, and/or
  in national security systems?
- Does the vulnerability, if left unpatched, impose significant risk?
- How much harm could an adversary nation or criminal group do with
  knowledge of this vulnerability?
- How likely is it that we would know if someone else was exploiting it?
- How badly do we need the intelligence we think we can get from exploit-
  ing the vulnerability?
- Are there other ways we can get it?
- Could we utilize the vulnerability for a short period of time before we
  disclose it?
- How likely is it that someone else will discover the vulnerability?
- Can the vulnerability be patched or otherwise mitigated?

These are obviously relevant questions. But the answer to any one of
them is essentially unknowable. How do you assess "significant risk"? You
have to know how many other systems are susceptible, what kinds of systems, how damaging an attack would likely be, how to assess damage, and
who would likely use the exploit. And you would have to know this not
just for the United States, but around the world, and not just for now, but
for the near- to mid-future. Bounded rationality is the idea that decision
making is limited to the information available, the cognitive limitations of
the deciders' minds, and the time available to make the decision. The more
complicated the situation, the less information, and the more limited the
mindset, the worse the decision will be. This is the insight behind Professor
Charles Perrow's work on "normal accidents." Perrow's seminal 1984 work
builds on the concept of bounded rationality to show how multiple and

---

[39] R. Gallagher and G. Greenwald. "How the NSA plans to infect 'millions' of computers with malware." *The Intercept.* March 12, 2014. firstlook.org/theintercept/2014/03/12/
nsa-plans-infect-millions-computers-malware/

unexpected failures are built into society's complex and tightly coupled systems. Such accidents are unavoidable and cannot be designed around.

There is not only a data problem, there is a political problem. An agency that wants to "Collect It All" is making hacking decisions essentially unsupervised by Congress, the courts, and the public. Moreover, there is no other agency in the US government charged with securing communications networks to argue the other side. The only agency responsible for network security and information assurance is the NSA itself.

The US Department of State has a broader – and, importantly, a civilian-oriented – understanding of the importance of network security. The Department of State's website says that:

> Internet freedom is a foreign policy priority for the United States, and has been for many years. Our goal is to ensure that any child, born anywhere in the world, has access to the global Internet as an open platform on which to innovate, learn, organize, and express herself free from undue interference or censorship.[40]

The Federal Trade Commission is also increasingly active in security matters. It understands that protecting consumers means both requiring and encouraging encryption, better software, and more. The US government shouldn't be in the business of squirreling away vulnerability data that could make the global network more secure. But if that is what we are going to do, then the process to make the decisions about when to stockpile and when to disclose must include the State Department, the Federal Trade Commission, and other political entities whose job it is, not to attack the network, but to protect the public's security and civil rights. Only then could the decision-making process have a hope of properly assessing risk and reward.

Any notion of national security has to include preserving and protecting Internet freedom. On this view, security means improving Internet access for all, protecting and enabling free expression and political uses of the network, encouraging continued economic growth through free flow of information, and ensuring data availability. Our national interest demands access to information and the network, resilience, privacy, anonymity, and the ability to speak and to innovate for people around the globe. Network reliability and security is an essential part of this. The NSA's efforts to create a network that the US military can take down at will

[40] See US Department of State. "Internet Freedom." www.state.gov/e/eb/cip/netfreedom/index.htm

means creating a network that others – governments, groups, lone attackers – can take down at will, too. It would be tragically short-sighted if we were to continue to undermine the valuable, generative characteristics of the Internet without serious deliberation about and deep understanding of what we are giving up.

The NSA has offered the public an exceptionally narrow view of network security. It's dominated by the surveillance mission and by the agency's tight connection to military leadership and authority. The military idea is that "cyber" is a domain like air, sea, land, or space. What makes these domains secure is American hegemony over them. General Michael Hayden, the former NSA and CIA director, has said that America should treat communications networks like we treat these other domains. The goal is to both ensure use of the Internet at times and places of our choosing while denying access to our adversaries at times and places of our choosing.[41]

But the majority of people around the globe rely on the same cryptographic algorithms, operating systems, and Internet routers that nation-states use. Breaking network security breaks banking, shopping, communications integrity, privacy, and tools that protect Americans as well as citizens of other nations. If the US military exercises control over US airspace, it does not necessarily make European airspace more vulnerable to attack. But hacking the Internet such that the United States can deny adversaries the ability to securely and persistently use it necessarily creates vulnerabilities that those same adversaries, and others, can use against us.

Today, military and civilian networks are the same thing. US and global networks are the same thing. And you can't hack the network to ensure surveillance and still secure the network to prevent hacking. Hawkish cybersecurity rhetoric has polluted the conversation about modern security, and enabled our government to infect the Internet backbone with botnets, malware, broken routers, and weak encryption.

We all use the same network to communicate. Attackers can study the technology and find flaws. Those flaws can be used against terrorists, foreign governments, dissidents, journalists, and regular people alike. Security vulnerabilities are agnostic. If the NSA can break in or

---

[41] M. Hayden. Interview with M. Hujer and H. Stark. "Former NSA Director: 'Shame on us.'" *Der Spiegel*. March 24, 2014. www.spiegel.de/international/world/spiegel-interview-with-former-nsa-director-michael-hayden-a-960389.html

decrypt, then, so can other spies. Over time, the attacks will get easier, because of increasing computing power, or computing knowledge or both. Techniques once limited to foreign intelligence or terrorism will be used in run-of-the-mill investigations and then eventually be discovered and adopted by criminals.

There is another problem with the NSA's hacking. It has emboldened China and other nations to use their hacking capabilities against our government, our companies, and their own people.[42] For years, US officials have been warning about Chinese state-sponsored hacking. We've accused China of attacking military contractors like Lockheed Martin and Northrop Grumman, to steal intellectual property. We claim China was behind a 2007 hack of Defense Secretary Robert Gates' office. We blame China for hacking Google, stealing source code, and forcing the Internet company to reduce its operations in that nation. China allegedly hacked noted security company RSA. RSA's products protect computer networks at the White House, the CIA, the NSA, the Pentagon, the DHS, most top defense contractors, and a majority of Fortune 500 corporations.[43]

There is little we can do to deter Chinese hacking. We can't arrest the people at the keyboard and bring them to trial. We can't necessarily prove that the hackers are the agents of the Chinese government. We are in something of digital cold war with Beijing. Managing this problem is a serious US concern, especially given our dependence on digital networks and how much our sophisticated technology companies have to lose in the world market. President Obama and China's president, Xi Jinping, have begun talks about limiting the cyber conflict.

But now that the world has discovered that we are also hacking, then the United States has less standing to complain about what the People's Republic of China (PRC) is doing. We've squandered our moral authority. As Google CEO Eric Schmidt said in August 2014, in a Stanford University conversation with former Secretary of State Condoleezza Rice, "we've been hacked by the best. We've been hacked by the PRC and we've been hacked by the NSA."

---

[42] N. Weaver. "A close look at the NSA's most powerful Internet attack tool." *Wired.* March 13, 2014. www.wired.com/opinion/2014/03/quantum/

[43] M. J. Gross. "Enter the cyber-dragon." *Vanity Fair.* August 2, 2011. www.vanityfair.com/news/2011/09/chinese-hacking-201109

American officials have long considered Huawei a security threat for its allegedly close ties to the Chinese government. We have claimed that Huawei is particularly susceptible to Chinese pressure to create "back doors" in its equipment that could allow the Chinese military or Beijing-backed hackers to steal corporate and government secrets from Huawei customers and networks dependant on Huawei devices.

But even as the United States made a public case about the dangers of buying from Huawei, classified documents have shown that the NSA was creating its own back doors, not only in Cisco routers, Belgacom, and other companies, but also in Huawei's networks. "Many of our targets communicate over Huawei-produced products," the NSA document said. "We want to make sure that we know how to exploit these products," it added, to "gain access to networks of interest." The idea was that when Huawei sold equipment to other countries, if the NSA knew the vulnerabilities, or introduced some, then American spies would have access to these other nations' computer and telephone networks to conduct surveillance. The knowledge could also be used to conduct cyber attacks and bring down those networks.[44]

Now that we've expressed interest and aptitude in router hacking, the United States is far less likely to be able to demand that the Chinese government stop what it is doing. We are witnessing a race to the bottom, compromising the security of people around the globe.

Policy makers will eventually take up the problem of communications security. Congress is faced with the FBI's claims about its surveillance capabilities "going dark" as the public implements stronger encryption. Government agents press for changes to the Federal Rules of Criminal Procedure that will allow them to hack into networks and private computers. The United States now faces a critical information security choice: will it adopt policies that foster a global digital ecosystem that is more secure? Or, in the name of surveillance, will we push less secure, wiretap friendly technologies into the market? The President's Review Group on Intelligence and Communications Technologies unanimously recommended in their December 2013 report that the US government should "(1) fully support and not undermine efforts to create encryption standards; (2) not in any

---

[44] D. E. Sanger and N. Perlroth. "NSA breached Chinese servers seen as a security threat." *The New York Times.* March 22, 2014. www.nytimes.com/2014/03/23/world/asia/nsa-breached-chinese-servers-seen-as-spy-peril.html?_r=1

way subvert, undermine, weaken, or make vulnerable generally available commercial software; and (3) increase the use of encryption and urge US companies to do so, in order to better protect data in transit, at rest, in the cloud, and in other storage." The Review Group is right. We need to investigate the damage from the NSA's and the FBI's security policies and put policies into place that incentivize government agencies to make the network more, not less, secure.

17

The Future of Surveillance

There are two competing visions of the world we live in today. In one view, the world is a very dangerous place and massive surveillance reduces the risks from terrorism and serious crime. Governments need all the information they can get to figure out who the bad guys are and capture them before it is too late. I've argued that this vision is overblown. It has been promulgated by television shows and cable news and relied upon by government officials who believe in their hearts that they and their colleagues are well-meaning people who would only use the massive powers they have for good, and never for evil.

The countervailing view is the one I have set forth in this book. We are living in a golden age for surveillance. Technological development, government secrecy, and a legal vacuum have conspired to give the intelligence community unprecedented insight into and power over private conduct. Government agents are using this power as government agents always have: to monitor and hinder individuals and groups that seek political and social change. Only by making surveillance expensive again can we realign government agents' incentives to focus on only true threats to our national interest and public safety. Making surveillance expensive and properly aligning interests will require a combination of legal changes and technological development. Neither of those things will happen without public demand.

As Chapter 12 shows, an almost necessary prerequisite for rolling back surveillance is public outcry following a scandal. The Snowden documents provide that scandal. But people are not as outraged as they might be. This book seeks to help people understand the massive scale of surveillance, so massive that a vast amount of data about regular people is captured in the net. It does not matter if you are essentially law-abiding, or if you are an American. Once the government has the data, its ability to use it is largely unchecked. This information is power.

Properly understood, the scope of modern surveillance should be as scary or scarier than COINTELPRO and the abuses of the Watergate era.

Yet, Americans are frustrated with the options for real political change. The conversation in Washington is circular and insular. The technology and law are complicated. The Big Surveillance lobby – national security officials, law enforcement, and the companies that sell spy technology to governments – are powerful and secretive.

Still, we can and should fight to reform the current surveillance system. The year 2017 presents a fantastic opportunity for reform. Section 702 and the remainder of the FISA Amendments Act are set to expire in December of 2017. If Congress does nothing, section 702 will end. So either section 702 dies, or Congress must act, either to renew the provisions as they are, or to reform them. Thanks to the deadline, reformers have an opportunity to improve the legal structure under which surveillance takes place and specifically to rewrite or rescind section 702.

This chapter talks about what the public should demand in 2017 and beyond. First, reformers should focus on reducing secrecy. Secrecy is perhaps the biggest systemic problem we can fix. In the dark, illegality and misconduct fester. Opportunities for reform are cut off because no one knows that changes need to be made.

Second, we need to strengthen inter-branch oversight, while also asking why such oversight has been so anemic in the past. We need to discard the false confidence that the days of political spying and civil liberties abuses are behind us. Oversight processes under President Obama have functioned as a compliance regime, designed to catch insiders who do not follow the rules. But to avoid abuses, oversight needs to do more. It has to be designed to uncover and stop a president who implements illegal or illegitimate spying.

Third, we have to understand the risks and rewards of surveillance better. Ultimately that means limiting the scope of collection, and updating our laws to take account of the power of metadata and the interests of foreigners. Government needs to take a serious look at what surveillance can and cannot do, and what other, more targeted, investigative techniques might be more effective. Official faith that surveillance stops terrorism is misguided. American spies should be working on limiting collection of irrelevant data while improving other intelligence tools, such as developing relationships with minority communities. History shows that intelligence agencies would have been wise to listen better when family members – for example, the father in the case of Mr. Abdulmutallab, the so-called underwear bomber – and foreign governments – for example, Russia in the case of the Boston Marathon bombing – come forward to report their concerns.

Finally, this chapter will take a closer look at what these three general insights mean in the specific context of the December 2017 sunset of the FISA Amendments Act.

Ending Secret Law and Increasing Public Accountability

Today, we have secret law that impacts privacy, civil liberties, and political freedoms around the world. Secret law is almost like no law at all. Government officials can change it in secret. Government officials can violate it in secret, and there are no ramifications for doing so. Secret law is anathema to a democracy. There is no way elected officials can be accountable to voters if no one knows what is going on.

Of course, some surveillance activities are legitimately secret, the disclosure of which would harm public interests without improving accountability, civil liberties, or human rights. But our secrecy goes too far. Government must act lawfully, but the public has no way of knowing what those laws are. Further, on a global network, the surveillance methods aimed at terrorists can affect everyone else. Given these realities, it is obligatory that the public be aware of and engaged in setting counterterrorism policies, especially those involving surveillance.

First, targets should have greater opportunity to learn that they have been spied on and to force the government to delete irrelevant data. Keeping the individual targets of surveillance secret at least for some period of time can make good sense under an otherwise balanced regime. Under the Wiretap Act, Title III orders are sealed, but people who have been eavesdropped upon must eventually receive notification that their conversations were intercepted. But in many criminal investigations and routinely in intelligence investigations, the affected individuals are never informed that they were spied on, nor are they notified what the government has done with the data that investigators collected. The law could provide people who are no longer, or who never were, targets with notice and an opportunity to review and delete the data about them that has been unnecessarily collected. It would also enable people to bring legal challenges to questionable surveillance, clarifying the law.

The public should demand that all FISC opinions interpreting statutes or the Constitution quickly be declassified and released with only minimal redactions. Currently, the intelligence community has been picking and choosing which opinions to release, thereby controlling what people know about surveillance laws and sculpting public opinion. This gamesmanship is unacceptable. The opinions should be released across the board.

FISC judges should also be required to *write* opinions if assessing the legality of novel spying practices. Recall that, in 2006, Judge Malcolm Howard didn't bother writing such an opinion when approving the phone call dragnet under section 215. Declassification of opinions alone would not have revealed the way American spies decided to misuse the statute. Alternatively, surveillance orders like the ones Judge Howard did sign, properly redacted to mask legitimate targets, should also be made publicly available.

The executive branch should also declassify and disclose more Office of Legal Counsel opinions. OLC opinions tell the story of how the executive branch over time uses the law to build, or to limit, the national security state. These opinions show what the laws Congress passes and the rulings courts issue actually mean to American spies. Given the power of these opinions to both authorize surveillance and immunize officials, the public needs to know what those opinions say.

Protecting journalists and whistleblowers is also an essential part of creating a system of public accountability. Without national security whistleblowers like Thomas Drake, William Binney, Thomas Tamm, Mark Klein, and Edward Snowden – and the journalists who reported their stories – the public would not have known about illegal, excessive, and unsupervised surveillance. Yet, Thomas Drake, the NSA employee who worked with the *Baltimore Sun* to expose the economic waste that came from the NSA's infatuation with privacy-invasive domestic surveillance tools, was prosecuted. Thomas Tamm, the OIPR attorney who revealed the NSA's warrantless wiretapping program, was long the subject of investigation.[1] William Binney, who intelligence officials suspected of leaking information because of his internal complaints that the NSA wrongly had given up on the more privacy-protective ThinThread tool in favor of the TrailBlazer boondoggle, faced armed FBI agents one morning when getting out of the shower. Meaningful legal protection for whistleblowers is critical. Right now, we don't have it. Whistleblower protection rules only apply to people who report higher up in the chain of authority. If the illegal commands come from the top brass in the intelligence community, or from the

---

[1] C. Savage. "Ex-Department of Justice Lawyer faces penalties in leak of NSA program." *The New York Times.* January 27, 2016. www.nytimes.com/2016/01/28/us/politics/ex-department-of-justice-lawyer-faces-penalties-in-leak-of-nsa-program.html

president herself, that narrow reporting channel isn't going to be effective. Legitimate whistleblowers need to believe they will be protected and not prosecuted if they come forward to report illegal surveillance. For that, we should consider changing our laws to protect whistleblowers from professional and legal retaliation, especially if they report to officials in other branches of government.

Oversight

Oversight – involvement by all three branches of government in policing surveillance – is one of the few tools that the law has to guard against official misconduct. Today, intelligence officials point to the web of complex rules and regulations, the compliance reports and the documentation, the training and the stratification of analysts, to show how completely policed surveillance practices are. There is a vast bureaucracy to train agents and monitor their compliance with hundreds or thousands of rules and policies in the name of complying with the rule of law. These internal policies, while useful in preventing some abuses on an individual level, are no substitute for robust inter-branch oversight.

Internal Oversight

Internal oversight is important. The internal oversight mechanisms we have today are designed to monitor compliance and to catch the wayward employee from abusing his access. To some extent they are effective in accomplishing that goal. Of course, they could be better. For example, it should be impossible to wiretap Washington D.C. merely by typing 202 into a terminal, regardless of whether the goal was the lawful one of surveilling Egyptians or the illegal one of spying on Americans.

Former NSA cryptographer William Binney's view is that the NSA pretends that it's difficult to exclude US data, but in reality they have made choices that mean domestic collection is inevitable. For example, the phone network has a numeric system for routing calls, but that the NSA does not use this system to exclude US calls – ones where the number starts with +1. Binney also points out that Internet regulatory groups divide the world of Internet addresses into regions but the NSA makes no use of this regional classification to exclude Americans.[2]

---

[2] A. O'Brien. "Retired NSA technical director explains Snowden docs." *alexaobrien.com*. September 30, 2014.

There is no reason why the technology the NSA uses could not be designed with American privacy in mind. The agency's failure to do so – choosing TrailBlazer over ThinThread, or using an interface that allows Washington D.C. to be mistakenly wiretapped – results in inadvertent over-collection that both intelligence and law enforcement can then exploit behind closed doors. When judges and policy makers consider whether the NSA should be allowed to conduct surveillance as it does – performing "about collection" or conducting multi-hop data analysis, for example – the answers must be informed by deeper understanding of the privacy-enhancing tools that the NSA could have implemented, but decided not to.

But the internal oversight procedures we have today cannot effectively stop executive branch officials from violating the law when directed to do so at the highest levels. When President Bush ordered the NSA to implement STELLARWIND, the Attorney General and NSA attorneys did so. No amount of compliance process imposed inside the intelligence community is going to stop that kind of thing from happening again.

To accomplish this goal of president-proof surveillance policy, spying programs should be subject to broader debate within the executive branch. Oversight conducted only by agencies inside the intelligence community fails to take competing public interests into account. For at least some practices, the NSA and Cyber Command should have to respond to the concerns of civilian agencies in the executive branch. For example, when the issue is whether and when American spies should disclose computer security vulnerabilities, there should be multiple agencies with different agendas in the room to ensure that consumer security, human rights, and innovation interests are considered along with surveillance goals. When the issue is what data to share with other nations, military interests are not the only interests to take into account. The Department of State has broad insights into our relationships with other countries. It is also charged with understanding how they treat their citizens and whether our collaboration with foreign governments will harm American interests in the long term. These considerations should be part of any decision-making process about information sharing.

Ultimately, only robust external oversight is going to ensure that presidents are legally accountable to Congress, to courts, and to the people. External oversight is the only way to design surveillance to be president-proof. External oversight helps ensure that the statutes Congress passes are not misinterpreted. It holds the president accountable for her decisions. It enables the government to take countervailing interests like privacy, human rights, economic competitiveness, and international affairs, into consideration when making surveillance decisions.

Unfortunately, history suggests that both Congress and the federal courts have done a terrible job of overseeing modern surveillance, and it is not entirely American spies' fault. Congress members do not show up for top-secret briefings. They do not insist that intelligence officers provide honest answers to hard questions. The FISC judges approve unprecedented surveillance practices based on flimsy reasoning. When the NSA has violated the FISC's rules, the FISC has changed those rules to normalize the violations and allow the data collection to continue unabated.

Improving oversight is not just about giving Congress and the courts the *authority* to approve or review spying practices. Political science professor Michael J. Glennon has written about the ways that national security oversight in the United States has failed. His research shows that the established intelligence community is an entrenched bureaucracy that is insulated from political changes in Congress or in the White House, and only marginally impacted by judicial oversight. In sum, Glennon concludes that "[j]udicial review is negligible; congressional oversight is dysfunctional; and presidential control is nominal."[3] We need to take that lesson seriously, or the oversight that reformers mandate will be processed without substance. The goal must be to increase the *capability and incentives* to serve as a check on spying. It is not clear how to do that. But if surveillance hawks who get themselves appointed to congressional intelligence committees continue to be the dominant overseers of surveillance programs, then Congress will continue to fail to demand much political or legal accountability from American spies.

Oversight by Congress

The executive branch should be required to inform Congress when surveillance rules change, whether by executive order, presidential policy directive, or otherwise. The president should have to inform Congress when she initiates new spying programs. When Office of Legal Counsel opinions justifying surveillance proposals are written, Congress should be given a review copy. Some may argue that reporting to Congress interferes with the president's exercise of her authority under Article II of the Constitution. But overseas surveillance directly affects even American

---

[3] M. J. Glennon. "National Security and Double Government." *Harvard National Security Journal* 1 (2014).

privacy. At the very least, our elected representatives need to better understand the scope of data collection and its impact on the citizenry.

Today lawmakers are severely constrained in their efforts to stop illegal, abusive, or unwanted programs. Legislators cannot discuss classified issues even with other members of Congress outside of a secured facility. Lawmakers cannot rely on their staffers for research assistance unless the staffers have security clearances. Big Surveillance supporters like the Director of National Intelligence James Clapper, Senators Feinstein and Chambliss, and Representatives Gowdy and Rogers were free to offer reassuring but misleading statements to the public describing our surveillance practices and the safeguards in place. But Big Surveillance opponents like Senator Wyden could only issue vague, ominous warnings, restrained by confidentiality obligations. During the Patriot Act reauthorization debate in 2011, Senator Wyden could only warn, "[w]hen the American people find out how government has secretly interpreted the Patriot Act, they are going to be stunned and they are going to be angry."[4] It took the Snowden documents to reveal to the public what Senator Wyden was talking about.

Ultimately, though, Congress will not be incentivized to conduct robust oversight and limit excessive spying until and unless the American public strongly wants it. Members of Congress have relationships with national security officials, defense contractors that sell surveillance equipment, and with federal and state law enforcement. Americans are afraid that they will be the victims of crime or a terrorist attack, but not that they will be politically. There is little downside for lawmakers to keep saying yes to ever more surveillance unless Americans see this differently.

Oversight by Courts

The secretive FISC is the primary judicial overseer of modern surveillance. Secrecy is itself a huge problem. But given the role that the FISC is playing in modern surveillance, American law should empower FISC judges to do more than just sign off on the spying proposals that come before them.

In the 1978 Foreign Intelligence Surveillance Act, Congress created the FISC and empowered it to secretly approve foreign intelligence targets for surveillance. But today, FISC judges are interpreting statutes and

---

[4] "In Speech, Wyden Says Official Interpretations of Patriot Act Must Be Made Public." Office of Senator Ron Wyden. Press Release. May 26, 2011. www.wyden.senate.gov/news/ press-releases/in-speech-wyden-says-official-interpretations-of-patriot-act-must-be-made-public

the Fourth Amendment, thereby making law. A secret court should not be empowered to do this. The FISC should return to its role as a mechanism for quickly and confidentially approving targeting proposals from American spies. The role of assessing whether surveillance practices are lawful belongs to the public court system and not to the FISC.

Second, the FISC would benefit not only from more open debate about surveillance policy, but also from a robust adversarial process. To that end, the USA Freedom Act of 2015 provided that the FISC should appoint *"amicus curiae"* or "friend of the court" counsel when considering novel spying programs or significant interpretations of law. This *amicus* counsel is charged with being an advocate for protecting individual privacy and civil liberties. A civil liberties advocate is a good idea, but will likely have limited impact on the court. In a democracy, a handful of people cannot effectively represent the public interest on a case-by-case basis. Legal interpretations are best formed, not by one or two smart people arguing over secret law and classified facts behind closed doors, but by robust and informed public debate and fact-finding.

Nevertheless, the *amicus* role before the court could be useful and should be strengthened. Today, the FISC judges have discretion whether or not to proceed with appointing an *amicus*.[5] Congress could *require* that a public interest advocate counsel be appointed in certain circumstances. The advocates will need access to prior FISC opinions, as well as relevant facts. Today, the FISC judge has discretion over whether to reveal facts and case law to the advocate. Instead, the advocate likely needs to be able to compel the government and the FISC to disclose relevant information. Without this authority, FISC judges and intelligence lawyers may not disclose relevant information that could make a difference in the case. Take, for example, the 2007 Yahoo! challenge to programmatic content spying. In that case, it was not until 2014 when the FISC declassified documents from the challenge, that the Yahoo! lawyers got to see the information the intelligence community had provided to the court. The documents included certifications, procedures, declarations, and other FISC decisions about the level of oversight for certifications. The FISC did not give Yahoo! these documents at the time. As a result, the government was able to make false assertions that may have impacted judicial rulings. For example, the FISCR relied on the government's representation that "it does not maintain a database of incidentally collected information from nontargeted

---

[5] USA Freedom Act codified at 50 U.S.C. § 1803.

United States persons, and there is no evidence to the contrary."[6] That claim wasn't true. The government had such a database compiled during STELLARWIND. But without discovery, Yahoo! could not help ensure the FISCR relied on accurate information.

As another example, in 2011, FISC Judge Bates accepted the NSA's claim that its "about collection" is an unavoidable by-product of Upstream surveillance technologies. Partially on that basis, the FISC allowed "about collection" to continue. An *amicus* counsel would want to challenge that assertion and ask the NSA to present evidence to support that claim, and would likely need to call expert witnesses to rebut it.

Congress could also give the *amicus* counsel the ability to appeal when a FISC judge does not adopt her reasoning. Currently, on the rare occasion that the government loses before the FISC, it can appeal. But if the people's Fourth Amendment rights are diminished, no one may appeal. This situation results in a one-way ratchet in favor of more surveillance. If the *amicus* counsel could appeal, that dynamic would be thwarted. Without the ability to compel disclosure, to cross-examine, to present evidence, and to appeal, the amicus can play a meaningful, but only moderately effective, role.

Some have suggested that another way to improve the FISC would be to change the way judges are selected for service on the court. Judicial selection processes, without other reforms, are unlikely to change the subservience the FISC has shown to the executive branch. The problem does not appear to be that FISC judges are too deferential to the government due to ideological commitments. Rather, the FISC is hobbled in its oversight by both dependence and fear. FISC judges have to take the NSA's word on technological and factual matters. For years, the judges believed what the intelligence community lawyers told them about how the domestic dragnets and Upstream surveillance worked. Only around 2009, after Bush was out of office and the Obama Administration was in, did the FISC judges start getting reports about how the NSA had been disobeying court-established rules in all three programs. The FISC was wholly dependent on the information that the NSA officials provided. FISC judges do not seem to have the ability to compel the NSA to answer its questions or to follow up to ensure that their orders are obeyed. Ultimately, the biggest problem with the FISC is that even in the face of

[6] *In re Directives Related to [redacted] Pursuant to Section 105B of the Foreign Intelligence Surveillance Act*, No. 08-01 (FISCR August 22, 2008) p. 26. nsarchive.gwu.edu/NSAEBB/ NSAEBB436/docs/EBB-021.pdf

persistent misconduct and misrepresentations, and regardless of political party, FISC judges are highly deferential to executive branch claims
that surveillance is necessary. The judges do not want to be responsible
for either ending the programs or for punishing administration officials
responsible for unlawful conduct.

The history of surveillance law shows that courts can be meaningful
protectors of civil liberties. We need to figure out why that is not the role
the FISC has reliably played, and encourage the FISC judges to perform
their oversight role more effectively. At a minimum, the judges need to
be empowered with information, expertise, and arguments. But the history of FISC acquiescence with massive surveillance programs – and its
endorsement of weak legal reasoning to get there – suggests that we need
something more. Perhaps with less secrecy in the system, the pressures of
public accountability will encourage judges to do real work. That means
writing opinions, reasonably interpreting the law, conducting fact finding,
consulting with colleagues, asking for input from *amicus* counsel, and disclosing relevant information to the rare private litigant who appears before
the court. These things are necessary if the FISC is to oversee surveillance,
ensure that intelligence operations follow the law, and identify the areas
where the law is fuzzy or absent and American spies' surveillance capabilities or limitations should be made clear.

The Risks and Rewards of Surveillance

The discourse on surveillance policy too often presumes that more surveillance will be an effective counterterrorism or crime-stopping measure.
In reality, the intelligence community has failed to develop any metric for
assessing whether the hundreds of millions of dollars spent on surveillance programs has been a good investment or not. Further, as discussed
in Chapter 6, massive surveillance creates a signal-to-noise problem; there
may be too many false positives in the sea of information. Government
officials fail to acknowledge to the outside world that this problem exists,
even as analysts struggle with it internally.

Together, the CIA and the NSA spend around 16 billion dollars a year on
information collection, processing, and exploitation.[7] Without the ability
to compel disclosure, to cross-examine, to present evidence, and to appeal,
the amicus can play a meaningful but only moderately effective role. By

---

[7] *The Washington Post.* "$52.6 billion: The Black Budget". August 29, 2013. www.washington-
post.com/wp-srv/special/national/black-budget/

spending the money on surveillance, we have foregone other national security opportunities like improving port security or tracking chemical weapons. Policy makers need create a methodology for assessing the value of surveillance programs.

In the future, there is going to be more intelligence agency demand for broad datasets. At the same time, it is going to be more difficult to make sense of such information. As the US Signals Intelligence Division Director of Analysis and Production said in a 2011 interview:

> We need to piece together the data. It's impossible to do that using traditional methods. Strong selectors – like phone numbers – will become a thing of the past. It used to be that if you had a target's number, you could follow it for most of your career. Not anymore. My daughter doesn't even **make** phone calls, and many targets do the same. Also, the commercial market demands privacy, and this will drive our targets to go encrypted, maybe into unexploitable realms. Our nation needs us to look for patterns surrounding a particular spot on Earth and make the connections – who can do that if not us? And we can't do it using traditional methods.[8]

Will intelligence agencies actually be able to use mass surveillance and modern data science to identify lone wolf terrorists, previously unknown terrorist groups or plots, or people likely to commit terrorist acts in the future? As discussed in Chapter 9, government programs may offer the public this hope, but some kinds of data mining could never reliably be used to identify potentially dangerous people. Our legal and policy systems do a poor job of ferreting out scientific claims. Legislatures funded and forensic experts routinely offered false testimony in hair and bite mark comparison analysis for decades.[9] Other techniques such as handwriting analysis, ballistics analysis, shoe and tire print analysis, bullet-lead analysis, and the certain arson investigatory techniques are also of dubious reliability.[10] Today, we cannot currently reliably predict who might be

---

[8] "Is there a sustainable Ops tempo in S2? How can analysts deal with the flood of collection? – An interview with [redacted]." *SIDToday*. April 6, 2011. Emphasis in original. www.eff.org/files/2015/06/15/20150528-intercept-is_there_a_sustainable_ops_tempo_in_s2_how_can_analysts_deal_with_the_flood_of_collection.pdf

[9] S. Hsu. "FBI admits flaws in hair analysis over decades." *The Washington Post*. April 18, 2015. www.washingtonpost.com/local/crime/fbi-overstated-forensic-hair-matches-in-nearly-all-criminal-trials-for-decades/2015/04/18/39c8d8c6-e515-11e4-b510-962fcfabc310_story.html

[10] S. Hsu. "Forensic techniques are subject to human bias, lack standards, panel found." *The Washington Post*. April 17, 2012. www.washingtonpost.com/pb/local/crime/forensic-techniques-are-subject-to-human-bias-lack-standards-panel-found/2012/04/17/gIQAD-CoMPT_story.html

dangerous or become dangerous in the future, and we might never be able to do so. Where a program is based on data mining techniques, Congress and the courts should ask for rigorous scientific testing before approving analysts' use of a technique meant to produce actionable results.[11]

Finally, our national security efforts need to be driven by realistic assessments of risk and not by movies, television, and cable news. We are more likely to be killed by falling furniture, and vastly more likely to be killed by cars, than by terrorism. If Americans understood this fact, perhaps we would we be more circumspect with our tax dollars, our national security policies, and our surveillance practices. Every dollar spent on mass surveillance is a dollar that the government could have spent on preventing heart disease, reversing global climate change, or making our highways safer.

Updating Our Laws to Take into Account the Power of Metadata

Currently, American law enshrines lesser privacy protections for the collection of metadata than it does for the content of communications in both law enforcement and intelligence investigations. That differential treatment no longer makes any sense in a world of Big Data analytics. Metadata is extremely revealing about people's personal relationships, religious beliefs, and political activities. At the same time, statistical insights show that metadata analysis is more misleading than enlightening when it comes to finding unknown terrorists in a haystack of information, and that it is likely to always be so. The disparate treatment of metadata and content no longer makes sense, and the law should be updated to protect personal and sensitive information more generally.

This is a job for Congress. In 2016, Congress considered an amendment to the Electronic Communications Privacy Act, which would clarify that government access to email and location information requires a search warrant. Congress could also amend surveillance laws to enhance the protection of metadata information that is not the content of communications. Meanwhile, the Supreme Court is questioning the continued viability of the so-called third party doctrine under which information that can be called metadata has been subject to warrantless collection. The Supreme Court may eventually reject the third party doctrine, or the metadata/

---

[11] See National Research Council. "Protecting Individual Privacy in the Struggle Against Terrorists: A Framework for Program Assessment." (Washington, D.C.: National Academies Press, 2008), p. 46. www.nap.edu/openbook.php?record_id=12452&page=46

content distinction such that the Fourth Amendment once again serves as a check on government power.

The Interests of Foreigners

Surveillance focused on foreigners impacts American interests in a number of ways. Is it worth it for us to continue that surveillance unabated? As discussed in Chapter 7, American rights rise and fall with the rights of foreigners. If we fail to protect their rights, then we also compromise our own privacy. Our interconnected world no longer allows us to remain provincial about civil liberties. The Five Eyes intelligence agencies are swapping data about each others' citizens, which turns us all into foreigners with little or no rights. Further, American interests are served by the spread of freedom of expression and civil liberties around the world. Having a dual standard with foreigner's rights contradicts American efforts to exercise much needed moral leadership.

The December 2013 report from the President's Review Group on Intelligence and Communications Technologies, "Liberty and Security in a Changing World," recognized that consideration of the privacy and civil liberties rights of non-US persons is important. In particular, the Board suggested – among other recommendations – that surveillance of foreigners:

- must be directed exclusively at protecting national security interests of the United States or our allies;
- must not target any non-US person based solely on that person's political views or religious convictions; and
- must not disseminate information about non-US persons if the information is not relevant to protecting the national security of the United States or our allies.

In response to the political outcry, the Obama Administration moved to provide some assurance to foreigners. But the protections of PPD-28 – generally that "[p]rivacy and civil liberties shall be integral considerations in the planning of U.S. signals intelligence activities" – only apply to bulk-collected data. Selector-based collection, no matter how broad, does not receive the same considerations under that policy.

Given the different interests a government has in surveillance of citizens and noncitizens, and given the long history of differential treatment, developing meaningful standards for protecting foreigners will be challenging. Will we allow surveillance for trade negotiations, commodity markets, and the like? If so, how do we protect regular people from our government and their own? This issue will come up in 2017, as we consider whether to keep any version of section 702, and whether to rein in surveillance under EO 12333.

FISA Amendments Act Reform

In December 2017, the FISA Amendments Act and section 702 will sunset. Congress must decide whether to renew the law,[12] reform it, or kill it.[13] Currently, section 702 allows the NSA to wiretap communications to or from and collect the emails and other stored data of noncitizens located in other countries for foreign intelligence purposes. If section 702 dies, the NSA and the FBI will still be able to wiretap foreigners and collect their communications from service providers. However, they will not be able to do so for any foreigner talking about any foreign intelligence matter. Nor will they be able to collect foreigners' data from Internet companies based on directives and selectors without FISC supervision. Instead, if the intelligence agencies follow the law, they will have to provide probable to a cause that the foreigner is an agent of a foreign power in order to get a warrant for the surveillance.

This limitation would be a great comfort to everyday people from other countries who do not want to be casually subjected to US government investigation. The NSA would still conduct surveillance on foreigners talking to other foreigners through US Internet chokepoints under its transit authority, as well as through network points outside the country under EO 12333. And it would, absent reforms to EO 12333, still collect Americans' international communications, albeit only from points overseas. The intelligence agencies would have less access to stored electronic data involving the conversations of foreigners who are not agents of foreign powers or suspected terrorists. Finally, by requiring search warrants for surveillance when Americans are talking to foreigners, ending section 702 would bring spying practices back in line with the protections of the Fourth Amendment. Expiration of section 702 may mean that some

---

[12] E. Nakashima. "McConnell bill would extend NSA surveillance." *The Washington Post*. April 22, 2015. www.washingtonpost.com/world/national-security/mcconnell-introduces-bill-to-extend-nsa-surveillance/2015/04/21/fa4b66aa-e89d-11e4-aae1-d642717d8afa_story.html

[13] Letter to Director James R. Clapper, October 29, 2015. www.brennancenter.org/sites/default/files/analysis/Coalition_Letter_DNI_Clapper_102915.pdf

foreign intelligence is lost, but there are economic, diplomatic, and civil liberties gains to be had in exchange.

Purpose of Collection

Short of ending section 702's warrantless wiretapping, there is much that Congress could do to limit its scope without losing any national security advantage warrantless wiretapping may convey to American spies. Average foreigners have legitimate concerns about being spied on even though they are neither terrorists nor agents of foreign powers. Broad surveillance of foreigners for general foreign intelligence purposes increases the likelihood that the program will pick up Americans, too. Finally, massive surveillance may overwhelm relevant information with irrelevant data, making it less useful than more targeted collection in counterterrorism efforts. These factors argue in favor of narrowing the scope of section 702. Today, section 702 can be used if a "significant purpose" of the collection is foreign intelligence, which can include topics like trade disputes and the price of oil. We could limit the approved purposes for section 702 collection to spying on foreign governments and potential terrorists, or to topics more closely connected to our national security interests like counterterrorism and counterproliferation.

The double standard for Americans and foreigners is less and less politically viable. The Court of Justice of the European Union (CJEU) ruled in *Schrems v. Facebook* that section 702 violates the rights of European citizens under EU privacy law. As a result, the CJEU invalidated the data protection Safe Harbor, on which American companies relied in order to do business in Europe in the course of providing email, social networking, and other online services globally. The pending remedial proposal, called the *Privacy Shield*, does almost nothing to ameliorate the problems the CJEU identified with section 702 in *Schrems*. Without some other means of harmonizing EU and US law, American companies again will be at legal risk when doing any business in the European Union. So, international pressure is on to fix section 702, not just for Americans but for foreigners, too.

Upstream and Abouts

One of the most contentious aspects of section 702 is Upstream surveillance. In Upstream, the NSA exploits its technical position by scanning foreign-to-foreign messages on US networks, thereby collecting

Americans' international messages. Upstream has serious constitutional defects. The NSA's machines scan the contents of all of the communications passing through the collection point, and the presence of the selector or other signature that justifies the collection is not known until after the scanning is complete. It is arguably an illegal search to scan messages when the government has no idea whether or not they contain the selector. Doing so is analogous to the government opening all letters to read them to see whether they contain interesting or relevant content.

In response, some argue that since only a robot "reads" the documents and innocent information is never revealed to a human, the scan is not a search. The querying software, like a drug-sniffing dog, only identifies hits, and thus is not a search. Electronic searches for foreign intelligence are not like dog sniffs, however. Unlike the hypothetical drug dog, foreign intelligence selectors identify more than just contraband. They also identify legal conduct, like talking to or about a foreign intelligence target. Further, warrantless dog sniffs are unconstitutional when they target a highly protected area like a home.[14] Private papers, like homes, are specifically mentioned in the text of the Fourth Amendment, and the Constitution may well treat them with the same consideration. A warrant could well be required even for a robotic search.

A related constitutional problem is "about collection." The NSA is scanning both the transactional information and the contents of messages to see whether they contain the email address, IP address, or other selectors associated with section 702 targets. The NSA then collects not only the messages sent to and from a target's email address, but also messages sent between nontargets that mention the selector.[15] The NSA claims that "about collection" is a natural by-product of how it conducts Upstream surveillance and that it cannot avoid "about collection" without interfering with its collection based on "to" and "from" email addresses. Computer science academics have questioned this claim, saying that given the way that the Internet and modern traffic filtering tools work, the claim that the NSA is helpless to stop about collection is suspicious. And civil libertarians bristle at the collection. Why is it appropriate for NSA computers not only to read through the messages of nontargets, but also for the agency to then collect and use these messages simply because people mentioned the target selectors? No court has ever approved warrantless surveillance of two nontargets based on the content of their conversation. Further,

---

[14] *Florida v. Jardines,* 569 U.S. 1 (2013).
[15] PCLOB 702 Report at 10, 38.

"about collection" results in massive over-collection. "About collection" can capture purely domestic messages when they happen to be routed overseas, as well as multi-communication transactions (MCTs).

Serious reform of section 702 should mean ending both Upstream and "about collection."

Minimization and Back Door Searches

The nature of intelligence collection is broad, as is necessary to understand post-collection usage rules are necessary, though not sufficient, for real reform. To this end, the FISC should have greater control over establishing and enforcing minimization procedures. Under section 702, the judges are only allowed to ask whether the government's proposed minimization procedures "fit the definition" of minimization rules. That is, the court can ask whether the rules are "reasonably designed" but not whether they are effective or whether they could be improved.

There are several ways in which the procedures could be improved. First, FISC judges should have more authority to sculpt and improve the rules. The judges should be able to require reporting, not just ask nicely for it as Judge Bates had to do in 2011, to investigate whether the NSA is following the rules.

Next, minimization procedures could be designed so that government agents may not take advantage of data they were not authorized by statute to intentionally obtain. By prohibiting use of over-collected information – domestic messages and inadvertently collected data – minimization procedures could encourage the government to implement more discriminating surveillance technologies.

Minimization procedures could also require the government to take steps to improve the public understanding of surveillance. For example, the law could require that affected people be informed that their records were collected by the government at a point in the investigation when it is safe to do so.

Perhaps most importantly, minimization procedures should require that collected data only be used for its authorized purposes. The NSA is providing unminimized PRISM data to the CIA and the FBI.[16] The CIA and the FBI have rules for searching this data and can look for information

---

[16] "Report on the Surveillance Program Pursuant to Section 702 of the Foreign Intelligence Surveillance Act," Privacy and Civil Liberties Oversight Board, July 2, 2014, p. 53 (footnotes omitted).

about specific Americans, in accordance with each agency's mission.[17] The FBI can warrantlessly search through the vast PRISM database for information about criminal activity. The agents are piggybacking on the NSA's foreign intelligence-justified collection to get warrantless access to Americans' private information for criminal fishing expeditions.

In reforming section 702, the public should insist that Congress end these kind of backdoor searches. We can do this in several ways. First, we could cut off the FBI's access to the raw data. FBI access to data would be limited to only those circumstances where the NSA analysts happen upon evidence of a crime or seek to share data for national security purposes. The Office of the Director of National Intelligence purportedly took a step in this direction in 2015. Robert Litt reported that section 702 information about a US person would not be introduced as evidence against that person in any criminal proceeding except (1) with the approval of the attorney general, and (2) in criminal cases with national security implications or certain other serious crimes.[18] But this voluntarily adopted usage limitation does not appear to have been implemented in the FBI minimization procedures. So, the ODNI could unilaterally and secretly reverse course and allow the FBI to recommence using the data in any criminal case. Neither the attorney general nor the FISC would necessarily know.[19] Moreover, Litt's promise does not stop the FBI from looking for any kind criminal conduct. Once it finds signs of some wrongdoing, agents may then use parallel construction techniques to come up with other evidence

---

[17] Id., pp. 7–8. For a discussion of the mechanics of querying, see p. 55.

[18] See ODNI Signals Intelligence Reform 2015 Anniversary Report. icontherecord.tumblr. com/ppd-28/2015/privacy-civil-liberties. In particular, according to Bob Litt, the General Counsel of ODNI: Under the new policy, in addition to any other limitations imposed by applicable law, including FISA, any communication to or from, or information about, a US person acquired under Section 702 of FISA shall not be introduced as evidence against that US person in any criminal proceeding except (1) with the prior approval of the Attorney General and (2) in (A) criminal proceedings related to national security (such as terrorism, proliferation, espionage, or cybersecurity) or (B) other prosecutions of crimes involving (i) death; (ii) kidnapping; (iii) substantial bodily harm; (iv) conduct that constitutes a criminal offense that is a specified offense against a minor as defined in 42 U.S.C. 16911; (v) incapacitation or destruction of critical infrastructure as defined in 42 U.S.C. 5195c(e); (vi) cybersecurity; (vii) transnational crimes; or (vii) human trafficking. ODNI General Counsel Robert Litt's As Prepared Remarks on Signals Intelligence Reform at the Brookings Institute (February 4, 2015). icontherecord.tumblr.com/post/110632851413/ odni-general-counsel-robert-litts-as-prepared

[19] J. Laperruque. Revelations from the Newly Declassified FISC Opinion on Section 702. www.justsecurity.org/30776/revelations-newly-declassified-fisc-opinion-section-702/. April 27, 2016.

that the government can use to prosecute the person. The FISC *amicus* advocate appointed in November of 2015 to consider privacy and civil liberties concerns with new and classified minimization procedures warned that this is exactly what the new policies would allow.[20]

As an alternative, and with the intention of stopping fishing expeditions, a judge could assess whether there is probable cause for the FBI searches of PRISM data. Two members of the PCLOB recommended that a FISC judge review and approve identifiers before they may be used to query data collected under section 702 for a foreign intelligence purpose, other than in exigent circumstances or where otherwise required by law.[21] A regular judge in the public court system could also assess probable cause and issue warrants for searches intended to find evidence in criminal cases. It is dangerous to allow the government to create a historical record of much of what its citizens do just in case it wants to take a look and use the data later. As we saw in Chapter 9, US census data collected for one reason was repurposed to help accomplish the internment of Japanese citizens during the World War II era. And as we saw in Chapter 17, at least one court in *Ganias* has said that the Fourth Amendment doesn't allow the government to store data indefinitely in the anticipation that it might one day use it against somebody. Given the scope of criminal law, there will likely be something suspicious in the database about everyone. But at least requiring a warrant would avoid suspicionless fishing expeditions, that is, if American spies obey the limitation.

EO 12333 Reform

Executive Order 12333 surveillance also has been the subject of public outcry. Despite the fact that collection takes place overseas or only seeks foreign data, it impacts the privacy of Americans, as discussed in Chapter 7. One proposal to remedy this problem is to extend some of the current section 702 rules that purport to protect Americans to EO 12333 spying. That would mean a FISC judge reviews the purposes of surveillance, as well as the minimization and targeting procedures.

---

[20] Ibid.
[21] "Report on the Surveillance Program Pursuant to Section 702 of the Foreign Intelligence Surveillance Act," Privacy and Civil Liberties Oversight Board, July 2, 2014, p. 14 (footnotes omitted). (Separate Statement of Board Members Medine and Wald). For more detail on how querying works under Section 702, see "Report on the Surveillance Program Pursuant to Section 702," pp. 55–60.

The PCLOB is reviewing EO 12333 and will likely consider the merits of FISC involvement in EO 12333 programs. However, the chief lawyer for the ODNI opposes the idea, giving some indication of the intelligence community position. ODNI attorney Robert Litt has said that FISC review of EO 12333 efforts would be a substantial burden given the scope of collection. He pointed to the role that the NSA plays in battlefield intelligence to make the case that speed is often a necessity.[22] The PCLOB and Congress are in the process of investigating and reporting on EO 12333. With that information in hand, the public can consider whether to scale back the collection, the use or both of data, whether to limit surveillance in friendly nations, and whether to regulate how American spies may search what they gather.

Transparency

Another area for reform as Congress considers the renewal of the FISA Amendments Act in 2017 will be transparency. How much surveillance is the NSA doing and how many Americans are affected? There are two sources for this information: US companies and the intelligence agencies themselves. Over the past few years, US companies have started to issue "transparency reports." These reports reveal the number of government demands for data, the kinds of data disclosed, and with what legal process. A coalition of companies negotiated with the US government to report data, but the intelligence community has so far only agreed to permit public disclosures in aggregate ranges measured in thousands. However, even if these businesses were allowed to report with more granularity, there is a limit to what sense the public can make from these numbers. Remember that former NSA attorney Inglis told Congress in 2013 that there were only 300 selectors used on the section 215 phone call database. But as Chapter 7 showed, given the multiple hops that the NSA was entitled to search, those 300 selectors put scores more Americans under government scrutiny. We've been told that there are approximately three section 702 certifications and 100,000 targets. These numbers may sound reassuring in a world of 4 billion people. But if one of those targets is "the French government" or "the United Nations," then millions of people's privacy could be compromised.

[22] S. Nelson. "Whistleblower debates top spy lawyer over surveillance order." *U.S. News & World Report*. September 19, 2014. www.usnews.com/news/articles/2014/09/19/whistleblower-debates-top-spy-lawyer-over-surveillance-order

More transparency is required to understand the scope of these programs. Congress might seek to know how many selectors the intelligence community uses. For each target, are there three or four, or 10,000 email addresses under investigation? Also, how accurate are the selectors? If the *Washington Post* statistical analysis discussed in Chapter 13 holds true throughout the section 702 database, then nine out of ten people are not targets. How many innocents are being spied on? And how many of those are Americans?

Gag orders are another area ripe for reform. National security letters legally compelling companies to disclose a wide range of records and other data types may be issued by FBI agents without any court oversight. These letters, as well as search warrants and section 215 orders, often come with gag orders prohibiting the recipients from telling anyone that they have received the surveillance demand. That means that the individuals who are the subject of the surveillance may never know it. Such secrecy makes sense when dangerous people are under investigation, but it also inhibits average people from being able to protect their rights, from arguing that the request is overbroad, or from asserting that there is no basis for the demand.

These orders go well beyond keeping the target of the investigation in the dark. The companies aren't allowed to say that they've received an order, never mind for whom or for what. The public can't know how many orders there are, what companies are subject to them, or how broad the requests are. All this uncertainty has contributed to an atmosphere of mistrust. Internet companies have said that they think that the public would be reassured if it knew how few such requests the companies received. Experts are less sanguine, noting all the ways in which numbers can be misleading. Nevertheless, companies have tried to inform their users without violating gag orders in an effort to build trust and to allow the affected party opportunity to vindicate her rights. For example, Twitter has challenged gag orders in court, saying that they violate the company's freedom of speech, and other communications companies have rallied around the lawsuit.[23] Microsoft filed a lawsuit against the government arguing that gag orders violate the company's First Amendment right to inform its users about its compliance with surveillance demands, as well as the customers' Fourth Amendment rights to notice of searches and seizures. But, for now, gag orders stand. Reform efforts should eliminate permanent gag orders.[24]

***

[23] *Twitter v Holder*, No. 14-04480 (N.D. Cal. October 7, 2014).
[24] *Microsoft Corporation v. US Department of Justice*, No. 2:16-cv-00538 (W.D. Wash. April 14, 2016).

Twenty years ago, I decided to study areas of law related to the Internet. It was a time when people thought that Internet activity would be difficult to trace or control. "On the Internet, Nobody Knows You're a Dog," a phrase drawn from a 1993 New Yorker cartoon, captured this idea. Some celebrated the hope that online anonymity might create a society where people were valued for the content of their minds and character, and not judged based on race, gender, nationality, or other provincial concepts of the predigital world. Some feared that anarchy would reign in a world where governments could not readily identify wrongdoers.

Today, no one asks whether the government can regulate the Internet. Today, people ask "what will the Internet look like when every government in the world is regulating it." Today, we know that the Internet has been a boon for surveillance. The surveillance capabilities of American spies expanded thanks to technological and business developments that have made information gathering comprehensive and inexpensive. As a result, modern surveillance has expanded the scrutiny to which minority groups have always been subject. Modern surveillance also sweeps into its net people who were traditionally left alone by their government, meaning that groups that in the past were largely free from government attention are now pervasively monitored.

At the same time, Congress granted intelligence and law enforcement greater permission to access and use this data through legislation like the USA PATRIOT Act and the FISA Amendments Act. In secret, American spies went even further. Via controversial classified interpretations of section 215 of the Patriot Act, the pen register statute, the so-called third party doctrine, the content versus metadata distinction, and the foreign intelligence exception to the Fourth Amendment's warrant requirement, they successfully created new, secret rules extending their surveillance powers.

We soon will have an opportunity to restore the balance that has been lost. In December of 2017, section 702 of the FISA Amendments Act is due to sunset, and Congress will decide whether to renew it, reform it, or end it. We need to reduce secrecy, reject massive collection in favor of targeted collection wherever feasible, strengthen inter-branch oversight, and learn to intelligently assess the risks and rewards of surveillance.

Today we live in a golden age for surveillance, when American spies have more capabilities and fewer legal constraints than ever before. Since the golden age for surveillance is a product of both legal and technological developments, technological reform is also essential. As I argue in Chapter 16, the government should not undermine information security in the name of greater surveillance. The public needs to be able to easily encrypt its communications to protect them from opportunistic collection and suspicionless review. Encryption also helps protect potential targets – political activists, human rights workers, journalists, and religious, sexual, and social minorities – from surveillance by misguided or oppressive regimes.

Civil libertarians know that achieving any of these reform proposals will require talented advocates, intelligent legal and policy analysis, and hard work. It will also require the engagement of an informed public. In his recent book, *Engines of Liberty*, Professor David Cole writes about what it takes to convince courts to protect constitutional liberties. Cole points out that constitutional rights are not necessarily something that the majority of voters will support. In fact, the goal of much of the Bill of Rights is to protect minority communities and viewpoints from the predations of the majority. Nevertheless, campaigns to establish or protect civil rights in law will fail without public support. Creating social change is a group effort, albeit one that takes sophistication and dedication. "If you care about constitutional rights," Cole argues, "the way forward should be clear: find or found associations of like-minded citizens, engage broadly and creatively, and do not leave constitutional law to the lawyers, much less the judges."[25]

Reform will not necessarily come swiftly. But it will not happen at all unless the public has the information and the expertise to effectively work together to change the way American spies do business. My goal in writing this book was to give readers that information and expertise. Now, let's get to work.

[25] D. Cole. *Engines of Liberty* (New York: Basic Books, 2016) p. 229.

GLOSSARY OF SELECTED TERMS

BULLRUN   Joint NSA and GCHQ effort to undermine and weaken cryptography standards and tools.

CALEA, Communications Assistance to Law Enforcement Act of 1994   US federal law that requires telephone networks to be wiretappable with the assistance of the provider.

CAPTIVATEDAUDIENCE   NSA software that takes over a targeted computer's microphone and records conversations taking place near the device.

EO12333, Executive Order 12333   Foreign US spying takes place under a presidential order called Executive Order 12333 (EO 12333, pronounced "twelve triple three").

FISA, The Foreign Intelligence Surveillance Act of 1978   US federal law that prescribes procedures for the physical and electronic surveillance and collection of "foreign intelligence information" between "foreign powers" and "agents of foreign powers".

FISA Amendments Act, Section 702   Section 702 permits the programmatic and warrantless acquisition of phone call, email, and other communications targeting noncitizens located overseas and includes collection of messages to, from, or about entities of foreign intelligence interest.

Five Eyes   An intelligence alliance comprising Australia, Canada, New Zealand, the United Kingdom, and the United States. These countries share information pursuant to the multilateral UKUSA Agreement, a treaty for joint cooperation in signals intelligence.

FLAME   NSA software that tricks users into installing it by masquerading as a Microsoft software update.

FOGGYBOTTOM   NSA software that records the users' Internet browsing history and collects login details and passwords used to access websites and email accounts, then sends those login credentials to NSA.

GROK   An NSA TAO software implant used to log keystrokes, creating a record of everything the target types.

GUMFISH   NSA software that can covertly take over a computer's web-cam and snap photographs. The software makes sure that the webcam's light doesn't go on so that the target has no way of knowing the camera is on and recording.

MAINWAY   Database of telephone records. The bulk collection of telephone call records from Verizon Business Services was one source of raw intelligence for MAINWAY.

Metadata   Internet metadata can include information about the sender and receiver of information, such as the caller or person called, or the To and From fields in emails.

MUSCULAR   The NSA and GCHQ have jointly operated this program to intercept data from Yahoo! and Google networks.

NUCLEON   Database of spoken words from intercepted telephone calls.

PCLOB, Privacy and Civil Liberties Oversight Board   An independent agency within the executive branch of the US government, established by Congress in 2007 to advise the executive branch and ensure that concerns with respect to privacy and civil liberties in the United States are appropriately considered in the development and implementation of all laws, regulations, and executive branch policies related to terrorism.

Pen Register/Trap and Trace (PR/TT)   An electronic device that records all numbers called from a particular telephone line or similar dialing, routing, addressing, or signaling information derived from Internet usage.

PRISM   The PRISM program collects message content from US technology companies.

Regin   GCHQ malware used to attack a Belgian telco.

SALVAGERABBIT   NSA software that steals data from removable flash drives that connect to an infected computer.

SIGINT, Signals Intelligence   The name for intelligence gathering by interception of signals, whether communications between people (communications intelligence – abbreviated to COMINT) or from other electronic signals.

STELLARWIND   The code name of a secret National Security Agency (NSA) program approved by President George W. Bush shortly after the September 11, 2001 attacks. The program collected email communications, telephone conversations, financial transactions, and Internet activity and was revealed by Thomas Tamm to the *New York Times*.

Tailored Access Organization (TAO)   NSA's elite hacker division.

ThinThread   An NSA data analysis tool created by William Binney and Ed Loomis with built-in privacy protections for US persons, subsequently discontinued.

Turbine   A network of active command and control servers around the world that can be used for "industrial scale exploitation."

Upstream   The Upstream program collects communications transiting the Internet via commercial partners code named FAIRVIEW, STORMBREW, BLARNEY, and OAKSTAR.

USA PATRIOT Act, section 215   US federal law that expanded the sweep of Foreign Intelligence Surveillance Act orders to compel production of business records and other tangible objects. The provision was used to justify the NSA's domestic telephone calling record dragnet.

XKEYSCORE   An NSA tool for searching and analyzing global Internet data.

FURTHER READING

Alexander, M. *The New Jim Crow: Mass Incarceration in the Age of Colorblindness* (New York: The New Press, 2012).

Bamford, James. *The Puzzle Palace: Inside the National Security Agency America's Most Secret Intelligence Organization* (New York: Penguin Books, 1983).

Body of Secrets: Anatomy of the Ultra-Secret National Security Agency (New York: Random House, 2002).

The Shadow Factory: The Ultra-Secret NSA from 9/11 to the Eavesdropping on America (New York: Doubleday, 2008). Kindle Edition.

Eichenwald, K. *500 Days: Secrets and Lies in the Terror Wars* (New York, NY: Simon & Schuster, 2012).

Goldsmith, Jack. *The Terror Presidency* (New York: W.W. Norton & Company, 2007).

Greenwald, Glenn. *No Place to Hide: Edward Snowden, the NSA, and the U.S. Surveillance State* (New York: Metropolitan Books, 2014).

Hager, Nicky. *Secret Power: New Zealand's Role in the International Spy Network* (Nelson, New Zealand: Potton & Burton, 1996).

Harris, Shane. *@War: The Rise of the Military-Internet Complex* (New York: Houghton Mifflin Harcourt, 2014).

Kris, David and J. Douglas Wilson. *National Security Investigations and Prosecutions*, 2nd ed. (Eagan, MN: Thomson West 2012).

Risen, James. *Pay Any Price: Greed, Power, and Endless War* (New York: Houghton Mifflin Harcourt, 2014).

Savage, Charlie. *Power Wars: Inside Obama's Post-9/11 Presidency* (New York: Little, Brown and Company, 2015) Kindle Edition.

Silverglate, Harvey. *Three Felonies a Day* (New York: Encounter Books, 2011).

Weiner, Tim. *Enemies: A History of the FBI* (New York: Random House, 2013).

Legacy of Ashes: The History of the CIA (New York: Anchor Books, 2008).

INDEX

public accountability in, 292
regulation of, 31–32
warrantless wiretapping and, 31–32,
233
tax audits, surveillance and, 135–38
Tea Party movement, 135, 146
technology
civil liberties and, 1
growth of mass surveillance and, 3,
24–26
terrorism and limits of, 94–95
telephone call data collection. *See also*
Section 215 (USA PATRIOT Act),
See also mobile phones
categories of, 28–30
Congressional and court cooperation
on, 178–86
continued justification for, 85–90
Fourth Amendment protections and,
13–14, 187–91, 200–01, 224–32
government collection of, 9–10,
54–55
history of surveillance using,
175–76
key escrow technology and, 264
limits in counterterrorism of, 80–85
NSA global surveillance of, 19–24
privacy protections and, 60–62
reasonable expectation of privacy
standard and, 29–30, 178–86
Senate investigation into collection
of, 10–17
STELLARWIND violations
of, 192–96
third party doctrine and, 187–91
Terror Presidency, The (Goldsmith), 177
terrorism
criminal violence *vs.*, 90–98
definitions of, 5n. 1
by Islamic non-state groups, 142–45
legal definition of, 91–92
mass surveillance and detection
of, 90–98
public perceptions of, 138–40
surveillance policies as response
to, 67–74
Terrorist Surveillance Program (TSP),
17, 207, 252

Terrorists Identities Datamart
Environment (TIDE), 78
The Wire (television series), 87
ThinThread project, 46–49, 295
third party doctrine
Fourth Amendment protections
and, 225
phone data and email
privacy, 219–21
phone data collection and, 57–60,
189–91
phone data collection and, 242
STELLARWIND
investigation, 194–96
This American Life (radio program), 143
Three Felonies a Day (Silverglate), 129
TIDE (Terrorists Identities
Datamart Environment). *See*
Terrorists Identities Datamart
Environment (TIDE)
Title III (Wiretap Act), 180–81, 187–91,
205
torture, terrorism as justification for, 92,
158, 223
Total oil and gas company, 110
tower dumps, of mobile phone
data, 54–55
TrailBlazer surveillance tool, 47, 50,
295
transit authority, expansion of, 210
transparency in surveillance, proposals
for, 310
Transportation Security Administration
(TSA), 93
Tsarnaev, Dzhokhar, 77–79
Tsarnaev, Tamerlan, 77–79
TURBINE system, 268
Twitter, 87, 169–70
Tye, John, 22, 110, 111, 152

US Constitution, surveillance regulation
and. *See also* Fourth Amendment,
See also First Amendment
US National Counterterrorism
Center, 78
USS Cole, attack on, 72
Udall, Mark, 83, 254
UK-USA Agreement, 163–65